Decision Making Support Systems:

Achievements, Trends and Challenges for the New Decade

Manuel Mora
Autonomous University of Aguascalientes, Mexico

Guisseppi A. Forgionne
University of Maryland, Baltimore County, USA

Jatinder N. D. Gupta
University of Alabama in Huntsville, USA

IDEA GROUP PUBLISHING
Hershey • London • Melbourne • Singapore • Beijing

Acquisition Editor:	Mehdi Khosrowpour
Senior Managing Editor:	Jan Travers
Managing Editor:	Amanda Appicello
Development Editor:	Michele Rossi
Copy Editor:	Elizabeth Arneson
Typesetter:	Tamara Gillis
Cover Design:	Integrated Book Technology
Printed at:	Integrated Book Technology

Published in the United States of America by
Idea Group Publishing (an imprint of Idea Group Inc.)
701 E. Chocolate Avenue
Hershey PA 17033
Tel: 717-533-8845
Fax: 717-533-8661
E-mail: cust@idea-group.com
Web site: http://www.idea-group.com

and in the United Kingdom by
Idea Group Publishing (an imprint of Idea Group Inc.)
3 Henrietta Street
Covent Garden
London WC2E 8LU
Tel: 44 20 7240 0856
Fax: 44 20 7379 3313
Web site: http://www.eurospan.co.uk

Library of Congress Cataloging-in-Publication Data

Decision making support systems : achievements, trends, and challenges for the new decade / [edited by] Manuel Mora, Guisseppi A. Forgionne, Jatinder N.D. Gupta.
     p. cm.
  Includes bibliographical references and index.
  ISBN 1-59140-045-7 (hardcover)
   1. Decision support systems. I. Mora, Manuel, 1961- II. Forgionne, Guisseppi A., 1945- III. Gupta, Jatinder N.D., 1942-

T58.62 .D424 2002
658.4'03--dc21   2002027310

eISBN 1-59140-080-5

British Cataloguing in Publication Data
A Cataloguing in Publication record for this book is available from the British Library.

Dedication

"I dedicate my editorial work and chapter to my parents Dn. Guillermo Mora (=) and Dña. Magdalena Tavarez, and to my sisters and brothers by their permanent support in my life; to my friends Paola, Mabel, Rosario, Mary, Lolita and the priest Artemio Romo by his kind friendship; to the professors Dr. Francisco Cervantes and Dr. Ovsei Gelman by the trust on my current research endeavor; to my colleagues co-editors Dr. G. Forgionne and Dr. J. Gupta by sharing their experience with me in this editorial project; to my professor at ITESM and UNAM by the strong academic preparation taught me and to the UAA for providing me a nice place to work and doing research. I thank also to my students by encouraging me to improve my knowledge and to the eminent scientific Herbert A. Simon (=) by his kindness to advise me via email with key ideas in the starting point of my doctoral dissertation. Finally I spiritually thank to the Lord God and the S.V. Maria for the blessings to complete this book and my doctoral dissertation on time." **Manuel Mora**

"I dedicate my part of the book to my mother Mary for her support and encouragement over the years and to my Lord and Savior Jesus Christ for providing the spiritual and intellectual guidance to complete the endeavor." **Guisseppi A. Forgionne**

"I dedicate my work to my wife Harsh and the memory of my parents, Babu Ram and Soshila Gupta, for their guidance, support, and encouragement throughout my life and enabling me to undertake and complete such tasks. In addition, I dedicate my work to numerous friends and mentors who have shaped my thought processes and provided continuous inspiration to do my best at all times in my life." **Jatinder N. D. Gupta**

September 2002

Decision Making Support Systems:
Achievements, Trends and Challenges for the New Decade

Table of Contents

SECTION III: ADVANCED IT FOR DMSS

SECTION IV: EVALUATION AND MANAGEMENT OF DMSS

SECTION V: CHALLENGES AND THE FUTURE OF DMSS

Preface

Decision making support systems (DMSS) are information systems designed to interactively support all phases of a user's decision making process. There are various notions about all aspects of this definition. They can be for individual, or group usage. Support can be direct or indirect. The decision making process can be viewed in various ways. User-computer interaction can have a variety of dimensions. The information system offering the support can involve many technologies drawn from several disciplines, including accounting, cognitive science, computer science, economics, engineering, management science, and statistics, among others.

Because of the various perspectives and dimensions involved in decision making support, the field has evolved in a variety of directions. These directions have offered different focuses and contributions. While being effective and beneficial, this disparity has created much confusion about the theoretical basis, architectural form, support mechanisms, design and development strategies, evaluation approaches, and managerial and organizational aspects of decision making support systems. This book, which we have titled *Decision Making Support Systems: Achievements, Trends and Challenges for the New Decade,* is an attempt to alleviate some of the confusion.

Thus, this book aims to demystify DMSS by considering various phases involved in the development and implementation of them. The book's mission is to present the core and state-of-the-art knowledge about decision making support systems (DMSS). In the process, we hope to: (a) provide a compendium of quality theoretical and applied papers on DMSS, (b) help diffuse scarce knowledge about effective methods and strategies for successfully designing, developing, implementing, and evaluating of DMSS, and (c) create an awareness among academicians and practitioners about the relevance of DMSS in the current complex and dynamic management environment.

The presentation is divided into five sections. In the first section, labeled *Foundations and Architectures of DMSS*, we present the theoretical basis for decision making support and the architectures that have been proposed to deliver the theory in practice. There are four chapters in this first section.

In chapter 1, the main architectures of DMSS developed during the last 15 years are presented and their advantages and disadvantages for supporting the decision making process are analyzed. Because none of the stand-alone DMSS architectures supports the entire process in an integrated and complete manner, an integrated architecture is proposed and discussed. Implications of DMSS architectures for researchers and practitioners for leading to better design, development, and robust implementation of DMSS are finally suggested.

Chapter 2 discusses a multidimensional framework for categorizing DMSS, originally proposed by Power. This framework is based on four characteristics: 1) the dominant component and driver of decision support, 2) the targeted users, 3) the specific purpose of the system, and 4) the primary deployment technology. With this framework, researchers and practitioners can improve their understanding of DMSS and can establish a common framework for classification and discussion.

A special architecture of DMSS, called spatial decision support systems (SDSS), is analyzed in chapter 3. Spatial applications represent an area of information technology (IT) application with a significantly different history from the other DMSS discussed in this book. However, the distinct contribution of SDSS to decision making is the ability of these systems to store and manipulate data based on its spatial location. SDSS is useful in a wide range of government and business activities. Untapped potential uses to enhance the decision making process are suggested finally.

The last chapter of this section, chapter 4, endeavors to provide a technical definition of DSS relying upon human decision making. It is argued that although there are good functional definitions of what DSS should do, an understandable definition involving human reasoning is still lacking. Therefore, this chapter attempts to bridge the gap between human reasoning and the understanding and design of DSS. The chapter first presents a description of the human process of decision making. A semiformal definition of DMSS is then developed and finally a brief discussion about DSS architecture is analyzed. The ultimate goal of this chapter is paving the way to better understanding and design of future DSS.

The second section of the book is called *Applications of DMSS*. As the label indicates, this section presents new and unique applications of the decision making support system concept. Six chapters detail these new DMSS applications.

In chapter 5, a real case of a DMSS to control routes of a regional railway system is presented. Competitive pressures in all systems of transport for passengers and goods require improved and effective use of all available resources to keep service reliability and availability, which ultimately have a strong impact on the quality perceived by users. Thus, the development of DMSS for this type of scenario is especially interesting. This chapter reports design issues and implementation experiences gained during its development. It also shows that DMSS are useful tools for mission-critical online processes.

Another real application of a DSS in the context of urban transportation, called *Navigate UTOPIA,* is reported in chapter 6. This area is particularly well suited to be supported by a DMSS through a multi-criteria approach, given the complexity and interaction involved with a series of economic, ecological, social, and political subsystems and the large number of stakeholders involved. In addition to the realized capabilities of *Navigate UTOPIA*, the chapter also focuses on the user behavioral issues related to its development. Learned lessons about the intense interaction with potential DSS users during the DSS construction phase, particularly when these include stakeholders with limited technical training, are discussed.

Chapter 7 describes the development of an expert support system oriented to quality management for a regional bank. This chapter shows that expert systems technology is still useful. Its technical construction is possible through a structured development process. The DMSS assists the teams to determine which problems to address and what data to collect in order to incrementally improve the business processes of the bank. For that reason, the DMSS provides decision support, interactive training and expert advice.

In chapter 8, a specific DMSS tool for the creation of guidelines for better DMSS in the domain of health informatics is reported. For that reason, this chapter presents an extended ontology for a DMSS founded on related research in information systems and artificial intelligence and on several case studies in health informatics. The ontology explicates relevant constructs and presents a vocabulary for a DMSS. It also emphasizes the need to cover environmental and contextual variables as an integral part of decision support systems development and evaluation methodologies. With the inclusion of specific domain, application, and knowledge aspects, it is claimed that more successful systems could be developed. However, other complications arise. This chapter discusses these complications and their managerial and practical implications.

An exploratory analysis of how knowledge management (KM) practices can enhance the decision-making process in pharmaceutical firms is reported in chapter 9. The complexity of the pharmaceutical industry, from the hard science of drug research and development to the psychology of marketing, places special decision making demands on managers. Since knowledge is considered a core resource to make good decisions, and pharmaceutical firms rely on innovation and collaboration activities that are knowledge intensive activities, then, KM becomes an essential practice for DMSS development.

Chapter 10 reports a case study of how DMSS support a leader organization in the entertainment industry. The core advanced IT of the DMSS presented is data warehousing (DW), which could be considered to be the most important development in decision support over the last decade. DW is being used to support many important organizational strategies and initiatives, such as the balanced score card, electronic commerce (both B2C and B2B), and customer relationship management (CRM). CRM is designed to attract new customers, enhance relationships with existing customers, and reduce customer attrition. This case describes how the organization has deployed DW and DMSS to support their business strategy. Special attention is given to the use of IT to support "closed loop marketing." The impacts of IT-based initiatives are discussed. Finally future directions and lessons learned are given.

The third section of the book is titled *Advanced IT for DMSS*. This section presents state-of-the-art information technologies that have been developed to improve the efficiency and effectiveness of decision making support systems. Some of the technologies are variations on existing hardware and software concepts. Others are new, unique, or innovative. These advanced IT developments are offered in six (6) separate chapters.

In chapter 11, a large-scale and multiyear project in the military context based on multiagent systems, called *SENTINEL*, is described. It was designed to computerize the strategic and tactical planning processes of the U.S. Coast Guard (USCG). This large-scale project required the creation of several distributed decision support systems (DDSS) for human participants acting at different levels of the USCG hierarchy. This chapter describes the objectives, the peculiarities, and the constraints of the task environment, as well as the solution to some problems that are fundamental and ubiquitous in many real-time, spatially and temporally distributed multiagent systems.

In chapter 12, a conceptual knowledge warehouse architecture is posed for the extraction, storage, analysis and understanding of explicit knowledge. Knowledge warehouses (KW), similar to the data warehouses, could provide knowledge and support to the entire enterprise decision making process. The proposed KW architecture consists of an object-oriented knowledge base management system module (OO-KBMS), a knowledge analysis workbench, and a communication manager. The proposed KW architecture is unique in that it proposes support for all four phases of the knowledge spiral in a decision support system, especially in model-based decision support. Finally, practitioner and research implications are reported.

Chapter 13 reports a technique to develop expert systems (ES) called ripple down rules (RDR). This chapter shows that an ES can generate negative perceptions in the practitioner and academic community. While ES had shortcomings, there are successes and ES research is alive. A reason for the limited use of ES is reported as the high complexity for its development and in particular due to the knowledge acquisition phase. Consequently this chapter describes a knowledge representation and acquisition technique, i.e., RDR, that tackles head-on the limitations of first-generation ES while avoiding some of the new problems introduced in second-generation ES. Finally, emerging trends and future directions of ES research are given.

A general information framework of e-management for knowledge-based modeling of customer responsive systems is reported in chapter 14. This framework integrates intelligent information support, group decision making, and agreement modeling for a supply chain network. Through the proposed framework, it is possible to experiment with various types of behavior patterns that may emerge through interaction of virtual enterprise members and apply lessons learned in developing robust e-management models. Global firms that compete in a business environment based on complex collaborative relationships need frameworks to deploy adequately the underlying information technology infrastructure to support their business strategies. This chapter offers a conceptual mechanism for providing such support.

A new kind of DMSS based on synthetic characters is reported in chapter 15. Synthetic characters are intelligent agents able to show typical human-like behavior by means of natural language interaction. This chapter shows how a particular highly interactive kind of intelligent agent, i.e., the synthetic characters, can support the decision making process. It also discusses general characteristics of a decision making model and the architecture and processing flow of DEMON (DEcision-Making OrgaNizer), a decision support agent currently under development. Finally, research and practical implications are given.

In Chapter 16, a novel advanced IT approach is presented: the narrative-based information systems (NBIS) approach. Since DMSS are focused on improving the effectiveness of the decision making process and are based on the accuracy of the resulting information, the presentation language of a DMSS, a part of the user interface, is critical for successful DMSS operation. Narratives and stories could be incorporated to achieve greater meaning and understanding of the presentation language of a DMSS. A conceptual model of NBIS is examined and used to outline areas for further research. Finally, theoretical and practical implications for DMSS developments are discussed.

The fourth section of the book is called *Evaluation and Management of DMSS*. This section offers some new or innovative ways to evaluate the effectiveness of decision making support systems. This section also presents managerial issues that are created or resolved by the implementation of these systems. Four chapters are used to present the material.

Chapter 17 reports a conceptual scheme called the decision support systems research (DSSR) framework. The DSSR framework was developed to integrate theoretical constructs from various information systems areas into a coherent theme with the objective to improve the quality of the DMSS. This DSSR framework can be used as the basis for the identification and selection of a hierarchy of factors potentially affecting the quality of DMSS development. The DSSR framework is used in tandem with the generic software quality metrics framework specified in the IEEE Standard 1061-1992. The usage of these frameworks to identify system quality factors is demonstrated in the context of military research and development projects.

In chapter 18, a national-based descriptive study on the usage and practices of executive information systems (EIS) is reported. EIS have been widely used in multinational organizations located in highly developed nations. In emergent economies, their usage is still limited. This chapter reports the findings from a survey study conducted in an emergent economy country. Following the work line manifested in the preceding research, this chapter aims at undertaking a comparative analysis between the reported situation of EIS and the results obtained in similar descriptive studies.

Based on the Rockart's critical success factor (CSF) approach, chapter 19 puts forward a practical method to guide the development of executive information systems (EIS) in organizations. This method extends the current theory of EIS by using the concept of the *dashboard of information* to show how an enterprise-wide approach to the development of more effective decision support for managers can deliver tangible benefits without requiring the time-consuming and single-decision focus of the traditional development methods. This method also attempts to leverage the latest computing technologies now available for the development of such systems, notably graphical user interfaces (GUI), data warehousing (DW) and OLAP. The proposed approach is illustrated by examples of dashboard developments, which show how managers should carry out the analysis and development of such a system in their own organizations, business units or functional areas.

In chapter 20, an extensive literature review of the main contributions and limitations of the factor-based (FB) and stage-based (SB) approaches conducted in the DMSS implementation research is presented. It is argued that despite the claimed benefits of stand-alone and integrated DMSS, the rate of implementation failures is still high. Therefore, in practice, the number of DMSS installed and adequately used has been far less than expected. Under the premise that DMSS implementation is a process of high complexity, it is claimed that FB and SB approaches must be complemented with other research approaches in order to capture the full complexity of the whole phenomenon. The authors propose the systems approach as this emergent research methodology. Finally, conclusions and directions for further research are given.

The fifth, and last, section is titled *Challenges and the Future of DMSS*. As the title suggests, this last section identifies key challenges for management, organizations, and other entities that are presented by decision making support systems. The section also discusses the main trends in DMSS research and practice. A unique feature of this last section is that it reports the opinions of leading DMSS researchers and practitioners regarding the challenges and opportunities that exist in the field.

Chapter 21 describes a study of how two advanced technologies, simulation and geographic information systems, can be integrated to support a critical complex management process like evacuation and emergency planning and management. The aim is to provide decision support for emergency prevention or mitigation, response and recovery. At present, this process widely relies on computer-aided emergency management systems which gather and analyze information and data on hazardous emissions, geological activity, meteorology, demography, and geography. Therefore, deployment of advanced IT for DMSS is attractive but it is also complex. This chapter identifies and analyzes the challenging issues faced in using the above two technologies. It focuses on the behavioral and decision making processes of the various players in the evacuation system, logistics, generating realistic scenarios for testing out contingency plans, and the validation of such computer-based decision support tools. Future trends in technology and the evolution of emergency planning and management processes are also discussed.

Based on Kant, Hegel, Locke and Liebnitz mental models, chapter 22 reviews the inquiring models with a view to provide an analytical framework for knowledge creating and sharing activities. Knowledge management (KM) has been identified as a critical activity for decision-making, since it includes task solving activity which requires high-quality knowledge as input. This chapter provides a review of the KM concepts and perspectives, with an introduction to knowledge management systems (KMS) and related technologies. The importance of a knowledge base for knowledge management (KM) and knowledge sharing (KS) activities is illustrated for a hypothetical firm. Effective knowledge sharing or better knowledge utilization can result in increased organizational capabilities as defined by competitiveness, efficiency, competency, and creativity. Emergent DMSS based on KMS is finally suggested as a key research topic.

The last chapter of the book, chapter 23, attempts to summarize the achievements of decision making support systems and outlines the future opportunities and challenges. It does so by inviting and synthesizing the opinions of the experts in this exciting and emergent field of study. From this chapter, is it clear that DMSS have been useful in a variety of situations and have provided significant support to technical, managerial, and executive decision making efforts. This chapter also reports that while much has been accomplished in this field, considerable work still needs to be done, including the explicit consideration of the DMSS implementation issues in a global context.

We believe that the book will be a comprehensive compilation of DMSS thought and vision. There is a thorough presentation on all phases of decision making support, newly reported applications in DMSS in a variety of areas, unique information technologies for improving DMSS design, development, and implementation, unique strategies for measuring DMSS effectiveness, and new methodologies for managing DMSS in practice. The presentation illustrates the concepts with a variety of public, private, societal, and organizational applications, offers practical guidelines for designing, developing, and implementing DMSS, offers measures to effectively evaluate and manage DMSS, and presents expert opinion about the future of DMSS.

Readers of the text will gain an understanding of, among other things: (a) decision making concepts in organizations, (b) DMSS types, (c) DMSS integration strategies, (d) ESS, IDSS, MSS, and DTS architectures, (e) intelligent agents, RDR-based expert systems, synthetic characters, NIBS and other innovative AI-based approaches, (f) system simulation, (g) DMSS system design and development, (h) DMSS effectiveness measurement, (i) organizational and management issues and impacts, (j) DMSS implementation barriers, and (k) future DMSS trends. Thus, this will facilitate the development and implementation of decision making support systems within any organization. It is hoped that the book will enable the business community to start benefiting more widely from this powerful technology.

This understanding of various phases of DMSS should benefit undergraduate and graduate students taking decision making support systems courses and practitioners seeking to better support and improve their organizational or individual decision making process. Hopefully, the book will also stimulate new research in DMSS by academicians and practitioners.

Acknowledgments

This book would not have been possible without the cooperation of many people: the authors, reviewers, our colleagues, and the staff at Idea Group Publishing (IGP). The editors would like to thank Mehdi Khosrow-Pour for inviting us to produce this book, Jan Travers for managing the project and Michele Rossi as development editor for answering our questions and keeping us on schedule. The resources that the staff at IGP provided assisted us enormously.

Many of the authors of chapters in this book also served as reviewers of other chapters, and so we are doubly appreciative of their contribution. We also acknowledge our respective universities for affording us the time to work on this project and our colleagues and students for many stimulating discussions. Finally, the authors wish to acknowledge their families for providing time and support for this project.

Manuel Mora
Autonomous University of Aguascalientes, Mexico

Guisseppi A. Forgionne
University of Maryland, Baltimore County, USA

Jatinder N. D. Gupta
University of Alabama in Huntsville, USA

SECTION I

FOUNDATIONS AND ARCHITECTURES OF DMSS

Chapter I

An Architecture for the Integration of Decision Making Support Functionalities

Guisseppi A. Forgionne
University of Maryland, Baltimore County, USA

ABSTRACT

Various information systems have evolved to support the decision making process. There are decision support systems (DSS), executive information systems (EIS), artificially intelligent systems (AIS), and integrated combinations of these systems. Each of the individual systems supports particular phases and steps of the decision making process, but none of the individual systems supports the entire process in an integrated and complete manner. The integrated systems alleviate the support deficiencies, and each of the integration approaches has specific advantages and disadvantages. By studying these advantages and disadvantages, researchers and practitioners can better design, develop, and implement robust decision making support systems. This chapter facilitates such study by presenting and illustrating the underlying information system architectures for robust decision making support.

INTRODUCTION

Because of the importance to individual, group, and organizational success, information systems research has examined ways to improve support for decision making for the last three decades. The research has generated a variety of information systems designed, developed, and implemented to provide the necessary support. In the process, there has been an evolution from simple data access and reporting to complex analytical, creative, and artificially intelligent support for decision making (Holsapple & Whinston, 1996).

Much of the research and practice has occurred in specific disciplines, such as computer science, information systems, management science, and psychology, among others. Often, researchers and practitioners in one discipline have been unaware of important developments in the others. The independent disciplinary research and practice has led to a duplication of effort and a loss of synergy. As a result, there has been a proliferation of independent individual systems that support decision making in a fragmentary and incomplete manner.

Value can be created by identifying decision making support requirements and developing information systems that provide the necessary support in a comprehensive and integrated manner (Forgionne & Kohli, 1995; Kumar, 1999). This chapter addresses these issues by formalizing the decision making process, isolating the phases and steps that require support, examining the information systems that have been created to provide the support, identifying the shortcomings in the support, and proffering decision making support systems that can close the gaps. Since the issues involve information and decision technology, the focus will be on decision making support system architectures and their role in decision making support.

BACKGROUND

Several frameworks have been developed to describe the human decision making process. The most popular is Simon's three-phase paradigm of intelligence, design, and choice (Simon, 1960). This paradigm seems to be the most general, implying virtually all other proposed frameworks, and the Simon paradigm appears to have best withstood empirical testing (Borenstein, 1998; Martinsons, Davison, & Tse, 1999). Such scrutiny, however, has suggested the expansion of the basic formulation to conclude with an implementation phase.

Decision Making Process

During the intelligence phase, the decision maker observes reality, gains a fundamental understanding of existing problems or new opportunities, and acquires the general quantitative and qualitative information needed to address the problems or opportunities. In the design phase, the decision maker develops a specific and precise model that can be used to systematically examine the discovered problem or opportunity. This model will consist of decision alternatives, uncontrollable events, criteria, and the symbolic or numerical relationships between these variables. Using the explicit models to logically evaluate the specified alternatives and to generate recommended actions constitutes the ensuing choice phase. During the subsequent implementation phase, the decision maker ponders the analyses and recommendations, weighs the consequences, gains sufficient confidence in the decision, develops an implementation plan, secures needed financial, human, and material resources, and puts the plan into action.

Figure 1 summarizes the phases and steps within the phases of the decision making process (Forgionne, 2000). As this figure illustrates, the decision making process is continuous, even though the process involves discrete phases and steps.

Figure 1: Decision Making Process

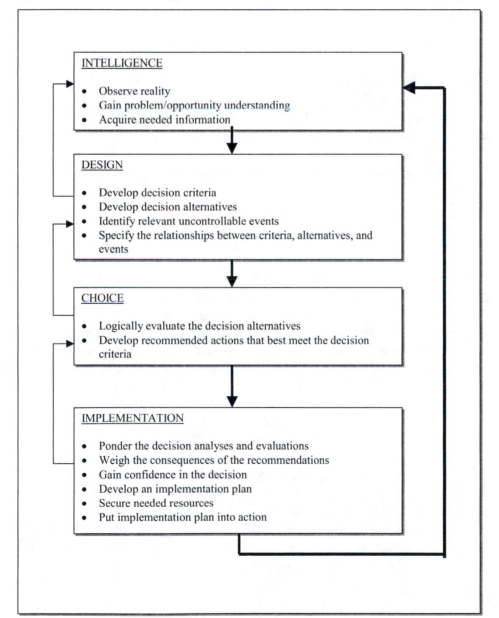

After the final choice is implemented, the decision maker should observe the new reality and, where appropriate, follow through with intelligence, design, choice, and implementation. Moreover, phase analyses may suggest the need for revisions at preceding phases. For example, analyses during choice may necessitate adjustments in the previous design. Such continuous monitoring and adjustment is similar to Simon's review phase.

Conceptually, the decision making process applies in the same manner to individual or group decision making. In practice, group decision making must accommodate the communication-intensive aspects of cooperative problem-solving within and between organizations, use structured techniques to support voting, ranking, rating, and other methodologies for developing a consensus, and provide group and organizational collaboration support (Sauter, 1997).

Process to Outcome Link

While some phases may be performed concurrently, decision making fundamentally is a sequential process. Design will require intelligence. Choice should not proceed without design. Implementation follows choice. Similarly, many steps within the phases typically must be performed sequentially. For example, decision alternatives must be evaluated before a recommendation can be developed.

Since an outcome can occur only after the final choice has been implemented, the decision outcome will be a function of (largely explained by) the decision making process. There can be an outcome to the organization (for example, improved performance) or the decision maker (for example, learned skills and abilities). That is, the decision outcome is defined as the set of results accruing to the organization and decision maker. The decision making process can be defined as the set of its phase activities, while each phase can be defined as the set of its step activities.

The process to outcome link suggests that outcomes to the decision maker and organization will depend on the completion of the process steps and phases (Forgionne, 1999). By specifying these steps and phases, the decision maker can identify the activities that must be measured to evaluate decision outcomes properly (Raghunathan, 1999). Such a specification ascertains the nature of the outcomes that must be measured. After the measurements are made, the outcome, phase, and step relationships will help to isolate the specific causes for particular decision outcomes (Balasubramanian, Nochur, Hendersen, & Kwan, 1999; Siskos & Spryridakos, 1999).

It should be noted that the process to outcome link is independent of the specific decision approach or context. For example, many observed decision processes are political, with managers making up their mind first and trying to justify their opinions with further information gathering. Similarly, since the outcome of a decision is a consequence of the alternatives selected and the events that occur, a seemingly good selection can produce very bad outcomes if events are unforeseen or improperly specified. Nevertheless, the outcome still results from the process utilized, whatever its form.

MAIN THRUST OF THE CHAPTER

A variety of individual information systems have been offered to support users during the phases and steps of the decision making process (Mirchandani & Pakath, 1999). Much can be learned about this support by examining the architectures of the offered individual systems. In the examination, particular information systems have been grouped into broader categories because the support functionality within categories is similar, if not identical. For example, since expert and case-based reasoning systems both rely on captured knowledge to provide support, these systems are categorized as knowledge-based systems (KBS). Similarly, neural networks and genetic algorithms both mimic physical learning and adaptation to provide support, so these systems are categorized as machine learning systems (MLS). Other forms of artificial intelligence, such as speech recognition and robotics, are excluded from the examination because they do not directly support the human decision making process.

Issues, Controversies, and Problems

Decision making support has evolved over time and across disciplines. Initial support was offered by a DSS, with the typical architecture shown in Figure 2. In the typical DSS, the problem-pertinent data and models are captured and stored as inputs in the system. The decision maker utilizes computer technology to: (a) organize the data into problem parameters, (b) attach the parameters to a model, (c) use the model to simulate (experiment with) alternatives and events, and/or (d) find the best solution to the problem. Results are reported as parameter conditions (status reports), experimental forecasts, and/or recommended actions. Feedback from the user-controlled processing guides the decision maker to a problem solution, and created information and knowledge are stored as additional inputs for future or further processing. Applications have incorporated some or all of the typical DSS functionality.

The DSS concept presumes that the problem pertinent data and models have been created and made available to the system prior to user processing (Hooghiemstra, Kroon, Odijk, Salomon, & Zwaneveld, 1999). It also assumes that the user can utilize the computer technology to perform the technical processing operations and computations required by the system (Lawrence & Sim, 1999). In fact, DSS users rarely have the technical skill to recognize, capture, and process pertinent data and models or to interpret the results of the models' processing within the problem context. Providing technical assistants has alleviated but not resolved these prob-lems, and such an approach has created additional implementation barriers. In short, the DSS concept offers little direct support for the intelligence, early design, and implementation phases of decision making.

Problem-pertinent data will be available from external as well as internal sources. To be useful for decision making, these data must be identified, located, captured, stored, accessed, and interpreted (Seely & Targett, 1999). Data ware-

Figure 2: Decision Support System (DSS)

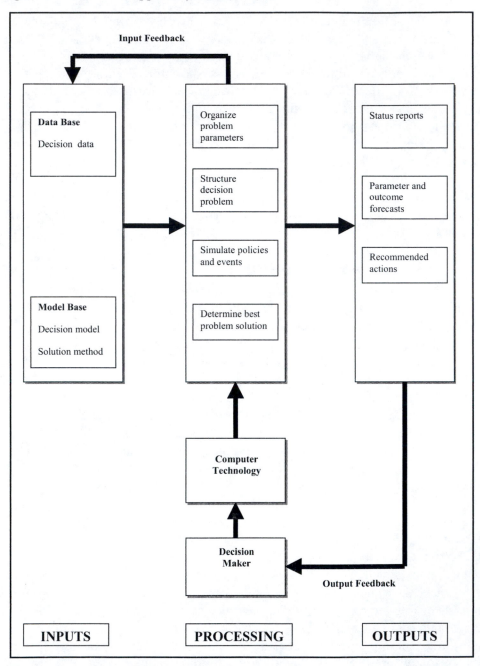

housing can be used to facilitate access and reporting, while data mining can help with the interpretation function.   The EIS concept, with the typical architecture shown in Figure 3, can deliver these data access, reporting, and interpretation functions to the decision maker in an intuitive and appealing manner.

As Figure 3 illustrates, a typical EIS captures and stores as inputs, either physically or as views of the data warehouse, problem-pertinent external and internal data, the descriptive statistical models needed to organize the data, and the statistical or other mathematical models that will be used to mine the captured data. The

Figure 3: Executive Information System (EIS)

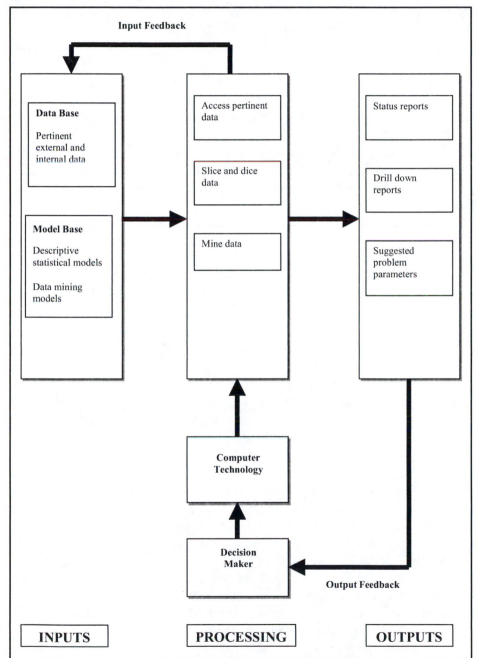

decision maker utilizes computer technology to: (a) organize the data into specified broad categories, (b) view (slice and dice) the data from interesting perspectives, (c) generate "warnings" for the decision maker by scanning current trends, and (d) mine the data for less obvious relationships. Results are reported as category summaries (status reports), sliced and diced details (drill down reports), and/or suggested problem parameters (events). Feedback from the user-controlled processing guides the decision maker to a general problem understanding, and the created parameters are stored as additional inputs for future or further processing.

Applications have incorporated some or all of the typical EIS functionality. For example, a geographical information system (GIS) can be thought of as an EIS that focuses on data access and reporting functionality for problems that involve spatial dimensions or can usefully be examined in a spatial manner. In this case, pertinent data would also include spatial information, such as the location of regions and the geographic attributes of the regions.

The user should exit EIS (or GIS) processing with a general understanding of the problem or opportunity and with relevant problem information (such as general objectives, range of decision alternatives, and range of pertinent events). Additional decision analysis beyond EIS (or GIS) processing will be required to explicitly formulate the problem and complete the decision making process. Put another way, an EIS (or GIS) directly supports only the intelligence phase of decision making.

Technical and domain expertise will be needed to recognize, formulate, and solve most complex and significant decision problems or opportunities. Although such expertise will be available within and outside an organization, the expertise may be difficult, costly, and time-consuming to locate, access, and utilize. The corresponding knowledge, however, can be acquired, embedded within a KBS, and the system can be used to capture, store, and deliver the expertise to the decision maker (Ayyub, 2001). Figure 4 shows the typical architecture for a KBS.

As Figure 4 indicates, a typical KBS captures and stores as inputs problem-pertinent knowledge, either from experts, cases, or other sources, and the models (inference engine or reasoning mechanisms) needed to draw problem solution inferences from the knowledge. The decision maker utilizes computer technology to: (a) access problem knowledge, (b) structure the problem facts, and (c) simulate expertise. Results are reported as problem conditions (status reports), decision advice, and/or explanation for the solicited facts and the rendered advice. Feedback from the user-controlled processing guides the decision maker to useful decision alternatives, a system evaluation of the alternatives, and a selection of the most preferable alternative. Created knowledge is stored as an additional input for future or further processing. In other words, a KBS directly supports some of the design and most of the choice phases of decision making. Specifically, a KBS facilitates problem structuring and the evaluation and selection of alternatives.

Since decision making is a sequential and continuous process, learning will be essential to the successful completion of the process. Users will learn from their interactions with a KBS (or other individual decision making support system) and, in

Figure 4: Knowledge-based system (KBS)

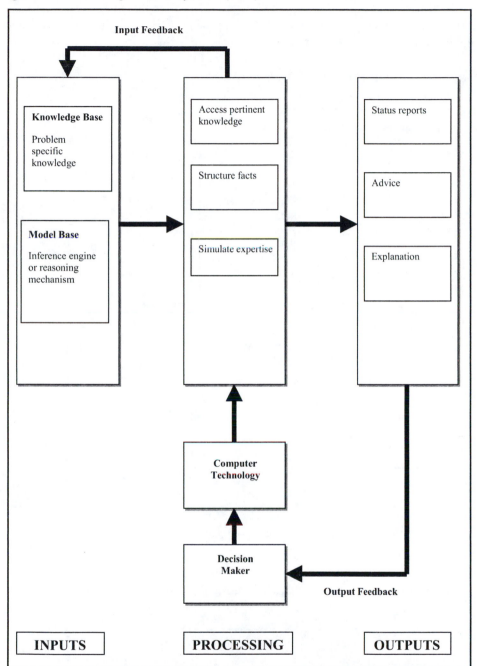

the process, gain skills that can be applied to future decision making tasks. Applying learning to the solution of the current problem, however, often will require system support (Steiger, 1998). Machine learning systems can provide such support by mimicing the learning processes of physical systems.

Figure 5 gives the typical architecture of a machine learning system.   As this figure illustrates, a typical MLS captures and stores as inputs problem-specific data and learning models (such as neural networks and genetic algorithms). The decision maker utilizes computer technology to: (a) organize the problem data, (b) structure

Figure 5: Machine Learning System (MLS)

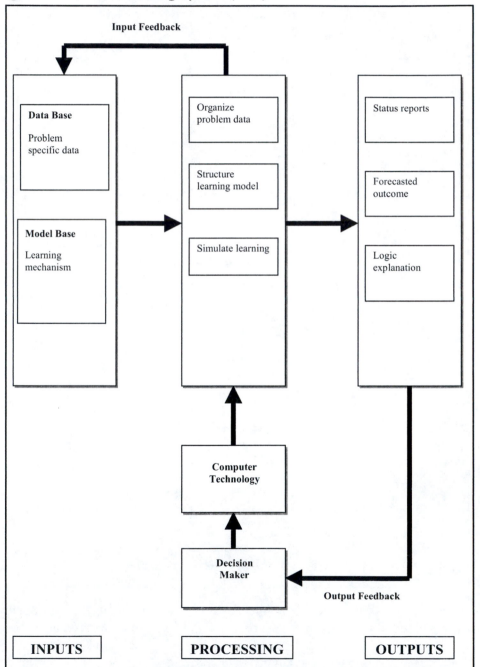

(operationalize) the learning model, and (c) simulate learning. Results are reported as problem conditions (status reports), forecasted problem outcomes, and/or an explanation of the learning logic. Feedback from the user-controlled processing guides the decision maker through the systematic and logical evaluation of alternatives required during the choice phase of decision making and provides additional problem-specific data. Created problem data are stored as additional inputs for future or further processing.

Besides learning, creativity often is needed to successfully complete the decision making process (Keys, 2000). While the previous systems free decision makers to concentrate on the creative aspects of decision making, they do not provide direct support for the creative process (Savransky, 2001). Since decision makers may not be inherently creative, support for creativity can considerably enhance their decision making process. A creativity enhancing system (CES), with the typical architecture shown in Figure 6, offers such support (Forgionne, Clements, & Newman, 1995).

Figure 6 shows that a typical CES captures and stores as inputs problem-specific ideas and concepts and creativity enhancing tools. Ideas and concepts may come from conventional wisdom, documents detailing standard operating procedures, case studies, or other sources, while creativity enhancing tools include morphological analysis, metaphors, divergent thinking mechanisms, brainstorming, calculus, and other methodologies. The decision maker utilizes computer technology to: (a) organize (chiefly, categorize and classify) the problem ideas and concepts, (b) structure ideas and concepts into problem elements and relationships, and (c) simulate conceptual problem solutions. Results are reported as problem elements (status reports), the problem's conceptual structure (criteria, alternatives, events, and relationships), and/or forecasted outcomes from the conceptual analyses. Feedback from the user-controlled processing guides the decision maker through the design stages of the decision making process and identifies the parties affected by the conceptual analyses. This identification helps the decision maker to develop an implementation plan and put the plan into action. Created problem elements and structures are stored as additional inputs for future or further processing.

The major individual systems and their primary and direct support are summarized in Table 1. An examination of this table shows that none of the individual systems offers complete and integrated support for all phases and steps of the decision making process. In some cases, such support may be unnecessary. For ill-structured, complex, and significant problems, especially at the strategic level, the decision maker will need assistance during the entire decision making process. This realization has encouraged researchers to seek the synergistic effects that can be achieved by combining the functionalities of the individual systems. The result has been the development of the various integrated systems for decision making support, summarized in Table 2.

As Table 2 indicates, each integrated system, such as an ESS or MSS, integrates the functionality of particular individual systems to provide decision making support.

Figure 6: Creativity Enhancing System (CES)

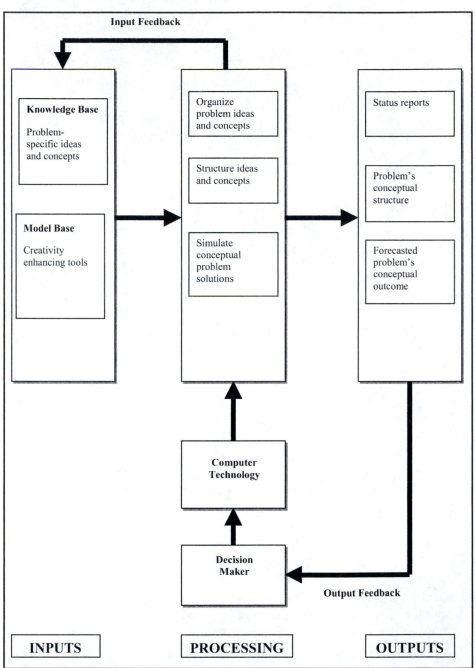

While the integrated functionality has created more complete and unified decision making support, the suggested synergies still leave significant gaps in decision making support. For example, an IDSS still leaves gaps in design support, while an MSS does not provide creativity support. With even more system choices available than previously, the decision maker and/or staff are forced to match the relevant functionality with his/her/their decision making support needs. Decision makers and/or staff may be ill-equipped to make these selections and design, build, and implement the desired system.

Table 1: Individual decision making support systems

System	Type	Support
Decision Support System (DSS)	Individual	Specifying relationships between criteria, alternatives, and events; choice
Executive Information System (EIS) and Geographic Information Systems (GIS)	Individual	Intelligence; developing decision criteria; identifying relevant uncontrollable events
Knowledge-Based System (KBS)	Individual	Develop decision alternatives; choice
Machine Learning System (MLS)	Individual	Logically evaluate decision alternatives
Creativity Enhancing System (CES)	Individual	Design; develop an implementation plan; put implementation plan into action

Table 2: Integrated decision making support systems

System	Type	Support
Intelligent Decision Support System (IDSS)	Integrates the functions of DSS and KBS (and/or MLS)	Developing decision alternatives; specifying relationships between criteria, alternatives, and events; choice
Executive Support System (ESS)	Integrates the functions of DSS and EIS (and/or GIS)	Intelligence; developing decision criteria; identifying relevant uncontrollable events; specifying relationships between criteria, alternatives, and events; choice
Whole-Brained Decision Support System (WDSS) and Group Decision Support System (GDSS)	Integrate the functions of DSS and CES	Gain problem/opportunity understanding; design; choice
Management Support System (MSS)	Integrates the functions of DSS, EIS (and/or GIS), and KBS (and/or MLS)	Intelligence; design; choice

Solutions and Recommendations

An alternative strategy is to create one decision making support system that synthesizes the main features and functions from Table 1 and 2's decision making support systems but which can be tailored to the particular requirements of the user faced with a specific decision problem or opportunity. A decision technology system (DTS) has been proposed to support this alternative strategy. Figure 7 gives a generalized architecture of a DTS.

As Figure 7 illustrates, a DTS has three major inputs. There is a data base, knowledge base, and model base. The data base contains the data directly relevant to the decision problem, including the values for the uncontrollable events, decision alternatives, and decision criteria. The knowledge base holds problem knowledge, such as formulas for converting available data into the problem's parameters, guidance for selecting decision alternatives and problem relationships, or advice in interpreting possible outcomes. The model base is a repository for the formal (tabular, graphic, conceptual, or mathematical) models of the decision problem and the methodology for developing results (simulations and solutions) from the formal models.

Decision makers utilize computer technology (hardware and software) to process the inputs into problem-relevant outputs. The DTS can use problem ideas, concepts, and knowledge drawn from the knowledge base to assist users in performing these processing tasks. Processing will involve:

(a)   organizing problem parameters—accessing the data base, extracting the decision data, and organizing the information in the form needed by the solution model and methodology;

(b)   structuring the decision problem—accessing the model base, retrieving the appropriate decision model, and operationalizing (attaching organized parameters to) the decision model;

(c)   simulating policies and events—using the operationalized decision model to perform the computations needed to simulate outcomes from user-specified alternatives and then identifying the alternative (or alternatives) that best meets the decision criterion (or criteria) among those tested; and

(d)   finding the best problem solution—accessing the model base, retrieving the appropriate solution method, and using the retrieved method to systematically determine the alternative (or alternatives), among all possible alternatives, that best meets the decision criterion (or criteria).

Processing will generate status reports, forecasts, recommendations, and explanations. The status reports will identify relevant uncontrollable events, decision alternatives, and decision criteria and show the current values for these problem elements.   Forecasts will report the events and alternatives specified in the simulations and the resulting projected values of the decision criteria. The recommendations will suggest the values for the decision alternatives that best meet the decision criteria and the corresponding criteria values under current and forecasted values for the uncontrollable events. Explanations will justify the recommendations and offer advice on further processing. Such advice may include suggestions on interpreting the output and guidance for examining additional scenarios.

The DTS provides both input and output feedback to the user. Input feedback from the processing provides additional data, knowledge, and models that may be

Figure 7: Decision Technology System (DTS)

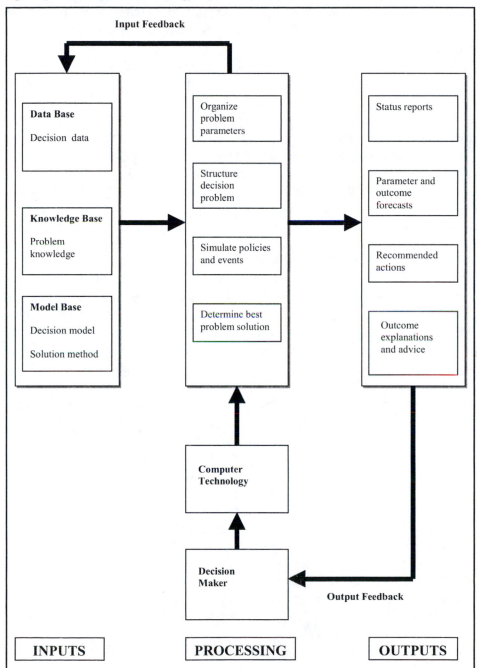

useful for future decision making. Output feedback (which can include outcomes, cognitive information, task models, and what-if, goal-seeking, and other types of sensitivity analyses) is used to extend or modify the original analyses and evaluations.

In practice, a decision maker may desire all or only some of the functionality involved in Figure 7's general DTS architecture. This figure, then, can serve as a guideline to tailor system design and development for the specific decision problem. Starting with basic decision making support, such design and development may evolve into the general architecture as the decision maker's needs and requirements mature.

Figure 7's general DTS architecture can support all phases of the decision making process in a complete, integrated, and continuous manner. Critical problem data can be captured in a DTS data base. The DTS can be used to organize this captured information, generate timely focused reports, and project trends. Such processing helps the decision maker to quickly monitor the decision environment, set objectives, and evaluate the processed information for opportunities or problems, thereby supporting the intelligence phase of decision making.

Accounting, economic, and information science constructs, OR/MS models, and statistical methodologies can be captured in a DTS model base. The DTS, augmented by the managers' (or perhaps staff) insights and judgements, can be used to process these captured constructs and models into criteria, events, and alternatives needed to formulate a model of the decision problem. Additional processing with the captured statistical methodologies can estimate the parameters required to operationalize the formulated decision problem model, thereby supporting the design phase of decision making. The formulated models, again augmented by the managers' insights and judgements, are used to evaluate alternatives in a systematic and analytic fashion and to recommend alternatives, thereby supporting the choice phase of decision making.

Decision technology systems (DTS) can provide the analyses in vivid detail with tables, graphs, and other supporting material. Such supporting material will increase the decision maker's confidence in the recommendations, improve the decision maker's perception of support system effectiveness, and enable the decision maker to better explain, justify, and communicate the decisions during implementation, thereby supporting the implementation phase of decision making.

DTS interactive feedback loops make it relatively easy for management to support the decision making process in a continuous and dynamic manner. Along with the original analyses and evaluations, the feedback loops also increase the users' confidence in the recommendations and enable the decision maker to better explain, justify, and communicate the decisions during implementation.

By organizing captured data, generating timely focused reports, and projecting trends, the DTS provides problem-specific information. Structuring the decision model with the DTS accesses virtual expertise that helps the user to gain knowledge about the decision problem. DTS simulations, optimizations, and sensitivity analyses transform the knowledge into wisdom (understanding and insight) about the problem and its solution.

FUTURE TRENDS

Realizing the DTS promise presents significant technical and management challenges, problem-pertinent data, models, and knowledge must be identified, located, retrieved, and captured. Intelligent data warehousing and mining can support the data retrieval tasks, and it may be possible to adapt these methodologies for model and knowledge retrieval support. Differences in data, knowledge, and model structures, however, may necessitate the development of new methodologies for knowledge and model retrieval tasks.

Integration offers an additional challenge. Currently, there are tools available to support some, but not all, of the integration tasks involved in DTS. Most of these tools rely on a linked approach, with several individual systems offering inputs for output processing by the others. For example, an EIS tool may be used to generate data for a DSS generator, and the DSS generator, perhaps with the aid of an ES shell, may be used to evaluate alternatives. In other cases, the integration may proceed in an embedded fashion with one system consisting of modules or components that share the relevant information and processing task to achieve the decision making support. In the future, we can expect the integrated system to include modules that will eliminate or greatly reduce existing support gaps.

Also, it will be challenging to collect and deliver the tools and to manage the design, development, and implementation effort. Agents and object-oriented methods can be used to capture the tools and make them available for system operation. The resulting system, however, will profoundly challenge the nature of the decision maker's work as well as altering the structure of the organization. By providing complete and integrated decision making support, a DTS will enable the decision maker to perform technical tasks previously outsourced to specialists. The result may be an organization with fewer hierarchical levels and smaller staffs.

Further, it will be necessary to strongly integrate the DTS with other information systems that: (a) provide the data for the decision analyses (such as transaction processing and management information systems) and (b) communicate findings and suggested actions to affected parties (such as groupware and other management communication systems). While such intersystem integration is commonplace among the individual decision making and the data processing and communication systems, this intersystem sharing will be even more crucial for DTS success. That's because a DTS has wider and deeper information requirements than an individual or less integrated decision making support system.

CONCLUSION

Over the years, support for decision making has taken a variety of forms. As the forms have evolved, decision making support has become more comprehensive and integrated. Today, there are many system choices available, and matching the appropriate system to the particular problem or opportunity has created a new task for management.

The evolution has illustrated the synergistic value that can be achieved through higher levels of functional integration. This chapter has presented a DMSS architecture, the DTS, that can offer a mechanism to consolidate the advances and promote a revolution in management. The proposed system has also created significant research opportunities—determining the best integration strategy, identifying the best design and development tools to achieve the strategy, and examining the impact of integrated decision support on management, decision making, and organizational structure, among others. It also clarifies the needs to: (a) have effective and efficient information reporting and communication systems in place and (b) integrate the decision making support systems with information reporting and communication systems.

REFERENCES

Ayyub, B. M. (2001). *Elicitation of expert opinions for uncertainty and risks.* Andover, UK: CRC Press.

Balasubramanian, P., Nochur, K., Henderson, J. C., & Kwan, M. M. (1999). Managing process knowledge for decision support. *Decision Support Systems, 27*(1-2), 145-162.

Borenstein, D. (1998). Towards a practical method to validate decision support systems. *Decision Support Systems, 23*(3), 227-239.

Forgionne, G. A. (1999). An AHP model of DSS effectiveness. *European Journal of Information Systems, 8*, 95-106.

Forgionne, G. A. (2000). Decision-making support system effectiveness: The process to outcome link. *Information Knowledge Systems Management, 2*(2), 169-188.

Forgionne, G. A., Clements, J. P., & Newman, J. (1995). Qualitative thinking support systems (QTSS). *Journal of Decision Systems, 4*(2), 103-137.

Forgionne, G. A., & Kohli, R. (1995). Integrated MSS effects: An empirical health care investigation. *Information Processing and Management, 31*(6), 879-896.

Holsapple, C. W., & Whinston, A. B. (1996). *Decision support systems: A knowledge-based approach.* New York: ITP.

Hooghiemstra, J. S., Kroon, L. G., Odijk, M. A., Salomon, M., & Zwaneveld, P. J. (1999). Decision support systems support the search for win-win solutions in railway network design. *Interfaces, 29*(2), 15-32.

Keys, P. (2000). Creativity, design and style in MS/OR. *Omega, 28*(3), 303-312.

Kumar, R. L. (1999). Understanding DSS value: An options perspective. *Omega, 27*(3), 295-304.

Lawrence, M., & Sim, W. (1999). Prototyping a financial DSS. *Omega, 27*(4), 445-450.

Martinsons, M., Davison, R., & Tse, D. (1999). The balanced scorecard: A foundation for the strategic management of information systems. *Decision Support Systems*, *25*(1), 71-88.

Mirchandani, D., & Pakath, R. (1999). Four models for a decision support system. *Information & Management*, *35*(1), 31-42.

Raghunathan, S. (1999). Impact of information quality and decision-maker quality on decision quality: A theoretical model and simulation analysis. *Decision Support Systems, 26*(4), 275-286.

Sauter, V. (1997). *Decision support systems*. New York: Wiley.

Savransky, S. D. (2001). *Engineering of creativity: Introduction to TRIZ methodology of inventive problem solving*. Andover, UK: CRC Press.

Seely, M., & Targett, D. (1999). Patterns of senior executives' personal use of computers. *Information & Management*, *35*(6), 315-330.

Simon, H. (1960). *The new science of management decision*. New York: Harper & Row.

Siskos, Y., & Spyridakos, A. (1999). Intelligent multiple criteria decision support: Overview and perspectives. *European Journal of Operational Research*, *113*(2), 236-246.

Steiger, D. M. (1998). Enhancing user understanding in a decision support system: A theoretical basis and framework. *Journal of Management Information Systems*, *15*(2), 199-220.

Chapter II

Categorizing Decision Support Systems: A Multidimensional Approach

D. J. Power
University of Northern Iowa, USA

ABSTRACT

This chapter summarizes a multidimensional approach to categorizing specific decision support systems (DSS) developed in Power (2002) and related works. The suggested approach or expanded framework emphases evaluates DSS in terms of one primary dimension and three secondary dimensions. Managers and analysts need to examine what drives the DSS and provides the dominant functionality of the system. Then a DSS can be further categorized in terms of targeted users, purpose of the system and primary deployment technology. The framework can improve discussions about DSS and assist in organizing our current knowledge about DSS.

INTRODUCTION

To some people, a discussion of categories or types of decision support systems may seem largely an academic exercise. To others such discussions have the potential to improve our understanding of these important computerized systems intended to support decision making. The need for typologies and especially "new" typologies is an ongoing debate in many disciplines. But classifying things has been occurring in science for hundreds, if not thousands, of years. In general, classification helps create order and helps the classifier and others using a framework transmit information to those interested in the phenomenon. A classification scheme or framework can help one view the world more systematically. A number of DSS typologies have been proposed in the past 30 years, but technology developments and new applications suggest that an expanded framework is needed. Also, an expanded framework can help decision makers and DSS developers explain and categorize potential DSS projects as well as existing decision support systems. A rigorous, clearly defined conceptual framework can provide guidelines for making such categorizations.

This chapter summarizes and discusses a multidimensional framework for categorizing DSS based on four characteristics: 1) the dominant component and driver of decision support, 2) the targeted users, 3) the specific purpose of the system and 4) the primary deployment technology. The goal of the chapter is to help people categorize decision support systems using the expanded, multidimensional conceptual framework proposed by Power (1997, 2000, 2001, 2002). This framework has also been discussed in the electronic newsletter DSS News and at the Web site dssresources.com.

BACKGROUND

Researchers in many fields have worked to develop meaningful typologies that help organize our knowledge about the world. Their experiences suggest that gaining acceptance of a new framework is often difficult and controversial. Hall (1972), in a review of organization typologies, argued that many classification schemes are an oversimplification of the observed phenomenon and only focus on a single characteristic. He argues the "essence of the typological effort really lies in the determination of the critical variables for differentiating the phenomena under investigation" (p. 41).

Efforts to develop taxonomies or typologies can be based either on deduction or induction. Typologies based on induction are often derived from empirical research. The framework summarized in this article has been developed deductively. The initial focus was on using the characteristics and critical variables in prior classification schemes to create a more comprehensive framework. A number of questions were addressed: What characteristics are relevant to creating a typology of decision support systems? What are the critical characteristics that differentiate one decision support system from another? What characteristic makes a DSS a member of a specific category of decision support systems? Are the variables in the framework important for building successful DSS? Finally, can one measure or evaluate the variables when examining a specific DSS?

The terms frameworks, taxonomies, conceptual models and typologies are often used interchangeably. Taxonomies classify objects and typologies show how mutually exclusive types of things are related. The general desire is to create a set of labels that help people organize and categorize information. Sprague and Watson (1996) argued typologies, frameworks or conceptual models are "often crucial to the understanding of a new or complex subject." A good framework shows the parts of a topic or phenomenon and how the parts interrelate and operate in the context of an observed phenomenon or object.

A new framework can also be useful because many poorly defined terms are currently used for specific types of decision support systems that need to be categorized. For example, the terms business intelligence, collaborative systems, data mining, data warehousing, knowledge management and online analytical processing (OLAP) are all used by some vendors and managers to label DSS and decision support software. Software vendors use these more specialized terms for both descriptive and marketing purposes. What term we use for a system or software package is important in studying these systems and making sense out of what has been deployed and what capabilities various software products can provide managers and organizations. Some DSS are subsystems of other information systems and this structural design adds to the complexity of categorizing and identifying DSS. In general, decision support systems are a broad category of information systems. One reason we study DSS is to understand how they differ from other information systems.

The information systems called decision support systems are not all the same. What managers, vendors and consultants call DSS can "take on many different forms and can be used in many different ways (Alter, 1980, p. 71)." DSS differ in terms of capabilities and targeted users of a specific system and in terms of how the DSS is implemented and what it is called. Some DSS focus on data, some on models and some on facilitating communications and collaboration. DSS also differ in terms of targeted users; some DSS are intended for one "primary" user and used "standalone" for analysis and others are intended for many users in an organization.

Holsapple and Whinston (1996, pp. 178-195) identified five specialized types of DSS: text-oriented, database-oriented, spreadsheet-oriented, solver-oriented, and rule-oriented DSS. Donovan and Madnick (1977) classified DSS as institutional or ad hoc DSS. Institutional DSS support decisions that are recurring. An ad hoc DSS supports problems that are not anticipated and that are not expected to reoccur. Hackathorn and Keen (1981) identified DSS in three distinct yet interrelated categories: personal DSS, group DSS and organizational DSS.

In 1980, Steven Alter explained an empirically derived taxonomy of decision support systems. His taxonomy is based on the degree to which DSS output can directly determine a decision. The taxonomy is related to a spectrum of generic operations that can be performed by decision support systems. These generic operations extend along a single dimension, ranging from extremely data-oriented to extremely model-oriented decision tasks. DSS may involve retrieving a single item of information, providing a mechanism for ad hoc data analysis and pre-specified aggregations of data in the form of reports or "screens." DSS may also include estimating the consequences of proposed decisions and proposing decisions. Alter categorized DSS into seven distinct types: file drawer systems, data analysis systems, analysis information systems, accounting and financial models, representational models, optimization models, and suggestion models. Alter's dissertation research (1975) remains the cornerstone for future research and theory development on types of decision support systems.

AN EXPANDED FRAMEWORK

A new, broader typology or framework is needed today because decision support systems are much more common and more diverse than when Alter conducted his research and proposed his framework. The 1980 typology is still relevant for categorizing some types of DSS, but not for all decision support systems.

Traditionally, academics and practitioners have discussed building decision support systems in terms of four major components: 1) the user interface, 2) the database, 3) the models and analytical tools, and 4) the DSS architecture and network (cf. Sprague & Carlson, 1982). This traditional list of components remains useful because it identifies similarities and differences between categories or types of DSS and it can help managers and analysts build new DSS. The following expanded DSS framework is primarily based on the different emphases placed on DSS components when systems are actually constructed. This characteristic, the importance of components of a DSS, was identified as a major differentiating variable. Many DSS seem to derive their functionality primarily from one major component. To keep the number of categories in a new framework manageable, Alter's 1980 typology was simplified into three types of decision support systems: data-driven, model-driven and knowledge-driven.

The expanded framework focuses on one major dimension with five categories and three secondary dimensions. The major characteristic in the framework is the dominant technology that drives or provides the decision support functionality. Five generic categories based on the dominant component are discussed in this section: communications-driven, data-driven, document-driven, knowledge-driven, and , model-driven decision support systems. Some DSS are hybrid systems driven by more than one major DSS component. The following expanded DSS framework helps categorize the most common DSS currently in use.

Communications-driven DSS include systems built using communication, collaboration and decision support technologies. These systems were developed first in the mid-1980s and they do not fit within those DSS types identified by Alter.

Data-driven DSS include file drawer and management reporting systems, data warehousing and analysis systems, executive information systems (EIS) and spatial decision support systems (SDSS). Business intelligence systems linked to a data warehouse are also examples of data-driven DSS. Data-driven DSS emphasize access to and manipulation of large databases of structured data and especially a time series of internal company data. Simple file systems accessed by query and retrieval tools provide the most elementary level of functionality. Data warehouse systems that allow the manipulation of data by computerized tools tailored to a specific task and setting or by more general tools and operators provide additional functionality. Data-driven DSS with online analytical processing (OLAP) provide the highest level of functionality and decision support that is linked to analysis of large collections of historical data (cf. Dhar & Stein, 1997).

Document-driven DSS integrate a variety of storage and processing technologies to provide complete document retrieval and analysis. A search tool that creates text summaries and rates document relevance provides decision support functionality, but the dominant component is the document base. Examples of documents that might be included in a document database include policies and procedures, product specifications, catalogs, and corporate historical information, including minutes of meetings, corporate records, and important correspondence (cf. Fedorowicz, 1993; Swanson & Culnan, 1978).

Knowledge-driven DSS or what Alter termed suggestion DSS can suggest or recommend actions to managers. These DSS contain specialized problem-solving expertise. The "expertise" consists of knowledge about a particular domain, understanding of problems within that domain, and "skill" at solving some of those problems.

Model-driven DSS include systems that use accounting and financial models, representational models, and optimization models. Model-driven DSS emphasize access to and manipulation of a model. Simple statistical and analytical tools provide the most elementary level of functionality.

Data-driven, document-driven and knowledge-driven DSS need specialized database components. The model component provides the dominant functionality in a model-driven DSS. Finally, the communications and networking component is the key driver of communications-driven DSS.

Each generic category of DSS can be targeted to various user groups, including internal and external stakeholders. Each DSS can have a specific or a very general purpose. Finally, each category of DSS can be deployed using a mainframe computer, a client/server LAN, or a Web-based architecture. In this expanded framework, DSS should also be categorized on these secondary dimensions. Most DSS are intra-organizational DSS designed for use by individuals in a company, but the rapid growth of the Internet is making it easier to implement interorganizational DSS targeted to customers or suppliers. General-purpose DSS software helps support broad tasks like project management and decision analysis, or it serves as a DSS generator to build a specific category of DSS. Some DSS software supports a very narrow, specific purpose and should be referred to as a function-specific or industry-specific application. Finally, even though Web technologies are the leading edge for building DSS, traditional programming languages or fourth-generation languages are still used to build DSS. Mainframe and client-server technologies remain important DSS enabling technologies. So DSS can and should be categorized in terms of targeted users, purpose and the technology used to implement the system.

One can and should use all four dimensions in the framework to categorize a specific system. Some specific questions for identifying the DSS type include: What is the dominant component and driver of decision support? Who is the targeted user group? What is the purpose of the DSS? and What is the enabling technology used for implementing the system? The answers to these questions should help classify the proposed DSS or the DSS product a vendor is trying to sell or an existing system that was previously implemented in a company. For example, a manager may want to build a model-driven, interorganizational, product design, Web-based DSS. Or a company might currently have a data-driven, intra-organizational, ad hoc query, client/server-based DSS. Or a manager may have built a model-driven, marketing management, sales forecasting, spreadsheet-based DSS that is no longer meeting his needs. Some managers use multiple DSS and using the proposed framework can help them understand how the various DSS differ and how they are similar.

CONCLUSIONS

This chapter attempted to summarize a rigorous, clearly defined conceptual framework that can be used for categorizing decision support systems. Discussion and debate and efforts to use the framework can improve it and make it more useful for both research and practice. One can hope that the above discussion and framework improves our understanding of computerized systems intended to support decision making. In 1982, Sprague and Carlson concluded "DSS comprise a class of information system that draws on transaction processing systems and interacts with the other parts of the overall information system to support the decision-making activities of managers and other knowledge workers in organizations" (p. 9). Almost 20 years later, DSS still comprise a class of information system intended to support the decision-making activities of managers. The concept has been buffeted by the hyperbole of marketing people and technologies have improved and changed. Without a doubt we have major conceptual overlap problems related to terms associated with computerized decision support, and we still have too much hype and too many marketing terms for decision support software that sound too good to be true. But the basic underlying concept of supporting decision makers remains important.

Does the expanded DSS framework (Power, 2002) summarized in this chapter improve our understanding of various decision support systems? From my biased perspective, it seems to meet this goal. The framework will certainly evolve and empirical testing can add value to it. Much remains to be done. In many ways, the era of decision support is only just beginning. The Model-T era of DSS is ending and the mass customization era is beginning. Academics and practitioners still have much to learn. What are the unanswered questions about this framework that need to be resolved in future papers and in empirical studies?

First, there is a serious measurement and evaluation issue—How does one conclude which component is the dominant component of a DSS? One of the major concerns is learning enough about complex DSS to evaluate them using the framework. Second, there are important technology issues—Is it necessary to distinguish the different technologies for developing DSS? How can and should the enabling technologies be categorized? Is it adequate to consider only four or five categories like mainframe-based, client-server, stand-alone PC, Web-based, and perhaps emerging like handheld PCs? There is a related technology issue—Is there an important difference between a Web-based and a Web-enabled DSS that draws on legacy data sources on mainframe computers?

Third, the major issue of system boundaries must be addressed in any analysis of information systems—Can an information system have multiple decision support subsystems and if so, is it reasonable to assert that the dominant component in each subsystem may differ?

The framework seems usable in its present form despite these unresolved issues. Perhaps a good conceptual framework can stimulate research about decision support systems—Ask yourself, "What do we really know about using technology to support decision makers?"

REFERENCES

Alter, S. L. (1975). *A study of computer aided decision making in organizations.* Unpublished doctoral dissertation, MIT.

Alter, S. L. (1980). *Decision support systems: Current practice and continuing challenges.* Reading, MA: Addison-Wesley.

Dhar, V., & Stein, R. (1997). *Intelligent decision support methods: The science of knowledge.* Upper Saddle River, NJ: Prentice Hall.

Donovan, J.J., & Madnick, S. E. (1977). Institutional and ad hoc DSS and their effective use. *Data Base, 8*(3).

Fedorowicz, J. (1993). A technology infrastructure for document-based decision support systems. In R. Sprague & H. J. Watson *Decision Support Systems: Putting Theory into Practice* (3rd ed., pp. 125-136).

Hackathorn, R. D., & Keen, P.G.W. (1981, September) "Organizational Strategies for Personal Computing in Decision Support Systems," MIS Quarterly, pp. 21-27.

Hall, R. (1972). *Organizations: Structure and process.* Englewood Cliffs, NJ: Prentice Hall.

Holsapple, C.W., & Whinston, A. B. (1996). *Decision support systems: A knowledge-based approach.* Minneapolis, MN: West Publishing Co.

Power, D. J. (2000). "What is a DSS?" DSStar, The On-Line Executive Journal for Data-Intensive Decision Support, Vol. 1, No. 3, October 21, 1997 .

Power, D. J. (2000). "Web-Based and Model-Driven Decision Support Systems: Concepts and Issues," Proceedings of the 2000 Americas Conference on Information Systems, Long Beach, California, August 10-13.

Power, D. J. (2001). "Supporting Decision-Makers: An Expanded Framework," In Harriger, A. (Editor), e-Proceedings (ISSN 1535-0703), 2001 Informing Science Conference, June 19-22, Krakow, Poland.

Power, D. J. (2002). *Decision support systems: Concepts and resources for managers.* Westport, CT: Quorum Books.

Sprague, R. H., & Carlson, E. D. (1982). *Building effective decision support systems*. Englewood Cliffs, NJ: Prentice Hall.

Sprague, R. H., & Watson, H. J. (1996)(eds.). *Decision support for management*. Englewood Cliffs, N.J.: Prentice Hall, Inc.

Swanson, E. B., & Culnan, M. J. (1978). "Document-Based Systems for Management Planning and Control: A Classification, Survey, and Assessment." MIS Quarterly, December, pp. 31–46.

Chapter III

Spatial Decision Support Systems

Peter B. Keenan
University College Dublin, Ireland

ABSTRACT

Many types of challenging problems faced by decision makers have a geographic or spatial component. Spatial decision support systems (SDSS) can effectively support this class of problem. This represents a growing class of DMSS, taking advantage of the increasing capability of technology to deal with spatial data. SDSS is characterized by the use of significant amounts of public data external to the organizations that use it and the increasing availability of such spatial data facilities wider use of such systems. This chapter describes spatial systems, their history, their relationship to other systems, their mean areas of application and their future development.

INTRODUCTION

Spatial decision support systems (SDSS) provide computerized support for decision making where there is a geographic or spatial component to the decision. Computer support for spatial applications is provided by systems based around a geographic (or geographical) information system (GIS) (Keenan, 2002). Spatial applications represent an area of information technology (IT) application with a significantly different history from the other decision making systems discussed in this book. There are a variety of definitions of GIS (Maguire, 1991); these generally identify a GIS as a computer system that facilitates the display and storage of geographically or spatially related data that allows the integration of this data with nonspatial (attribute) data. A GIS has a sophisticated data manager that allows queries based on spatial location. The GIS interface facilitates interaction with this database. A GIS can be distinguished from a simple map display program that lacks these query features. The acronym GIS has also been used as an abbreviation for geographical information science, referring to a body of research on techniques for processing geographic information. A geographic information system employs these techniques. In common usage the expression GIS refers to a computer system, and this convention will be used in this text.

The distinct contribution of GIS to decision making lies in the ability of these systems to store and manipulate data based on its spatial location. Spatial data is of interest in a wide range of government and business activities. Early areas of GIS application included primary industries such as forestry and mining. An important area of GIS application is the transportation field, both in the design of transport infrastructure and in the routing of vehicles that use this infrastructure. More recent developments have included the use of GIS for location analysis and related problems. These include a variety of business and government applications, such as the siting of public facilities (Maniezzo, Mendes, & Paruccini, 1998) or large retail outlets (Clarke & Rowley, 1995). GIS continues to grow in importance, playing a central role in the provision of new services such as mobile telephony. Mobile commerce is an emerging field, largely distinguished from electronic commerce by the presence of a locational element (MacKintosh, Keen, & Heikkonen, 2001). In this environment the importance of GIS and spatial decision making systems can only increase.

ORIGINS OF SDSS

GIS was first used in the 1950s in North America, largely for the automated production of maps. The 1960s saw the introduction of many of the basic concepts in GIS, although their widespread implementation awaited further developments in computer technology. Consequently, more powerful computers were needed, as relatively large volumes of data characterize spatial applications when compared to conventional business data processing. Therefore, the development of sophisticated GIS applications required the introduction of computer systems that had the necessary speed and storage capacity to process queries on the larger quantities of data involved. In the early years of GIS use, these systems required the use of powerful and expensive mainframe computers and could not be easily used in a flexible way.

In the 1970s the concept of decision support systems (DSS) began to develop in the information systems (IS) community, notably with the work undertaken at the Massachusetts Institute of Technology (Gorry & Scott-Morton, 1971; Little, 1971). By the early 1980s there were many books and papers published in the DSS field (Alter, 1980; Bonczek, Holsapple, & Whinston, 1981; Sprague, 1980) and DSS had become a recognized part of IS. DSS had evolved out of the business data processing tradition and usually dealt with the financial and operating data associated with business use. The volumes of data involved with such systems were relatively small compared with those in the geographic domain. As computer systems became more powerful, some DSS type applications evolved that used map display or employed spatial information. A good example is the Geodata Analysis and Display System (GADS) (Grace, 1977), which was used for routing applications. Nevertheless, the technology it used had limited graphics and inadequate processing power to exploit the full potential of spatial applications.

While these developments in DSS were taking place in the IS community in the 1970s, a largely separate trend of development took place in GIS, with developments largely concentrated on geographic data processing applications (Nagy & Wagle, 1979). Spatial applications had placed heavy demands on the technology, and this slowed the progression from data processing to decision support applications. However, over time improving computer performance led to increasing interest in spatial what-if analysis and modeling applications. The idea of a spatial decision support system (SDSS) evolved in the mid-1980s (Armstrong, Densham, & Rushton, 1986), and by the end of the decade SDSS was included in an authoritative review of the GIS field (Densham, 1991). This trend was evident in the launch of a research initiative on SDSS in 1990 by the US National Center for Geographic Information and Analysis (Goodchild & Densham, 1993).

Consequently, by the early 1990s SDSS had achieved a recognized place in the GIS community and was identified by Muller (1993) as a growth area in the application of GIS technology. The delay in the recognition of SDSS, compared to other DSS in other domains reflects the greater demands of spatial processing on IT. Nevertheless, despite these developments SDSS does not occupy a central place in the GIS field, and many introductory GIS textbooks do not mention SDSS at all (Bernhardsen, 1999; Clarke, 1997). This may reflect a feeling among many in the geographic disciplines that SDSS applications involve a diversity of techniques from different fields largely outside the geography domain.

Less attention was paid to SDSS within the DSS research community until the mid-1990s when some work in this area began to appear (Wilson, 1994). One of the first papers in an IS-related publication illustrated the effectiveness of SDSS technology (Crossland, Wynne, & Perkins, 1995). Recently the benefits of SDSS for both inexperienced and experienced decision makers (Mennecke, Crossland, & Killingsworth, 2000) were discussed in *MIS Quarterly*.

DEFINITION OF SDSS

While an increasing number of GIS-based applications are described as SDSS, there is no agreement on what a SDSS exactly constitutes. Partly this reflects the varying definitions of DSS in the DSS research community. However, disagreement on the definition of SDSS also arises from the separation of GIS research from other DSS-related research. To a large extent the term SDSS is used in the GIS research community with little reference to the DSS field generally, and this is reflected in the diversity of applications that describe themselves as SDSS. Many widely accepted definitions of DSS identify the need for a combination of database, interface and model components directed at a specific problem (Sprague, 1980). However there is ongoing debate about the proper definition of DSS, with continuing ambiguity in the use of this term by academics and practitioners. Surveys have shown that many systems described as being DSS generally do not fully meet the definition, while other systems meet the definition of DSS without being described as such (Eom, Lee, Kim, & Somarajan, 1998). In a similar way the term SDSS may be used to describe DSS applications with a simple mapping component where little or no GIS technology is used.

The simplest perspective on the definition of SDSS is that a GIS is implicitly a DSS, as a GIS can be used to support decision making. This type of informal definition is also used in other fields; Keen (1986) identified a trend for the use of any computer system, by people who make decisions to be defined as a DSS. Many GIS-based systems are described as being DSS on the basis that the GIS assisted in the collection or organization of data used by the decision maker. In this context GIS may have contributed to these decisions, but it is questionable if it can be viewed as a system for supporting decisions. The view of GIS as a DSS derives from the perspective of the limited set of users in geography and related fields. For this group, the standard functions of GIS provide the bulk of the information for their decision making needs. A critical limitation of this point of view is that the ultimate potential for SDSS use greatly exceeds this set of traditional users. The wide range of techniques from operations research, accounting, marketing, etc., needed for this broader set of users is unlikely ever to be included in standard GIS software.

A more academic approach is to seek to justify GIS as DSS in terms of the definition of DSS. From this perspective it is possible to argue that a GIS already meets the requirement of being a DSS, as GIS contains an interface, a database and some spatial modeling components. The view of GIS as a DSS has some support in the well-established definitions of DSS. Alter (1980) proposed a framework for DSS that includes data-driven DSS that do not have a substantial model component. GIS could be regarded as an analysis information system in Alter's framework, as the database component, rather than a modeling component, is central to standard GIS software. Mennecke (1997) sees SDSS as an easy-to-use subset of GIS, which incorporates facilities for manipulating and analyzing spatial data. The view that SDSS is a subset of GIS reflects the need for decision makers to focus on their specific problem, and their lack of interest in GIS features outside this domain. This view suggests that the techniques needed for SDSS are already within the GIS domain and that a subset of these techniques can be applied to a particular problem. As the features of a standard GIS are directed at the needs of its traditional users, it is this group that is most likely to subscribe to the view of SDSS being merely a subset of the larger GIS field.

Some authors in the GIS field have looked to the classic definitions of DSS (Keen & Scott -Morton, 1978; Sprague, 1980) and found that GIS lacks the modeling component needed to be accepted as a DSS (Armstrong & Densham, 1990). From this viewpoint SDSS requires the addition of modeling techniques not found in basic GIS software. This position sees SDSS in general, not as a subset of GIS, but as a superset formed by the intersection of GIS and other techniques. This point of view seems to this author to be the most flexible one, where GIS is regarded as a form of DSS generator (Sprague, 1980) to which models can be added to made a specific DSS (Keenan, 1996).

ALTERNATIVE PERSPECTIVES ON SDSS

The different perspectives that exist in relation to SDSS definition can be illustrated by the problem represented in Figure 1. A decision maker might use the basic functionality of a GIS to identify areas liable to flooding along the banks of a river. This would provide information such as the area affected by a given rise in the water level or the new width of the river. This information could be the main input required for some types of decision and for this type of decision maker the GIS software might be said to be acting directly as a SDSS. Another user might wish to identify the sections of road affected by areas liable to flooding along the banks of a river. In turn, this could be used to identify the buildings affected by the flood. The area liable to flood and the relevant road sections could be identified by an appropriate sequence of GIS operations. If this type of decision were made frequently it would be useful to employ a macro to automate the sequence of spatial operations required. Reports could be produced listing the streets in the affected area and quantifying the number of people at risk. One example of the use of a subset of GIS commands to build a specific SDSS might be the inclusion of appropriate reports and customized commands in a set of specific macros. Such a system would employ a database, would use spatial models and an appropriate interface and might be considered to be a DSS in terms of the traditional definitions. This approach has considerable value, but is limited to the functions represented in the macro languages of the GIS software.

A more complex problem is to identify an appropriate evacuation sequence and emergency vehicle routing plan for districts that might be affected by flooding (Figure 2). This would require quite complex modeling techniques; the spatial tools of the GIS would provide the input to this analysis. In this case additional modeling software is needed and it must be integrated with the GIS. This additional software might be a separate modeling package or might make use of custom programs written in a third-generation programming language. This is an example of extending the GIS by using it as a generator for a SDSS. Emergency evacuation (Cova & Church, 1997; de Silva & Eglese, 2000) is one important example of such a problem where this type of synthesis is needed and where complicated modeling is required.

A DSS is a specific system designed for a user familiar with the information and modeling aspects of the specific problem. A DSS is not a black box; it should provide the user with control over the models and interface representations used (Barbosa & Hirko, 1980). SDSS users come from different backgrounds and this has

Figure 1: Areas liable to flooding along a riverbank

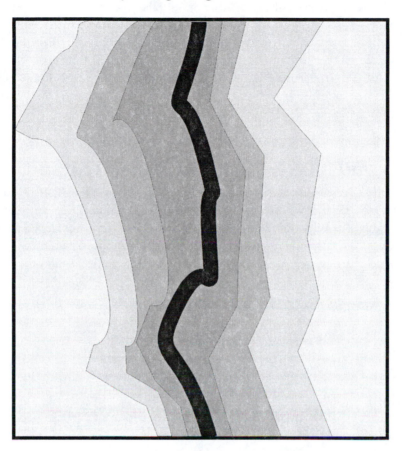

implications for the type of system that they use. Those from a geography background have a good knowledge of the data and models underlying the GIS and are generally concerned with activities which predominately use these types of models. Such users will expect to be able to exert effective control over the specialized spatial models in the GIS. This user is most likely to see a GIS, perhaps with some customized macros, as constituting a SDSS.

Where GIS is only one component of a more complex decision making system, the users may have less interest in the purely geographic issues in the system. For this class of decision maker, the aim of the system builder must be to cater for the problem representation of the user, the logical view of the problem, rather than provide a system too closely related to the physical geographic data. Different users should have different system representations and operations, in a similar way to the concept of subschemas providing a distinctive presentation of a database to a user. This class of user will not be interested in all of the data in a GIS and the full range of GIS operations need not be made available. Different users of a given type of information may be accustomed to quite different presentation formats for the information. This diversity of user requirement places important demands on the design of the components of the SDSS, not only the interface but also the database and modeling components (Grimshaw, Mott, & Roberts, 1997). Flexibility is a key requirement of the GIS software used to build a specific system of this type, as interaction with other software is needed to extend the GIS for the specific problem. A successful SDSS must provide system builders with the flexibility to accommodate user preferences and allow users to employ the form of interaction that they are most comfortable with.

FUTURE PROSPECTS FOR SDSS

A number of potential directions can be identified when looking at the future prospects for SDSS development. Improvements in standard GIS software might increase the range of people who could easily use it directly for decision making. Superior customization features in GIS software might allow easier modification of GIS for specific decisions. Enhanced features for interaction with other software

Figure 2: Identification of route to visit roads affected by flooding

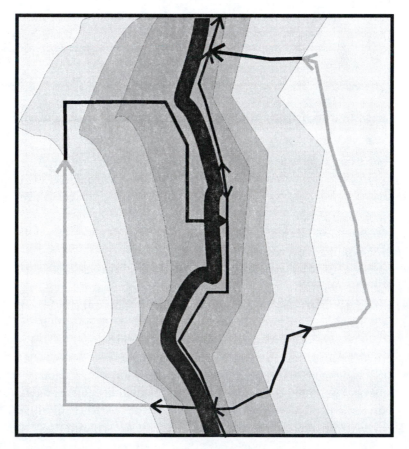

might allow GIS to be readily extended to form a large variety of SDSS applications. Future developments are likely to encompass all of these trends, with different groups of users taking advantage of these changes.

A number of different categories of GIS software exist. At the top end, large powerful packages exist, capable of dealing with large amounts of data, for example, the ESRI ArcInfo software. This powerful software is not always easy to use for decision making purposes but has the capacity to model large geographic areas. Below this level there are a number of user-friendly desktop software applications, for instance, ESRI Arcview (ESRI) or Mapinfo (Mapinfo), which are more often associated with decision making applications. Each new version of these products has additional features and improved interface design, allowing these applications to assist in the decision making needs of an increasing set of users. Those users who find GIS directly usable will typically use only a few of the many additional features offered, reflecting the viewpoint of SDSS as a subset of GIS. Further development is likely to take place in the design of techniques to make this functionality accessible to less experienced users. This might include the addition of artificial intelligence features to allow the software to better implement typical user operations. As these systems become more capable, more users will find them directly useful for decision making.

GIS vendors have recognized the importance of making their software flexible and customizable. Many of the off-the-shelf products are simply one of many possible configurations of the underlying tools with which the software is built. Those wishing to build SDSS, either third parties or users themselves, can provide alternative configurations directed at supporting specific decisions. In a similar way, interfaces are provided for other programs and a variety of third party add-ons exist for specialized purposes. The GIS vendors are moving their products towards commonly recognized standards; for example, ESRI, the largest GIS vendor, has moved its products to a Visual Basic for Applications (VBA) based scripting language. All vendors provide products that support popular software interchange standards such as Object Linking and Embedding (OLE). Adherence to these standards has facilitated the development by third-party developers of a large range of specialist add-ons for GIS products. For instance add-ons for ESRI products include tools for mapping crime, for managing electricity grids, for planning new road developments and for dispatching fire engines.

Another technical development of interest is the extension of GIS techniques to the Internet. Internet standards have some limitations for use in spatial applications, but new software and plug-ins continue to be developed. Current applications offer map display but frequently fall short of providing comprehensive GIS functionality. Future developments offer the possibility of a distributed SDSS that could connect with datasets held at distant locations on the Internet. In this scenario multiple specific SDSS applications might use the Internet to share the geographic data that they have in common.

This author suggests, therefore, that SDSS development in the future will predominately use relatively complex combinations of GIS and other forms of DSS tools. SDSS will support a wide range of problems and users, with quite different systems being used in each situation. Spatial applications have largely been used in the past for problems where the manipulation of spatial data was the key or only information component of the decision to be taken. This type of decision required a system that provided users with full control over the spatial operations in the system. This group of users will continue to use these systems and will be able to exploit technology-driven enhancements in the capability of GIS.

In the future, traditional SDSS applications will be extended to the large number of potential applications where the spatial information is only an interim stage or a subset of the information required for the decision. This will require the construction of systems where users can concentrate on the variables of interest in their decision while other processing is performed without the need for extensive user interaction. These systems will incorporate research and techniques from fields quite separate from the traditional geography-based disciplines that initially used SDSS. This may lead to some fragmentation of the SDSS field, a trend long noted in the DSS field generally. This trend will increase the sense of separation between SDSS and the GIS field on which it is based. This reflects similar trends in other decision making systems where systems draw from fields such as database management or operations research. Decision making applications exploit a synthesis of techniques, without necessarily representing a new breakthrough in the fundamental reference disciplines. Research work continues in new models for these reference disciplines that may in the future be incorporated into decision making systems. The separation of fundamental principles from applications, geographic information science for spatial applications, allows a focus on user-oriented applications. This will allow new types of users and a wider range of decisions to be effectively supported.

As the market grows, GIS software will become less expensive and easier to use and will continue to be used directly for decision making by those in the traditional geo-spatial disciplines. Better integration of models and GIS will extend SDSS applications to a range of applications where GIS has not played a full role in the past. Examples of this would include routing and location problems, which have a long tradition of the use of mathematical techniques. It has long been recognized that these techniques can be greatly enhanced when coupled with the spatial interface and database processing found in GIS software, but this integration still has some way to go. The increased availability of user-friendly SDSS will allow other less technical business disciplines such as marketing to start to exploit spatial modeling for the first time. This will allow exploration of the spatial component of business relationships, which rarely takes place at present.

CONCLUSION

Spatial decision support systems represent an important and growing class of decision making system. SDSS has its origins in disciplines related to geography and will continue to play an important role in these areas. However a wide range of potential applications exist outside the traditional geographic domains. Support can be provided to a much larger range of decision makers in these new fields if GIS software can be better integrated with other modeling software. Standard business computers are now powerful enough to run these more complex applications. As the market for spatial information grows, spatial data is becoming more widely available and less expensive. This is providing a critical mass for new applications; in response to these opportunities GIS vendors are enhancing both the direct capabilities of their software and the potential to integrate that software with other types of software and applications. This will benefit those potential users who currently lack comprehensive computer support for examination of the spatial dimension of their decision making and who as a result often largely neglect this component of their decisions. This untapped body of potential SDSS users promises a bright future for this class of system.

REFERENCES

Alter, S. (1980). *Decision support systems: Current practice and continuing challenges*. Reading: Addison-Wesley.

Armstrong, A. P., & Densham, P. J. (1990). Database organization strategies for spatial decision support systems. *International Journal of Geographical Information Systems, 4*(1), 3-20.

Armstrong, M. P., Densham, P. J., & Rushton, G. (1986, March). *Architecture for a microcomputer based spatial decision support system.* Paper presented at the Second International Symposium on Spatial Data Handling.

Barbosa, L. C., & Hirko, R. G. (1980, March). Integration of algorithmic aids into decision support systems. *MIS Quarterly, 4*, 1-12.

Bernhardsen, T. (1999). *Geographic information systems: An introduction.* (2nd ed.). Wiley.

Bonczek, R. H., Holsapple, C. W., & Whinston, A. B. (1981). *Foundations of decision support systems*. Orlando: Academic Press.

Clarke, I., & Rowley, J. (1995). A case for spatial decision-support systems in retail location planning. *International Journal of Retail & Distribution Management, 23*(3), 4-10.

Clarke, K. C. (1997). *Getting Started with Geographic Information Systems*. Upper Saddle River, NJ: Prentice Hall.

Cova, T. J., & Church, R. L. (1997). Modelling community evacuation vulnerability using GIS. *International Journal of Geographical Information Science, 11*(8), 763-784.

Crossland, M. D., Wynne, B. E., & Perkins, W. C. (1995). Spatial Decision Support Systems: An overview of technology and a test of efficacy. *Decision Support Systems, 14*(3), 219-235.

de Silva, F. N., & Eglese, R. W. (2000). Integrating simulation modelling and GIS:

Spatial decision support systems for evacuation planning. *The Journal of the Operational Research Society, 41*(4), 423-430.

Densham, P. J. (1991). Spatial decision support systems. In D. J. Maguire, M. F. Goodchild, & D. W. Rhind (Eds.), *Geographical Information Systems, Volume 1 : Principles* (Vol. 1, pp. 403-412). Longman.

Eom, S. B., Lee, S. M., Kim, E. B., & Somarajan, C. (1998). A survey of decision support applications (1988-1994). *Journal of the Operational Research Society, 49*(2), 109-120.

ESRI Corp, Redlands, CA , USA (*http://www.esri.com*).

Goodchild, M., & Densham, P. (1993). *Initiative 6: Spatial decision support systems (1990-1992)*. Santa Barbara, CA: National Center for Geographic Information and Analysis.

Gorry, A., & Scott-Morton, M. (1971). A Framework for Information Systems. *Sloan Management Review, 13*, 56-79.

Grace, B. F. (1977). Training Users of a prototype DSS. *Data Base, 8*(3), 30-36.

Grimshaw, D. J., Mott, P. L., & Roberts, S. A. (1997). The role of context in decision-making: Some implications for database design. *European Journal of Information Systems, 6*(2), 122-128.

Keen, P. (1986). Decision support systems: The next decade. In E. McLean & H. G. Sol (Eds.), *Decision Support Systems: A decade in perspective*: North-Holland.

Keen, P. G. W., & Scott-Morton, M. S. (1978). *Decision support systems: An organizational perspective.* Addison-Wesley.

Keenan, P. (1996). Using a GIS as a DSS generator. In J. Darzentas, J. S. Darzentas, & T. Spyrou (Eds.), *Perspectives on DSS* (pp. 33-40). University of the Aegean, Greece.

Keenan, P. B. (2002). Geographic Information Systems. In H. Bidgoli (Ed.), *Encyclopedia of Information Systems*. San Diego, CA: Academic Press.

Little, J. D. C. (1971). Models and managers: The concept of a decision calculus. *Management Science, 16*(8), 466-485.

MacKintosh, R., Keen, P. G. W., & Heikkonen, M. (2001). *The Freedom Economy: Gaining the mCommerce Edge in the Era of the Wireless Internet*: McGraw-Hill.

Maguire, D. J. (1991). An overview and definition of GIS. In D. J. Maguire, M. F. Goodchild, & D. W. Rhind (Eds.), *Geographical Information Systems, Vol. 1: Principles* (pp. 9-20). Longman.

Maniezzo, V., Mendes, I., & Paruccini, M. (1998). Decision support for siting problems. *Decision Support Systems, 23*(3), 273-284.

Mapinfo. MapInfo Corp, Troy, NY, USA (http://www.mapinfo.com).

Mennecke, B. E. (1997). Understanding the Role of Geographic Information Technologies in Business: Applications and Research Directions. *Journal of Geographic Information and Decision Analysis, 1*(1), 44-68.

Mennecke, B. E., Crossland, M. D., & Killingsworth, B. L. (2000). Is a map more than a picture? The role of SDSS technology, subject characteristics, and problem complexity on map reading and problem solving. *MIS Quarterly, 24*(4), 601-604, 625-629.

Muller, J.-C. (1993). Latest developments in GIS/LIS. *International Journal of Geographical Information Systems, 7*(4), 293-303.

Nagy, G., & Wagle, S. (1979). Geographic data processing. *Computing Surveys, 11*(2), 139-181.

Sprague, R. (1980). A framework for the development of decision support systems. *MIS Quarterly, 4*(1).

Wilson, R. D. (1994). GIS & decision support systems. *Journal of Systems Management, 45*(11), 36-40.

Chapter IV

From Human Decision Making to DMSS Architecture

Jean-Charles Pomerol
Université Pierre et Marie Curie, France

Frédéric Adam
University College Cork, Ireland

ABSTRACT

In this chapter we begin by featuring the main characteristics of the human decision process. Then, from these traits, we separate the decision process between diagnosis and look-ahead. We explain why DMSSs are mainly look-ahead machines. We claim that look-ahead is generally performed via heuristic search and "what-if analysis" at different cognitive levels. This leads to a functional definition of DMSSs and to different architectures adapted to heuristic search and moreover, paves the way for an analysis of the decision support tools.

INTRODUCTION

From a philosophical standpoint, decision making has always been regarded as a specifically human activity reflecting the ability of human beings to exercise judgement and freely decide to act in a certain chosen way. However, this reality has not always been acknowledged in science, and other human activities, such as language, have been studied for a long time in the context of the study of how the brain works (the discovery of Broca's areas in 1861 indicates the beginnings of the investigation of the structure of the brain) whereas we are only at the beginning in our investigations of decision making. Thus, the study of decisional biology (Damasio, 1994; Damasio, Damasio, & Christen, 1996) only emerged as a topic of research in the 1990s. This is all the more surprising given the persuasive argument of Damasio et al. (1996) that, "Decision making is, in fact, as defining a human trait as language."

We would argue that decision making and subsequent actions, and especially the earlier stages of the process whereby individuals reflect on their goals and the desired outcomes of their actions, are typically human activities. In terms of decision making, human beings are totally opposed to animals for which action is a direct and unambiguous consequence of the stimuli they perceive in their environment, because for humans, there is an extra layer of look-ahead reasoning between the acquisition of data (the inputs or stimuli) and the resulting action. There are still some instinctive and intuitive reactions in human behaviour, but they are closely related to some biological processes (e.g., closing down the windpipe when drinking, breathing and such other reflex behaviour as pulling one's hand away from the fire). Thus, in human beings, action is mediated by reflection and this intellectual stage is what gives us freedom to explore the wide universe of what may happen (or *look-ahead*; see Pomerol, 1997) as opposed to just recognition-primed action, to use the term coined by Klein (1993). This, as we shall show in the next section, is the key stage of decision making.

For a long time, operational research systems, MIS and DMSS were developed without any reference to human behaviour as optimising tools relying on rational models. This led to systems more prone to data crunching than to alleviating the stress inherent in decision making and supporting decision makers. For this reason, it quickly appeared that MIS systems were not going to be used by managers and some authors were prompt to deplore the side effects of "management MIS-information systems" (Ackoff, 1967). In particular, these systems turned out to aggravate rather than solve the problem of information overload and resulted in managers being swamped in data but starved for information. Tony O'Reilly, the managing director of Heinz, described the problem with modern information systems as,

> The first thing that strikes me about information systems is that we are getting too much information. Much of this data is only partly digested and much of it is irrelevant to what I believe to be the fundamental objective of business information which is simplification.

Thus, what is mostly needed is the development of systems that are able to translate raw data—facts and figures taken at random in the heaps of management information reports or in the organisation's data warehouse—into information, a set of meaningful data organised and presented in a way that enhances its relevance to a particular problem. This resulted in IS researchers turning to the concept of decision support system (DSS), which was first coined by Gorry and Scott-Morton (1971), thereby focusing the attention of IS researchers and practitioners on the decision making processes of managers and acknowledging, at last, the importance of decision making as a separate activity for human beings at large and managers in particular.

Even though there are good functional definitions of what DSS should do, a readily understandable definition taking into account the specificities of human reasoning is still lacking. In this chapter we try to bridge the gap between human reasoning and the understanding and design of DSS. We start from a description of the human process of decision making, then we give a semiformal definition of decision making support systems (DMSS) and we finish with a few words about the architecture of such systems.

BACKGROUND—HUMAN DECISION

The Decision Process

Let us start from the assumption that any decision has its origin in a dissatisfaction. *Let us call this dissatisfaction a decision problem.* The dissatisfaction arises from the difference between the current state of affairs and another, not yet existing, more desirable state of affairs (see Figure 1). The notation "state of world" or sometimes "nature state" refers to the seminal work of Savage (1954).

It is worth noting that the personal dimension of decision making is at the core of the above process because what one person wants may not be desirable for another. In addition, it is important to realise that, whereas the current state is perceived as being perfectly definite for a sane person in a context where things are known with certainty, this is no longer true in case of uncertainty. Difficulties may also arise with the evaluation of the desirable state when it involves many different attributes that are not fully compatible (*e.g.*, get better wages and more free time).

Figure 1: The decision problem

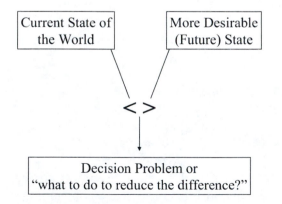

Before making a decision, the subject explores the current state. It is a common view that the present shapes the future and is shaped by the past. For this reason, let us agree that *the current state contains information about the past and the present*. In other words, the subject knows a part of what happened before and has his own perception of what occurs now. Then, keeping in mind his perception of the current state, the subject tries to identify it with reference to his own experience. *This means that we can assume that the subject has recorded many situations or states he has already met or has learned about. Let us call these states "recorded states."*

The first phase of decision, then, consists in finding one or several recorded states close to the perceived current state. Depending on the context and complexity of these states, this operation can be denoted "pattern matching" or "diagnosis." In artificial intelligence (AI), the expression "pattern matching" is generally reserved for the recognition of a simple pattern, whereas "diagnosis" is used for the identification of more complex states. In terms of control, one uses the terms *state-estimation problem* or simply *observation*. Finally, in some cases, it is very difficult to know what happened and what the exact status of the situation we are dealing with is. Thus, we cannot dismiss the possibility of a subject identifying various possible current states with estimated probabilities. In such cases, the diagnosis is uncertain.

Sometimes, it is possible to draw up a so-called **causation table**, following a term coined by Thomson and Tuden (1959), relating the current state S_i, the action A_j and the outcome OC_{ij}. In some very simple cases, for any S_i, there exists a unique action A_i which produces the best outcome we denote this action $A_i = \varphi(S_i)$.

To complete this simple picture we have just sketched, we have to introduce one additional central concept in decision making, namely, the inherent *uncertainty of the future*.

Uncertainty in Decision Making

Starting with the concept of uncertainty, we must realise that future states are obviously not known with certainty. Making decision A_j may result in the future state F_1 in some cases and, in some other, F_2. Suppose that F_1 is desirable whereas F_2 is a very negative outcome; then the decision becomes difficult. In some cases, the probability of occurrence of F_1 vs. F_2 is known because the events are frequent (*e.g.*, the probability for a train in a given railway network being delayed may be known since there are many trains each day) but, in many cases, it is very difficult to obtain common, shared probabilities, each human subject having his own. This is the reason why they are called **subjective probabilities**. Many researchers have also advocated that there is no probability at all and various models have been proposed to take into account the representation of uncertainty in the mind.

In any case, let us denote E (for **expectations**) a representation of future events uncontrolled and uninfluenced by the subject (states of nature with probabilities in decision theory). Depending on the various expectations and on the action carried out, many states are attainable with different probabilities. The set of all the "recognised future states attainable from the diagnosed current state" can be viewed as the **outcome set** in decision theory. The **preferences** of the subject apply to this set and, by a regressive reasoning, the preferred outcome defines the action to be chosen (decision). We may think of the elements of the outcome set as the possible **goals** of the subject. Thus, in our scheme, the goals are defined among the attainable states, the difficulty being that it is not easy to determine what is or what is not attainable. It depends on the actions and expectations. In other words, a goal is the result of a complex alchemy, combining possible actions, recorded experiences, expectations and preferences. We can summarise the situation in a diagram (see Figure 2).

Figure 2 deserves some comments. We have drawn a line from the preference box to the actions because many people consider that it is possible, to some extent, to define the actions according to the preferences. First define what you want, then define the actions to reach it ! This is expressed in current research, originated mainly by Keeney (1988, 1992), about value-driven thinking. Here attention is drawn to the fact that the action (or alternative) set is not given and can be changed during the process of reasoning. It has been often observed that many real decision makers are over-constrained in their perception of the alternative set and study just a small subset of the possible alternatives. The classical decision theory assumes that the actions are known, even though it has long been recognised that the design of the actions itself is an important step in the decision process (Simon, 1977).

In some cases, it is also defensible to draw a line from the preferences to the expectation box. This may be regarded as a psychological bias because it means that

Figure 2: The decision process (adapted from Pomerol, 1997)

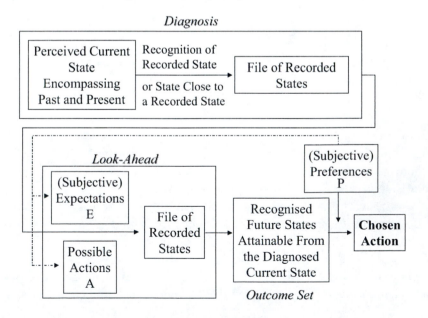

the future is seen according to the preferences. This is probably a frequent situation to be avoided in rational decision making as well as the inverse effect of influencing the preference by expectations. The latter can be regarded as a kind of framing effect (see, e.g., Berkeley & Humphreys, 1982; Tversky & Kahneman, 1987, for a discussion). Rationally, preferences should be independent of expectations.

Also, the subjects' preferences may influence the diagnosis process and the file of the recorded states (memory). Numerous psychological biases are observed in this domain (Bell, Raiffa, & Tversky, 1988; von Winterfeldt & Edwards, 1986). Another simplification in Figure 2 is that the decision process may appear as being "linear." This is not the case and many backtracks can occur, especially when the subject becomes aware that the attainable future states are not satisfactory. Moreover, in many actual organisational settings, due to feedback phenomenon, it is not always possible to distinguish an event from an outcome. For example, in an oligopolistic market, is price rising (or decreasing) an event (uncontrolled and uninfluenced) or an outcome? In many cases, the decision makers and the modellers do not know, on the one hand, where to set the limit of the model and the time horizon because, depending on the level of analysis, any significant decision may have far-reaching consequences (see Berkeley & Humphreys, 1982, for a discussion about the *small world assumption*), and on the other hand, the line between events and outcomes is rather thin and vague due to human being agency.

In Figure 2, we have sketched what may be regarded as a realistic human decision process, tracking the main components of decision reasoning. For the sake of simplicity, we have divided the process into two main parts, diagnosis and look-ahead. It is, of course, not always easy to separate these two but, from an engineer's point of view, it facilitates the design of systems aimed at supporting the process of decision making.

Diagnosis, Classification and Decision

The first phase of the decision reasoning process is the diagnosis. The problem is to recognise, as accurately as possible, the current state (including the past). It may entail certain elements (*e.g.,* the present president of France is Jacques Chirac) or uncertain elements (*e.g.,* the Earth has entered an era of increasingly high average temperature). Contrary to the classical model of decision theory (Savage, 1954), it is of practical importance to distinguish between the current state and the future ones because the former is generally known with more certainty than the latter.

The main point is that the current state may be subject to evaluation and comparison. For example, in process control, one can measure the present tempera-ture, stress, etc., so that the current state is characterised by a vector of many different values of measurement. Assume that the number of actions is finite and that we face the simple case in which there exists a function φ (see Section 1.2). The decision maker then chooses the action $\varphi(S_i)=A_i$, based on the attributes characterising S_i. In other words, he has to determine whether $S_i \in \varphi^{-1}(A_j)$ or not. Assuming that $\varphi^{-1}(A_j)$, for j=1,...., n, realises a partition of S, the decision problem is solved. Going

Figure 3: The simplified decision process

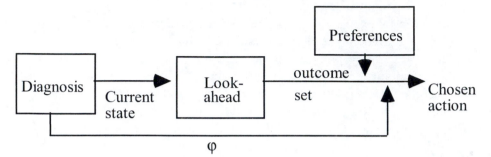

back to Figure 2, we can simplify it as Figure 3. The function φ shunts the "look-ahead" step. Things are often not so simple but, in a lot of cases, the previous simple scheme works and the decision problem amounts to affect a vector of R^n to a class. ***Thus, in simple cases, decision is a mere classification problem.*** We discussed in Pomerol (1997) more in-depth the relationships between classification and decision making as well as the function of expert systems as classifiers.

DECISION MACHINES, WHAT-IF ANALYSIS AND LOOK-AHEAD—A PRIMER FOR DECISION MAKING SUPPORT SYSTEMS (DMSS)

Having recalled the main steps and features of the human decision process (i.e., diagnosis and look-ahead) let us see now what are the most appropriate systems able to support this process. We start with diagnosis machines and continue with an idea which is well-known in the DMSS community: "what-if" analysis. Then we finish with the concept of look-ahead machines, which encompasses the very problem of human decision making.

Decision Machines

A decision machine is an automaton adhering to one-to-one correspondence between the diagnosed current state and an action. As said before the word "decision" is, in this case, improper because the decision has already been made by the designer of the system. However, when people are unaware of the program or when it is so sophisticated that it is impossible to look through its operations, one can refer to these as decision machines. A decision machine may therefore be regarded as a program performing the function φ of Figure 3. As such most of the decision machines are mere classifiers which link a recognised state to an action. Numerous such machines already exist in the context of almost continuous decision (control of industrial processes, underground or train driving, and so on). We have already seen that, in this context, the look-ahead phase is very reduced.

However, even with a programmed decision machine relating the current state to an action, one does not capture all the complexity of human decisions. Such systems may also have some undesirable effects. In human decisions, it may happen that nobody wishes, for various organisational reasons, to embody the decision process in a computer program. This is a first obstacle on the road to a "decision machine." The main difficulty is that in many concrete situations the set of all the possible current states cannot be described either extensionally or intentionally. Thus, the human decision maker is always indispensable, working in an interactive way with the machine, mainly because unexpected (not programmed) states might occur. Emergency and accident cases were created by the bad recognition of the current state (wrong diagnosis) by the subject (Boy, 1991). The designers of decision support systems are therefore confronted with the paradoxical problem of developing systems capable of helping people in situations that neither the user nor the program can foresee. This is one of the most difficult challenges in the development of decision support systems.

"What-If" Analysis

Although various previous attempts have been made to cope with uncertainty, many decision makers are not satisfied with the proposed methods. In most cases, the dissatisfaction stems from what we have identified as **look-ahead reasoning** (Figure 2). It means that, in real situations, the events are either very interdependent and/or the probabilities remain unknown (*e.g.*, what is the probability that the price of oil will be higher in three months than today?). Another difficulty is predicting or even identifying all the possible reactions of other agents, especially in a competitive setting. The ability to envision the future seems to be a phylogenetic acquisition. The capacity for anticipation exists only in most advanced animals. Even for human beings, the capacity for anticipation and the ability to decide against immediate short-term advantage to pursue future gains seem to be, at least, components of intelligent behaviour performed in special, identified locations in the brain (Damasio, 1994). This kind of multi-criteria choice function between two criteria, short-term gains and long-term advantages, seems to be impaired in some illnesses and addictions. Pomerol (1997) regards this basic multi-criteria choice as a basic expression of rationality. This is consistent with Damasio's view: "Will power is just another name for the idea of choosing according to long-term outcomes rather than short-term ones" (Damasio, 1994, p. 175). Whether the multicriteria long-term *vs.* short-term choice is correlated to computational skills, language and emotion is open for debate.

The basis of this anticipating behaviour seems to be the capacity of the human mind in placing itself into a nonexisting (future or past) situation and chaining (just as in language) foreseen events resulting in scenarios (see Calvin, 1991, for an evolutionary perspective). A well-known neurobiologist recently said that:

> In summary all of the above considerations point to the necessity and take
> into account the fact that the brain is: 1) a predictive biological machine, 2)
> a simulator of action in order to predict the consequences of action by

referring to past experience, and 3) probably using for these purposes inner loops in which action is simulated (and not represented) in extremely specialised circuits.

In this perspective, "free will" is nothing other than the capacity to internally simulate action and make a decision, i.e., selectively remove inhibitions at many levels of the central nervous system and generate an executed or imagined action (Berthoz, 1996). This kind of prospective reasoning may be interpreted as a "what-if" analysis which was regarded for a long time as the main function of decision support systems (DMSS). *We claim that the basis of the human ability to perform look-ahead reasoning is the "what-if" analysis.* The same idea may be viewed from the point of view of scenario scrolling. This is the popular reasoning of the type: "If I do that, they will react like this, and I will do this" and so on. What is important in scenario reasoning is to be able to develop many scenarios and to assess, at least approximately, their probabilities (which is an impossible task for the human mind). Thus, *supporting people in decision making amounts to mainly helping them foresee the consequences of their choices* (Hatchuel, 1994).

In any case, "what-if" analysis, or more accurately "scenario reasoning," should produce two outputs: all possible outcomes at a given horizon and the probability or plausibility of each outcome. The decision maker exercises his preferences on probabilistic outcomes (preferably multi-attribute), then makes his decision and implements the resulting actions in accordance with the chosen scenario. Let us notice that dealing with probabilistic outcomes supposes that the subject is able to make trade-offs between the value of a given outcome and its risk (this trade-off is generally hidden in the utility function). Unfortunately, for non-aided decision makers, scenario reasoning may lead to a combinatorial explosion such that it is often impossible to handle long, precise and diverse scenarios (Pomerol, 2001). This is the very reason why support from machines is necessary.

Look-Ahead Machines

Two capabilities appear to be necessary in a look-ahead machine: (1) the ability to combine many actions and events (with probabilities or similar measures), and (2) the ability to imagine the possible actions and to anticipate all possible reactions of the other agents and/or nature. According to Figure 2, this "imagination" ability is simply provided by the file of recorded states, such that, for a given subject, all possible events and reactions of the other agents are drawn from a set of memorised items. In any case, it has been claimed that forecasts never predict what is really new (see Hogarth & Makridakis, 1981; Makridakis, 1990; Mumpower, 1987). It is therefore unlikely that look-ahead machines might escape this weakness, although it would clearly be nice if they could foresee what has already happened at least once somewhere! Another reason for using recorded states is that human forecasts are often too optimistic because human beings remember success more easily than failures (Kahneman & Lovallo, 1993). The intrinsic difficulty of forecasting (Hogarth & Makridakis, 1981; Makridakis, 1990) is the main weakness of many formalised planning processes. This is particularly true for long-term or strategic planning. Mintzberg (1994) provides a good overview of the main flaws of strategic planning.

Bearing in mind that the basis for scenario building is often restricted to the set of recorded actions, events and situations (i.e., states), what are the candidates for look-ahead machines? At first glance, they are of two types: simulation machines and decision support systems (DMSS).

A simulation machine or simulator is a machine in which a real industrial or social process has been modelled on a reduced scale (using concepts or devices such as nodes; links and flows as arcs between the nodes, treatments associated with the nodes). Then, some initial data and parameters are fed into the simulator and the user observes the evolution of the variables he is interested in. One of the most interesting features of this technology is that some variables characterising uncertain events are randomly fed into the system according to a given law of probability. Then, the simulator produces random variables whose mean and standard deviation, for example, can be observed.

Simulation seems to be the only way of looking ahead when it is impracticable to model the process completely via "hard modelling" (equations, rules, etc.). This impossibility generally stems from the entanglement of causes and consequences. It is very difficult to arrive at a satisfactory model of a process that has many intertwined feedback loops. The problem of feedback loops in look-ahead reasoning deserves some brief comments. It has been observed many times that subjects are insensitive to the implication of feedback when medium or long delays occur between a decision and its effects (Kleinmuntz, 1985, 1993; Sterman, 1989). Decision makers generally fail to see the ramifications of a decision as soon as a delayed feedback occurs. One of the few ways to sensitise decision makers to feedback is to use system dynamics as initially described by J. Forrester (see, for example, Wolstenholme, 1990). Studying the dynamics of the variables of the model via simulation allows a progressive understanding of how a modification of the input variables leads to possibly very counterintuitive effects, caused by no obvious feedbacks. In case of delayed feedbacks and/or tangled retrograde effects, assuming that no causal model exists, nobody can really anticipate the future states of the system without simulation. But when it is possible to develop at least a partial model of the given process, it is possible to exploit it by developing a DMSS.

Research and development conducted by one of the authors in the DMSS area over a period of many years led to the conclusion that *DMSS are look-ahead machines* designed to perform an exploration at several cognitive levels (see in the next section). At the data level, it is called "what-if" or sensitivity analysis. Roy (Courbon, Dugois, & Roy, 1994; Roy, 1998) has also described another type of "what-if" analysis called *robustness analysis*. In robustness analysis, the question raised by the decision maker is "What input modifications can a decision endure before really becoming bad?" It differs from sensitivity analysis, which looks for the largest modification of some input that leaves a decision unchanged. For an example of robustness analysis, see Pomerol, Roy, Rosenthal-Sabroux, and Saad (1995).

At the model level, heuristic search allows the decision maker to explore different types of models to look ahead among the many possible situations that may occur. Findler (1995) provides a good example of such "anticipating functions" in a DMSS for air traffic control. One of the two working stations in his system is used to display the consequences of the tentative decisions. In a DMSS, the model as a whole (or meta-model) is never complete, but it is completed by the decision maker's interaction (Pomerol, 1992). In such a system, one specific operation is often left to the decision maker: to perform the numerous evaluations that occur along the exploration process. In evaluating the plausibility of a model and expressing preferences about different outcomes, the decision maker expresses his preferences, which only he knows about. In this same vein, an interpretation of interactivity relies upon the idea that the function φ in Figure 3 does not incorporate the preferences. Thus the interactive process in a DMSS is intended to allow the decision maker to elicit his preferences by an interactive search. This idea has been strongly advocated in multi-criteria analysis (see Pomerol & Barba-Romero, 2000; Roy, 1990).

In the process of preferences elicitation, a DMSS designer must acknowledge that the preferences involved in the decision maker's mind are certainly multi-attribute (which excludes any simple utility function) and personal. Many multi-criteria DMSS (for a survey, see Pomerol, 1993; Pomerol & Barba-Romero, 2000) have been designed which do not incorporate this idea. They try to model and impose an aggregation of the multi-attribute preferences in order to make the decision. Very few of them are in use. Rather than focusing on choice, designers would be better advised to help managers envisage richer scenarios by enabling them to produce and to handle complex actions and situations (Pomerol, 1993; Pomerol, 2001; Pomerol, Roy, Rosenthal-Sabroux, & Saad, 1995).

Let us illustrate the above ideas with a final example. Assume that you are the CEO of a small company trying to make a decision about a big investment. To do that, you use a spreadsheet (spreadsheets are prototypical and the most used type of DMSS). The first task of our CEO is to create a model of his business. He then explores various sets of data and parameters and evaluates the result according to several attributes (gains, productivity, payback time, etc.). He evaluates each situation and will make his decision (for example, adopt the investment budget) according to the data which produces the most "satisfying" outcome, having made a trade-off between gains and risks (or probabilities of success). In the case in which no set of data is satisfying, the decision maker may continue his reasoning by trying other models (see Figure 6). We have not made mention of the fact that the CEO has to evaluate the quality of the model (this evaluation may depend on his preferences and experience).

This idea of allowing extended and simple exploration at the data level has became one of the most common feature of executives information systems (EIS) in the shape of multidimensional spreadsheets. A multidimensional spreadsheet uses a simple data cube to generalise to n dimensions the two-dimensional tables used by managers. Each cell in the model represents one item of data such as a monthly sale for a specific product on a specific market for a particular year. Users can then manipulate the data cube to display the information they want as a two-or-three dimensional table depending upon the mode of representation available. An example of a data cube is presented in chapter 19 of this book.

This method of manipulation of the data is particularly useful for organisations which deal with many products on many markets because it considerably eases the tasks of consolidation of accounting results and the forecasting/planning process. Individual markets and individual products can be monitored by managers without any additional burden for the operators who prepare the information displays. Furthermore, the data cube, once developed by an expert, can be used by managers in their own time to explore complex scenarios and run what-if or goal seek analyses that would involve too many variables and rules for a *pen and paper* approach.

This small example shows the range of tasks that can be modelled in a typical DMSS (business, process, etc.) and the parts which are left to the decision maker (mainly evaluation or, in some sense, the expression of his preferences). The contribution of AI to DMSS is its ability to put forward better and more sophisticated representations allowing more complex states and reasoning to be handled. AI also contributes to the modelling process of unstructured tasks, for example, via expert system technique. It has given rise to many "intelligent" DMSS involving knowledge bases (see Klein & Methlie, 1990, Lévine & Pomerol, 1989; Turban, 1988).

DEFINING DECISION MAKING SUPPORT SYSTEMS

A Functional Definition for DMSS

There are many ways to conceive of and technically describe DMSS, but whatever way is selected, a number of difficulties must be addressed. The first difficulty is that DMSS are more often than not, ad hoc systems designed for a particular purpose. This leads to definitions of DMSS which state that "DMSSs are systems which are intended to support a decision maker" or "... that enable manager to solve problem, in their own personalised way" (Parker, 1989). Many of these typical "textbook" definitions turn out to be tautological and not really helpful neither for the purpose of teaching student what DMSS are about or for the purpose of developing better systems.

Keen and Scott-Morton's book from 1978 presents a comprehensive sample of the definitions and ideas relying upon functional views put forward by IS researchers in the 1970s. These ideas are suitably summarised in the following quote from Keen and Scott-Morton:

Decision support implies the use of computers to: (1) assist managers in their decision process for semi-structured tasks, (2) support rather than replace managerial judgement and (3) improve the effectiveness of decision making rather than its efficiency. (p. 1)

The obvious drawback of such definitions is that, while they clearly describe what a DMSS is meant to do, they are weak at describing how it should do it and do not provide any clear guidelines from DMSS development or usage. According to Naylor (1982), this lack of formal theorisation of what DMSS should do greatly contributed to the relative lack of success of the DMSS concept. During the 80s, many authors attempted to go beyond the limitations inherent in such definitions and to put forward new ideas about the design and development of DMSS applications (Bonczek, Holsapple, & Whinston, 1981; Lévine & Pomerol, 1989; Sprague & Carlson, 1982). These new definitions were more or less inspired by artificial intelligence (see next subsection), while the functional perspective was changed by the introduction of the concept of EIS (see section 7 of this chapter). Since then, other concepts have been proposed either on the technological (OLAP, data warehouse) or conceptual side (groupware, drill down, exception reporting, ...), but this does not affect the question of the nature of decision making support and of the design of executive systems with clear decision making relevance.

DMSS as Information Processing System

Bonczek, Holsapple, and Whinston (1981) were the first authors to introduce the idea of artificial intelligence (AI) in DMSS theory and to regard DMSS as special kind of information processing systems (IPS) as described by Newell and Simon (1972). This novel vision of DMSS amounts to viewing DMSS applications as essentially problem-solving applications. Their vision of DMSS is illustrated in Figure 4, which shows the typical structure of a DMSS application.

In conformity with Newell and Simon's (1972) model, the IPS features a processor (the PPS), memories (the KS) and an input/output device (the LS). Starting from Bonczek, Holsapple, and Whinston's model and specifying that processing within the DMSS takes place according to some operational models, we are led to the vision of Sprague and Carlson (1982) of a DMSS based on representation, operations, memory aids and control mechanisms (aka ROMC). The main contribution of Sprague and Carlson was to emphasise the importance of two additional factors: (1) the role of the representation—a certain structure applied to the data, and (2) the issue of control—the methods available to the decision maker to use and control the DMSS, i.e., how the DMSS supports the decision making process.

In a simplified diagram, Sprague (1987) illustrated his vision of DMSS as a system with memories (a database), its operation performed according to pro-grammed models and a dialogue device (see Figure 5).

It is worth noting that the all-important concept of control has disappeared from this diagram, despite the acknowledgment of its importance for the successful use of the DMSS application. Lévine and Pomerol (1989, 1995) reintroduced the control

Figure 4: Structure of a DSS according to Bonczek et al. (1981)

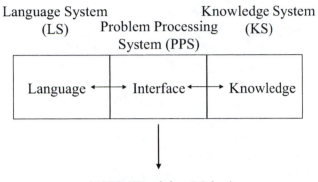

USER (Decision Maker)

Figure 5: A DSS according to Sprague (1987)

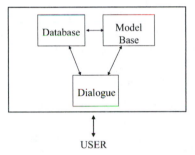

USER

aspect of DMSS in their vision of DMSS (1989, 1993). They proposed regarding the decision maker's search for support during his usage of the DMSS as a heuristic search. In other words, they proposed that using a DMSS amounts to performing a heuristic search up to the moment where the decision maker feels that he has gathered sufficient knowledge to make a decision.

Levine and Pomerol (1995) suggested that this heuristic search may, in fact, occur at different levels. These representation levels initially described by Humphreys and Bekerley (1985) are characterised by a level of abstraction and a specific way of thinking so that the different levels can be compared from two points of view, the degree of abstraction of the problems tackled and the degree of formalisation of the problems. Humphreys (1989) later described how problem solving involves passing through the five levels from the highest to the lowest level of abstraction. These five levels are described in the next subsection.

Representation Levels in DMSSs

The five representation levels can be illustrated with Humphreys and Bekerley's (1985) description of the problem handling process:

(1) At the highest level, representations are mainly cultural and psychological; managers are more or less aware of what a problem involves, but its expression is mostly beyond language. It is at this level that the problem is shaped.

(2) At this level, the representations become explicit and the problem can be broken down into a number of subproblems, some of which can be formalised. The structuration of the problems is still partial rather than detailed and managers will refer to "the marketing function" or "the marketing process" without being able to formalise processes in greater details.

(3) At this level, decision makers are able to define the structure of the problems they must solve. They are able to put forward models that can be used for the investigation of the alternatives they will pursue.

(4) At this level, the decision makers will perform sensitivity analysis with the models they have defined in the previous stage so as to determine which input values are the most suitable.

(5) Finally, at the lowest level, managers decide upon the most suitable values and the representation of the problem they must solve is stable and fully operational.

The process described by Humphreys is a top down process whereby the structuration of the concepts investigated is refined from one level to the next until decisions can be made. As noted by Lévine and Pomerol (1995), Levels 1 and 2 are generally considered as strategic levels of reflection handled by top executives, whereas the remaining three levels correspond to more operational and tactical levels. It is worth noting that, at the top-level, the decision maker has total freedom to decide on a direction to follow. This is obviously a very important stage of the decision making process as the only factors limiting the horizon of the decision maker are either psychological (unconscious) or cultural (e.g., his educational background). In human decision making, this step of shaping the framework for further studying the problem appears under the name "setting the agenda" (Simon, 1997) or "problem setting" (Checkland, 1981). The role of the person who shapes the problem, the "problem owner" in Checkland's words, is very important for the follow-up of the decision and action although there are still few operational tools addressing the question (see Landry, Pascot, & Briolat, 1985). As noted by Pomerol (1994), this stage is all the more important in that it conditions the outcome of the decision making process. Simon (1997, p. 296 *et seq*.) reports an experiment proving that accountants set as an accounting problem the same problem that sales supervisors would set as a sales problem, and so on. Avenues that are not envisaged at that stage are unlikely to be explored at a later stage. The manager's vision of the problem is then considerably refined at the second level to prepare for the formalisation of the third level, where the manager enters the realm of "hard system thinking" and where the representations and computational models must be fully stabilised. At the remaining levels, the manager will define the processing to be applied to the data and identify the most appropriate input values of the model. The refining process from top cognitive level to lower ones can also be interpreted as a decision process, in which high level decisions shape the decision framework, within which smaller decisions are then made leading to actions, which are the ultimate level. This refinement process in decision making was also described by Simon (1977, p. 44).

Based on this view of DMSS, we can conclude that existing DMSS applications often cover Levels 3, 4 and 5 and neglect the two initial levels, which, admittedly, are much more problematic to handle.

Towards a Contingency View of DMSS

The advantages of the vision of DMSS described in the previous section can be summarised as follows (after Lévine & Pomerol, 1995):
(1) It takes into account the problem of representation levels.
(2) It accounts for the continued success of spreadsheet-based DMSS applications, which are still the most used DMSS.
(3) It enables researchers to analyse the classical "what-if" analysis as a heuristic search for better insights (generally about future outcomes or look-ahead)
(4) It provides some insights into the reasons why the human decision maker is so important in the decision making process; i.e., to express his preferences and to evaluate the outcomes generated by the DMSS.

Such a vision of DMSS can be used to put forward a definition or description of decision support systems which takes into account the representation level at which the DMSS is going to be used by managers/users. *This definition states that a DMSS is an information processing system (IPS) which is designed so that the decision maker can perform a heuristic search at any representation level.* At the lower levels (3,4 and 5), the model in the DMSS is virtually complete and the system may be able to deliver a complete solution ready to be implemented. By contrast, at the higher levels (1 and 2), the model, only present in the manager's mind and in an incomplete form, is not available for modelling and the decision making process must be enacted as a dialogue between the DMSS and the decision maker. An important consequence of this definition is that the interaction which takes place between the DMSS and the manager is fundamentally different at the lower levels and at the higher levels. At the lower levels of abstraction, the exchanges between the IPS and the manager are limited to data entry and output of results, whereas, at the higher levels, they must enable the control of the often abstract heuristic search described in the previous section.

Naturally, it must be acknowledged that the development of DMSS applications aimed at the first and second levels is very ambitious. According to Humphreys (1989), the second level is the realm of problem-structuring languages and it is not clear what the first level may involve. This issue can only be resolved by investigating two important aspect of DMSS applications: (1) the ability of the underlying models to accurately describe reality and (2) the architecture of DMSS systems and the interaction between their components. These two aspects of DMSS are the foci of the next two sections of this chapter.

IMPLEMENTATION AND THE ROLE OF MODELS IN DMSS

As was illustrated in the previous section, models constitute a very important component of DMSS applications. The support that the decision maker gets from the DMSS he is using comes mainly from the ability of the model to accurately represent and simulate reality. In the words of Keen (1987), models are active in the search for solution, a vision in sharp opposition with the idea that DMSS merely follow the reasoning of the decision maker. The idea that reality can actually be modelled in the model of a DMSS raises a specific problem: If the models get to such a level of sophistication, what role will the human operator play and will the DMSS still need to be interactive? This underlines the limits of current knowledge in relation to models: Models are, at best, incomplete (when not totally wrong) and can only provide partial support to the decision maker. As such, the model encompasses the processing that can be applied to the data, a processing which reflects the knowledge of the developers of the system.

In this section, we will refer to models as a plural because DMSS applications typically include a set of different models which are called upon at different stages of complex decision making processes or, alternatively, are used selectively depending upon the preferences of the decision makers. In this case, the DMSS application will organise linking and passing parameters between the different models and provide an interface for the dialogues between the user and the DMSS's models.

Implementation

In the early days of DMSS modelling, systems were often geared towards the solution of one specific problem and were therefore based on a stable representation of this problem; i.e., a single model. These models, which were often very large, were solved according to a sequential series of specific steps: (1) initiation of session, (2) acquisition of the data, (3) execution of the model and (4) presentation of results. This sequence is similar to that followed by many optimisation machines. There are many difficulties with this optimisation view, of which two are major problems. The first one is that data acquisition often needs a human intervention especially when vision (e.g. handwritten material) is involved. The fact that a human operator must remain in the loop for data acquisition and interpretation calls for interactive systems, because if a human being is useful for data input why not utilise him for the reasoning as well (see Pomerol, 1990).

The second problem comes from the difficulty inherent in changing any organisational process without a specific preparation. Some authors have referred to integrate as an *unfreezing* step prior to the implementation of systems that introduce significant changes to work practices (see Schein, 1961, for the Lewin-Schein model and also Pomerol, 1990, for similar experiences with expert systems). Indeed, there are many examples of implementations of new information tools which turned out to be quickly discarded by their users because they required changes to work practices, an increase in operator skill, or training or aimed at increasing the degree of control of management over their subordinates (Cooper & Zmud, 1999).

Another source of modification for the way DMSS applications operate came from user feedback. The old-fashioned attitude to DMSS development whereby the analysts gathered information about the problem that must be solved and then retired to their offices to create the model and the interface of the system is no longer acceptable. These practices resulted in many failures of DMSS application because users refused to use the systems that were developed for them or refused to follow the procedures specified by the developers. Problems would arise in cases where models were developed without adequate attention being paid to current organisational practices and new procedures were too radically in conflict with these practices. It follows that current practice must be used as a basis for the way the DMSS will ultimately be used. This largely explains why expert systems modules, which give their users more flexibility in the choice of the methods followed, have rapidly become essential components of DMSS.

As a conclusion, the two main hurdles that DMSS developers must overcome are: (1) the creation of a nonlinear method of solving problems and (2) the resistance of system users to change the way they work. These two obstacles can be addressed by establishing proper dialogue between the user and the system. The progressive or evolutive development as advocated by Courbon (see Sprague & Carlson, 1982) is another potential answer to the problems of user involvement and better prediction of the future uses of the system. The interactivity of the DMSS will condition the degree of control the user has over the process of decision support and, ultimately, the degree of confidence the users have in the system.

An interactive session will typically be based on a number of stages: (1) the user calls the decision support application, (2) the data are acquired either from a database or from a series of answers provided by the user, and (3) the processing of the data begins. In this last stage, users retain control over the operations taking place. They can interrupt the process, go back, follow a different lead by altering input data or modifying their initial answers and terminate the analysis at any stage they like. Partial and final results can be stored and compared with the results of other simulations. Such an interactive model is obviously much richer than any linear model described above; it is also much more in keeping with the way decision making takes place among managers.

Multi-Models DMSS

Models are stored in the DMSS's model base together with the programmes applicable to the data processing required for these models. This model base also contains information about the input and output values of each model and the other variables which it uses for its calculations. In simple DMSS applications relying on one single model, the only exchanges that take place are the exchanges of data between the database and the model. In multi-model DMSS, there is a need to integrate models in a coherent set so that they are able to draw their information from the same data set (in order to avoid the duplication of data) and share their results. This creates a dilemma for DMSS developers who are tempted to develop each model with its own data and its own conversations in isolation from the other models. While this is easier to implement, this may limit the usefulness of the DMSS application considerably because managers never think about one side of their knowledge in isolation from the rest of what they know. The DMSS will not be efficient if much time is wasted transferring data from one model into another one and updating input data and other shared variables. The system must therefore be able to switch from one model to another midway through processing data rather than run programmes in isolation. Some authors advocate for a kind of hyper-modeling which would be able to organise the cooperation between models (see, Chang, Holsapple, & Whinston, 1983, e.g. Moore & Chang, 1983).

It is worth noting that the process of heuristic search, which is the rule at the data level ought to also be the rule at the model level. We saw that the decision maker using a DMSS performs an exploration among the data as exemplified in spread-sheets. Some DMSS have an easy-to-use modelling language enabling users to modify the model just like they would do it in a spreadsheet. Thus, the decision maker can change the model when he thinks that changing the data only will not be sufficient to arrive at a solution. Thus, DMSS can be defined as a system which allows interactive heuristic search at two levels: the data level and the model level, as illustrated in Figure 6. Figure 6 shows that there are two degrees of freedom in using a spreadsheet, which explains its success as a DMSS.

They are many types of modeling that can be used at the model level (see Adam & Pomerol, 2000). Also, this gives rise to a variety of different system architectures for DMSS which are presented in the next section.

Figure 6: Using a spreadsheet as a two-level DMSS

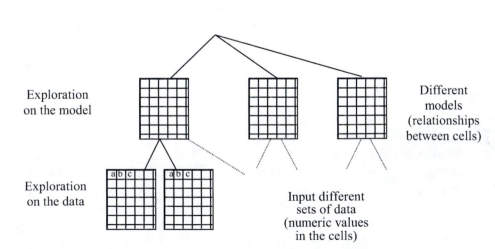

ARCHITECTURES FOR DMSS

In the previous paragraphs, we distinguished three fundamental components of DMSS: (1) the database, (2) the model base and (3) the interface/dialogue modules. In practice, it may not always be so easy to distinguish between these components, but this basic architecture is nevertheless helpful in highlighting the basic issues in DMSS design and, in particular, the requirements in terms of integration of the functions of DMSS. Based on the above, we can describe three main types of architectures commonly used for DMSS: (1) the network of agents, (2) the centralised architecture and (3) the hierarchical architecture. These are studied in the next three subsections.

Networks of Agents or Network Architecture

In a DMSS of this kind, each model has its own database and its own integration and dialogue modules so that it represents a relatively independent agent; i.e., some kind of autonomous sub-DMSS. The control of the network of agents is carried out by a special integration module (Figure 7) which is not aware of the processing going on in the individual agents and merely manages the exchanges of data between the other components. The main advantage of this architecture resides in its great modularity, i.e., the ease with which additional modules can be built into the system. It remains that this ease of development is obtained at the expense of the integration between the components, which is only minimum.

It remains that the network of agents is an open and adaptable architecture where modifications can be made within agents without affecting the other agents in the DMSS.

Figure 7: A network of agents

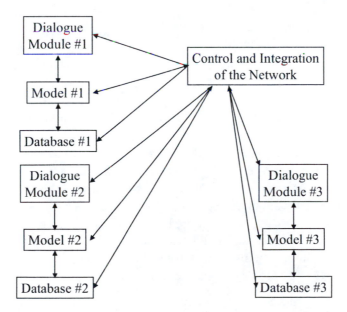

Figure 8: A centralised DMSS

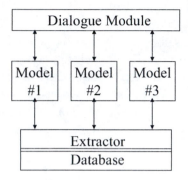

Centralised Architecture

In this structure, all modules rely on a centralised dialogue module and a single database (Figure 8). The main advantage of such architecture resides in the excellent integration between the modules that it enables. The unique dialogue module is a source of comfort for the user and the look and feel of the system is the same throughout. In addition, the unique database considerably facilitates the exchanges of data between modules. Control definitely resides with the user and is enforced by the dialogue module.

The main drawback of such architecture is its lack of flexibility. Indeed, the design of the dialogue and control module can be very complex if it is to allow the same level of interaction between the user and the individual modules as, for example, a network of agents. This lack of flexibility will become very obvious as the DMSS evolves to accommodate additional models and the dialogue and control module and the database must be rewritten or redesigned fundamentally to reflect these changes.

Hierarchical Architecture

In many ways, the hierarchical architecture is similar to the centralised architecture. The main differences are that the dialogue module is divided into specific sub-modules and that the database contains two layers with a view to facilitating the modification of the DMSS (which is the main weakness of the centralised architecture).

The dialogue function of the DMSS is divided up into two layers. The top layer is the general dialogue module which is concerned with the communication between the system and the user and the communication between modules. The second layer is composed of a series of model-specific dialogue modules which serve as interface between each model and the rest of the application. The overall control of the DMSS is taken care of by a supervisor module which acts as an intermediary between the model-specific dialogue modules and the general dialogue module and coordinates the switches between modules. In this case, the models do not exchange any data or parameters among themselves and neither do their dedicated databases (Figure 9). It is worth noting that, even though the supervisor's role seems to be comparable to that of the network controller in Figure 8, they differ quite fundamentally. In order to perform its task the supervisor must be aware of the nature of the data manipulated and the computations taking place within each of the models, a requirement that does not exist for a network controller.

Hierarchical architectures have been used in many existing DMSS applications, especially in cases where the different models in the systems are radically different in their structure and the way they operate. In such cases, it becomes interesting to separate the models and to give them access to the data they can process only.

In this kind of DMSS, the user controls the application through the supervisor, which has its own dialogue routines and enables the switch between models. The search for specific results (e.g., what-if analysis), by contrast, is done at the level of individual models. Some data exchanges among the different models can be organised using the supervisor, which may copy the data from one model into its own dedicated database before passing them across to another process in another model.

This kind of architecture tends to cumulate the advantages of the networked and centralised architecture: unique dialogue module giving a consistent interface and greater ease of use to the user, and possibilities to exchange data and excellent integration on the one hand and ease of adaptation and further development on the other hand. In the case where additional models must be added or removed, modifications must only be reflected in the supervisor and its two associated components (dialogue and dedicated database).

The strengths and weaknesses of the three architectures presented above are summarised in Table 1.

Figure 9: A hierarchical DMSS

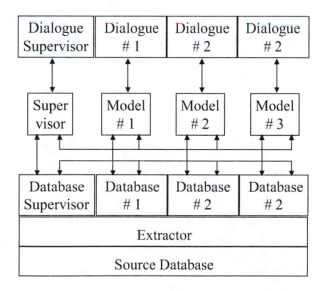

Table 1: Strengths and weaknesses of existing DMSS architectures

	Strengths	Weaknesses
Network of agents	Open architecture Very adaptable	Low integration Lack of consistency in the dialogues Difficult to exchange data Control difficult to implement
Centralised architecture	High integration Dialogue consistency Ease of data exchanges Ease of development	Modifications difficult, especially when adding new modules Lack of model-specific data
Hierarchical architecture	High integration Dialogue consistency Ease of development Very adaptable Ease of use	Supervisor and data extractor difficult to program for further evolution of the DMSS

Turnkey DMSS

Turnkey DMSS are systems which include fully developed models and complete databases and can immediately be used by a decision maker. They are opposed to DMSS generators, which enable a user to develop a system to support a decision. DMSS generators are dealt with in the next subsection.

In turn-key DMSSs, the number of different models is often small, or even limited to one. The flexibility does not reside in the choice of many models, but in the ability to change a large number of parameters within these models, to run a wide range of simulations and to provide a wide variety of interpretations. The type of problems best handled by such DMSS will involve repetitive decisions with a specific approach to decision making; e.g., the selection of manuscripts by a publisher (100 different books accepted per year, a wide but known set of parameters and a formal presentation of each case). The value of such a system will reside in its ability to enable a subtle interpretation of the selection rules so that the decisions made are not stereotypic. This flexibility will be obtained by enabling the decision maker to include a wide range of parameters and variables in his or her analysis so that many different scenarios (i.e., paths to a decision) can be followed and the outcome of the evaluation is directly related to the specificity of each book.

At the end of the day, the flexibility of turn-key DMSS must rest with the decision maker. The quality of his intuition and the amount of knowledge he possesses about the problem must be allowed to contribute to the decision making process, which requires that the DMSS is open to new inputs and new parameters and that the interface between the user and the system enables a high degree of interaction.

DMSS Generators

DMSS generators are systems that can be used to quickly develop a DMSS of a certain kind or for a certain kind of task; e.g., the production of economic forecasts. This type of system enables users to build a number of statistical or economical models based on existing templates and to adapt them to a specific decision situation.

In a generator, flexibility is a function of the number of templates of models available. The dialogue module must also be able to accommodate a great variety of types of interaction and handle many types of messages. Naturally, the flexibility of such systems also resides in the ability of the user to implement some variations in the inputs and variables used by the system, as is the case in a turn-key DMSS. In other words, a DMSS generator is a system which gives users the capability to modify the structure of models. As such, it is very close to expert systems generators.

At the same time, the development of DMSS applications is not so straight-forward that one DMSS generator will offer solutions for all problems. A given generator will always be geared toward the support of a certain kind of decision situation and the models it proposes might not be very varied. In many cases, the models proposed will be similar and offer the user the capability to change the parameters used in a certain type of model rather than radically change the structure of the model.

Toolboxes

An alternative to turnkey DMSS applications and DMSS generators which brings more flexibility to the user has been suggested. It consists in providing users with a set of tools aimed at enabling them to develop their own DMSS application from scratch. In some cases, this is achieved by providing a toolbox, made up of more or less directly usable building blocks, whereas in other cases, it is achieved by providing a complete development environment not very different from modern programming packages available under Windows (e.g., Visual Basic). These development environments include screen generators, code generators, libraries of code and models and a database engine. Special programming languages may be included in order to enable users to code their models in the form of programmes or routines.

Such environments are naturally going to require greater skills from end users, especially technical knowledge and programming skills, if users are to be able to develop complete DMSS from scratch. The alternative to such an increase in the skill base of end users would be to conceive code generators of the kind used in software engineering, a concept which is still out of reach at this point in time.

In terms of databases, it is easier to see how automated environments can be provided to DMSS users-developers whereby most of the technical tasks of designing and creating the database structure are taken care of by the software and not the user. This is already the case in some of Microsoft point-and-click database environments.

FUTURE TRENDS—EXECUTIVE INFORMATION SYSTEMS, OLAP AND GROUPWARE

Following the limited success of DMSS-type systems with the highest levels of managers in organisations, researchers have also explored a number of other avenues to support top managers with computers putting forward a large number of very diverse concepts such as EIS, ESS, groupware or workflow automation systems (Baecker, 1993; Harvey & Mickeljohn, 1991; Marca & Bock, 1992; Watson, Rainer, & Koh, 1991). Decision support systems have turned out to be used more widely by middle managers and for the monitoring of straightforward tasks than the traditional literature on DMSS had predicted. Some problems have also been reported with the way in which DMSS applications are developed; most of them being the product of end-user approaches rather than the result of cooperation between the IS staff and managers from other functional areas (Fahy & Murphy, 1996).

Another significant weakness of DMSS, as regards executive use, resides in the lack of confidence of executives in their models. The idea that decision makers need sophisticated models is probably wrong. People in charge of the preparation of decisions would probably be able to understand and use smart models, but the high-level executives who most commonly have the final say are far too busy to train with and use involved systems. On the contrary, they appear to prefer simple systems that they trust and understand and that display very timely "punchy" information. Trust in the models used is one of the important factors of acceptance identified by many empirical studies (see Pomerol & Barba-Romero, 2000, ch. 11, for some references). More often, the data required to make the best decisions already reside in some form or another in the database of the organisation and what is really needed is a device to filter, display and warn executives about the most important variances.

This resulted throughout the '80s in a shift from DMSS systems including sophisticated prescriptive models to simpler systems with more attractive display and dialogue functions. For executives, a mere information filter seems more valued than high-level, involved models and quick reaction to problems is more useful than sophisticated look-ahead; at least executives seem to think so! This also justifies the increased popularity of the concepts of data warehousing or data mining, which both emphasise the ability of organisations to make the fullest use of the information they already possess before they spend time prospecting for more.

As a result, the emphasis in information systems design has shifted towards systems that provide managers with the information they require in a broader sense than just one specific decision and that support their communication needs. Executive information systems (EIS) and executive support systems (ESS) have been put forward as the solution to the problems of information provision to senior managers (Rockart & DeLong, 1988). Scott-Morton (1984) has defined executive support systems as being focused on a manager's or a group of managers' information needs across a range of areas. He added the following comment: Rather than being limited to a single recurring type of decision, ESS incorporate in one system the data and analytic tools to provide information support for many managerial processes and problems. (Scott-Morton, 1984)

Many researchers in the area have been prompt to point out the numerous benefits which will accrue to organisations which implement EIS competently (Paller & Laska, 1990): (1) an increased span of control available "from the keyboard"; (2)

a saving in time enabled by the possibility to get an answer quicker not only because the data are already in the corporate database, but because new software allows managers to formulate their requests directly into a language that the machine can understand; (3) unlimited access into the corporate data resources guided by several levels of summary data authorising managers to "drill down" into layers of data to the level of detail they need; and (4) easy-to-use access to external sources of information now widely available (Economic Intelligence Unit, 1991).

A number of examples of successful EIS systems have been presented in the literature (see Courbon, 1994, and the references therein). The AIMS system developed by British Airways is interesting because it was a very early example of ESS (1982). It was originally designed for the top managers of the company, but now has more than 250 regular users. In other cases, ESS has become a presentation tool which optimises and synthesises top managers' access to the information available in their organisation. A new trend appears to design EIS as dashboards helping to follow a business's "critical success factors" (Adam and Pomerol, 2002).

Other researchers have expressed concerns related to the excessive concentration on systems dedicated to the support of individual managers. This is the reason why many studies are now focussed on the development of cooperative systems (Greenberg, 1991) and computer supported co-operative work—"the scientific discipline that motivates and validates groupware design." There is little consensus as to what CSCW involves and many definitions have been put forward. For practical purposes, Greenberg's (1991) vision of the field of CSCW seems helpful in an attempt to operationalise further studies in the area of groupwork support by computer systems. According to him, the field of CSCW studies and produces theories of how people work together and how the computer and related technologies affect group behaviour (Greenberg, 1991).

As a result, a number of researchers have studied groups and the effect of computer mediation on the pattern of interaction between individuals within groups (Hiltz & Johnson, 1990; Hiltz & Turoff, 1985; Nunamaker, 1989). Another perspective consists of finding new architectures which allow cooperative work and collaborative work. One can find a comparative view of the different types of systems in Pomerol and Brézillon (1998). Jones and Jacobs (2000) presents an overview of cooperative problems and models. Also, much research now focuses on the sociological aspect of information (e.g., Brown & Duguid, 2000). All these new trends attempt to capture the problem of decision support not for an isolated decision maker but for an individual immersed in sociological interaction. These perspectives would deserve another chapter.

CONCLUSION

In this chapter, we endeavour to give a technical definition of DMSS taking into account the specificities of human decision making. What is so particular in human decision is the look-ahead process often illustrated by scenario thinking and resulting in a multi-attribute choice balancing between short-term desires and long-term advantages. This balancing process can be supported by tools allowing a heuristic search at different cognitive levels. The search stops when a satisfying trade-off has been attained. This introduces DMSS as look-ahead machines and paves the way to better understanding and design of future DMSS.

REFERENCES

Ackoff, R. L. (1967) Management misinformation systems. *Management Science,* 14(4), 147-156.

Adam, F., & Pomerol, J.-Ch. (2000). Decision making and decision support systems. In P. Finnegan & C. Murphy (Eds.), *Information Systems at the Core.* Dublin: Blackhall Publishing.

Adam, F., & Pomerol, J.-Ch. (2002). Critical Factors in the Development of Executive Systems—Leveraging the Dashboard Approach, in this volume.

Baecker, R. M. (1993). *Groupware and computer supported cooperative work.* San Mateo, CA: Morgan Kaufmann Publishers.

Bell, D., Raiffa, H., & Tversky, A. (1988). *Decision making, descriptive, normative and prescriptive interactions.* Cambridge, UK: Cambridge University Press.

Berkeley, D., & Humphreys, P. (1982). Structuring Decision Problems and the "Bias heuristic." *Acta Psychologica,* 50, 201-252.

Berthoz, A. (1996). Neural basis of decision in perception and in the control of movement. In Damasio, A.-R., Damasio, H., & Christen, Y. (Eds.), *Neurobiology of Decision-Making.* Springer, 83-100.

Bonczek, R.-H., Holsapple, C.-W., & Whinston, A.-B. (1981). *Foundations of decision support systems.* New York: Academic Press.

Boy, G. (1991). *Intelligent assistant systems.* New York: Academic Press.

Brown, J. S., & Duguid, P. (2000). *The social life of information.* Boston, MA: Harvard Business School Press.

Business Intelligence (1990, 1991) *The Executive Information Systems Report.* London: Business Intelligence.

Calvin, W. -H. (1991). *The ascent of mind: Ice age, climate and the evolution of intelligence.* New York: Bantam Books.

Chang, A. -M., Holsapple, C.W., & Whinston, A.B. (1993). Model management issues and directions. *Decision Support Systems 9,* 19-37.

Checkland, P. D. (1981). *Systems Thinking, Systems Practice.* Chichester: John Wiley & Sons.

Cooper, R. B., & Zmud, R. W. (1990). Information technology implementation research: A technological diffusion approach. *Management Science 36,* 123-139.

Courbon, J.-Cl. (Ed.).(1994). Executive information systems. Special Issue *Journal of Decision Systems,* 3(4), 255-383.

Courbon, J.-Cl., Dubois, D., & Roy, B. (1994). Autour de l'aide à la décision et de l'intelligence artificielle, Rapport LAFORIA/IBP 94/01.

Damasio, A. R. (1994). *Descartes' Error*. New York: Pitman and Sons.

Damasio, A. R., Damasio, H., & Christen, Y. (1996). *Neuro-biology of Decision Making*. Berlin: Springer.

Economic Intelligence Unit (1991). *Executive Information Systems*, Special report # S123, *Management Guides*: London.

Fahy, M. & Murphy, C. (1996). From end-user computing to management developed systems. In Dias Coelo, Jelassi, Konig, Krcmar, O'Callagnan, Saaksjarvi (Eds.) *Proceedings of the 4th European Conference on Information Systems*, Lisbon, Portugal.

Findler, N.-V. (1995). Trade-off issues in a predictive man-machine environment. *Journal of Decision Systems*, *4*(3), 225-239.

van Gigch, J.-P. (1987). Rationalities and metarationalities in organisational decision making. In J.-P. van Gigch (Ed.), *Decision Making about Decision Making, Metamodels and Metasystems*, Abacus Press, pp. 241-255.

Gorry, A., & Scott-Morton, M. (1971). A framework for management information systems. *Sloan Management Review*, *13*(1), 55-70.

Gorry, A., & Scott-Morton, M. (1989). Retrospective commentary on the Gorry and Scott-Morton framework. *Sloan Management Review*, *31*(1), 58-60.

Greenberg, S. (1991). Computer-supported cooperative work and groupware. In Saul Greenberg (Ed.), the *Computer and People Series*, pp. 1-7.

Harvey, J., & Mickeljohn, M. (1991). *The EIS Report*. London: Business Intelligence.

Hatchuel, A. (1994). Apprentissages collectifs et activités de conception, *Revue Française de Gestion*, Juin-Juillet 1994, pp. 109-120.

Hiltz, S., & Johnson, K. (1990). User satisfaction with computer-mediated communication systems. *Management Science*, *36*(6), 739-764.

Hiltz, S., & Turoff, M. (1985). Structuring computer-mediated communication systems to avoid information overload. *Communications of the ACM*, *28*(7), 680-689.

Hogarth, R. M., & Makridakis, S. (1981). Forecasting and planning: An evaluation, *Management Science*, 27, 115-138.

Humphreys, P. (1989). Intelligence in decision making—A process model. In G. Doukidis, F. Land, & E. Miller (Eds.), *Knowledge-based Management Systems*. Chichester: Hellis Hovwood.

Humphreys, P., & Bekerley, D. (1985). Handling uncertainty: Levels of analysis of decision problems. In G. Wright (Ed.), *Behavioural Decision Making*. London: Plenum Press.

Jones, P. M., & Jacobs, J. L. (2000). Cooperative problem solving in human-machine systems: Theory, models, and intelligent associate systems. *IEEE Transactions on Systems Man and Cybernetics*, 30, 397-407.

Kahneman, D., & Lovallo, D. (1993). Timid choice and bold forecast : A cognitive perspective on risk taking. *Management Science*, 39, 17-31.

Keen, P. G. (1987). Decision support systems: The next decade. *Decision Support Systems*, 3, 253-265.

Keen, P. G., & Scott-Morton, M. S. (1978). *Decision Support Systems: An Organisational Perspective.* Reading, MA: Addison-Wesley.

Keeney, R.-L. (1988). Value-driven expert systems for decision support. *Decision Support Systems*, 4, 405-412.

Keeney, R.-L. (1992). *Value-Focused Thinking.* Boston, MA: Harvard University Press.

Klein, G. A. (1993). A recognition-primed decision (RPD) model of rapid decision in action. In Klein, G.A., Orasanu, J., Calderwood, R. & Zsambok, C.E. (Eds.), *Decision Making in Action: Models and Methods.* New York: Ablex.

Klein, M., & Methlie, L. B. (1990). *Expert Systems, A Decision Support Approach.* Reading, MA: Addison-Wesley.

Kleinmuntz, D.-N. (1985). Cognitive heuristics and feedback in a dynamic decision environment. *Management Science*, 31, 680-702.

Kleinmuntz, D.-N. (1993). Information processing and misperceptions of the implications of feedback in dynamic decision making. *System Dynamics Review*, 9, 223-237.

Landry, M., Pascot, D., & Briolat, D. (1985). Can DSS evolve without changing our view of the Concept of "Problem?" *Decision Support Systems* 1, 25-36.

Lévine, P., & Pomerol, J.-Ch. (1989). *Systèmes interactifs d'aide à la décision et systèmes experts.* Paris: Hermès.

Lévine, P., & Pomerol, J.-Ch. (1995). The role of the decision maker in DSS and representation levels. In *Proceedings of the 29th Hawaii International Conference on System Sciences* (Vol. 3), Nunamaker Jr., J. F., & Sprague, R. H. (Eds), IEEE, 42-51.

Makridakis, S. (1990). *Forecasting, Planning and the Strategy for the 21st century.* New York: The Free Press.

Marca, D., & Bock, G. (1992). *Groupware: Software for Computer Supported Cooperative Work.* Los Alamitos, CA: IEEE Computer Society Press.

Mintzberg, H. (1994). *The Rise And Fall Of Strategic Planning.* New York: Free Press.

Moore, J.H., & Chang, M. (1983). Meta-design considerations. In J.L. Bennett (Ed.), *Building Decision Support Systems,* 173-204, Reading, MA: Addison-Wesley.

Mumpower, J.L. (1987). Very simple expert systems: An application of judgment analysis to political risk analysis. In Mumpower, J.L., Phillips, L.D., Renn, O., & Uppuluri, V.R.R. (Eds.), *217-240, Expert Judgment and Expert Systems.* Berlin: Springer.

Naylor, T. H. (1982). Decision support systems or whatever happened to MIS? *Interfaces*, *12*(4), 92-94.

Newell, A., & Simon, H. A. (1972). *Human Problem Solving.* Englewood Cliffs, NJ: Prentice-Hall.

Nunamaker, J.-F. (1989). Group decision support systems (GDSS): Present and future. *IEEE Transactions on Engineering Management*, 11, 6-17.

Paller, A., & Laska, R. (1990). *The EIS Book: Information Systems for Top Managers*. New York: Business One, Irwin.

Parker, C. (1989). *Management Information Systems*. New York: McGraw Hill.

Pomerol, J.-Ch. (1990). *Systèmes experts et SIAD : enjeux et conséquences pour les organisations*, *TIS* 3, 37-64.

Pomerol, J.-Ch. (1992). Autour du concept de décision assistée par ordinateur, *Revue des systèmes de décision*, 1, 11-13.

Pomerol, J.-Ch. (1993). Multicriteria DSSs : State of the art and problems. *Central European Journal for Operations Research and Economics*, 2(3), 197-212.

Pomerol, J.-Ch. (1994). Le monde de l'aide à la décision, LAFORIA—Working Papers Series, Number 94/20, 1-26.

Pomerol, J.-Ch. (1997). Artificial intelligence and human decision making. *European Journal of Operational Research*, 99, 3-25.

Pomerol, J.-Ch. (2001). Scenario development and practical decision making under uncertainty. *Decision Support Systems*, 31, 197-204.

Pomerol, J.-Ch., & Barba-Romero, S. (2000). *Multicriterion Decision Making in Management: Principles and Practice*. New York: Kluwer.

Pomerol, J.-Ch., & Brézillon, P. (1998). From DSSs to cooperative systems: Some hard problems still remain. In D. Dolk (Ed.), *Proceedings HICCS 31*, IEEE Pub., 5, 64-71.

Pomerol, J.-Ch., Roy, B., Rosenthal-Sabroux, C., & Saad, A. (1995) An intelligent DSS for the multicriteria evaluation of railway timetables. *Foundations of Computing and Decision Science*, 20(3), 219-238.

Rockart, J., & DeLong, D. (1988). *Executive Support Systems: The Emergence Of Top Management Computer Use*, New York: Business One Irwin.

Roy, B. (1990). Decision-aid and decision-making. In readings in *Multiple-criteria Decision Aid*, C.A., Bana e Costa (Ed.), 17-35. Berlin: Springer-Verlag.

Roy, B. (1998). A missing link in OR-DA: Robustness analysis. *Foundations of Computing and Decision Science* 23, 141-160.

Savage, L. J. (1954). The Foundations of Statistics. New York: John Wiley & Sons.

Schein, E. H. (1961). Management development as a process of influence. *Industrial Management Review* 2, 59-77.

Scott-Morton, M. (1984). The state of the art of research in management information systems. In Rockart & Bullen (Eds.), *The Rise of Management Computing*, (chap. 16). New York: Irwin.

Simon, H.-A. (1977). *The New Science of Management Decision*. Rev. ed., Englewood Cliffs, NJ: Prentice-Hall.

Simon, H.-A. (1997). *Administrative Behavior*, 4ième édition (first edition 1947), New York: Free Press.

Sprague, R. (1987). DSS in context. *Decision Support Systems*, 3(2), 197-202.

Sprague, R., & Carlson, E.D. (1982). *Building Effective Decision Support Systems.* Englewood Cliffs, NJ: Prentice Hall.

Sterman, J.-D. (1989). Modelling managerial behavior: Misperceptions of feedback in a dynamic decision-making experiment. *Management Science,* 35, 321-339.

Thompson, J.-O., & Tuden, A. (1959). Strategies, structures and processes of organisational decision. In *Comparative Studies in Administration,* J.D. Thompson, P.B. Hammond, R.W. Hawkes, B.H. Junker, & A. Tuden (Eds.), 195-216. Pittsburgh: University of Pittsburgh Press.

Turban, E. (1988). *Decision Support and Expert Systems.* London: MacMillan.

Tversky, A., & Kahneman, D. (1987). In RM Hogarth & MW Reder (Eds.), *Rational choice: The contrast between economics and sociology,* 67-94. Chicago: University of Chicago Press.

Watson, H. J., Rainer Jr., R. K., & Koh, C. E. (1991). EIS: A framework for development and a survey of current practices. *MIS Quarterly,* 15, 13-30.

von Winterfeldt, D., & Edwards, W. (1986). *Decision Analysis and Behavioral Research.* Cambridge: Cambridge University Press.

Wolstenholme, E.-F. (1990). *System Enquiry—A System Dynamics Approach.* New York: John Wiley.

SECTION II

APPLICATIONS
OF
DMSS

Chapter V

DSS for Rescheduling of Railway Services Under Unplanned Events

B. Adenso-Díaz, J. Tuya, M. J. Suárez-Cabal and M. Goitia-Fuertes
Universidad de Oviedo, Spain

ABSTRACT

In the daily activity of railway transport, the need to make decisions when faced with unforeseen incidents is a common event. Quality of service my be affected by decisions that are made by delays or cancellations. In this multi-objective scenario, there is a need to combine affecting the majority of passengers as little as possible with the minimization of costs. Therefore it is necessary to design planning algorithms taking into account factors such as the availability of engines and the quality of service. This chapter presents the design and implementation experience of a practical case developed for the Spanish Railway Company. With this tool, a DSS was put into service that guides the person in charge as to which measures to adopt with respect to the events that have arisen. The information employed is obtained by means of heuristic search algorithms based on backtracking for the exploration of the solutions space.

INTRODUCTION

The constant increase in competitiveness in all systems of transport, both passenger and goods, requires improved, effective use of all the available resources, as well as permanent adaptation to changing user needs. All this is needed without losing sight at any time of service reliability and availability, since these have a direct impact on the quality perceived by the user. Thus, the development of decision-aiding systems for this type of scenario is especially interesting.

One important aspect related to the difficulty of the solution is that related to the topology of the tracks, since when an incident is produced, some of the units which were scheduled to circulate, both on the stretch involved as well as on other tracks, may be affected. At the same time, since this is a multi-objective scenario, there is a need to combine affecting the majority of passengers as little as possible with the minimization of costs.

In order to determine the best measures to take in such events, it is useful to design planning algorithms that take into account factors such as the availability of engines and the quality of service by means of an efficient search in the solutions tree.

This chapter presents the design and implementation experiences of a practical case developed for the Spanish National Railway Company, in use in its regional lines in the Principality of Asturias (Northern Spain). With this tool, an original decision support system was put into service that guides the person responsible for the network, via tables and graphs, with respect to which measures to adopt with respect to the events that have arisen. The information employed is obtained by means of heuristic search algorithms based on backtracking and pruning for the exploration of the solutions space.

This application enables the user to define the characteristics of the incident produced and the input constraints. As output, the user receives a series of solutions with their associated costs. The analyst may then select each of these solutions so as to observe the actions proposed by the system and the layout of the grid solution resulting from the application of said actions, to finally choose among them.

The chapter is structured in the following way. Similar experiences in the resolution of this type of decision problem are described next. Subsequently, a detailed description of the problem to be solved is given, as well as the algorithm designed to solve it. The chapter ends with a description of the implementation experiences and our conclusions.

BACKGROUND

As mentioned above, in the day-to-day activity of railway transport, the need to take decisions when faced with unforeseen incidents is a common event, with such decisions affecting the quality of the service due to the delays or cancellations they provoke. Given that these are complex systems of transport, the different policies employed may be classified according to the different desired levels of planning (Crainic, 2000):

- Strategic: The aim is to adopt long-term decisions (for instance, the planning, design and evolution of the actual network or the acquisition of resources).
- Tactical: The aim is to adopt medium-term decisions such as the coordination of the different existing resources.

- Operational: These are short-term decisions, such as, for example, the definition and adjustment of timetables. This is the type of problem that we shall focus on.

In order to adequately define any of these policies, it is of interest to possess *decision support systems* (DSS) that provide the users with an aid in their daily work of decision taking. The development of this type of system to assist in problems of analysis, solutions building and decision taking is presently one of the major challenges in this type of management (Rawlings, 1994).

In general, decision support systems are made up of three components: data, dialog and model (Sprague, 1980). In some applications in the railway sector, the dialog component together with that of data directly constitutes the decision support system, sometimes integrated in a GIS environment (Fitzgerald & Brewington, 1997), enabling the entire railway network that is the object of analysis to be visualized and managed.

On other occasions, other authors have used simulation models to design interactive decision support systems in railway environments (Bell & O'Keefe, 1995; Ceric, 1997; Chau, 1993), thus permitting responses to "what-if" queries or to be used for training those responsible for the networks.

However, the majority of research into decision support systems applied to railway traffic control systems is aimed, as in other types of problems, at the use of more or less complex models that lead to automatically obtained solutions, employing different types of approaches:

- The algorithmic approach: Using algorithms from mathematics, computer science and operations research, these obtain an overall optimum with respect to an objective function, taking into consideration a number of restrictions (Balakrishnan, Magnanti, & Mirchandani, 1997; Fernández, de Cuadra, & García, 1996; Magnanti & Wong, 1986; Zwaneveld, Lroon, & Ambergen, 1996).
- The heuristic approach: This aims at obtaining good, though not necessarily optimum, solutions using techniques from artificial intelligence and human expert knowledge in the form of expert system rules, fuzzy logic, etc. (Adamski, 1992; Fay, 2000; Schäfer & Pferdmenges, 1994).
- Mixed approaches: These combine the two aforementioned approaches, applying heuristics to algorithms with the aim of reducing the high computational cost of the latter.

Nonetheless, when trying to resolve problems of an operational type as in our case, one of the critical factors is always the response time, which should not exceed a few minutes. It is hence logical to employ mixed approaches. Missikoff (1998) combines an object-oriented architecture with optimization techniques and heuristics to design controllers that enable train timetables to be maintained in the presence of disruptions and delays, identifying anomalies and resolving conflicts. On the other hand, Martinelli and Teng (1996) employ neuronal nets to obtain the composition of trains. This enables good solutions to be obtained in a short space of time, thus being able to respond effectively to changes in conditions. Another example is that proposed by Fay (2000), who applies fuzzy rules in a model based on Petri networks in order to carry out and adjust the dispatching of trains, taking into account all the costs as well as the delays. This third aforementioned approach is also the one followed in our study.

THE CASE OF THE SPANISH REGIONAL RAILWAYS

This study arose in response to the need on the part of the Regional Operations Headquarters of the National Railway Network in Asturias to design a system capable of taking decisions with respect to the modification of timetables after possible interruptions in the line or other incidents until the regular timetables are established again. Said system should provide the person in charge at that moment with the necessary assistance to take decisions with respect to actions that imply the suspension of services and the reassignment of railway units. Similar systems were not available by the national company in any of its lines.

Achieving high levels of punctuality (efficiency in the times of passing each control point in the average working day) and regularity (fulfilling the daily offer of services) is one of the objectives of the project. A decrease in the delay of a train translates directly into a cost saving, since it signifies saving in energy consumption, equipment cost, availability of machines and an improvement in the quality of the service offered to clients. Any anomaly in the network can affect the fulfillment of both measures, hence the need for a system that defines forms of action to minimize the consequences.

Given the combinatory nature of the problem (there are many possible alternatives, such as delaying the departure of a service[1] until the unit that has suffered the delay reaches the departure station; withdrawing the affected service; withdrawing a service so as to send this unit to carry out another one with a higher priority; transferring units from one line to another; etc.), the person in charge of the network encountered serious difficulties in analyzing the best decisions to take, i.e., those that affect the least possible number of passengers. The objective was therefore to create a DSS that included a search algorithm which provides the best solutions for minimizing the total delay of trains, whilst fulfilling the defined restrictions.

The railway network of Asturias covers a total of 151.7 km, of which 120.5 are double-track lines. There is a daily offer of 181 services, which supposes an approximate total of 22,213 passengers transported daily. These services are carried out by 14 units, there being an additional 3 reserve units waiting to be employed in any contingency. Initially, each unit has a series of services assigned to it that belong to the routes of one particular line (there are three lines in the region of Asturias). Hence, each line is covered by a fixed number of units, and each service has pre-

Table 1: Lines and distribution of passengers

Line	Origin-Destination	Length (Km)	Passengers	Passengers (Km)	Average journey (Km)
L1	P. Los Fierros – Oviedo - Gijón	75.5	6,454	143,840	22.3
	Gijón – Oviedo - P. Los Fierros		6,854	151,130	22.0
L2	El Entrego - Oviedo	29.6	1,148	26,567	19.2
	Oviedo - El Entrego		1,312	29,709	18.2
L3	San Juan de Nieva - Oviedo	33.6	2,933	56,224	19.2
	Oviedo - San Juan de Nieva		3,154	57,497	18.2
	TOTAL	151.7	22,213	468,822	21.1

assigned a "*shift unit*" that will cover it, coordinated with the other assignments that this unit has to complete for other services.

With respect to passengers, Table 1 shows how 40% of these transit through the station at Oviedo (the region's capital). For this reason, the railway network of regional trains in Asturias is considered to have a radial configuration, with its center in Oviedo.

Due to this structure of the railway network of Asturias, the problem of incidents is exacerbated. All the lines concur in one common station, such that all the trains pass through it, without there being any alternative way of linking two diametrically opposed stations or stations belonging to different lines. The high number of services offered each day has also to be taken into consideration, which multiplies the set of trains affected when any anomaly occurs.

We may define *incident* as any event that alters the daily schedule of the trains, provoking shortcomings in the fulfillment of regularity and punctuality (problems of derailment, lack of personnel, problems in the power system or with the signals, etc.). Incidents may be classified according to their origin, their average duration, their consequences, etc. For each case that we deal with, we shall distinguish between two possibilities:

- Total-line-interruption incident. This type of incident is produced in stretches of single-track line and hence supposes a total interruption at said point. Traffic is paralyzed at this point until it is corrected.
- Partial interruption incident. This is produced on a double track, it being possible to run on one of the lines. In this case, traffic is not totally paralyzed and the most important factor will be to adjust the crossovers on the line with traffic.

In order to minimize the consequences generated by incidents, a search heuristic algorithm was designed, based on backtracking, that enables both energy as well as equipment costs to be reduced by taking into consideration the availability of machines and which also considers another important factor: the maintenance of service quality, i.e., the fulfillment of train timetables and punctuality.

THE DESIGNED ALGORITHM

It is possible to offer MILP formulation to this problem of rescheduling timetables (Adenso-Díaz, González, & González, 1999). However, given the combinatory nature of the problem, these formulations are not useful from the practical point of view of obtaining solutions in reasonable times.

With regards the application of the results generated by the system, we can think of a solution as an assignment of one of the units available in the network (or a dummy in the case of cancellation) for each of the services that are potentially affected by the incident (i.e., those that are active at the time of the anomaly or which are due to depart during a specific time horizon, T, after it is produced). This assignment implies a specific delay in the execution of each service (null if the service can be executed by the assigned unit just at the time this should be carried out according to the regular timetable). Note that with the current data available to the system with respect to the network and incidents, it is possible to calculate the time needed to transfer any unit between any stations whatsoever and thus the associated delays.

To explore possible alternative actions, an exhaustive procedure would consist of the development of a search tree. One possible implementation would be to represent each service by a node, emerging from which would be a series of branches according to the following logic (Figure 1):

- A branch that corresponds to the shift unit (the desirable alternative, as it does not represent an alteration in the original plans).
- N branches corresponding to the remaining units available to carry out the service (units that could carry out this service with a delay below a predefined threshold of 30 minutes).
- A branch that indicates that the service will be cancelled.

Expanding the branches and carrying out an in-depth search would generate all the possible solutions. However, the size for real problems would make a complete search impossible, and so it is necessary to develop pruning and expansion algorithms for the branches that allow real problems to be solved in a practical way.

Figure 1: Structure of each node in the search tree

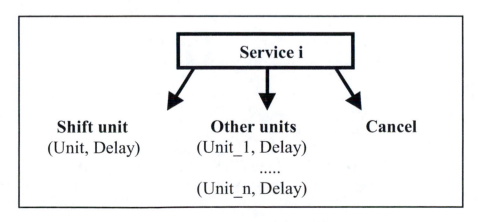

The following is a detailed description of the implementation:

1 – The trains with a departure time later than the DEPARTURE_TIME of the incident are selected, up until a time horizon, T. (This horizon is always less than 24 hours, since timetables would then begin to be repeated cyclically, even though there are a number of hours, generally during the night, when services are interrupted in order to clean the units). The services in this time horizon are the only ones to form part of the solution. In order to expand the tree, ordering is done according to the departure time, breaking ties depending on priority.

2 – Following this order, branches are generated for each service in accordance with the following logic:

♦ If the delay for the shift unit is zero, a branch is generated for this unit and no branching is carried out for the others (it is the most desirable assignment, as mentioned above).

♦ If there is a nonzero delay when assigning the shift unit, the following cases are considered, in this order, bearing in mind that: *i)* the units for which the delay caused by fulfilling the assignment is greater than the MAXIMUM_ALLOWED_DELAY will not then be considered and *ii)* on creating a branch in which the unit must be moved empty, if this movement together with the previous ones in the partial solution is greater than a predefined threshold, then this branch will not be expanded either.

{A. POSSIBILITY OF CARRYING OUT THE SERVICE WITHOUT A DELAY}

A1. If an available unit exists at the train's station of origin, the tree is expanded into two branches: the shift unit and another branch representing one of the units available in the station (any one of them).

A2. If no unit exists at the station, but there are units available that on being moved to the station of origin may carry out the service without a delay, the shift unit is branched and another branch is expanded corresponding to one of the units that has to be moved (in the case of there being several, with preference the reserve unit which is nearest).

{B. IMPOSSIBILITY OF CARRYING OUT THE SERVICE WITHOUT A DELAY}

B1. If no unit exists that can carry out the service without a delay, the shift unit is branched, and another two branches are extracted corresponding to moved units that can carry out the service. In this case, the system selects the two units, should they exist, that cause the least delay (as long as this is less than the MAXIMUM_ALLOWED_DELAY and less than the delay of the shift unit).

There are some other rules that enable the size of the tree to be reduced:

• When exploring each of the branches of the tree to obtain solutions, if all the shifts have zero delay, this means that the grid is already stabilized, and therefore there is no need to expand more branches for the problem we are studying.

• When exploring a branch, if the *cost of the solution* is greater than the most costly of the N best existing solutions, this branch is pruned and the solution is discarded. If it is less, the most costly solution is substituted by the newly found, less costly solution.

• An empty movement of a unit is defined as the time that a unit takes to move from its station of origin to another destination without making any intermediate stops and with no passengers on board. When performing the solutions search, an accumulation is made of the empty movements that units make to the stations of origin of the trains. A threshold is established that, if exceeded when exploring a branch, causes said branch to be pruned and the solution to be discarded.

In order to evaluate which alternatives are the best ones to offer to the person in charge of the network, the cost of a solution needs to be defined. To do this, not only should the delays of each train be taken into account, but also the priority and number of passengers of the services have to be considered. A short delay in a priority train with many passengers may be more detrimental than a longer one in a train with less importance. The cost associated with each service will be 0% if no delay is suffered and 100% if it is eliminated. Thus the degree of fulfillment with respect to the number of passengers on a train and the priority of the train may be calculated as:

$$Cost\_serv = \frac{Pass\_serv}{Max\_pass} * \frac{(Max\_priority + 1) - Priority\_serv}{Max\_priority} * \frac{Delay\_serv}{Max\_delay}$$

where *Max_pass* is the maximum number of passengers on any service; *Max_priority* is the greatest priority (in this case, it has been assumed that priorities may be 1, 2 or 3, being 1 the greatest); *Max_delay* is the maximum delay that a train may suffer with respect to its departure time without being suspended (30 minutes).

The overall cost of a solution will thus be:

$$Cost\_solution\% = \frac{\sum_{j=1}^{n} Cost\_serv(j)}{n} * 100$$

IMPLEMENTATION AND EXPERIENCES

As well as the model, the user interface is a key element for the success of the DSS, above all when the final user is not an expert in the use of computers. In our case, there are a series of informative-type screens p_r at provide information with respect to the state of the network, the location of trains, etc. A second set of screens permit incident data to be input and enable the recommendations generated by the system to be read. Figure 2 shows the initial screen of the process, via which the incident is parameterized: the type of incident is defined, and other parameters are set that will have an influence on the solution obtained, the scope of the incident is indicated (total or partial interruption in the line), the time that it occurred and its estimated duration, as well as other data related to the location of the event and its repercussions.

The options that the analyst wishes to employ when generating solutions are also introduced (on the right of the screen): it may occasionally be desirable to consider different solutions in which one alternative is always that of canceling services; it might also be desirable to use units that are in reserve. Other parameters are likewise input, such as the threshold for the time of empty journeys, the time horizon T of the services to consider, and the number of desired solutions.

Once all this data has been input, the algorithm is executed and the solutions generated are displayed, ordered according to their cost and in various formats (Figure 3). For each solution, the services that have been affected are specified, indicating whether they will be cancelled or which unit will carry out the service and with what delay (in the case of the delay being at a station other than that of the station of origin, this station is also indicated).

Figure 2: Screen for inputting incident data

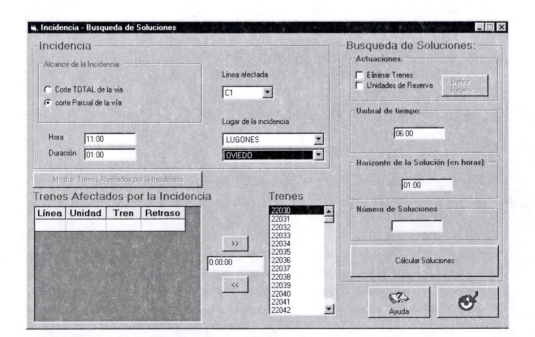

Seeing that railway personnel are used to visualizing services via grids, the system allows the solutions to be visualized using this form of representation (Figure 4), by means of which the operator observes, according to the different colors used, which services are cancelled (in thick red), comparing these with the standard timetables.

Finally, it should be noted that the developed tool is intuitive to use so as to facilitate as much as possible the work by personnel untrained in the use of computers. In order to achieve this goal, we collaborated closely with the personnel of the railroad company, who furnished the guidelines to follow at all times with respect to the way of presenting the information and the design of the screens.

DIFFICULTIES IN IMPLANTATION

On many occasions, the main problem during the start-up of a DSS is related to the rejection expressed by its end users (Adenso-Díaz, González, & González, 1991). This is due to factors such as their loss of power in the taking of decision within the structure of the firm or because of distrust with respect to its use. In the present case, as we are dealing with decision making in which the difficulty of analyzing the alternatives is highly complex (to which we must add the necessary speed in taking decisions), we received the unconditional collaboration of the person responsible for

Figure 3: Example of a screen in which five different solutions are offered; the second column indicates the cost, and the top row, the services affected with their assignment of units

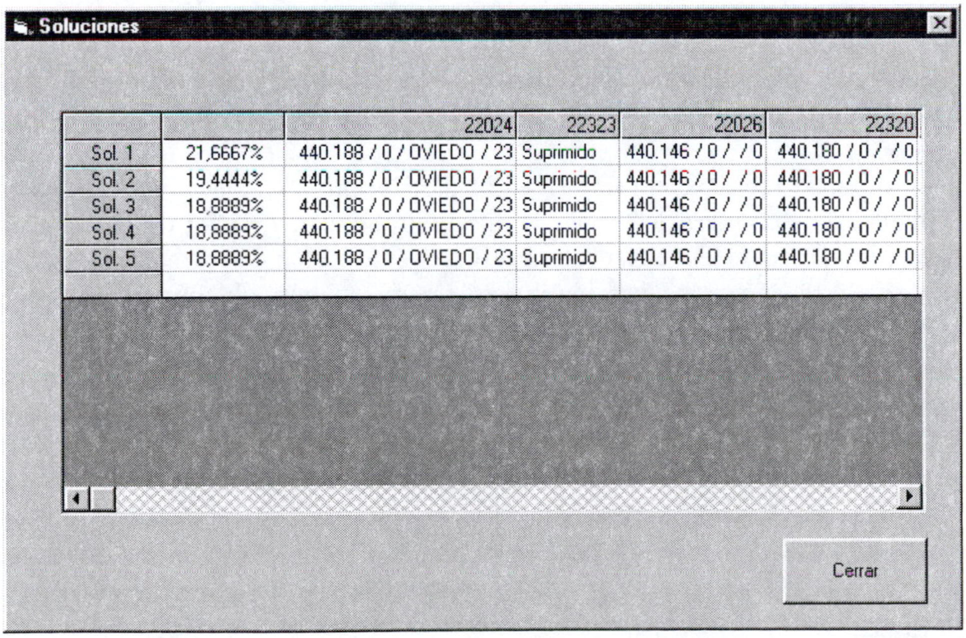

Soluciones			22024	22323	22026	22320
Sol. 1	21,6667%		440.188 / 0 / OVIEDO / 23	Suprimido	440.146 / 0 / / 0	440.180 / 0 / / 0
Sol. 2	19,4444%		440.188 / 0 / OVIEDO / 23	Suprimido	440.146 / 0 / / 0	440.180 / 0 / / 0
Sol. 3	18,8889%		440.188 / 0 / OVIEDO / 23	Suprimido	440.146 / 0 / / 0	440.180 / 0 / / 0
Sol. 4	18,8889%		440.188 / 0 / OVIEDO / 23	Suprimido	440.146 / 0 / / 0	440.180 / 0 / / 0
Sol. 5	18,8889%		440.188 / 0 / OVIEDO / 23	Suprimido	440.146 / 0 / / 0	440.180 / 0 / / 0

Cerrar

Figure 4: Grid associated with a solution, indicating delays and cancellations with respect to official timetables

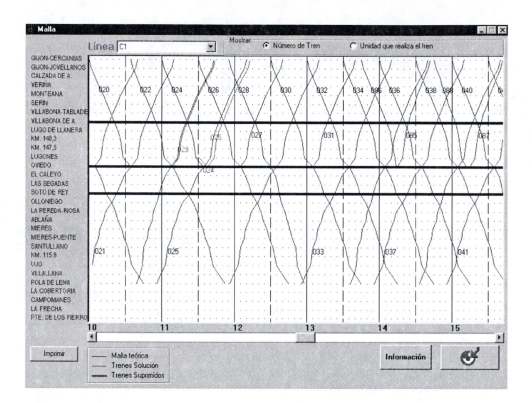

the network, which facilitated the speed of start-up and a design that is more adjusted to real needs, since he realized the personal benefits he would receive after implementation.

As far as the development phase of the algorithm is concerned, the major difficulty obviously resides in the definition of the heuristics for developing the branches and pruning. Deficient design gives rises to search spaces that are too large and which slow down the decision-making process excessively. In our case, when faced with real problems, no more than 2 or 3 minutes are needed until the system offers solutions, a time that adapts to the requirements of the users.

CONCLUSIONS

This chapter offers details of the development of a system for supporting in decision making that, on the basis of information with respect to the units and timetables stored in the database, guides the person in charge of the network via tables and grids that represent the possible solution to minimize online the effects of incidents that occur.

The actions to carry out so as to guarantee the efficient functioning of the railway network are then determined using the solutions obtained together with this person's experience. The goal is thus to decrease to the utmost the cost of reassigning units to carry out these services, at the same time as increasing the quality of the service and minimizing train delays as much as possible. The response times obtained when faced with real problems adjust to the operating needs of the railway network.

Similar solutions developed so far differ from this one in the goal and the problem tackled. Previous approaches (as those cited above or some other commercial software that can be found in the market, most of them based on constraint programming) faced mainly the problem of timetable construction and service planning. However, for our algorithm that information is just an input: it works initially with standard timetables that it must change after unplanned events occurring in the network. The difficulty of the latter problem is its online nature, while in the former that is not the case and therefore is not the case for the approaches developed for it.

Looking at the further research to be developed, we can identify several open points. Firstly, pruning of the search tree is always a task that can be improved. New opportunities can be found to reduce the searching time by analyzing the specific characteristics of the problem, which is also depending on the railway network. In addition, although in this project the people in charge of the network were actively participating, the man-machine interface needs more research in this type of DSS. The online nature that we have mentioned makes even more important than in other systems the quick access to the information and a full solutions visualization. He or she must decide in just a few minutes what action to take, and there are many data to consider from the computer system.

ENDNOTE

[1] The following is a list of railway terms used in this chapter:

- **Service:** the transit of passengers, defined by the departure time, station of origin, arrival time, destination and all the intermediate stations.
- **Unit:** a train formed by an engine and wagons for transporting passengers, which provides different services during a day.
- **Shift:** the set of services that are carried out by a particular unit during a day.
- **Grid:** the graphical representation of the trains; time is represented on one axis and the stations on the other; thus visualizing which station each train reaches and at what time (see example in Figure 4).

REFERENCES

Adamski, A. (1992). Real-time computer aided adaptive control in public transport from the point of view of schedule reliability. In *Proceedings of the CASPT'91*, (p. 278-295) Lisbon.

Adenso-Díaz, B., González, M. O., & González, P. (1999). On-line timetable rescheduling in regional train services. *Transportation Research-B, 33*(6), 387-398.

Adenso-Díaz, B., Sancho, F., García, R., & Larrañeta, J. (1991). A dynamic scheduling and control system in an ENSIDESA steel plant. *Interfaces, 21*(5) 53-62.

Balakrishnan, A., Magnanti, T. L., & Mirchandani, P. (1997). Network design. In M. Dell'Amico, F. Maffioli, & S. Martello (Eds.), *Annotated bibliographies in combinatorial optimization* (pp. 311-334). NY: Wiley.

Bell, P. C., & O'Keefe, R. M. (1995). An experimental investigation into the efficacy of visual interactive simulation. *Management Science*, 41, 1018-1038.

Ceric, V. (1997). Visual interactive modeling and simulation as a decision support in railway transport logistic operations. *Mathematics and Computers in Simulation*, 44, 251-261.

Chau, P. J. K. (1993). Decision support using traditional simulation and visual interactive simulation. *Information and Design Technologies*, 19, 63-76.

Crainic, T. G. (2000). Service network design in freight transportation. *European Journal of Operational Research*, 122, 272-288.

Fay, A. (2000). A fuzzy knowledge-based system for railway traffic control. *Engineering Applications of Artificial Intelligence*, 13, 719-729.

Fernández, A., de Cuadra, F., & García, A. (1996). SIRO—An optimal regulation system in an integrated control centre for metro lines. In *Proceedings of the COMPRAIL '96* (pp. 299-308) Berlin.

Fitzgerald, J. W., & Brewington, J. S. (1997, July). The GIS-based Rail Crossing Decision Support System for the North Carolina Department of Transportation. In *Proceedings of the 1997 ESRI User Conference*. San Diego.

Magnanti, T. L., & Wong, R. T. (1986). Network design and transportation planning: Models and algorithms. *Transportation Science, 18*(1), 1-55.

Martinelli, D. R., & Teng, H. (1996). Optimization of railway operations using neural networks. *Transportation Research, 4*(1), 33-49.

Missikoff, M. (1998). An object-oriented approach to an information and decision support system for railway traffic control. *Engineering Applications of Artificial Intelligence*, 11, 25-40.

Rawlings, D. (1994) Control center of the future gives operators the means to regulate effectively. *Railway Gazette International, 150*(9), 583-590.

Schäfer, H., & Pferdmenges, S. (1994). An expert system for real-time train dispatching. In *Proceedings of the COMPRAIL '94* (pp. 27-34) Madrid, Spain.

Sprague, R. H. (1980). A framework for the development of decision support systems. *Management Information Systems Quarterly*, 4, 1-26.

Zwaneveld, P. J., Lroon, L. G., & Ambergen, H. W. (1996). A decision support system for routing trains through railway stations. In *Proceedings of the COMPRAIL '96* (pp. 219-226) Berlin.

Chapter VI

Using Decision Support Systems to Help Policy Makers Cope With Urban Transport Problems

Francesco Mazzeo Rinaldi and Donald Bain
European Commission Joint Research Centre, Italy

ABSTRACT

More than 70% of Europe's population lives in urban areas. Transport pollution contributes significantly to severe health problems in many European cities. The impacts of air pollutants are particularly severe in busy city centres, where congestion creates long queues of stationary traffic pumping fumes onto streets crowded with pedestrians. Although improvements in vehicle technologies have led to steady reductions in pollutant emissions, the decrease has been slower than expected due to the ever-increasing transport demand.

Getting urban transport "right" is a challenging task for decision-makers given the number of policy areas affected, the large range of stakeholders and the high political sensitivity of almost any option adopted (including "do nothing"). Ultimately any decision must rest with the skills and informed judgement of the decision-maker or decision college. It remains difficult.

The work presented shows the development of a DSS called Navigate Utopia. It is a web-style tool based on Multicriteria Analysis which has been developed to allow policy-makers to explore and evaluate the numerous new transport technology options already available or on the point of entering the market.

Navigate Utopia draws on practical experience derived from previous case studies in Europe, giving guidance on how these can best be applied to specific urban situations and providing tools to understand what the effects might be. It considers also the wide range of new and improved propulsion systems currently coming on stream and draws together findings from a wide range of disciplines to address the complex issue of how to ensure successful market entry of new transport technologies.

INTRODUCTION

Within the research community applying multi-criteria approaches to decision support systems (DSS) there is extensive debate on issues of theory. These range from comparing the respective merits of the predominantly "Anglo-Saxon" multi-criteria decision making (MCDM) and the essentially "European" multi-criteria decision aid (MCDA) (Roy, 1985) to such matters as the possibilities of incorporating behavioural research findings (Stewart, 2000) and the consequences of ignoring ethical and normative concerns (Henig, 2001; Rauschmayer, 2001). In this chapter we try to bring this often rarefied debate into the realm of practical decision enhancement by stressing the importance of intense customer interaction during the decision support system (DSS) construction phase.

To achieve this we focus on a particular software product called Navigate UTOPIA. This is a decision support tool, incorporating an MCDA, developed as part of the European Commission's UTOPIA project. (UTOPIA = Urban Transport: Options for Propulsion systems and Instruments for Analysis.)

Although most of what follows relates to the problems of urban transport policy it is not transport per se which concerns us in this chapter.[1] The focus is more general and concentrated on the benefits of intense interaction with potential DSS users, particularly when these include stakeholders with limited technical training.

As it happens transport decisions are particularly well suited to a multi-criteria approach (Bana e Costa, Nunes de Silva, & Vansnick, 2001; Bristow & Nellthorp, 2000; Modesti & Sciomachen, 1998; e.g., Roy & Hugonnard, 1982; Tsamboulas & Mikroudis, 2000) given their complexity, their interaction with a whole series of economic, ecological, social and political subsystems and the large number of stakeholders involved. Getting urban transport "right" is a challenging task for decision makers, given the number of policy areas affected, the large range of stakeholders and the high political sensitivity of almost any option adopted (including "do nothing"). Ultimately any decision must rest with the skills and informed judgement of the decision maker or decision college. It remains difficult.

This is also the type of decision where competing techniques, notably cost-benefit analysis, have been shown to be not only impractical but also liable to exacerbate the problems (Munda, Ni,jkamp, & Rietveld, 1994). In urban transport decisions it is critically important that ownership of the decision remains with the multiple stakeholders. Moreover hostility of many of these actors to any prescriptive or black box approach strongly favours MCDA (Paruccini, 1992). For these reasons this is a project which yields practical guidelines and new avenues for further research.

BACKGROUND

The UTOPIA project was a joint research venture undertaken by a consortium, including a major vehicle manufacturer, trade organisations, universities, research centres and government agencies from the main European Union (EU) countries. The project was part-sponsored by the European Commission's Transport Research Programme. While consortium partners had a variety of motives for participation the key objective of the project was to overcome the various barriers to deployment of innovative propulsion systems as means of resolving transport problems in Europe's cities.

It is widely accepted that urban transport pollution (incorporating emissions, noise and congestion) is a major factor in health problems, environmental degradation and global warming, to name but three of the key problems confronting city dwellers. At the same time technologies such as electrical and natural gas vehicles, fuel cells and hybrids already have the potential to effect dramatic improvements in the situation. Local city planners, however, have shown considerable reluctance to commit themselves to these still largely untried technologies, despite their apparent attractiveness. The task of the consortium was to bring together available information on the technological options, and on case studies where they had already been introduced, with a view to building confidence in these alternatives among local decision-makers.

Most consortium partners were information providers or validators. The role of the JRC (Joint Research Centre of the European Commission) was to provide the decision support tools, which would give eventual users direct and dynamic access to the results. The JRC was asked to participate because of its substantial experience in applying MCDA to large-scale environmental projects: There was unanimous agreement among consortium partners that urban transport decisions need multi-criteria solutions.

Originally we had intended to use a tool called NAIADE (Munda, 1995), which we had successfully used in a large number of projects, mainly in environmental and resource planning, but also in transport futures studies. As UTOPIA progressed, however, numerous changes in perspective had to be incorporated into the project. It rapidly became evident that the focus could not be limited to the propulsion technologies but needed to be extended to systems such as incorporating electrical vehicles with car-share schemes or developing new mobility packages. At the level of the DSS development we discovered, through extensive test runs with potential end users, that many of our initial assumptions regarding the nature of the users and their modes of using knowledge were severely flawed. In particular we found that NAIADE, while a powerful MCDA when used by skilled environmental planners, was too complex to engage the very varied groups of stakeholders involved in urban transport decisions. Instead we developed a new tool, MARPA, based on the reference point approach (see below).

CHARACTERISTICS OF NAVIGATE UTOPIA

Navigate UTOPIA can be used in two ways: evaluating options and surfing the UTOPIA information base. In both cases the user enters the information system through a choice of "doors," or starting points, depending on his/her major field of interest. Depending on the level of interest, introductory or more detailed information may be accessed. The connection with other aspects of the problem is highlighted offering the possibility of navigating through documentation, data and models in a Web-type approach.

In the evaluating options phase the user defines the transport applications to be targeted, identifying typical European urban transport systems, particular demand cases and transport services in line with the city's problems. Thereafter he or she identifies options, or potential solutions, involving new transport solutions and technologies. The user is then guided through evaluating the options in the context of his or her city by means of a set of criteria estimating environmental, market, economic and social impacts. He or she must:

1)   Choose the alternatives to be evaluated (new transport solutions and technology options) in the context of his or her city.

2)   Select from among a set of criteria to evaluate the different alternatives. Here the users can decide either to go for a detailed analysis, choosing among a list of specific sub-criteria, or go for a less detailed assessment using a set of mega-criteria.

3)   Describe the criteria (quantitatively or qualitatively) for assessing the impacts of each alternative.

4)   Set, according to the multi-criteria method, the reference point and the weight for each criterion selected, in order to introduce his or her preferences.

5)   The user will then make a ranking of options according to these preferences, analysing the most favourable options in terms of the stage of market implementation to assess the eventual need for a pilot project or pilot projects.

Surfing the UTOPIA information base allows the user to explore in a free and dynamic way the substantial information resources which have been created in this major project. The information base has multiple entry points which allow definition of the search according to the user's own priorities.

We will now present each of these two modes in greater detail.

A: Evaluation

Problem Context

The starting point here is an analysis of typical European urban transport systems in terms of urban travel patterns and the associated problems. A set of representative demand cases is presented (TNO, 1998), as in Figure 1.

Figure 1: Demand Case 1

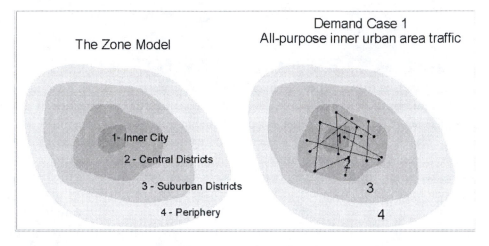

The Zone Model

Demand Case 1
All-purpose inner urban area traffic

1- Inner City

2 - Central Districts

3 - Suburban Districts

4 - Periphery

A second analysis focuses mainly on environmental impacts of urban transport systems and reviews the innovation processes and market acceptance factors (IER, 1999).

Based on an inventory of environmental impacts related to urban transport the indicators of particular interest to specific groups are identified. Legal standards related to environmental impacts from transport systems and the process of standard setting are reviewed, and different types of regulation are discussed with respect to the respective incentive for innovation processes.

Options

To examine the range of options available the user must first choose the demand cases closest to his or her specific urban transport setting. These demand cases have been selected so that they cover the main patterns of travel demand in European towns and cities. Next, a comprehensive list of propulsion systems, vehicle concepts and transport concepts is provided, together with accompanying descriptions (TNO, 1998; VW, 1998). The different characteristics of these systems and concepts are identified and presented in overviews.

Finally the system helps the user create a list of the most promising combinations (MPCs) of transport concepts, vehicle concepts and propulsion systems.

Evaluation Procedure

A systematic evaluation of public plans or projects has to be based on the identification and measurement of a broad set of criteria. Multi-criteria methods provide a flexible way of dealing with qualitative multidimensional environmental effects of decisions.

A set of evaluation criteria is presented in order to identify promising new transport solutions and technology options. The user is then guided interactively through a series of actions.

Figure 2: Interactive phase—formulation of alternatives

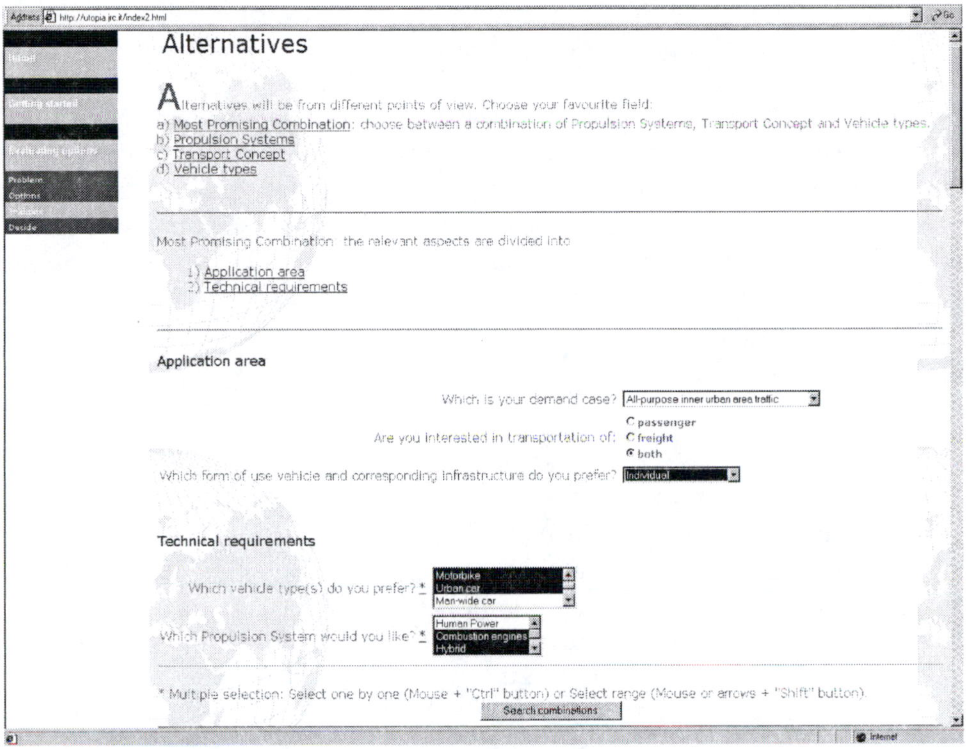

The main steps are:

1) Choosing the alternatives to be evaluated in the context of the user's city (Figure 2).

2) Selecting among a set of evaluation criteria to choose the different alternatives. Here the user can decide either to go for a detailed analysis, choosing among a list of specific sub-criteria, or opt for a less detailed set of main criteria.

3) Valuing the criteria (quantitatively or qualitatively) for assessing the impacts of each alternative. The user is responsible for assessing the impacts of each alternative. This can be done using either the user's personal knowledge and information, or through guidance, methods and tools provided by Navigate UTOPIA (e.g., the screening tools[2] presented in detail below). Each main criterion is linked to specific sources of information that help to describe it either quantitatively or qualitatively. The choice of using a dynamic and open way of assessing the impact of each alternative, rather than a more structured and rigid criteria quantification, comes from suggestions made by potential final users invited to attend focus groups across Europe (EST, 1999).

4) Setting, using the MARPA tool, the reference point[3] (Wierzbicki, 1980, 1982) and the weight for each criterion selected in order to identify his or her preferences. This step is taken only if the user wants to discriminate among the

selected criteria. There is a slight difference in fixing weights between main and sub-criteria. Using a sub-criterion requires first fixing weights relative to the criterion's family; in this way the final weight for each criterion is sub-criterion weight times family criterion weight in order to have total criteria weight normalised as one.

5)   Calculating, in order to obtain a résumé of settings and the final ranking.

The user is free to add both new alternatives and new criteria directly in the multi-criteria matrix. Then the user identifies a ranking of options, according to his or her preferences, analysing them in terms of the stage of market implementation to assess whether there is a need for a pilot project (Figure 3).

The basic philosophy behind MARPA is to generate efficient solutions by solving ordinary (single criteria) optimisation problems in the form of minimising the distance function:

$$\min_y d(y, \bar{y}) \forall y \in Y$$

after the construction of the evaluation matrix.

Here U is the set of feasible alternatives and $\bar{y}$ is a possible point in the criteria space. The distance function $d(y, \bar{y})$ measures how severely an alternative y deviates from the target $\bar{y}$. So the idea is that we search through the set of feasible alternatives U looking for the alternative $y^* \in Y$, which deviates least seriously from the target $\bar{y}$. By varying $\bar{y}$ and /or $d(.,.)$ it is possible to generate all efficient in general multiple criteria settings. Since the various criteria taken into account in evaluating the choice alternatives are likely to be measured in different units, the evaluation matrix needs to be normalised. The technique used here utilises the magnitude of individual scores (Carver, 1991), expressed as:

$$d_{ij} = \frac{c_{ij} - c_{rj}}{c_{i\max} - c_{i\min}} \qquad \text{where:}$$

d_{ij} is the distance of alternatives j from the reference point for criterion i and
c_{ij} is the score of alternatives j for criterion i,
c_{rj} is the score of the reference point for i,
$c_{i\max}$ is the maximum score for criterion i, *and*
$c_{i\min}$ is the minimum score for criterion i.

The deviation function is represented by the following formula:

$$d_j^p = \sqrt[p]{\sum_i d_{ij}^p} \quad \text{where:}$$

Figure 3: Interactive phase—multi-criteria analysis

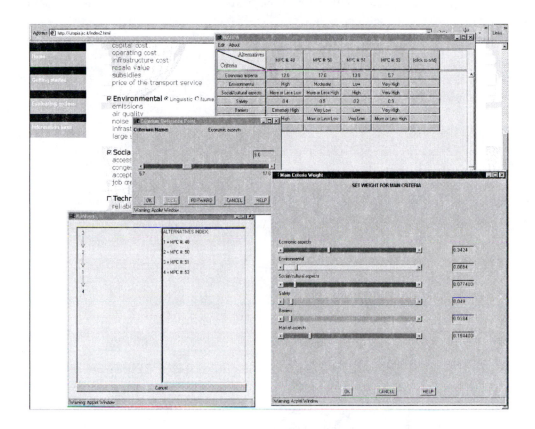

d_j^p is the distance of alternative j from the reference point,

d_{ij}^p is the distance of alternative j from the reference point for criterion i and in our case, and

$p = 2$ for the Euclidean metric.

The distance function is the aggregation function for the reference point method. The distance function might be corrected introducing the weight.

Deciding on a Pilot Project

Here the user can access the UTOPIA Guidelines whose main purpose is to provide advice on how to set up and run pilot and demonstration projects. The guidelines are derived from clean vehicle projects across Europe and link the various stages of decision making over the life-cycle of a project, from proposing an initiative through to evaluating the results and the options for follow-up work. Users of the guidelines learn how to avoid some of the common pitfalls encountered both in process of setting up and running a demonstration project and in the analysis of the results.

B: Surfing the Information Base

Surfing the UTOPIA information base gives the user access to all the data gathered and tools developed within the UTOPIA project. It includes information on the vehicle concepts, propulsion systems, alternative fuels and transport concepts. The UTOPIA information base also contains information at different levels of detail, according to choice, on the state of *market* implementation, possible *barriers*, relevant *policy options*, results from *case studies* and *environmental* issues.

The *market* starting point privileges in a nonrestrictive fashion consideration of the market potential of new propulsion and transportation systems (INSEAD, 2000) and helps policy and decision makers devise appropriate leverage actions to support the market penetration of the most promising systems. The framework is based on two assumptions: The first is that large-scale market diffusion is a smooth process in which the new technology progressively captures market segments of increasing size and importance as its performance increases and its cost decreases; the second is that this process of large-scale diffusion is nearly always preceded by an experimental phase of niche applications, where the effectiveness of the new transportation schemes is tested on a much smaller scale.

The *barrier* starting point focuses mainly on *social, institutional and political barriers* linked to the introduction of new transport systems, plus the results of a *survey among experts* with the main objective of identifying factors that influence the introduction of new propulsion systems in new and existing urban *transport modes* (passenger and freight) (TNO, 1998).

The *policy option* starting point describes different kind of "political tool" for introducing new propulsion and/or transportation systems, taking into account particular policy contexts (CERTU, 2000). State structure, the distribution of powers and competencies within the state and existing policies regarding clean technologies and sustainability for several EU member states are also described.

The *case studies* starting point presents several case studies from around Europe, describing the implementation of pilot projects (DITS, 2001). The goal of this starting point is to give support to transport planners, policy makers and fleet operators who want practical information on how other cities have dealt with similar problems.

The *environment* starting point introduces the environmental evaluation tools, or Navigate UTOPIA screening tools, that allow a simple and fast assessment of the environmental performance of different urban transport options. Technical details on these screening tools can be found in "Methodologies for Evaluating Environmental Aspects" (IER, 1999).

The *emission screening tool* (Figure 4) covers the full life cycle of the vehicles or transport systems, including not only direct emissions during transportation but also indirect emissions from vehicle manufacture, maintenance, fuel supply and scrap recovery.

When a technology is selected from the "technology" list and other parameters such as the transport distance or the country of electricity generation are defined, the

Figure 4: Navigate UTOPIA emission screening tool

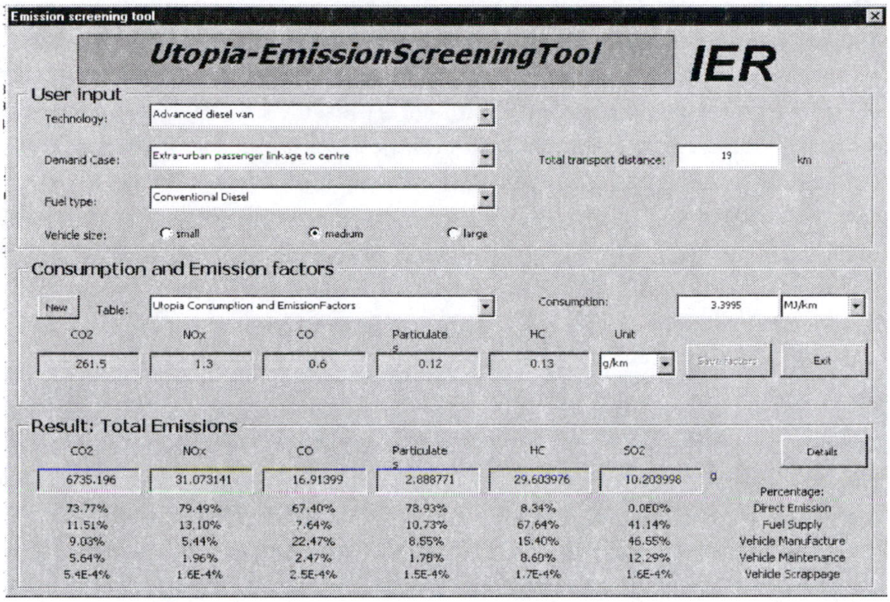

tool calculates and shows immediately the resulting emissions. The database provides emission factors and factors for consumption. These can be modified by the user.

The *air quality screening tool* prides assessment of concentration levels of air pollutants close to the road, thus addressing the needs of local city managers who have to ensure compliance with air quality standards. This tool is based on a model called MluS-92 (MluS, 1992).

The data inputs required by the model are the number of vehicles per day, the average emission factors in g/km on a specific road, and the average wind speed. The model estimates the annual mean of CO, HC, Nox, and particles.

The purpose of the *noise screening tool* is to provide a simple and easy-to-use tool that does not require complex input data from the user. The tool is based on the German "Directive for Anti-noise Protection along Roads" (RLS-90), published by the Road Construction Section of the German Federal Ministry of Transport. (Bundesminister für Verkehr, 1990).

The data input required by the tool are the number of vehicles per hour on a specific road, the percentage of heavy-duty vehicles within the traffic load, the max speed for different vehicle categories and some information on road characteristics (such as surface type, slope and distance from regulated crossings).

The *external cost screening tool* estimates the external costs resulting from a specific transport task, taking into account the emissions and the site-specific population density. The tool relies on a large number of case study results that have been derived from the EcoSense model developed within the EU-funded ExternE Project (European Commission, 1995). The large number of results from case studies performed within the ExternE study provided the opportunity to identify the key parameters determining the external costs and to establish a simplified parameterised model applicable within the Navigate UTOPIA framework.

The *pressure indicator screening tool* scores impacts of transport tasks by taking into account the potential environmental pressure on different environmental impact categories. The pressure indicator methodology is based on the environmental themes methodology (Heijungs et al., 1992) that has been developed for life cycle impact assessment.

OBSERVATIONS

As can be seen from the above, the data and the models available within the UTOPIA project have substantial breadth and complexity. From the focus groups and other interactions with potential users it became very clear that this complexity was an important barrier to acceptance. Much of the effort of the research team was therefore devoted to shaping the DSS towards customer preferences.

In this context it is important to note that the stakeholders involved in any major urban transport decision are extremely heterogeneous. They range from local residents and market stallholders through to motorists' lobbies, freight delivery services and local economic development agencies. Even within the municipal government structures, the transport planning department has to enlist support for any innovative proposal from other executive and policy departments, ranging from environmental health and social policy through to economic management and budgeting.

As a consequence the technical backgrounds of stakeholders and even of members of the governmental decision college are very varied. At the same time the high sensitivity of any course of action means that there is little tendency to adopt a "leave it to the experts" attitude.

In these circumstances even the concept of a formal DSS can meet with scepticism. As a result Navigate UTOPIA is not presented primarily as a decision support tool. Users tend to "discover" the interactive decision support features while using the tool as a Web navigator.

Given these constraints the DSS developer must exercise considerable flexibility and self-discipline. In this particular project it was even necessary, at a fairly advanced stage in the project, to jettison the developers' favoured system (NAIADE) in favour of MARPA. Not to have done so, taking the line that the problem should be shaped by the solution rather than vice versa, would have jeopardised the entire project.

FUTURE TRENDS

Development of the Navigate UTOPIA tool coincided with major advances in the Internet. These have transformed the whole context within which people approach information. There is a largely unconscious move from passive and highly structured absorption of information towards an interactive and serendipitous mode of knowledge discovery.

To keep abreast of this major shift in behaviour Navigate UTOPIA also evolved. The finished product is designed to be accessed not as a text (or even an interactive text) but as a Web site. While this involves challenges these are greatly outweighed by the advantages. Web browsing engages users and encourages them to extend their knowledge horizons. This less structured and curiosity-driven learning favours experimentation with DSS, even for those unfamiliar with the underlying philosophy. In particular the MCDA approach, which can readily be combined with the wealth of distributed information sources available on the Web, blends readily into this new information paradigm, (Paruccini, Haastrup, & Bain, 1997).

As the information available to decision-makers expands, the need for tools to make sense of it all will increasingly be felt. This makes it essential that DSS developers work in increasingly close concert with Web-designers.

CONCLUSION

Navigate UTOPIA has been designed and agreed with potential users in focus groups where participants have had the chance to discuss, confront and develop their ideas on the fundamentals of the proposed approach. This involvement of final users is an essential part of any integrated approach. Attempts to resolve issues characterised by conflict and uncertainty cannot depend on formal scientific enquiry alone, but require the inclusion of those affecting and affected by the issue of concern to supply knowledge and information in order to enhance understanding of the problem and potential responses. MCDA is particularly suited to this highly participatory process.

This type of DSS is strongly recommended in dealing with complex and politically sensitive problems even if the organisation and management, especially in running the focus groups, require time, additional skills and, in particular, a team predisposition to accept negative criticisms, to reformulate objectives if necessary and to redesign features of the tools or approaches proposed.

ENDNOTES

[1] For readers wishing a more specific discussion of decision problems in transport planning Krzysztof and Tkowski (1995) offer a classical systems engineering approach. In terms of DSS applications see Cascetta and Biggiero (1997); Fierbinteanu, Berkowicz, Hansen, & Hertel (1999); Cochran and Chen (1991); Jensen,(2001); and Bielli (1992).

[2] The Navigate UTOPIA screening tools are four models that help users to quantify the impact of various criteria.

[3] The multi-criteria method adopted in Navigate UTOPIA is the reference point (Wierzbicki, 1982), selected because it is not only simple and reliable, but was

also deemed particularly suitable for this specific application, taking into account the requirements of potential final users (as elicited in interviews). The Reference Point is an interactive method with which the user can identify a point in the space of the representative criteria considered relevant: this point is conventionally called the "reference point." This point does not coincide with a real existing solution but is the sum of the decision maker's aspirations. The user has to set his reference point for each criterion in order to compare the alternatives selected.

REFERENCES

Bana e Costa, C. A., Nunes da Silva, F., & Vansnick, J. C. (2001). Conflict dissolution in the public sector: A case study. *European Journal Of Operational Research, 2*(130), 388-401.

Bielli, M. (1992). A DSS approach to urban traffic management. *European Journal Of Operational Research, 1-2*(61), 106-113.

Bristow, A. L., & Nellthorp, J. (2000). Transport project appraisal in the European Union. *Transport Policy*, 7(1), 51-60.

Bundesminister für Verkehr. (1990). Richtlinien für den Larmuschutz an Straben. RLS-90.

Carver, S. J. (1991). Integrating Multi-criteria Evaluation with Geographical Information Systems, *International Journal of Geographic Information Systems*, 5(3), 321-339.

Cascetta, E., & Biggiero, L. (1997, June). Integrated models for simulating the Italian passenger transport system. Conference proceedings of Transportation systems—IFAC/IFIP/IFORS Symposium, first volume, Papageorgiou, M. & Pouliezos, A. (Eds.), Chania, Greece.

CERTU—Center for Studies on Urban Planning, Transport, Utilities and Public Constructions. (2000). The policy framework. Internal report for the EC, DG VII-funded UTOPIA project Work package 4.3.

Cochran, J. K., & Chen, M. T. (1991). An integrated multicomputer DSS design for transport planning using embedded computer simulation and database tools, *Decision Support Systems, 2*(7), 87-97.

DITS—Department of Hydraulic Transport and Street, University of Rome la Sapienza. (2001). Case Study Simulation. Internal report for the EC, DG VII-funded UTOPIA project. Work package 4.6.

EST—Energy Saving Trust. (1999). Stakeholder review of Evaluation Methodology. Internal report for the EC, DG VII-funded UTOPIA project. Work package 4.5.

ETSU—Energy Technology Support Unit. (2001). Demonstrating cleaner vehicles - Guidelines for success. Internal report for the EC, DG VII-funded UTOPIA project. Work package 6.1.

European Commission. (1995). Externalities of fuel cycles. European Commission, DG XII, Science, Research and Development, JOULE. ExterneE Project, Report no. 2 Methodology. Luxembourg, Office for Official Publication of the European Communities, EUR 16521 EN.

Fierbinteanu, C. (1999). A decision support systems generator for transportation demand forecasting implemented by constraint logic programming. *Decision Support Systems, 3*(26), 179-194.

Heijungs, R., Guinee, J. B., Huppes, G., Lankreijer, R. M., Udo de Haes, H. A., & WegnerSleeswijk, A. (1992). *Environmental life cycle assessment. Guide and backgrounds.* Leiden: CML, Leiden University.

Henig, M. (2001, Spring). Answer to Theo Stewart's article. *Newsletter of the European Working Group "Multicriteria Aid for Decisions," 3*(3), 2-3.

IER—Institute of Energy Economics and the Rational Use of Energy, University of Stuttgart. (1999). Methodologies for evaluating environmental aspects. Internal report for the EC, DG VII-funded UTOPIA project. Work package 4.4.

INSEAD. (2000). Assessing the market potential of new propulsion and transportation systems. Internal report for the EC, DG VII-funded UTOPIA project. Work package 4.2.

Jensen, S. S., Berkowicz, R., Hansen, H. S., & Hertel, O. (2001). A Danish decision-support GIS tool for management of urban air quality and human exposures. *Transportation Research. Part D: Transport and Environment, 6*(4), 229-241.

Krzysztof, G., & Tkowski, C. (1995). Optimal routing in a transportation network, *European Journal Of Operational Research, 2*(87), 214-222.

MluS. (1992). Merkblatt über die Luftverunreinigungen an Strassen. Forschungsgesellschaft für Strassen- und Verkehrswesen, Arbeitsgruppe Verkehrsführung und Verkehrssicherheit. Koeln (Cologne).

Modesti, P., & Sciomachen, A. (1998). A utility measure for finding multiobjective shortest paths in urban multimodal transportation networks. *European Journal Of Operational Research, 3*(111), 495-508.

Munda, G. (1995). *Multicriteria evaluation in a fuzzy environment. Theory and applications in ecological economics,* Heidelberg, Germany: Physica-Verlag.

Munda, G., Nijkamp, P., & Rietveld, P. (1994). Multicriteria evaluation in environmental management: Why and how? In Paruccini, M. (Ed.) *Applying multiple criteria aid for decision to environmental management.* Dordrecht, The Netherlands: Kluwer.

Paruccini, M. (1992). Decision Support Systems for Environmental Management, EUR 14087 EN, Ispra, Italy.

Paruccini, M., Haastrup, P., & Bain, D. (1997). Decision Support Systems in the service of policy makers, IPTS Report, 14, 28-35.

Rauschmayer, F. (2001, Spring). Nature *in* and nature *of* MCDA. *Newsletter of the European Working Group "Multicriteria Aid for Decisions," 3*(3), 1-2.

Roy, B. (1985). Methodologie multicritère d'aide a la decision, Economica, Paris.

Roy, B., & Hugonnard, J. C. (1982). Ranking of suburban line extension project of the Paris metro system by a multicriteria method. *Transportation Research*, *16A*(4), 301-312.

Stewart, T. (2000, Autumn). How should MCDA practice respond to behavioural research findings? *Newsletter of the European Working Group "Multicriteria Aid for Decisions,"* *3*(2), 1-2.

TNO—Netherlands Organization for Applied Scientific Research. (1998). Overview of promising transport modes related to transport concepts. Internal report for the EC, DG VII-funded UTOPIA project. Work Package 2.2.

Tsamboulas, D., & Mikroudis, G. (2000). EFECT—Evaluation framework of environmental impacts and costs of transport initiatives. *Transportation Research Part D: Transport and Environment*, *5*(4), 283-303.

VW—Volkswagen AG. (1998). Inventory of new propulsion systems. Internal report for the EC, DG VII-funded UTOPIA project. Work package 2.1.

Wierzbicki, A. P. (1980). The use of reference objectives in multiobjective optimisation. In *MCDM Theory and Application*, G. Fandel and T. Gal (Eds) (Vol. 177, pp. 468-486), Springer-Verlag.

Wierzbicki, A. P. (1982). A mathematical basis for satisficing decision making, *Mathematical Modelling*, 3, 391-405.

Chapter VII

Procedural Cuing Using an Expert Support System

Beverley G. Hope
Victoria University of Wellington, New Zealand

Rosemary H. Wild
California Polytechnic State University, USA

ABSTRACT

This chapter describes the development of a system to assist teams in determining which problems to address and what data to collect in order to incrementally improve business processes. While prototyping is commonly advocated for expert system development, this project used a structured development methodology comprising requirements analysis, knowledge acquisition, and system development. The knowledge acquisition phase resulted in a logical model, which specified the decision task and suggested a system structure. The field prototype developed from this model uses procedural cuing to guide decision makers through a decision making process. The system provides decision support, interactive training, and expert advice.

INTRODUCTION

Decision making support systems (DMSS) encompass a range of computer applications designed to assist managers at various levels in a variety of tasks including information management, people management, and production or process management. The ESS developed in this project assists teams in incremental business process improvement, specifically in selecting projects, developing measures, and designing data collection plans to measure and monitor processes. Incremental improvement is effected primarily at the operational level where many workers lack the necessary experience, skills, and knowledge. Consequently, they require an expert they can call upon for support. However, it is difficult, if not impossible, to have an expert available on an as-needed basis. Our solution to this problem was to provide workers with a computerized expert, an ESS, to guide them through a data-driven quality improvement process. The system, DATQUAL, uses procedural cuing to present the decision structure and guide teams through it. The result is a system which combines decision support, training, and expert advice for a complex task consisting of a series of decisions taken over an extended time period.

The research reported here completes the first phase of development leading to a model of the task domain, a supporting knowledge base, and a prototype system. In this phase we first identified the task through requirements analysis with a client firm. We then gathered knowledge and developed a conceptual model. The function of the conceptual model was to present the acquired knowledge in a way that allowed us to understand the task. The conceptual model formed the basis of a logical model, which added the hierarchical structure and detail required to encode the knowledge in a computer system. The outcome of this phase was a DMSS, which details a series of decision making events and suggests the data needed at each decision point.

The purpose of this chapter is to describe the development process involving the specification of the task, design of the system structure, and development of a field prototype. The chapter is organized as follows: First we describe the nature of DSS and ESS. We then discuss the development environment, describe the development process, and present the system models and structure. We conclude by summarizing the project and suggesting benefits and future directions.

DECISION MAKING AND EXPERT SUPPORT SYSTEMS

Decision Support Systems

One of the earliest attempts at describing the concept of decision support systems (DSS) was that of Gorry and Scott-Morton (1971). They describe these new systems as "interactive computer-based systems which help decision makers utilize data and models to solve unstructured problems." The significant concepts here include the use of *data* and *models* and their application to *unstructured problems*. Later, Keen and Scott Morton (1978) defined DSS as systems which "couple the intellectual resources of individuals with the capabilities of the computer to improve the quality of decisions. It is a computer-based support system for management decision makers who deal with semi-structured problems." In this later definition, suitable problem types are broadened to include *semi-structured problems*, and greater emphasis is given to the role of the *intellectual resources of individuals*. We also see a shift from solving problems to *improving the quality of* decisions for *management* decision makers.

Udo and Guimaraes (1994) identified perceived benefits of DSS in US corporations. The benefits included higher decision quality, improved communication, cost reduction, increased productivity, time saving, and employee and customer satisfaction. Again, we see the reference to improved decision quality—which may account for the cost reductions, increased productivity, and time savings—and find the addition of *employee and customer satisfaction.*

From these definitions we can extract several common elements:

1.   the use of data and models,
2.   a goal of effectiveness through improved decision quality,
3.   augmentation rather than replacement of the human in the decision making process,
4.   the application to unstructured or semi-structured problems,
5.   a primary use by management as decision makers, and
6.   an expectation of improved employee and customer satisfaction.

In contrast to the definitional approach to DSS, Turban and Araonson (2000) observe that DSS is a content-free term, which may mean different things to different people. Holsapple and Whinston (1996) also take a broad view of DSS in their six-category classification of DSS:

Text-oriented DSS allow documents to be created, retrieved, reviewed, and viewed as necessary to assist in decision making.

Database-oriented DSS make extensive use of data, query functions, and summary reports to assist decision makers.

Spreadsheet-oriented DSS emphasize the use of models to create, view, and modify data, most commonly quantitative data.

Solver-oriented DSS use algorithms and procedures contained in computer programs to perform computations for particular problem types, for example, linear programming.

Rule-oriented DSS may combine qualitative and quantitative rules, often in expert system format.

Compound DSS are hybrid systems incorporating features of two or more of the other five types.

We tend to agree with Turban and Araonson (2000) and Holsapple and Whinston (1996) in taking a broad view of decision support systems. Such systems might even include expert systems and would certainly incorporate the less intelligent expert support systems.

Expert Support Systems

Expert support systems assist decision makers by structuring complex problem solving tasks. They are not decision support systems in line with early definitions, that is, they do not make single-point decision recommendations or rank decision alternatives based on known data. Nor are they expert systems, that is, they do not reach conclusions by inference. Rather, they combine concepts and methods from both. In Holsapple and Whinston's (1996) DSS classification, they most closely approximate a rule-oriented DSS.

Expert Support Systems utilize Expert System knowledge representations, tools, and techniques but differ from Expert Systems in their functionality in that they require the human to do more of the work. Thus the emphasis in "expert support system" is on the *support* rather than on the *expert*; they support decision-making but do not make decisions. Since incremental process improvement calls for support in a complex series of decisions over an extended time period, an ESS was the alternative of choice in this task domain.

ESS and Procedural Cuing

The ESS developed in this research, DATQUAL, uses procedural cuing to guide teams. Silverman (1987, p. 80) notes that procedural cuing: Reminds the user of all the steps; suggests steps overlooked; provides step advice when requested; cues the user on the latest and most recent techniques and organizational changes.

DATQUAL uses a process of step decomposition to achieve procedural cuing. One way to understand this process is through an analogy of training someone to make the Italian dish lasagna. A lasagna expert (or ESS) might tell the cook to make and lay down alternating layers of pasta, vegetable/meat, and cheese—perhaps two of each—then bake the dish. If the cook is experienced, this may be enough information for him or her to complete the task. However, a novice cook may need to ask, "How do I make the pasta layer?" " ... the vegetable/meat layer?" or "... the cheese layer." Or the cook may need baking details such as temperature, time, or placement height in the oven. Our expert (or ESS) would need to decompose the queried steps into sub-steps, and some sub-steps might need to be further decomposed or explained.

We follow this decomposition process in providing support for data-driven process improvement. Users are initially provided with six major steps: identify output and customers, identify customer needs, determine what to measure, set standards, measure performance, and identify quality improvement opportunities. When a user is uncertain how to complete a step, the user can select that step and the step is decomposed to a series of smaller steps. Advice based on best practice is provided at each step and sub-step. In this way, users are cued as to the next step in the process and supported with further step decomposition where necessary. This not only helps to ensure that all steps are included and procedures followed, but also acts as a training tool for novices.

DEVELOPMENT ENVIRONMENT

To account for management responses to executive information systems, Eason (1992) presents a framework consisting of environment, task, users, and system. We use this framework to describe the development domain in this project.

Environment

The ESS was developed to meet the needs of a large United States savings and loan company. As system developers, we reported to the executive vice president (EVP) quality and to the senior vice president (SVP) quality service. The quality service team had responsibility for quality initiatives throughout the bank including the induction of new hires into the bank's culture, total quality management (TQM) philosophy, and a proprietary customer-perception model of quality based on Zeithaml, Parasuraman, and Berry (1990). An important organizational characteristic was the commitment of senior management to data-driven quality improvement and their endorsement of this system. The EVP quality commented that the ESS "will help to get everyone singing out of the same hymn book."

The system to be developed was aimed at the operational level. This is the level at which the organization's output is created and delivered, customers are served, advice is given, transactions are processed, and complaints are handled. It is also the level at which incremental process improvement takes place. Quality initiative at the bank had resulted in decision making responsibility being pushed down the organization, such that teams of nonmanagers were identifying and solving problems which were formerly the responsibility of management. For these teams to perform their new role efficiently, their members required new skills. Whereas managers at the strategic and tactical levels frequently had access to external consultants and internal specialists, this support was usually not available at the operational level. Consequently, expert support at the operational level was very much needed.

Task

The task addressed by DATQUAL is data-driven, operational-level process improvement. Process improvement is the foundation of all quality activity (Slater, 1991), and the foundation of process improvement is data. However, Easton (1993), a senior examiner for the Malcolm Baldrige Quality Awards, observes that operational workers often base improvement efforts on informal brainstorming rather than on data. He comments that many companies examined for the award avoided collecting data and consequently were ineffective at root cause analyses. Failure to correctly identify root causes of problems may result in failure to solve problems. In our own research, we have often observed workers collecting data, but in an unscientific manner, with little advance consideration of what data were important and no systematic plan for data collection and analysis.

Through prior research in organizations (Hope, 1997) and examination of the literature, we concluded that any DMSS should (a) provide support in the selection and use of data and quality improvement tools and (b) enable on-the-job training for workers. In other words, it should not only be prescriptive but should also help workers develop a mental model of the connection between data collection and analysis and the task of incremental process improvement.

Users

The system was to be used by individuals and teams throughout the bank. At the time of the development project the bank had around 80 quality improvement projects. Teams included entry-level and long-service employees, operational and middle-management employees, and individuals with varying educational and computer experience levels. Consequently, the DMSS would have multiple users with varying organizational knowledge and varying levels of computer literacy.

Although quality improvement was an important concept in the bank, it was not the core function. Consequently, system use would be intermittent. Unsophisticated, intermittent system users are prone to forget system functions between consultations. Therefore, system ease of use and ease of learning were considered essential.

System

To meet the needs of users and management, we required an easy-to-use system that would provide support, expertise, and training to users whilst also providing the consistency of approach desired by management. To achieve this, we chose to use procedural cuing embedded in a knowledge-based system.

Structuring the knowledge was an important design issue extending beyond the broad issue of what to represent to specific issues of how to use data structures. Two common forms of knowledge representation are rules and objects. These have been well understood for some time and we will not enter into a discussion of them here (see Buchanan & Smith, 1989; Rauch-Hindin, 1986). Hybrid systems combining objects and rules have been shown to provide improved naturalness, efficiency, and flexibility (Fikes & Kehler, 1985; Minsky, 1991). For these reasons, we sought a hybrid system.

The choice of software tool was important: A poor choice could lead to problems in future developments if it was discovered that desired functions could not be added. In our search, we required a system shell which met the following criteria:
1.   inexpensive,
2.   reliable,
3.   developer-friendly development interface,
4.   programming flexibility,
5.   good documentation,
6.   vendor support and maintenance,
7.   IBM PC platform for development and use, and
8.   potential for run-only systems.

The system chosen to meet these requirements was LEVEL5 object from Information Builders Inc. This is a high-level development environment providing object-oriented programming, logic capabilities, and database access. Development is aided by the provision of graphical display builders, editors, and debugging tools.

DEVELOPMENT PROCESS

The generally preferred methodology for expert system development is prototyping (Agarwal & Tanniru, 1992; Budde, Kautz, Kuhlenkamp, & Zullighoven, 1992; Budde & Zullighoven, 1992). Several advantages are claimed for prototyping: the ability to tailor systems to user needs, the obtaining of user support for the system, and prototyping's suitability for ill-structured problems due to its provision of concrete examples to which the expert(s) can react.

However, these advantages are lessened in development environments where there are multiple sources of expertise, multiple users, or a large problem domain. Where there are multiple sources of expertise, different heuristics may emerge to achieve similar goals and the knowledge engineer must cause these to converge for the purpose of system development. In the current project, the knowledge engineer had a good academic understanding of the issues, and the two primary field experts at the macro level, the EVP quality and the SVP quality service, held similar mental models. The problem of model convergence was not an issue.

Where there are to be multiple users with different characteristics and needs, tailoring the system to individuals' needs can be problematic. System developers may lack the time, budget, or ability to contact all potential users. In such cases, two alternatives are open to the developer: (1) develop a system with features and interaction modes to satisfy the needs of most users through definition of a stereotypic user, or (2) develop a system with an array of features and interaction modes from which the user may select to meet his or her needs. In the current project, senior managers defined system capabilities in the requirements analysis phase (see below). The interface was designed to meet the needs of most users based on what is already known from the literature on human-computer interaction.

Where the problem domain is large, prototyping can lead to an ill-structured and perhaps inaccurate knowledge base. Furthermore, use of procedural cuing implied a known or desired structure, which required specification, at least in outline, in advance of coding. Under these conditions, prototyping as a methodology seemed inappropriate and we employed a more structured method. The method consists of four stages with ongoing validation as shown in Figure 1. The stages covered in this chapter are requirements analysis, knowledge acquisition, and system development.

Requirements Analysis

Requirements analysis consisted of interviewing upper management at the bank including the EVP quality, SVP quality service, and several division heads. Agreement was reached on the overall functional requirements. These were:

1.   to support decision making in the task domain,
2.   to provide formal and informal training, and
3.   to provide expertise.

The benefits upper management sought from the system were:
1.   consistency throughout the organization in problem selection, data collection, and reporting,
2.   the obtaining of relevant and statistically valid data for quality improvement, and
3.   empowerment and training of workers.

Knowledge Acquisition

Knowledge acquisition consisted of interviews, record examination, group meetings, and examination of academic and practitioner literature. Interviews were conducted with employees at many levels, beginning with the EVP quality and extending to branch managers, tellers, and others as needed. Our interest was in what data these people felt they needed, why they needed it, how often they wanted to see it, and how they would use it. Records of existing data collection and analytic

Figure 1: Structured development process

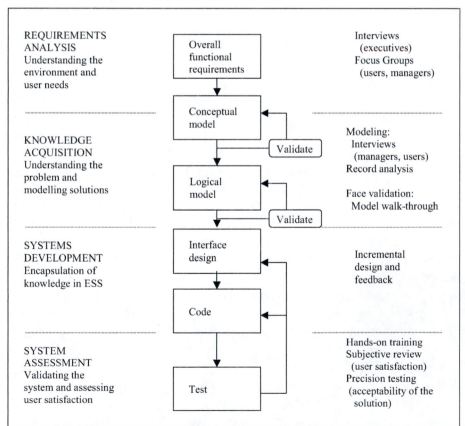

practices were examined to understand existing practices and to determine how improvements might be made in light of what is known in academe. Finally, groups of employees at the same level or performing the same job were used to provide feedback.

System Development

In addition to producing a usable system, system development was intended to clarify the model, to encourage full and clear specification of key concepts, and to force logical organization of knowledge. Davis (1989, p. 73) described the contribution of system development as follows:

> The programs we write will probably not be the ultimately important thing, though extensive pragmatic benefit may result from them. Perhaps more important will be the role of system construction in encouraging the accumulation, organization, systematization, and further development of knowledge about a task.

With the basic structure determined up front, system development was a straightforward task. When greater specification or clarification of knowledge was required during development, referral was made to selected users and to the literature on quality and measurement. Although a stepwise methodology is described, iteration between stages was required. For example, questions arose during system development which called for clarification (further knowledge acquisition). The resulting system was named DATQUAL to highlight its role in supporting data-driven quality improvement projects.

THE CONCEPTUAL AND LOGICAL MODELS

A major objective of the knowledge acquisition phase—and of the project in general—was to model the problem domain. This required a balance between the abstraction needed to make the model and resultant system applicable across divisions and the detail needed to make the system relevant and useful to those who consult it. The modeling process consisted of first developing a conceptual model, and subsequently deriving a logical model. The conceptual model links data needs to the quality improvement process, thereby encouraging practitioners to collect data for specific purposes rather than merely to "collect data."

From our field studies we identified three distinct levels of quality planning and implementation associated with the strategic, tactical, and operational levels of organizations. We found that even though quality is an organization-wide responsibility, the responsibility, tasks, and decision making requirements differed across the levels. Each level had different stakeholders, different measures of importance, and different data requirements. Consequently, the base model consists of three individual but integrated models. Our focus in this chapter is on the operational level.

The Conceptual Model

Figure 2 depicts the process model by which workers can identify quality improvement opportunities. The model defines these opportunities as situations where customer perceptions of performance differ from (are lower than) customer expectations. This may appear to be common sense, but we found both in the literature and field studies that common sense does not necessarily translate into common practice.

Figure 2: Conceptual model to identify quality improvement opportunities at the operational level

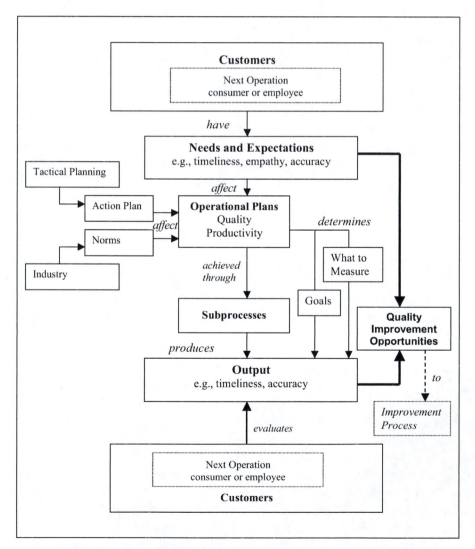

The model draws attention to the need for operational workers to identify their process output and the customers of that output. From our field studies we learned that operational workers seldom took into consideration the needs of internal customers. The model highlights the importance of internal customers. It allows operational workers to understand the impact of their work on others' work, a critical necessity of quality improvement stressed by Deming (1986). In addition, it forces workers to think in terms of processes rather than tasks, activities or hierarchies.

Another important aspect of the model is that it shows the relationship between operational units and the organization as a system. For example, the operational plan is influenced not only by customer needs, but also by industry norms and tactical level plans. Since the operational plan determines operational goals and suggests what needs to be measured, quality problems arising at operational levels may be traced back to constraints imposed by middle managers or external standards. The specification of all the inputs to operational plans may help operational workers to perform root-cause analysis more effectively.

A necessary precondition of system implementation was construction of a logical model. The conceptual model was a macro model: Implementation required a model which detailed steps and sub-steps.

The Logical Model

Derivation of the logical model was a stepwise process. First we extracted the major steps from the conceptual model, and then we defined the steps and sub-steps in more detail. Figure 3 presents the logical model for DATQUAL. The six major steps are shown in the vertical column at the left. To the right are the sub-steps or options offered in each step. A solid box represents a step or option a user can select, a circled "T" indicates availability of a tutorial, and a broken line box shows topics covered in a tutorial. The major steps are briefly described next.

Step 1, Identify Output and Customers: Our research showed that at the operational level the focus is on current output of subprocesses. Essentially in this step teams are asked to determine:
1. What do you produce?
2. For whom do you produce it?

This is not as obvious as it seems. Many quality improvement teams we visited omitted this step. Our logical model suggests teams may wish to use brainstorming and affinity diagrams to help identify and classify the outputs of the unit or sub-process, and the tutorials describe the techniques, their uses, and advantages.

Step 2, Identify Customer Needs: Field experts agreed workers must consider the needs of both external and internal customers. In this step teams must answer two basic questions:
1. What service attributes do customers consider important
2. What level of performance do they expect on these attributes

Figure 3: Logical model at the operational level

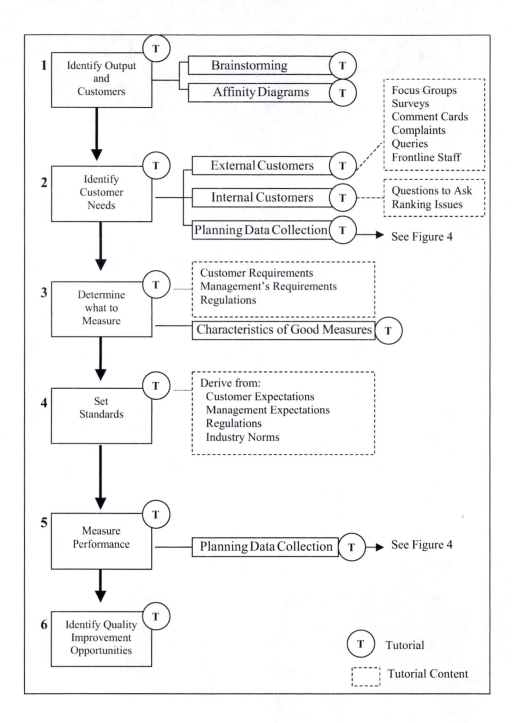

Associated tutorials describe common techniques used in the identification of external customer needs: focus groups, surveys, comment cards, complaint and query analysis, and listening to the insights of frontline staff. To identify the needs of internal customers, operational-level teams are advised to meet and talk with customers regularly, and the tutorials give advice on this.

Identification of customer needs is a major data collection point. Consequently, from this step of the logical model we provide access to a detailed module on data collection plans.

Step 3, Determine What to Measure: From field experts we learned that teams need to consider customer requirements, managerial requirements, and industry regulations when selecting measures. In a quality-focused organization, management and customer needs will be complimentary and both will exceed the requirements of regulations.

In addition to providing information on the determinants of measures, DATQUAL provides advice on the characteristics of good measures. These characteristics were synthesized from the literature on quality (see, for example, Case & Bigelow, 1992).

Step 4, Set Standards: Not surprisingly, data for setting standards come from the same sources that determine what to measure: customer expectations, management expectations, and regulations. In addition, some data can be obtained from industry norms. In the logical model we show these four sources of standards as topics in the tutorial at this step.

Step 5, Measure Performance: This is the second major data collection point in the models. Once again, teams are directed to the module on data collection plans.

Step 6, Identify Quality Improvement Opportunities: The final step in the process is the enumeration and selection of opportunities. Most of the work is done. The tutorial at this level simply reminds users of the steps they have completed and asks them to list all areas in which the measures of actual performance (Step 5) do not meet standards (Step 4). Since the standards are strongly influenced by customer expectations this amounts to identifying the areas in which the unit's performance is not meeting or exceeding customer expectations.

The process to plan data collection is detailed in Figure 4. The process focuses on four aspects of data collection: scope of the study, parameters to measure, data analysis requirements, and data collection resources. These are shown in the left vertical column of Figure 4.

Scope of Study: In this sub-step the team defines the limits of the study by defining the physical or process boundaries, the population of interest, and the time limit for the study. These are common considerations it setting boundaries for any experimental study. The associated tutorial briefly defines each term and gives examples to clarify each concept.

Parameters to Measure: In this sub-step teams select the attributes and variables to be measured and stipulate where in the process they will be measured. We found quality improvement teams collected almost exclusively attribute data, thereby excluding some of the rich information that can be obtained from variables data. The tutorial for this sub-step defines attributes and variables and provides examples. Advice is also provided on where in the process to collect data.

Data Analysis Requirements: In this sub-step, teams determine their data analysis needs with respect to frequency, types of comparisons to make, means of summarizing data, and the types of graphs and charts to use. The associated tutorial gives examples of comparisons that could be made, for example, trend analysis,

Figure 4: Logical model for data collection planning

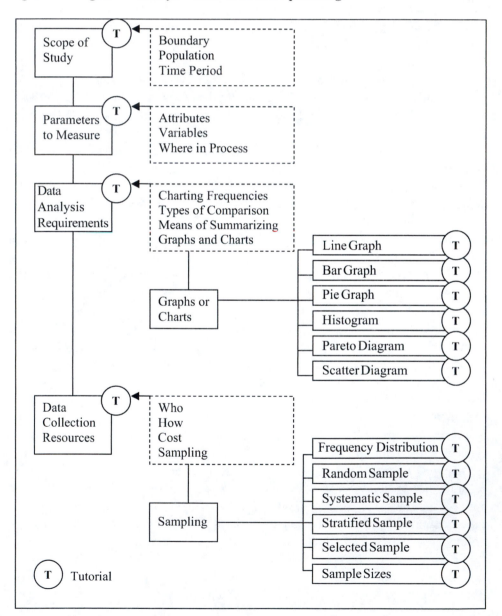

comparisons before and after interventions, comparisons by time periods such as time of day, comparisons by type and comparisons by location or group. Discussion of data summarization includes standard statistical measures. Charting (or graphing) is recommended as a way to visually show relationships, patterns, or trends so that data can be more readily understood and interpreted. The separate tutorial on graphing discusses the general characteristics of good graphs and provides construction guides for each chart type.

Data Collection Resources: In this sub-step teams define the resource requirements of their study in terms of people, equipment, money, and time. Advice is given on determining who should collect data and how the data should be collected to assist ease and accuracy of data collection and subsequent analysis. The issue of sampling is addressed in this step.

The logical model (Figures 3 and 4) represents the knowledge base developed for DATQUAL. From this model, the system was developed.

SYSTEM STRUCTURE

DATQUAL has 12 object classes, 150 object instances, and 40 methods. In addition, the application calls upon 87 external files. The three major object classes are: windows, displays, and display items. DATQUAL uses seven customized

Figure 5: A sample DATQUAL screen

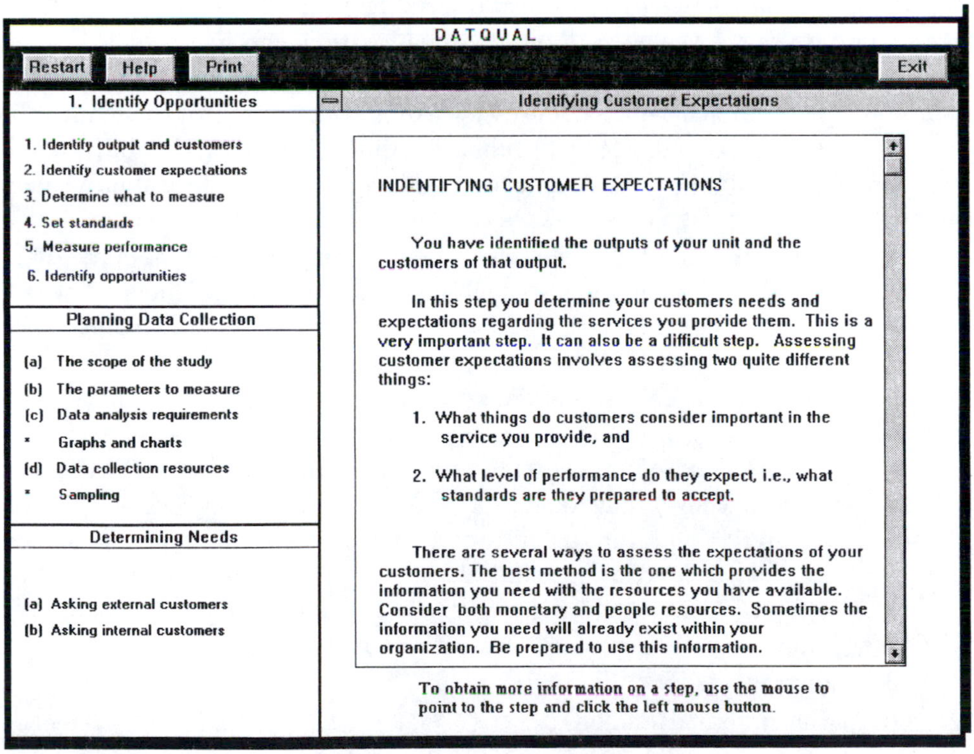

windows: a full-screen window, a smaller "help" window, and five windows designed to be displayed simultaneously during most of a consultation session. Displays are output to windows during runtime and are the primary informational object in DATQUAL. Each instance of the display class is a collection of display items such as text boxes, hyper-regions, picture boxes, and push buttons. During runtime, the application may also import specified files for display in text boxes or picture boxes.

The primary method used is the "When Changed" method. This causes DATQUAL to operate somewhat like a hypertext implementation. Indeed, hyper-regions underlying on-screen text provide the means of activating displays. An important difference is that in DATQUAL we leave the previous steps and sub-steps displayed on the side of the screen (Figure 5). Hypertext applications can cause novice users to become lost in a maze of screens. We wanted our users to retain a "sense of place" within a consultation session. By leaving step selections visible on the side of the screen we gave users a record of the step history, a sense of place within the application, and an ability to easily go back to previous steps or sub-steps. More importantly, concurrent display of step and sub-step breakdown would assist users in creating a mental model of the task domain, thereby achieving the training objective.

IMPACT OF THE SYSTEM

DATQUAL was developed primarily for proof of concept and assessment of the validity of the knowledge base that directs the user's learning process. The prototype has been presented to and used by many participants involved in the field studies. The responses, more anecdotal than formal, were favorable. Key respondents thought the system captured the essence of the quality improvement identification process. They also agreed that online, anytime, anyplace accessibility of the system would greatly encourage employee participation in the quality improvement process.

The ESS developed in this project provides operational workers the opportunity both to learn and use technical quality tools and to see the "bigger picture," which reinforces the importance of local decisions on the organization as a whole. The system helps operational workers use data effectively to make decisions that improve services, enhance customer satisfaction, and contribute to organizational survival.

The structure imposed on the quality improvement process by DATQUAL helps ensure consistency throughout the organization. Embedding decisions about data collection and use within the quality improvement process aids in the collection and analysis of relevant and meaningful data. The data definition process captured in the sub-step on data collection and analysis leads teams toward the collection of statistically valid data. The result is a system which provides:

1.   decision making support,
2.   formal and informal training,

3.   access to expertise on an ad hoc basis, and

4.   consistency of practices throughout an organization.

CONCLUSION

This chapter presented a structured approach to ESS development suitable for applications where there is a large problem domain with multiple experts and multiple users. In this approach, organizational requirements and knowledge are primarily obtained up front and system implementation follows. To develop the ESS, we first developed a conceptual model from a variety of knowledge sources. Key steps in the conceptual model were sequenced and detailed in a logical model that provided the structure needed to drive the computer implementation. To expedite system development we used a high-level expert system building tool to create an application that runs under Microsoft Windows.

Benefits were obtained from both the system's development and its implementation. Development benefits included a better understanding of the task through the analysis carried out during knowledge acquisition and modeling. New insights were gained by combining knowledge from several disparate sources: from the literature on quality, from standards and award criteria, and from experts in the field. The delineation of a strategy for improving service quality at the operational level will assist firms in their efforts to implement quality improvement systems.

Benefits from implementation include training, empowerment, and consistency of approach. DATQUAL simplifies a complex process by providing a logical sequencing of steps. For novices this acts both as a performance aid (consistency) and a training tool. On-the-job, context-based training is supplied in each DATQUAL consultation. The ordering of steps and the fact that recent steps and sub-steps remain visible on the screen help users to form a mental model of the task. Thus they can internalize the knowledge embedded in the system and become more effective members of quality improvement teams. DATQUAL tutorials also provide a language by which quality improvement can be understood and through which actions can be communicated. Above all, DATQUAL sells an idea—the idea that quality improvement is a data-driven process.

Another important benefit of implementation is empowerment. Implementing quality improvement projects that use objective data as their base requires special knowledge, skills, and abilities that many employees lack. DATQUAL empowers workers by providing support and encouraging consideration of all required steps. Where this can be accompanied by training, employee effectiveness and morale can be improved.

At an academic level, DATQUAL provides further evidence of the efficacy of procedural cueing in ESS. As early as 1987, Dillard, Ramakrishna, and Chandrasekaran described a frame-based ESS utilizing procedural cueing for military procurement. Their system was well received by the client organization and the academic community. The system developed in this research utilizes procedural cueing in a different task domain and using advanced object-oriented technologies. As such, it provides further evidence of the efficacy of procedural cueing as a means of providing intelligent support to industry.

Future development will include expansion of the field prototype and generalization of the system to other service industries. Given the team nature of quality improvement efforts, a potentially fruitful area for future research might be the development of a distributed group support system in this task domain.

REFERENCES

Agarwal, R., & Tanniru, M. (1992). A structured methodology for developing production systems. *Decision Support Systems*, *8*(1), 483-499.

Buchanan, B. G., & Smith, R. G. (1989). Fundamentals of expert systems. In A. Barr, P. R. Cohen, & E. A. Feigenbaum, (Eds.), *The handbook of artificial intelligence* (pp. 149-192). Reading, MA: Addison-Wesley.

Budde, R., Kautz, K., Kuhlenkamp, K., & Zullighoven, H. (1992). What is prototyping? *Information Technology and People*, *6*(2-3), 85-95.

Budde, R., & Zullighoven, H. (1992). Prototyping revisited. *Information Technology and People*, *6*(2-3), 97-107.

Case, K. E., & Bigelow, J. S. (1992). Inside the Baldrige award guidelines: Category 6: Quality and operational results. *Quality Progress*, *25*(11), 47-52.

Cole, R. E., Bacdayan, P., & White, B. J. (1993). Quality, participation, and competitiveness. *California Management Review*, *35*(3), 68-81.

Davis, R. (Ed.). (1989). Expert systems: How far can they go? (Part 2). *AI Magazine*, *10*(2), 65-77.

Deming, W. E. (1986). *Out of the crisis*. Cambridge, MA: Massachusetts Institute of Technology.

Dillard, J. F., Ramakrishna, K., & Chandrasekaran, B. (1987). Knowledge-based decision support systems for military procurement. In B. G. Silverman (Ed.), *Expert systems for business* (pp. 120-139). Reading, MA: Addison-Wesley.

Eason, K. (1992). Organizational issues in the use of decision support systems. In C. Holtham (Ed.), *Executive information systems and decision support systems*. London: Chapman & Hall.

Easton, G. S. (1993). The 1993 state of U.S. total quality management: A Baldrige examiner's perspective. *California Management Review*, 35(3), 32-54.

Fikes, R., & Kehler, T. (1985). The role of frame-based representation in reasoning. *Communications of the ACM*, *28*(9), 904-920.

Gorry, G. A., & Scott-Morton, M. S. (1971). A framework for management information systems. *Sloan Management Review*, *12*(1), 55-70.

Holsapple, C. W., & Whinston, A. B. (1996). *Decision support systems: A knowledge-based approach*. St. Paul, MN: West.

Hope, B. G. (1997). Performance measures for ongoing quality management of services. *Proceedings of the Australasian Evaluation Society 1997 International Conference,* 290-296.

Keen, P. G. W., & Scott-Morton, M. S. (1978). *Decision support systems: An organizational perspective.* Reading, MA: Addison-Wesley.

Minsky, M. (1991). Society of mind: A response to four reviews. *Artificial Intelligence, 48*(3), 371-396.

Parasuraman, A., Zeithaml, V. A., & Berry, L. L. (1994). Reassessment of expectations as a comparison standard in measuring service quality: Implications for further research. *Journal of Marketing, 58*(1), 111-124.

Rauch-Hindin, W. (1986). *Artificial intelligence in business, science, and industry.* Englewood Cliffs, NJ: Prentice Hall.

Silverman, B. G. (Ed.) (1987). *Expert systems for business.* Reading, MA: Addison-Wesley.

Simon, H. (1977). *The new science of management decision.* Englewood Cliffs, NJ: Prentice Hall.

Slater, R. H. (1991). Integrated process management: A quality model. *Quality Progress,* 1, 27-32.

Turban, E., & Araonson, J. E. (2000). Decision support systems and intelligent systems (6th ed.). Upper Saddle River, NJ: Prentice Hall.

Zeithaml, V.A., Parasuraman, A., & Berry, L.L. (1990). *Delivering quality service: Balancing customer perceptions and expectations.* New York, NY: Free Press.

Chapter VIII

On the Ontology of a Decision Support System in Health Informatics

Pirkko Nykänen
National Research and Development Centre for Welfare and Health,
Finland

ABSTRACT

A decision support system can be approached from two major disciplinary perspectives, those of information systems science (ISS) and artificial intelligence (AI). We present in this chapter an extended ontology for a decision support system in health informatics. The extended ontology is founded on related research in ISS and AI and on performed case studies in health informatics. The ontology explicates relevant constructs and presents a vocabulary for a decision support system, and emphasises the need to cover environmental and contextual variables as an integral part of decision support system development and evaluation methodologies. These results help the system developers to take the system's context into account through the set of defined variables that are linked to the application domain. This implies that domain and application characteristics, as well as knowledge creation and sharing aspects, are considered at every phase of development. With these extensions the focus in decision support systems development shifts from a task ontology towards a domain ontology. This extended ontology gives better support for development because from it follows that a more thorough problem analysis will be performed.

INTRODUCTION

Our current information society makes extensive use of information systems and technology. In the field of health care, information technology has been applied as long as computers have existed, and many types of information technology applications have been developed. The early applications in health care were restricted in scope, and they had an impact on only a few professionals. They were mostly targeted at automation of existing routines, rationing resources and ensuring quality. The shift to an information society has brought a qualitative change in this respect: The focus is now on the development of new information technology service products that can improve health care processes and their outcome. Current health care information systems and networks are large and they have wide-ranging impacts on people and organisations (Lorenzi, Riley, Southon, & Dixon, 1997).

An example of information technology applications in health care is decision support systems. Since the 1960s decision support systems have been developed in health care for such purposes as interpretation of findings and test results in patient care, selection of treatments, choice of tests or protocols for the patient case at hand, management of data and information, control of work flows and monitoring of patient care processes and their outcomes. Despite of the long history of availability and the type and amount of resources used, the results achieved have been rather low and dissemination of systems into health care practices has progressed slowly (Barahona & Christensen, 1994; Reisman, 1996). Numerous prototypical decision support systems exist, but very few of them have entered routine use. Some studies (Lundsgaarde, 1987; Pothoff 1988; Wyatt, Rothermund, Schwebel, Engelbrecht, & van Eimeren, 1987) showed that little more than 10% of medical decision support systems developed so far had been sufficiently developed to enter clinical use. In 1992 the 600 subscribers to the "artificial intelligence in medicine" mailing list reported only six systems to be in routine use (Heathfield & Wyatt, 1993).

This chapter deals with decision support systems in health care context. We are searching for answers to the following research questions:

*   What are decision support systems (DSS) in a health informatics context? Are they somehow different from information systems (IS) or knowledge-based systems (KBS)?
*   Do we need a special conceptualisation for a decision support system in health informatics as compared to those presented in related research areas?
*   Is health informatics a special field for application of decision support systems? Do we need special approaches and methodologies to develop and evaluate decision support systems in a health care context?

To find answers to the questions above, we analyse our case studies with decision support systems, and we use in the analysis conceptual definitions of a DSS and a KBS as presented in information systems science (ISS) and in artificial intelligence (AI). The purpose of this analysis is to identify relations between the theoretical approaches applied and practical implementations that could help to explain the successes and failures of decision support systems in health care.

ANALYSIS OF DSS CONCEPTUALISATIONS

Decision Support Systems—Information Systems

As early as 1970 Little described a decision calculus as a model-based set of procedures to assist a manager in his decision making. He wanted to utilise better management science models through effective computer implementations. Little was even then able to list the requirements for a successful decision support system: simple, robust, easy to control, adaptive, complete on important issues and easy to communicate with.

Scott-Morton developed in 1971 a pioneer DSS for marketing and production planning. Together with Gorry he gave the first definition for a decision support system in 1971. Their DSS framework maps the potential for computer support in management activities along two dimensions: structuredness of the task and level of managerial activity. Gorry and Scott-Morton saw that, based on this framework, decision tasks could be divided between a human decision maker and a computer system in many ways. In a structured situation all phases of decision making are structured and potentially automatable, and therefore the resulting systems are decision-making systems. In a semi-structured case, one or more of the intelligence, design and choice phases is unstructured. The unstructured case corresponds to Simon's (1981) unprogrammed situation. In semi- and unstructured situations there is need for decision support in order to extend the decision maker's capabilities or to improve the quality of the decision making process. Some researchers see that a DSS is useful only for the structured parts of decision problems, but humans must solve the unstructured parts. The line between structured and unstructured situations moves over time when problems are understood better, and this understanding brings structure to them.

From the early 1970s decision support systems research has grown significantly, and many definitions have been presented. Mostly definitions have paid attention to the task structuredness and the problem of distinguishing decision support systems from other management information systems or operations research models. Sprague and Carlson (1982) brought into the discussion the organisational context of a DSS by providing a practical overview on how organisations could build and utilise a DSS.

A major goal of decision support systems research is to develop guidelines for designing and implementing systems that can support decision making. Decision support systems can be designed and developed using different approaches and methods. A life cycle development methodology is often used and user participation in the development is emphasised. There are, however, problems with life cycle development methodology because it does not support well the typical design situation where users do not quite know their needs at the beginning and developers do not quite understand the users' needs. Adaptive design or incremental design using an evolutionary prototyping approach is often more suitable for DSS development because it supports learning during the development process.

Functionalism with a positivist epistemology has been the major approach applied in information systems science, also with decision support systems. Research has been largely focused on the DSS systems and models themselves rather than on the contextual aspects of the decision making processes in organisations. Development has been based on hard quantifiable data and information rather than on soft qualitative information. The goal has often been to find generic solutions by matching the type of the problem and the task of the system. Support has mostly been offered for individual decision making; only quite recently support has been offered to enterprise-wide or group decision making.

DSS research has been criticised for putting the major effort to the study of the choice phase in decision making and much less effort has been put to the intelligence and design phases. Winograd and Flores (1986) claimed that focusing on the choice phase in decision making is dangerous because it may mean selection of a solution without really thinking what the right solution might be. They advised to pay more attention to communication as a central element in organisational decision making.

Concepts Used in Defining a DSS in Information Systems Science

In Table 1 we summarise the definitions of a decision support system as found in information systems science textual sources.

In many of the definitions in Table 1, the problem type as well as system function and user (e.g., through usage pattern, interface or user behaviour) are explicitly

Table 1: Concepts used to define a decision support system in information systems science (further elaborated on the basis of Turban, 1988)

Source	DSS defined in terms of
Little, 1970	System function, interface characteristics
Gorry & Scott-Morton, 1971	Problem type, system function
Alter, 1980	Usage pattern, system objectives
Sprague, 1980	Task, users (knowledge workers), means (information technology)
Moore & Chang, 1980	Usage pattern, system capabilities
Bonczek, Holsapple, & Watson, 1981	System components
Keen, 1980	Development process
Turban, 1988	Problem type, usage pattern, system capabilities, system objectives
Sprague & Watson, 1989	Problem type, problem occurrence
Klein & Mehlie, 1990	System capabilities, system function (support), application tasks
Eierman, Niederman, & Adams, 1995	Environment, task, system capabilities, implementation strategy, system configuration, user, user behaviour, performance

included, but some definitions focus only on problem type and problem occurrence. Effects of interface characteristics on system design were emphasised early on, in 1970 (Little 1970). Sprague (1980) noted that a DSS is developed for a specific task in a knowledge worker's environment, and that information technologies are a means to develop a DSS. Moore and Chang (1980) noted that the structuredness concept in the Gorry and Scott-Morton framework cannot be general because structuredness is always in relation to the specific user (Moore and Chang 1980). In Keen's definition (Keen 1980) a DSS is seen as a product of a process where a user, a developer and a system itself exert mutual influence through adaptive learning and evolution. Eierman et al. (1995) pay special attention to the environment construct, which refers to the organisational context of the system's development and its use. This is a noteworthy addition to the Gorry and Scott-Morton framework. Eierman defines eight constructs and 17 relations between the constructs. These constructs attend also to the social and organisational aspects of system use, such as attitudes and motivation of the user as well as actions taken by the user. However, the focus in Eierman's analysis has been on two issues: system implementation and system use.

Table 1 shows that DSS approaches in ISS have been closely focused on development and implementation and on hardware and software issues rather than on decision makers and on decision processes. Keen (1997) has noted that the system, but not the decisions or the support, has been the focus in building the DSS. DSS technologies should not be the focus, but rather taken to be as means to develop better contexts for decision makers and DSS.

Decision Support Systems—Knowledge-Based Systems

The goals of artificial intelligence are to study human intelligence and to build computational models that can simulate intelligent behaviour (Lenat, 1975; Newell & Simon, 1976; Nilsson, 1974). AI can be seen as a science that studies solutions to complex or ill-structured problems using heuristics (Aliferis & Miller, 1995).

In many AI projects the goal has been to develop a model of a specific expert's expertise and to implement this model as an expert system. The object of such study has mostly been an expert task at an individual level decontextualised from the environment; in most developments the social and organisational contexts of decision making have not been considered.

Discussion on AI-based decision support systems, knowledge-based systems (KBS), or expert systems (ES) has largely concentrated on methodological aspects of decision support, asking such questions as: Is it better to use model-based or data-driven approaches to model and implement decision making algorithms?

Concepts Used To Define a KBS in AI

Concepts used to define a KBS in AI are presented in Table 2 as derived from textual sources.

We have included in Table 2 primarily the knowledge-level abstraction paradigms (Newell, 1982), because knowledge-level modelling has been the major approach applied in KBS to generalise and structure domain and task knowledge. These paradigms have made strong assumptions about domain knowledge, and therefore developers often had to select first the problem-solving paradigm and then define domain knowledge in terms of the method. Slowly, there has emerged the need to capture general concepts independent of what problem-solving method would be used. These efforts have gradually led to scalable architectures where reusable problem-solving methods and domain ontologies can be used. This kind of approach makes a distinction between the foundational domain concepts, inferences and problem solving that might be applied to those concepts (Musen, 1999). A good example of this approach has been the KADS model for knowledge engineering (Schreiber, Wielinger, & Breuker, 1993).

Additionally, we present in Table 2 the epistemological model (Ramoni, Stefanelli, Magnoni, & Barosi, 1990) and the development philosophy approach (Heathfield & Wyatt, 1993). In the epistemological model the term knowledge level has been replaced with epistemological level because inference structures, problem-solving methods and task features are also seen as elements at the knowledge level, in addition to domain knowledge. This approach proposes that a KBS contains two types of knowledge: knowledge about the domain (ontology) and knowledge about inference structures that are needed to execute a task to exploit the ontology. Therefore, in building a KBS we need to focus on the definition of the domain ontology and on the definition of the underlying inference structure.

The development philosophy approach is a pragmatic view covering the phases of DSS development from requirements analysis to evaluation and includes values and beliefs.

Table 2: Concepts used in AI to define a KBS

Abstraction paradigm or approach	KBS defined in terms of	Source
Heuristic classification	Feature abstraction, heuristic match, solution refinement	Clancey, 1985
Deep and shallow knowledge	Deep knowledge, causal relations, shallow knowledge	Keravnoe & Washbrook, 1989
Problem-solving method	Problem decomposition, domain independent strategies, sequencing inferences	McDermott, 1988
Generic tasks	Problem type, problem decomposition, task, ordering of tasks	Chandrasekaran, 1986
Epistemological model	Ontology, inference model, medical tasks	Ramoni et al., 1990
Development philosophy	Need, development methodology, methods, metrics, tools, integral evaluation, professional approach	Heathfield & Wyatt, 1993

The concepts detailed in Table 2 indicate that in AI a knowledge-based system or a decision support system is mostly understood to be a system that supports an individual's cognitive processes. The major focus in development has been on mimicking individual human intelligent behaviour by modelling tasks, knowledge and reasoning processes. The development philosophy approach aims at utilisation of software engineering approaches and experiences in KBS development in such a way that a professional, systematic methodology is used. However, the domain problem is still seen as an isolated and decontextualised one.

The object of a knowledge-based system has been construed as an expert task at an individual level decontextualised from the environment. Medical knowledge-based systems have mostly been expert systems developed to solve isolated medical decision making problems. The decision making context, i.e., the social and environmental variables, has mostly not been considered at all in the systems developed. The focus in the decision making process has been on the choice phase, and this has resulted in problems being matched to available tools. This way of proceeding puts the focus on the choice instead of on intelligence. The choice phase problems have been challenging for AI researchers and developers, but these choice phase problems may not have been driven by the interests and needs of health care professionals.

ANALYSIS OF OUR DSS CASE STUDIES

Support for Thyroid Disorders

Our first case study is a DSS developed for the interpretation of thyroid disorders (Nykänen & Nuutila, 1991). The decision model considers the clinical hormone tests, the clinical features and the genetic background of the patient as well as medication and the non-thyroidal illnesses of the patient. The combinations of the hormone assay results used are presented in Table 3 and the decision model for interpretation is presented in Figure 1.

From the ontological viewpoint the thyroid DSS case study covers aspects of development and evaluation and decision-making process. The applied four-phase

Table 3: Simplified combinations of hormone assay results

	S-TSH	S-T4 / S-fT4
Primary Hypothyroidism	↑	↓
Secondary Hypothyroidism	↓	↓
Primary Hyperthyroidism	↓	↑
Secondary Hyperthyroidism (rare)	↑	↑

Figure 1: Decision model for interpretation

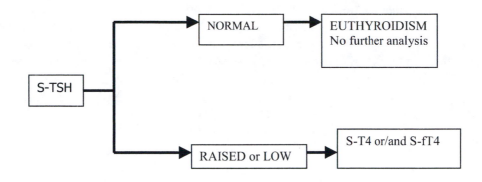

development and evaluation methodology is an AI-based approach for a knowledge-based system. The contextual aspects of the DSS were not considered and covered by the ontology applied.

In evaluating the DSS the preliminary exploration phase showed that the documents specifying user requirements worked well as a frame of reference in qualitative terms, but not well quantitatively. The specifications were incomplete; system performance, documentation and maintenance requirements were not documented at all in these specifications. Feasibility of the specifications was poor because of the lack of practical mappings from user requirements to software specifications. Neither cost-effectiveness nor viability of the system were considered at all.

Validity in application did not rate highly in this case study. The system classified correctly 98.6% of the test cases with suspected thyroid disease. This was less than the target correctness rate (99%). The failures were due to errors in data, in data entry and in definition of too broad diagnostic categories for classification. Broad categories were used because we would have required more detailed data and clinical information from the patient to be able to proceed to a more qualified classification. As a result, all those cases that could not be classified correctly were assigned to the class of nonspecific thyroid disorders. A commercial expert system shell was used in the development of the system, and the knowledge base was not checked for its validity. Functionality and usability of the thyroid system turned out to be poor, and the user acceptance of the system was also poor. The reasons for poor usability were the lack of navigation, inspection and updating options for the knowledge base. The system was very brittle, transferable for use only to an organisation where the same fixed strategy was in use for thyroid diagnostics. In the impacts phase it was found that a training effect was the major positive impact caused by the system. The training effect was seen in improved diagnostic accuracy in primary care and in the accumulation of knowledge on thyroid diagnostics in secondary care, especially in borderline and difficult cases. The training effect was caused by interpretative reports, which were sent by normal mail or e-mail to the primary care organisations. From these reports primary care physicians learned more about thyroid diagnostics and became more knowledgeable in the selection of tests to be performed. When the test selection strategies gradually became more accurate, the number of tests performed could be reduced. This resulted in better cost-effectiveness because the costs of tests were rather high and resources could be saved when only those tests were performed that were useful in the specific clinical situation.

The four-phase development and evaluation methodology proved not to function well in this case because the problems with the system's development were detected only in later phases. Errors should have been detected earlier; it would have saved time and resources. The methodology was not well suited for the development of knowledge-based systems because the knowledge acquisition phase and its validity checking were not explicitly included in the development life cycle. The system was connected with the laboratory information system in the hospital but the connection was very slow and difficult to use for the health care professional, and it worked only in one direction, from laboratory system to the KBS. The connection was used only to transmit the measured laboratory test results from biochemical analysers to the thyroid system for analysis and interpretation.

To summarise, the thyroid system helped users in primary care to deepen their understanding of thyroid diagnostics and to select better the tests to be performed. It also helped the specialist in the laboratory to concentrate on the borderline and difficult cases because the majority of the samples were normal and were correctly classified by the system. Though the acceptability of the system to the laboratory specialist was poor, the acceptability of the interpretative reports by the general practitioners was good. Our other study (Nuutila et al., 1991) on the clinical value of the system showed that in health centres 99% of the users read interpretative reports regularly and 60.4% considered these reports useful. In comparison, of the internists 79.5% read the reports regularly and 55.9% considered them useful. For these reasons clinicians considered the system a valuable support in their work.

Support for Post-Analytical Functionalities

In our second case study three DSS modules were developed for interpretation of laboratory test results and for alarming in the intensive care environment (Nykänen et al., 1993). The modules were integrated with an open laboratory information system architecture.

The thyroid decision model used in this second case study is described in Table 4. Both qualitative and quantitative variables were used. Quantitative data were classified into mutually exclusive decision ranges, which were locally modifiable; i.e., they were user-defined, fully revisable and age-specific. Qualitative data could be entered into the system in any combination by selecting the appropriate finding from the user-defined expandable lists of options. After data entry, the program obtained

Table 4: Qualitative and quantitative variables used in the thyroid decision support

Qualitative	Patient's sex
	Clinical details
	Drug therapy
Quantitative	Patient's age
	Serum total thyroxine concentration
	Serum thyrotropin concentration
	Serum free thyroxine concentration
	Serum free triiodothyroxine concentration

an interpretation from the observer and linked it to the data-derived rule so that an appropriate interpretation could be provided automatically whenever similar data were encountered (Nykänen et al., 1993).

Evaluation of the developed thyroid system with more than 3000 requests in a four-month period found that interpretations could be generated by the system for at least 90% of all requests. The remaining requests needed to be interpreted by a human expert.

With the intensive care DSS, interpretation of acid-base disorders was based on utilisation of the laboratory measurement results together with data recorded in the intensive care unit. Evaluation of the accuracy of the system resulted in 92.8% correct classifications with a test set of 194 cases. Two independent experts also tested the accuracy; levels of agreement between the independent expert, the system and between the different experts were found to be similar.

From an ontological viewpoint these intensive care case studies were ambitious attempts to cover contextual aspects of the decision making situation. We tried to build a model where information from the patient data monitoring system, electronic patient record, laboratory information system and human visual examinations were combined. This ontology was planned to represent the essential concepts and relationships in an intensive care decision making situation. Part of the ontology was taxonomies to bring order to the model and to present limited views of a model for human interpretation.

Generation of alarms and alerts in intensive care using laboratory data and clinical information proved to be a complex task due to the many variables that need to be included, due to the temporal aspects of the recorded data and due to high safety requirements. Two prototypes were developed and interfaced in a hospital with the laboratory information system, but the systems were used only in an experimental setting.

These developed DSS modules provided users of laboratory services, both in a specialised hospital unit and in primary care, with interpretations and suggestions on how to proceed with the specific patient case. The interpretations served as high-quality decision support for users. The modules were integrated with a telecommunication network, though they were originally designed as stand-alone systems. Integration was done using standardised components and open architecture specifications. An important aspect of these specifications was the standardised definitions for data and information exchange messages. When integrated with the laboratory information system, the developed systems did not add to the laboratory workload, but showed promise of improving laboratory efficiency (Nykänen et al., 1993).

Discussion on the Case Studies

Users' Problems

The developed, and to some extent evaluated, decision support systems in our case studies can be classified as knowledge-based systems, and they were targeted to support clinical decision making. They proved to be successful for the users in the management of information overload and in the interpretation of information so that it could be better utilised in clinical practice. Various users at different levels of health care were served through these systems. Specification of the systems' functions was based on the users' needs in the problem at hand. The major function of the developed systems was to enhance information from data and to transfer information to other health care units or primary care where expertise for interpretation was not available.

The evaluations performed in these case studies were restricted and were not reported to the users. No special attention was paid to how the evaluation studies and their results were documented so that users could understand them. In this respect users' needs were not served. On the other hand, users were involved in evaluations to some degree, and they received information and could give feedback for system developers on identified failures and needed improvements in the systems' functioning. Users, however, got no training or guidance for the future on how to evaluate decision support systems and which criteria and methods of evaluation to use, though there was a real user's need for that.

Developers' Problems

The developers' problems were mostly methodological. First, in developing decision support systems, the planned use environments determined the constraints for software and methodological choices. Use of a research-oriented, combined evaluation and development methodology and use of commercial expert system shells as software environments were not quite successfully combined. We were in a situation where problems were matched to tools and not vice versa, as it should have been done. Problems were especially encountered in interfacing the developed systems with the existing health care information systems environment.

Second, the developers' problems were related to the problem of how to integrate evaluation with the selected development methods. The used four-phase methodology integrates two different types of heuristics: that of sequential development and that of iterative development through prototyping. Checkpoints were defined at different phases of development to measure prespecified success or failure variables, and these measures were compared with the determined reference criteria in order to decide on how to continue with the development.

As developers we faced problems in this kind of situation. Although there were many technical and methodological possibilities and alternatives to choose from, the use environment imposed strict requirements and constraints for the selection of software and technology options. These requirements were in some degree even conflicting. Additionally, development was done in an evolving world, and emerging technologies were available and new modalities were arising. Therefore, we tried to apply as much as possible conventional approaches and standards so that the modules could be integrated with traditional legacy systems. This was not, however, always successful.

Remaining Problems

Though users' and developers' problems were in the main quite successfully served in our case studies, there still remained some problems which needed attention, but which were not recognised as problems while we were carrying out these case studies.

The first problem is that a decision support system was only implicitly conceptualised in these case studies. There was no explication of the concept. The contents of the concept "decision support system," particularly the type of system and the requirements for this type of system, were not explicated. This means that the essential variables, the task of the system and the role of the system in supporting decision making remained undefined.

The second problem is a natural consequence from the first, and it is also the same as with many early expert systems: decontextualisation of the system from its environment. While developing the system, the focus was on modelling the specific expert's expertise, or a few experts' expertise, in a defined task and that model was then implemented as an expert system. In the modelling and implementation processes, the decision making context and its social and environmental variables were not considered. From this it followed that the resulting system functioned well when seen as a problem solver for the specific problem, but when seen as a system in a real environment used by a human user, the system did not function well. This was because those system characteristics that would consider the environment and use contexts of the system, as well as the organisational context for knowledge and its use, were missing.

The third remaining problem is related to the evaluation and development methodologies. One essential feature for the development methodology is the possibility for evaluation during all development phases. Developing decision support systems for semi- and unstructured problems puts strenuous demands on development methodology and may even, depending on the type of the system, make it necessary to bring in additional developmental phases like knowledge acquisition, knowledge modelling, knowledge management, and knowledge validation. Also, another big problem is the lack of a generally accepted evaluation methodology. In these case studies, we did not have theoretical assumptions on how to connect evaluation and development successfully in the health care context.

EXTENDING A DSS ONTOLOGY WITH NEW VARIABLES

These case studies highlighted the need to consider the contextual aspects of decision support systems. In health care, decision support systems are developed and used as part of the health care environment and as part of the knowledge environment of the user. Therefore, we need such conceptualisation for a DSS that it covers the contextual aspects in the system's development, evaluation and use.

As contextual variables have not been considered during the development of decision support systems, the resulting systems have been brittle: They have functioned only in their development environment, and they have not been transferable to other organisational environments. On another level, this has also been a problem with DSS in general, as the contextual variables are mostly lacking from the DSS definitions (Tables 1 and 2). This is especially the case with medical expert or knowledge-based systems.

Reference Model for Information Systems Research

Ives, Hamilton and Davis presented in 1980 a model for information systems research and they defined variables that need to be considered with information systems. In their model, three information system environments (operations, development and user environments) and three information system processes (use, development and operation processes) and the information subsystem itself are defined, and all these defined entities exist within an external and organisational environment.

This model has exerted a big impact on information systems research because it can be used to understand and classify research approaches and to generate research hypotheses. What is important about this model is that it showed that the environmental variables and their relations to development, use and operation processes need to be taken into account in information systems development. We use this model as our reference when discussing the relevant variables and development and evaluation processes of decision support systems in the next subsections. The model, though it is abstract and has not been operationalised, helps us in identifying the relevant variables and in demonstrating the significance of environments and processes.

Decision Support System in Health Informatics

When comparing the Ives, Hamilton, and Davis (1980) model with the DSS and KBS approaches presented in Tables 1 and 2, we see that in information systems science, decision support systems research and development has been development-

and implementation-oriented, covering environment, process and information sub-system variables. The major focus has, however, been on development and user environment. In artificial intelligence, decision support systems research and devel-opment has been focused on the IS development environment and on information subsystem variables.

As a result of our case studies and of the analysis of definitions we propose that the Ives, Hamilton, and Davis (1980) framework be applied to the development of DSS in health informatics. And we propose to include some additional variables to the conceptualisation of a health informatics decision support system. These additional variables are presented in Table 5 and they are discussed in this subsection. From the variables of the Ives, Hamilton, and Davis model we have left out the operation environment and operation process variables which are not today as essential to information systems. They are even less relevant in the case of decision support systems as their operation is included in user environment and use process variables.

The environment variables presented in Ives, Hamilton, and Davis (1980) are essential for decision support systems, as systems are used by decision makers to support tasks and actions in a contextual situation, and they are developed with the express purpose of having effects and impacts on the environment. We propose to pay special attention to *user-system integrated behaviour* as part of the IS development environment. This variable emphasises the need to design and develop the system as part of the integrated knowledge environment of the user.

Environment variables have not been well covered in ISS-based DSS ap-proaches. For instance, in the Gorry and Scott-Morton (1971) framework for decision support systems, only a user environment variable was explicitly included, and implicitly development and operation environment variables were covered. Eierman et al. (1995) drew attention to the environment construct emphasising the need to consider the organisational and environmental context of system develop-ment and use. Eierman et al. however, did not include designers' or developers' attitudes in the presented constructs; neither problem type nor the system function were included. Eierman et al.'s results strengthen our analysis results that environ-mental aspects like organisational environment and structure, task characteristics and context have to be considered in DSS design and development.

In AI, task-specific approaches have been recently used in order to separate problem-solving methods and domain concept, and to be able to represent domain vocabularies and concepts as reusable ontologies (Musen, 1999). However, these task-specific approaches have not paid much attention to the contextual and environmental aspects of the task. Rather, domain ontologies have been used to represent fundamental domain concepts like classifications and taxonomies. In Table 2, only the development philosophy approach (Heathfield & Wyatt, 1993) drew attention to the context of the domain problem and its modelling.

In information subsystem variables, the *content* should specifically consider the *domain* that describes the domain vocabulary not included in the other variables in that group.

Table 5: Variable groups and variables for a decision support system

Environment variables	<ul><li>**External environment:** legal, social, political, economic, educational, resources, industrial environment of the system</li><li>**Organisational environment:** organisation's aims and objectives, tasks, structure, instability, management style and philosophy</li><li>**IS development environment:** development methods, techniques, development and design personnel with their assumptions and characteristics, organisation and management of the development work, user-system integrated behaviour</li><li>**User environment** users and their environment, users' characteristics, users' tasks, organisation of users</li></ul>
Process variables	<ul><li>**Development process:** resources and costs, participation, support and satisfaction</li><li>**Use process:** system usage, usage pattern, effects and impacts of system use on work performance and on productivity, on quality of decision making and work, user satisfaction</li></ul>
Information system variables	<ul><li>**Content:** information and knowledge achievable through the system, *Domain* describing vocabulary of the domain</li><li>**Representation:** formalisms, media and visualisation techniques</li><li>**Scale:** timestamps for representations</li><li>**Knowledge:** types, sources, validity of knowledge</li><li>**Application:** specialisation of the domain and task in the specific application</li></ul>

Domain consideration is needed because from the DSS conceptualisations in ISS and AI we found that definition of the problem that the system is planned to support is essential for a decision support system. Each DSS has a problem to address, which represents the existing need for the system. The purpose of DSS development is to have a system that solves or supports the solution of the underlying problem. This problem is contextual and domain-sensitive and characteristics of the problem are reflected in the resulting system. The domain defines the purpose for developing the system and its use from the environmental perspective.

An awareness of domain allows for the possibility that the focus in DSS development should be moved from the task analysis more to the direction of the domain analysis. Guarino (1997, 1998) has also raised the possibility that task ontology is an insufficient ontology for decision support systems in his studies of ontology-driven information systems. He concluded that there is a need to cover the aspects of domain and application area: a clear implication of our analysis of AI approaches. A DSS should not be an implementation of an expert task that is decontextualised from the environment, or from the domain, as has been the case with most medical expert systems developed, as we also found in our case studies.

In the information subsystem variables group we propose to add two new variables: knowledge and application.

- The *knowledge* variable indicates the characteristics of knowledge, i.e., type, sources, validity and acquisition method. Knowledge aspects are emphasised in AI-based approaches as seen in Table 2. A health informatics decision support system is not only managing data and information, but also knowledge. Knowledge models are developed during knowledge acquisition and the quality of the system depends on the quality of knowledge, type of knowledge and validity of knowledge.
  - ➢ The organisational context of knowledge is important to consider in the health care environment as knowledge is created and shared through various communication, learning and conversion processes (Boland & Tenkasi, 1995; Nonaka, 1994). When concepts are created and made explicit, they can be modelled and shared, first at the domain level and further at the application level. In a health informatics context, decision support systems are often targeted to function as means or facilitators for organisational knowledge creation, sharing and accumulation in the decision making context. A decision support system, developed through a development process in an environmental setting and used by users in their environment, should reflect through its characteristics, e.g., through an implemented knowledge model, its contextual and situational environment.
- As an information subsystem variable, the *application* variable specialises the domain environment in the specific application. The application variable is needed to take the contextual aspects into account at the system variables level. A DSS is an application which has a domain specified at a more general level, but the concepts relevant for this specific application need to be considered at the system level. For example, in our thyroid diagnostics case, the environmental domain and task are an internal medicine and interpretation task, and at the system level the application is thyroid interpretation.
  - ➢ Without specialising the domain and task to the system level through application, we would not be able to use shared concepts from the domain in the application and thus we would not have enough information for successful system development.

The discussed extensions to conceptualisation of a DSS present an ontology for a health informatics decision support system.

DISCUSSION

We have presented an ontology for a decision support system in health informatics that takes into account the defined variable groups. It was necessary to extend variable groups, as the contextual aspects had not been sufficiently considered with decision support systems. Failure to attend to these aspects was identified as a major reason for failures in our case studies.

The need to understand the contextual aspects of health information systems has been emphasised very recently also by "IMIA Working Group 13: Organisational Impact of Medical Informatics" (see e.g., Aarts & Peel, 1999; Berg & Goorman, 1999; Lorenzi, 1999). There is need to understand the context of clinical work as a prerequisite for successful implementation of information systems in health care. If such understanding exists, then it is reflected in the developer's work and, through his/her efforts, in the resulting system. Berg and Goorman (1999) emphasise, among others, that development of information systems in the health care context has a sociotechnical nature, and therefore successful development requires that developers understand the practises in the environment in which the systems are destined to function. Information in health care is in relation to the context where it is produced.

Also, a previous Delphi study (Brender, McNair, & Nöhr, 1999) identified as an important future research area in health informatics the context for application of decision support systems, i.e., how to integrate knowledge-based decision support with the clinical process. We can say that it is not only the clinical process, but the health care processes overall, that are related to decision support, depending on the case, and these processes we need to consider and understand.

On the Ontology

Does the presented ontology enable us to master such aspects of decision support systems that the other studied approaches are not able to cover? Does it provide us with better support for development, perhaps with better usability? And further, how valid and applicable is our ontology of a DSS?

We used as our reference the Ives, Hamilton, and Davis (1980) model. This model has been largely applied in information systems science, and it has proven to be useful in understanding problems. It has been widely accepted in the ISS research community to classify past research and to give directions for the future, though it is rather abstract and not operationalised.

The presented conceptualisation of a DSS applying the Ives, Hamilton and Davis (1980) model gives us possibilities to cover those aspects of DSS which have not been covered by earlier ISS-based or AI-based approaches. The contextual aspects of the domain, application and knowledge are covered. When the focus is moved to the direction of these issues, it means that domain and application characteristics, as well as knowledge creation and sharing aspects, are considered at every phase of development.

The presented conceptualisation gives better support for development because from it follows that a more thorough problem analysis will be performed. The environment and the domain are considered right from the beginning of the development. A more thorough problem analysis, on the other hand, means that more qualified resources may be required for development. However, with inclusion of domain, application and knowledge aspects, we are likely to be able to produce successful systems because their contextual environment is taken into consideration in system development, and the characteristics of the environment are reflected in the system qualities. One part of the development environment is the user-system integrated behaviour which puts the focus on the aspects of the integrated knowledge environment of the user.

When considering how valid and applicable our conceptualisation of a DSS is, we need to think about how the variables were found and how they were selected. The variables that have been selected for our conceptualisation of a DSS originate from three sources. First, they have been selected from the known variables of the Ives, Hamilton, and Davis (1980) model. Second, variables have been selected on the basis of our analysis of how a decision support system has been defined in areas of information systems science and artificial intelligence, Tables 1 and 2. This analysis found that some variables that are not present in the Ives, Hamilton, and Davis model should be included in the decision support system model in health informatics. Third, the results from our case studies confirm the need to include these additional variables. On this basis we have concluded that the environmental and contextual variables do have an influence on the phenomenon under study, i.e., on development and evaluation of decision support systems in health informatics. In this kind of decision, there is, of course, a possibility that we have forgotten some important variable that has not shown up during this experiment. We have classified this variable as unknown: It is interpreted as not having a big enough influence on the phenomenon under study. If the situation occurs that an unknown variable becomes known, then the conceptualisation should be modified on this basis, or new experiments carried out. This possibility would be a call for further research on the application of the ontology that we have presented on DSS development and evaluation.

Health Informatics Perspective

How does the presented ontology and framework contribute to health informatics research and practice?

Our DSS ontology builds a model of a DSS in health informatics and contributes to theory formulation in health informatics. When developing a decision support system in health informatics practice, important aspects to be considered are health care organisational context, and domain, application and knowledge aspects, as discussed earlier in this study. The ontology helps in drawing attention to these aspects during the problem formulation, development and evaluation phases.

Next, we look at our results in relation to the design science intent of information technology as discussed in March and Smith (1995). They describe that in information technology artifacts are created that serve human purposes. Design science products are of four types: constructs, models, methods and instantiations. Constructs or concepts form the vocabulary of the domain; a model is a set of propositions or statements that express relationships among the constructs or concepts. A method is a set of steps, an algorithm or a guideline used to perform a task. An instantiation is the realisation of an artefact in its environment. Building, or development, is a process of constructing an artefact for a specific purpose. Evaluation is a process of determining how well the artefact performs.

In this study we have produced the following research findings in the terms of March and Smith (1995): The DSS conceptualisation represents constructs. The DSS conceptualisation (ontology) represents also a model as it describes the relationships between the defined constructs. The DSS conceptualisation identifies relevant constructs and thus presents a vocabulary of a DSS in a health informatics domain. Are the created constructs better than the old ones, i.e., those presented in conceptualisations in ISS and AI areas? Our DSS conceptualisation gives a wider and a more dense classification for concepts than the other conceptualisations discussed, and its application domain is health informatics. The DSS conceptualisation is also a model, which describes the situation as problem and solution statements. Is this model better than the other ones discussed, e.g., the abstraction paradigms of AI? The DSS conceptualisation represents essential concepts and gives a structure to the presentation. The model can be used to build instantiations. If the model helps both user and developer better understand the problem at hand, or the developer to develop better instantiations based on better understanding, and as a result, the user will have a useful and usable system at his/her disposal, then we can obviously judge that the utility is better than that of the model we are comparing with.

The presented ontology for a DSS in health informatics contains more variables and viewpoints than those presented and discussed earlier in this study. Thus it may guarantee a more thorough analysis of the problem case, but it does have negative consequences, too. While forcing a deeper analysis, we increase the work of system developers and users. This might mean that system's development requires higher intellectual qualifications and a larger consumption of human resources. These requirements may not be easily met in a real-life situation. However, these results in their part support our additional finding that education and training in health informatics are important issues to be covered.

CONCLUSIONS

The approaches for DSS research in ISS have been focused on development and implementation and on hardware and software issues rather than on decision makers and on decision processes (Table 1). In AI-based approaches a DSS has been mostly understood to be a system that supports an individual's cognitive processes. The major focus in development has been on mimicking individual human intelligent behaviour by modelling tasks, knowledge and inference processes, and the domain problem is seen as an isolated and decontextualised one.

The presented framework presents a research agenda and an integrated framework for decision support systems in a health informatics domain. The earlier discussed DSS frameworks and approaches, presented in Tables 1 and 2, have been developed from particular viewpoints with a focus on defined sets of concepts. The presented framework of this study gives us possibilities to cover those aspects of DSS which have not been covered by earlier ISS-based or AI-based approaches. The presented conceptualisation applying the Ives, Hamilton, and Davis (1980) model puts the focus on environmental variables and on domain ontology, and thus it contributes to the DSS research in general, too. When the focus is moved to the direction of these issues, it means that domain and application characteristics, as well as knowledge creation and sharing aspects, are considered at every phase of development. The presented conceptualisation gives support for development because from it follows that a more thorough problem analysis will be performed.

The results of this analysis have some implications on research and development of decision support systems in health informatics:

- Focus on decision support systems development is proposed to be moved from task ontology towards domain ontology.
- Systems development is seen as a sense-making process, where the system designer helps the user to understand the system. This is needed to achieve an understanding of the domain problem and the purpose of the planned system.
- Consideration of environment, process and system variable groups during development and evaluation, and especially focusing on environmental variables, means that we are not any more developing isolated decision support systems, but systems that support decision making in a health care organisational context and in the user's domain, knowledge and application context.

Development and evaluation of information technology products, e.g. decision support systems, in health informatics require information and knowledge on the domain and methods of health informatics. Research and practice are the essential components of health informatics, and dialogue between these two is needed, and they both should be included in health informatics education.

REFERENCES

Aarts, J., & Peel, V. (1999). Using a descriptive model of change when implementing large scale clinical information systems to identify priorities for further research. *International Journal of Medical Informatics 56*(1-3), 43-50.

Aliferis, C. F., & Miller, R. A. (1995). On the heuristic nature of medical decision support systems. *Methods of Information in Medicine,* 34, 5-14.

Alter, S. (1980). *Decision support systems: Current practice and continuing challenges.* Reading, MA: Addison-Wesley.

Barahona, P., & Christensen, J.P. (Eds.). (1994). *Knowledge and decisions in health telematics.* IOS Press, Technology and Informatics 12.

Berg, M., & Goorman, E. (1999). The contextual nature of medical information. *International Journal of Medical Informatics 56,* (1-3), 51-60.

Boland, R.J., & Tenkasi, R.V. (1995). Perspective making and perspective taking in communities of knowing. *Organisation Science, 6*(4), 350-372.

Bonczek, R. H., Holsapple, C.W., & Watson, A.B. (1981). *Foundations of decision support systems,* Academic Press, NY.

Brender, J., McNair, P., & Nöhr, C. (1999). Research needs and priorities in health informatics—Early results of a Delphi study. In P. Kohol (Ed.), *Proceedings of Medical Informatics Europe 99* (pp. 191-196). IOS Press.

Chandrasekaran, B. (1986). Generic tasks in knowledge-based reasoning: High level building blocks for expert systems. *IEEE Expert,* 23-30.

Clancey, W. (1985). Heuristic classification. *Artificial Intelligence, 27,* 289-350.

Eierman, M. A., Niederman, F., & Adams, C. (1995). DSS theory: A model of constructs and relationships. *Decision Support Systems, 14,* 1-26.

Gorry, G.A., & Scott-Morton, M. S. (1971). A framework for management information systems. *Sloan Management Review, 3*(1), 55-71.

Guarino, N. (1997). Understanding, building and using ontologies: A commentary to *Using explicit ontologies in KBS development.* In *J Human and Computer Studies, 46,* 293-310.

Guarino, N. (1998). Formal ontology and information systems. In N. Guarino (Ed.), *Formal ontology in information systems* (pp. 3-15). Amsterdam: IOS Press.

Heathfield, H. A., & Wyatt, J. (1993). Philosophies for the design and development of clinical decision support systems. *Methods of Information in Medicine,* 32, 1-8.

Ives, B., Hamilton, S., & Davis, G. B. (1980). A framework for research in computer-based management information systems. *Management Science 26, 9,* 910-934.

Keen, P.G.W. (1980). Decision support systems: Translating useful models into usable technologies. *Sloan Management Review, 21*(3), 33-44.

Keen, P.G.W. (1997). Let's focus on action not info. http://www2.computerworld.com/home/cwlaunch.nsf/launch?RealForm&/home/print9497.nsf/ November 17, 1997.

Keravnoe, E., & Washbrook, S. (1989). Deep and shallow models in medical expert systems. *International Journal Artificial Intelligence in Medicine,* 1, 11-28.

Klein, M., & Mehlie, L. B. (1990). *Knowledge-based decision support systems with applications in business.* John Wiley & Sons, UK.

Lenat, D. B. (1975). The ubiquity of discovery. *Artificial Intelligence 9*(3), 257-285.

Little, J.D.C. (1970). Models and managers: The concept of decision calculus. *Management Science, 16,* 466-485.

Lorenzi, N. (1999). IMIA Working group 13: Organisational impact of medical informatics. *International Journal of Medical Informatics 56*(1-3), 5-8.

Lorenzi, N. M., Riley, R. T., Blyth, A.J.C., Southon, G., & Dixon, B. J. (1997). Antecedents of the people and organisational aspects of medical informatics. Review of the literature. *JAMA, 2,* 79-93.

Lundsgaarde, H. P. (1987). Evaluating medical expert systems. *Social Science and Medicine, 24*(10), 805-819.

March, S. T., & Smith, G. F. (1995). Design and natural science research on information technology. *Decision Support Systems, 15,* 251-266.

McDermott, J. (1988). Preliminary step toward a taxonomy of problem-solving methods. In S. Marcus (Ed.), *Automatic knowledge acquisition for expert systems* (pp. 225-254). Boston: Kluwer Academic Publishers.

Moore, J. H., & Chang, M. G. (1980). Design of decision support systems. *Database, 12*(1-2), 8-14.

Musen, M. A. (1999). Scalable software architectures for decision support. *Methods of Information in Medicine 38,* 229-238.

Newell, A. (1982). The knowledge level. *Artificial Intelligence, 18,* 87-127.

Newell, A., & Simon, H. (1976). Computer science as an empirical inquiry: Symbols and search. (1975 ACM Turing Award Lecture), *Comm ACM, 19*(3), 113-126.

Nilsson, N. (1974). Artificial intelligence. In J.L. Rosenfeld (Ed.), *Information Processing* (pp. 778-901). Stockholm: North-Holland.

Nonaka, I. (1994). A dynamic theory of organizational knowledge creation. *Organisation Science, 5*(1), 14-37.

Nuutila, P., Irjala, K., Viikari, J., Forsström, J., Välimäki, M., Nykänen, P., & Saarinen, K. (1991). Clinical value of the decision support system for the assessment of thyroid function. In K.P. Adlassnig, G. Grabner, S. Bengtsson, & R. Hansen (Eds.), *Proceedings of Medical Informatics Europe, Lecture Notes in Medical Informatics 45* (pp. 389-393). Berlin: Springer Verlag.

Nykänen, P., Boran, G., Pince, H., Clarke, K., Yearworth, M., Willems, J. L., & O'Moore, R. (1993). Interpretative reporting based on laboratory data. *Clinica Chimica Act, 222,* 37-48.

Nykänen, P., & Nuutila, P. (1991). Validation and evaluation of a system for thyroid disorders. *Expert Systems with Applications, 3,* 289-295.

Pothoff, P., Rothemund, M., Schwebel, D., Engelbrecht, R., & van Eimeren, W. (1988). Expert systems in medicine. Possible future effects. *International Journal of Technology Assessment in Health Care, 4,* 121-133.

Ramoni, M., Stefanelli, M., Magnani, L., & Barosi, G. (1990). *An epistemological framework for medical knowledge based systems.* Pavia University. Research Rep. (RIDIS-41-90).

Reisman, Y. (1996). Computer-based clinical decision aids. A review of methods and assessment of systems. *International Journal of Medical Informatics, 21*(3), 179-197.

Schreiber, A., Wielinga, B., & Breuker, J. (Eds.).(1993). *KADS: A principled approach to knowledge based systems development.* London: Academic Press.

Scott-Morton, M. (1971). *Management decision systems: Computer-based support for decision making.* Harvard University Press, Boston.

Simon, H. A. (1981). *The sciences of the artificial.* MIT Press, Cambridge.

Sprague, R. H. (1980). A framework for the development of decision support systems. *MIS Quarterly, 4*(4), 32-46.

Sprague, R. H., & Carlson, E. D. (1982). *Building effective decision support systems.* Englewood Cliffs, NJ: Prentice Hall.

Sprague, R. H., & Watson, H. J. (Eds.).(1989). *Decision support systems. Putting theory into practice.* Prentice Hall, USA.

Turban, E. (1988). *Decision support and expert systems: Management support systems* (1st ed.). Macmillan.

Winograd, T., & Flores, F. (1986). *Understanding computers and cognition: A new foundation for design.* Addison-Wesley.

Wyatt, J. (1987). The evaluation of clinical decision support systems: A discussion of the methodology used in the ACORN project. In J. Fox, M. Fieschi, & R. Engelbrecht (Eds.), *Proceedings of the Artificial Intelligence in Medicine, Lecture Notes in Medical Informatics 33* (pp.15-24). Berlin: Springer Verlag.

Chapter IX

Knowledge Management Support for Decision Making in the Pharmaceutical Industry

Rick Gibson
American University, USA

ABSTRACT

The purpose of this chapter is to explore the practical application of knowledge management as an aid to decision making by pharmaceutical firms which comprise an industry that seems very well suited for knowledge management investigation. Although researchers assert that knowledge management has moved beyond fad status to become mainstream, practitioners remain skeptical and express major concerns regarding the ambiguity surrounding the sub-discipline associated with the management of knowledge. The major players in the pharmaceutical industry have already implemented knowledge management systems and therefore may experience a competitive advantage over other pharmaceutical companies. No attempt will be made in this chapter to suggest how the lessons learned from the pharmaceutical industry can be generalized to other industries.

INTRODUCTION

The success of the global industrial economy suggests that a great deal is known about how to make good decisions regarding *financial* capital and tangible economic resources. Over the past decade, as management priorities have shifted to less tangible concerns (e.g., quality, service, innovation) that rely on *intellectual* capital, ideas and knowledge have emerged as key factors in the decision making process. Paradoxically, knowledge and uncertainty are both increasing at disquieting rates. Micklethwait and Wooldridge (1996) suggest this has forced companies to respond with dramatic changes to their organizational structures, but that manager's problems with knowledge persist—they need to learn how to "grow" and manage knowledge resources as well as they have grown and managed capital resources in the past.

Moreover, managers must also learn how to take advantage of those gifted few people who are born bright enough to make connections and generate ideas more rapidly and creatively than their coworkers. These workers need freedom, not structure, to keep their minds free and to keep their unique skills up-to-date. Too late, firms have realized that it is often the middle managers, lost in reengineering rightsizing reorganizations, who play an essential role in bringing together the people with such tacit knowledge.

The relative complexity of the pharmaceutical industry, which spans the challenging science of drug research and development and includes the psychology of indirect marketing, places special decision making demands on managers. Pharmaceutical companies must excel at innovation and collaboration; they are knowledge-intensive, which suggests that the use of knowledge management would be pioneered to facilitate innovation, proliferate best practices, and obtain and utilize competitive intelligence and knowledge from within and with their partners and alliances—in short, to make better decisions

The purpose of this chapter is to explore the practical application of knowledge management as an aid to decision making by pharmaceutical firms, which comprise an industry that seems very well suited for knowledge management investigation. Although researchers assert that knowledge management has moved beyond fad status to become mainstream, practitioners remain skeptical and express major concerns regarding the ambiguity surrounding the subdiscipline associated with the management of knowledge. No attempt will be made to suggest how the lessons learned from the pharmaceutical industry can be generalized to other industries.

BACKGROUND AND THEORETICAL FRAMEWORK

Knowledge in general and knowledge management in particular are complex, multifaceted concepts. Micklethwait and Wooldridge (1996) remind us that Peter Drucker coined the term knowledge worker in 1959 and has since argued that the real basis for sustained economic growth is not discovery of new technologies, but the invention of new (learning) organizations.

Pressman (2001) defines knowledge (see Figure 1) as associatively within multiple contexts, which is surpassed in usefulness only by wisdom—the creation of generalized principles based on existing knowledge from different sources. Analogously, "only connect" was the constant admonition of the great novelist E. M. Forster. This capacity to connect data dots to create information and knowledge may

Figure 1: Pressman's definition of knowledge

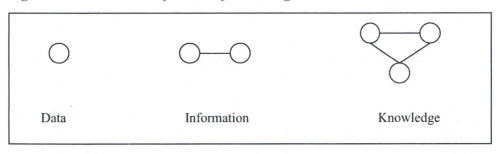

Data	Information	Knowledge

be instinctive to some individuals; in the extreme it may be part of the mystery we label as genius.

In the past few years there has been a growing interest in treating knowledge as a significant organizational resource. For example, Strassman (1999) provided a calculation of knowledge capital *per employee* at several major pharmaceutical firms, shown in Table 1.

Consistent with the interest in organizational knowledge as a resource and knowledge management, researchers have begun promoting a class of information systems, referred to as knowledge management systems, which have as their design objective the creation, transfer, and application of knowledge in organizations. However, rational managers are asking how can we measure and control something we cannot even yet define. The PricewaterhouseCoopers Technology Forecast 2001-2003 describes knowledge management as accurate, relevant, timely facts, enriched by expert insights to produce better solutions. Ribière (2001) suggests that everyone has their own definition of knowledge management, but suggests the following three are worth consideration:

1. "Knowledge management is the systematic, explicit, and deliberate building, renewal and application of knowledge to maximize an enterprise's knowledge related effectiveness from its knowledge assets" (Wigg, 1997).

Table 1: Calculation of knowledge capital per employee

Merck & Co.	$1,423,916
Glaxo Wellcome	$ 784,215
Abbot Laboratories	$ 702, 468
Johnson & Johnson	$ 582, 568
Warner-Lambert	$ 261,847

2.   "Knowledge management is the process of capturing a company's collective expertise wherever it resides—in databases, on paper, or in people's heads—and distributing it to wherever it can help produce the biggest payoff" (Hibbard, 1997).

3.   "Knowledge management is getting the right knowledge to the right people at the right time so they can make the best decision" (Pettrash, 1996).

It is this third definition that will serve to operationally define knowledge management for the conceptual purposes of this chapter—*knowledge management is getting the right knowledge to the right people at the right time so they can make the best decision.*

As useful framework for organizing this exploration of knowledge management in the pharmaceutical industry is that of a knowledge management episode, adapted from Holsapple and Joshi (1998) by Koch, Paradice, Bonsug, & Guo (2001).

According to Tiwana (2000), there are nine primary reasons (identified as "influences" in Figure 2 for implementing knowledge management systems:

1.   Companies are becoming knowledge-intensive, not capital-intensive. Knowledge is displacing capital and monetary prowess (Drucker, 1999).

2.   Unstable markets necessitate "organized abandonment" (Drucker, 1999). Markets might undergo changes and leave a company in a disastrous position; knowledge management helps prepare for such organization abandonment to help get out of projects that can pull your business down and get into others that can help maximize potential.

3.   Knowledge management lets you lead change so change does not lead you. Drucker (1999) says that no industry or company has a natural advantage or disadvantage; the only advantage it can possess is the ability to exploit universally available knowledge.

4.   Only the knowledgeable survive. The ability to survive is derived from a firm's ability to create, acquire, process, maintain, and retain old and new knowledge in the face of complexity, uncertainty, and rapid change (Dhurana, 1999).

Figure 2: Nine primary reasons for implementing knowledge management systems

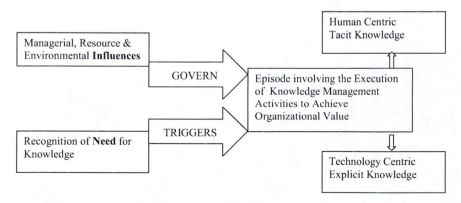

5.   Cross-industry amalgamation is breeding complexity.
6.   *Knowledge can drive decision support like no other.*
7.   Knowledge requires sharing environments.
8.   Tacit knowledge is mobile. Knowledge moves from one company to another when an employee shifts organizations.
9.   Your competitors are no longer just on the West Coast. According to Drucker (1999), we are becoming increasingly global and companies need to keep up with development threats and opportunities in other countries.

The sixth reason listed above—*Knowledge can drive decision support like no other*—is of particular interest when one considers a recent knowledge management research report (KPMG, 2000) suggesting that knowledge management has been adopted by 80% of the largest companies around the globe, and of these firms, almost 90% cited better decision making as the principal reason to pursue knowledge management.

Pfeffer and Sutton (2000) remind us that annual expenditures totaling billions of dollars are spent on training programs and management consultants in order to improve the organizational decision making process. They question why, given that knowledge of best practices is nearly ubiquitous, are so few organizations able to actually implement these best practices? Pfeffer and Sutton itemize some of the key reasons, which are behavioral and cultural in nature.

Other possible explanations emerge when we consider the inputs to the decision making process independent of individual behavior and organizational culture. The Corporate Executive Board (2000) reports the unfortunate paradox that results from the existence of two type of organizational information: structured (data, accounts, and transactions) and unstructured (documents, e-mails, presentations). In terms of volume of information, roughly 85% is unstructured, but in terms of information management spending 90% is on structured (see Figure 3).

Figure 3: Volume of information from two types of organizational information

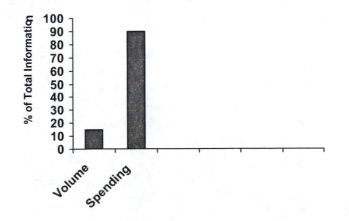

McKellar (2000) summarizes a survey from KPMG, which suggests that large companies have a high regard for knowledge management programs. Nearly 75% of those surveyed were looking to knowledge management to perform at least a significant role in improving competitive advantage, marketing and customer focus. About 65% expect knowledge management to benefit product innovation, revenue growth and profit. Nearly three quarters (71%) believe knowledge management leads to better decision making, and about 65% view it as achieving faster response to important business issues and better customer handling.

Some 75% of the respondents report the knowledge management decision driven by senior management or from the board level and that any such initiative must be company-wide. However, the KPMG study suggests that these decision makers view knowledge management only in terms of return on investment.

Of course, not all respondents reported success. Thirty-six percent of the KPMG study respondents reported the benefits failed to meet expectations for the following reasons:

- lack of user uptake owning to insufficient communication (20%)
- failure to integrate knowledge management into everyday working practices (19%)
- inadequate time to learn the system or the belief it was too complicated (18%)
- lack of training (15%)
- belief there was too little personal benefit for the user (13%).

The KPMG study identifies the organizations' failure to perceive the cultural implications of knowledge management. While such a program should remove employee frustration, only a third of the companies actually had knowledge management policies that spelled out the priority of knowledge elements, with less than a third (31%) rewarded knowledge working. Only 18% had a knowledge map that indicated what information is available. Moreover, according to the survey data, just 16% of the respondents of companies that either implemented (or considered implementation of) a knowledge management regime actually measure "intellectual capital," or the intangible value of knowledge, innovation and relationships.

Instead, the KPMG study concluded that companies view knowledge management issues as amenable to a purely technological solution. Accordingly, they have utilized information technologies: 93% use the Internet to access external knowledge; 78%, an intranet; 63%, data warehouse or mining; 61%, document management systems; 49%, decision support; 43%, groupware; and 38%, extranets. Only 16% of the companies have a system specifically designed for knowledge management.

The global pharmaceutical market is currently valued at over $250 billion a year. A key area for decision making in the pharmaceutical firms centers on innovation in terms of new drug discovery research and drug development programs. There is a compelling need to reduce research costs and shorten the research cycles that eventually lead to new drugs. Koretz and Lee (1998) focus on how knowledge management can add value to these programs, which typically require $350 million over 8-12 years to bring a drug to market. They suggest that drug development has three significant characteristics:

1. Effective drug development means making correct decisions to cease development of failures and accelerate development of successes as early as possible.
2. Drug development uses hundreds of individual contributors from dozens of disciplines and companies at geographically dispersed locations over many years.
3. *Label-driven* decision making centers on objectives that are derived from the desired label claims.

These characteristics confirm that drug development is a decision making process and that the basis for the decisions is especially difficult to manage.

Moreover, Koretz and Lee (1998) remind us that knowledge management is not new to the health care industry, but distinguish between passive and active knowledge management. Passive knowledge management is traditional with existing material entered into a knowledge management system, like MEDLINE. In a more active mode, knowledge management is used to drive the creation of information. For example, in a label-driven decision, supporting evidence is created and captured.

According to Davenport and Prusak (1998), companies can no longer expect the products and practices that made them successful in the past will make them successful in the future. Liebowitz (2000) noted both the value of knowledge management and investigated concerns and pessimism related to knowledge management initiatives at a pharmaceutical company. In terms of value, Pfizer attributes part of the success of Viagra to knowledge management. He concluded that although the potential exists for exploiting knowledge management, further education is needed. Other concerns are highlighted by Cuthbertson (1999), who credits the huge research and development costs as drivers for pharmaceutical firms to pursue knowledge management, but also credits concerns to prevent duplicative work, reduce development time and leverage internal resources to remain competitive. Further support for this comes from Forrester Research (2001), which suggests that drug manufacturers like Pfizer spend about 20% of their revenues on research and development and a new drug can cost up to $600 million and take more than 8 years in development.

According to a recent study (CGE&Y, 2000), pharmaceutical companies are rapidly globalizing in response to the perception that new emerging markets have more potential than the established mature markets of North American, Japan, and Europe. One consequence of a global strategy is the need to conduct simultaneous clinical trials in a number of countries so that drugs arrive on the market simultaneously in multiple countries and regions. An additional benefit is that testing new drug candidates against a more diverse range of population groups yields stronger results than do trials run only in a single, homogeneous population. The resulting complexity of running these clinical trials presents immense challenges for which knowledge management solutions are needed. In general, knowledge management offers companies greater consistency, quality, and speed in running any clinical trials.

In particular, knowledge management systems support the additional collaboration needed for the more complex, global clinical trials.

Knowledge management solutions can contribute to the sales and marketing effort for pharmaceutical firms. Studies (such as CGE&Y, 2000) stress the complexity of the marketing environment in which pharmaceutical companies must operate. Companies must build solid relationships with a very diversified group of customers, capture and analyze customer data, make these data available across the organization and to regulatory agencies, and synchronize complex marketing efforts that encompass a variety of markets. Most pharmaceutical firms have numerous sales and marketing groups that require coordination and collaboration. Sophisticated knowledge management techniques are needed so that knowledge is collected from all available sources including data stores, systems, file cabinets, and people and is stored in a knowledge repository to be used by individuals and teams to maximize their marketing effectiveness and efficiency. In addition, all knowledge in the repository must remain current and as it becomes obsolete, it must be removed or archived. Pfizer uses knowledge management to enhance their sales promotions—allowing their 2,700 sales representatives access to information about any specific drug, along with associated details about dosage, side effects, and treatment regulations.

In order to receive regulatory approval to market a new drug, pharmaceutical companies must amass a tremendous quantity of knowledge. They must compile and submit an assortment of document types ranging from preclinical studies, through clinical trial results, to post-trial statistical analyses. Barron (1998) reports that knowledge management technology is helping to solve many of the difficulties inherent in these regulatory and accountability processes for pharmaceutical firms. Several hundred thousand documents may be involved in this compliance process, and delays in the regulatory approval cycle can cost a pharmaceutical firm a million dollars a day or more.

Zimmerman (2000) observes that developing pharmaceuticals is a science that relies on efficient sharing of information beyond the organizational boundaries of an individual pharmaceutical company. For example, since drugs are marketed directly to consumers, advertising and marketing professionals can become part of the mix before a drug has even been approved by the Food and Drug Administration. For this reason, Web portals are gaining popularity as a tool for pharmaceutical firms to manage their knowledge assets. The Internet and intranets facilitate collaboration within the organization as well as with outside marketing coordinators, advertising executives and other stakeholders. In defining teams for collaboration, pharmaceuticals firms have begun to realign along therapeutic lines. For example, all members of a team involved with an arthritis drug—from scientists to marketers—work closely together as part of a business unit, rather than groups of scientists or groups of advertising reps working alone. Because the pharmaceutical industry is highly regulated, this abundance of knowledge must be shared both internally and externally.

Getting the right people involved from the beginning has been a big impetus for implementing knowledge management systems in the pharmaceutical industry. Pharmaceutical companies are increasingly finding the need to have a centralized repository for all their electronic documents, including word processing files, spreadsheets, clinical data, videos, voice mail and e-mail. Beyond the Food and Drug Administration requirement for more and more electronic submissions is the need to gather clinical data from physicians around the world and to cross-reference personnel applications so that they know who worked on a particular project, so that others at the company can tap into that person's knowledge for similar projects.

Tkach (2001) observes pharmaceutical companies have performed strategic moves such as outsourcing elements of the research and development value chain through collaborative relationships with dedicated biotechnology firms, university laboratories, and other pharmaceutical companies. These collaborative relationships need to be managed, which involves decisions on source selection, and demand an efficient transfer of knowledge from the outsource entities to the internal team.

Knowledge repositories can be used to lower risk exposure when companies address product risk as a major business factor. This is the case in the pharmaceutical industry, where documenting risk reduction is the key to new drug acceptance and where knowledge repositories have long played a key role. While the risks associated with preserving business documents have long been understood, knowledge management exacerbates them by capturing a much broader array of informal communications, transforming them into shared knowledge and business records (Silver, 1998).

Beyond Web portals there are various knowledge management tools available that have shown positive results. A good example is a knowledge management writing tool centered on a "seed document." This tool facilitates the collaborative efforts of drug development teams and helps team members engage in substantive conflict and reach consensus on difficult issues. The results are more useful with timely documentation that facilitates quicker drug approval (Bernhardt & McCulley, 2000).

Perhaps the real challenge in implementing knowledge management is less in the sending and more in the receiving, particularly the task of learning the processes of sense-making, understanding, and being able to make decisions and act upon the information available (Denning, 2000).

Cap Gemini Ernst & Young, conducted a study in 2000 involving interviews of CEOs and VPs of the 17 largest pharmaceutical companies such as the following: Abbott, Amgen, Bristol-Myers Squibb, Glaxo, Johnson & Johnson, Nestle, Pfizer, Rouche, Pharmacia & Upjohn. The results indicated that more than 65% of the leading pharmaceutical companies considered knowledge management as a strategic business objective, 29% thought that it is important, but not vital to their business objectives, and only 6% said that it is unimportant, but interesting (see Figure 4).

By comparison, 12% indicated that they consider knowledge management a core business activity and consider their company to be among the industry leaders,

Figure 4: Importance of knowledge management to business objectives

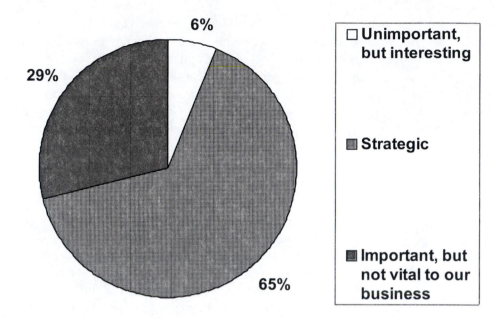

35% of the companies indicated that they have made significant progress in the knowledge management field but are not yet industry leaders, 41% indicated that they are minimally engaged in knowledge management activities, 6% said that they are not engaged in knowledge management activities, and 6% did not know.

Other significant findings from the Cap Gemini Ernst & Young (2000) study include:

- The technology to implement knowledge management is readily available, but additional changes are needed such as making knowledge collection and sharing behaviors an explicit part of the reward system, focusing on people, content, process, then technology, and providing rich, easily accessible external content.
- Knowledge management has sparked a revolution in the drug discovery process. Companies have found ways to industrialize the discovery process by automating various steps and performing the creation and evaluation steps in parallel rather than sequentially. This will help increase the speed of discovery and reduce the number of compounds that fail in clinical trials.
- Due to the knowledge management tools, drug discovery and consumer marketing will become simultaneous, parallel processes. This will bring a much closer integration between market knowledge and drug discovery, demanding corresponding organizational shifts to bring previously distant functions within the firm into closer collaboration.

- Implementing appropriate knowledge management solutions will be a key factor for leveraging the intellectual assets of scientists from across research specialties. These resources were developed over decades of experience and unavailable to smaller, newer competitors.

- Knowledge management facilitates the administration of clinical trials, which is among the most complex and challenging aspects of the pharmaceutical business. These trials vary in terms of length, cost, the difficulty of showing effectiveness depending on the patients' condition, and other major factors. In order to bring drugs to market simultaneously in multiple countries and regions, clinical trials must be carried out globally. In addition, carrying out trials in different countries allows companies to reach more robust conclusions about drugs' safety and effectiveness. Testing new drug candidates against a more diverse range of population groups yields stronger results than do trials run only in a single, homogeneous population.

- Pharmaceutical companies face a major decision when a drug has reached the point where it is submitted for regulatory approval. At this point, it already represents an enormous investment. It is imperative that companies minimize rejections by deciding to eliminate drug candidates that will fail clinical trials earlier in the pipeline and ensuring that filings are of the highest quality.

- Pharmaceutical companies confront some of the most complex marketing decisions faced by any industry. The target market for new drugs includes physicians, pharmacists, managed care companies and other organizations, and patients. Pharmaceutical companies address each of these audiences through multiple outlets and under a variety of circumstances. One of the most pressing challenges facing the industry is to present a single face to the customer across all these marketing channels. Knowledge management tools can solve that problem and can help support the gathering, interpretation, and dissemination of customer information. The availability of detailed information on diseases, drugs, and other medical issues over the Internet has created a newly informed customer base, presenting pharmaceutical companies with both challenges and opportunities.

In a case study (CGE&Y, 2000) on Roche Pharmaceuticals manufacturing division, it was shown that after 4 years of operating a knowledge management system the division had exceeded senior management's targets for cost, quality, and efficiency improvements. At the plant level, significant process and technical innovations have been developed, which they attribute to the knowledge management system. At the individual level, the employees use the knowledge management system on a daily basis to guide their decision making process and deepen their expertise. Companies such as KPMG, CGE&Y, and IBM are helping pharmaceuticals develop their knowledge-based systems and understanding of knowledge management. The major players in the pharmaceutical industry have already implemented these systems and therefore may experience a competitive advantage over other pharmaceutical companies.

FUTURE TRENDS

Silverstone and Karlenzig (1999) suggested the following future knowledge management trends:

- the rise of the corporate portal as the defining knowledge management application
- recognition of knowledge economics as the context for next-century business
- theory gradually being replaced by practical knowledge management
- continued application of knowledge management to customer relationship management.

Companies that apply knowledge management better than others will continue to have a competitive advantage. However, Murray, Allison, Greene, and Hekimian (2000) warn that knowledge is context-and time-dependent—what is knowledge today may not be knowledge tomorrow. Knowledge must be maintained through validation to preserve integrity and relevance.

Drucker (1993) highlighted the need for an economic theory that puts knowledge into the center of the wealth-producing process. What is still needed is an understanding of how knowledge behaves as an economic resource. Meanwhile, knowledge management practitioners apply basic management precepts. For example, the productivity of knowledge requires increasing the yield from what is known.

Technology is significant because it will force us to do new things, rather than enabling us to do old things better. It remains to be seen what new things we can do with knowledge management technology. Leonard-Barton (1995) asserts that there is a need for "T"-shaped skills—deep expertise in one discipline (the stem of the "T") combined with a sufficient intellectual range to relate that expertise to lots of other areas (the bar of the "T").

CONCLUSION

The conclusion reached through this research is that knowledge management holds the key to success for pioneering firms in the pharmaceutical industry. The early adopters of knowledge management technologies in that industry have showed that knowledge management implementation in the pharmaceutical industry can help:

- companies reduce drug research/development
- save money and time
- reduce product launch and marketing costs and time
- improve drug quality
- foster innovation
- enable global clinical trials to target world population
- analyze consumer data and build consumer relations.

Knowledge management pioneers need a passion for experimentation and a willingness to fail—this goes back to Chris Argyris's argument that failure is a better teacher than success due to the opportunity for double-loop learning, which allows people to question the assumptions behind the failures as well as the failures themselves. The collective willingness to fail may be missing in the pharmaceutical industry due to the unusually severe consequences of failure.

REFERENCES

Barron, J. (1998). KM: Healthy Rx for pharmaceutical firms. *KMWorld Magazine, 7*(1).

Bernhardt, S., & McCulley, G. (2000, February). Knowledge management and pharmaceutical development. *Journal of the Society for Technical Communication, 47*(1).

Cap Gemini Ernst & Young. (2000). *Pharmaceutical study.* Life Sciences Group.

Corporate Executive Board. (2000). Knowledge management intranets: Basic principles of information architecture. Working Council for Chief Information Officers.

Cuthbertson, B. (1999, January). Huge R&D costs lead drug companies to pursue KM. *Knowledge Management.*

Davenport, T., & Prusak, L. (1998). *Working knowledge: How organizations manage what they know.* Boston: Harvard Business School Press.

Denning, S. (2000). *The springboard: How storytelling ignites action in knowledge-era organizations.* Boston: Butterworth-Heinemann.

Dhurana, A. (1999). Managing complex production processes. *Sloan Management Review.* 85-97.

Drucker, P. (1993). *Post-capitalist society.* New York: HarperCollins.

Drucker, P. (1999). *Management challenges for the 21st century.* New York: HarperBusiness.

Forrester Research Press Release. (2001, March). Growing market pressures will force drug manufactures to evolve into flexible operating networks.

Hibbard, J. (1997). Knowing what we know. *InformationWeek* (October 20).

Holsapple, C., & Joshi, K. (1998). In search of a descriptive framework for knowledge management: Preliminary Delphi results. *Kentucky Initiative for Knowledge Management*, 118, 1-27.

Koch, H., Paradice, D., Bonsug, C., & Guo, Y. (2001). An investigation of knowledge management within a university IT group. *Information Resources Management Journal* (January–March, pp. 13-21).

Koretz, S., & Lee, G. (1998). Knowledge management and drug development. *Journal of Knowledge Management, 2*(2), 53-58.

KPMG Consulting. (2000). Knowledge Management Research Report.

Leonard-Barton, D. (1995). *Wellsprings of knowledge: Building and sustaining the sources of innovation.* Boston: Harvard Business School Press.

Liebowitz, J. (2000). Knowledge management receptivity at a major pharmaceutical company. *Journal of Knowledge Management, 4*(3), 252-257.

McKellar, H. (2000). KPMG releases KM report. *KMWorld Magazine.*

Micklethwait, J., & Wooldridge, A. (1996). *The witch doctors: What the management gurus are saying, why it matters and how to make sense of it.* London: Heinemann.

Murray, A., Allison, J., Greene, A., & Hekimian, A. (2000). KM conceptual framework and research road map. *Enterprise Knowledge Management Group.*

Pettrash, G. (1996). Managing knowledge assets for value. *Proceedings of the Knowledge-Based Leadership Conference.*

Pfeffer, J., & Sutton, R. (2000). *The knowing-doing gap: How smart companies turn knowledge into action.* Boston: Harvard Business School Press.

Pressman, R. (2001). *Software engineering: A practitioner's approach.* (5th Ed.). Boston: McGraw-Hill.

Quinn, J., Anderson, P., & Finkelstein, S. (1996, April). *Managing professional intellect—Making the most of the best.* Boston: Harvard Business Review on Knowledge Management.

Ribière, V. (2001). *Assessing knowledge management initiative successes as a function of organizational culture.* Unpublished doctoral dissertation, George Washington University.

Silver, B. (1998, January). KM's double-edged sword. *KMWorld Magazine, 7,* 1.

Silverstone, S., & Karlenzig, W. (1999, December). The 1999 KM year in review. *Knowledge Management Magazine.*

Strassman, P. (1999, December). What's the worth of an employee? *Knowledge Management Magazine.*

Tiwana, A. (2000). *The knowledge management toolkit.* New Jersey: Prentice Hall, PTR.

Tkach, D. (2001). IBM data management: Advances in knowledge management—KM for the pharmaceutical industry.

Zimmerman, K. (2000). Pharmaceutical firms discover the collaborative power of Web portals. *KMWorld Magazine.*

Chapter X

Customer Relationship Management at Harrah's Entertainment

Hugh J. Watson
University of Georgia, USA

Linda Volonino
Canisius College, USA

ABSTRACT

Data warehousing has significantly changed how decision making is supported in organizations. A leading application of data warehousing is customer relationship management (CRM). The power of CRM is illustrated by the experiences at Harrah's Entertainment, which has assumed a leadership role in the gaming industry through a business strategy that focuses on knowing their customers well, giving them great service, and rewarding their loyalty so that they seek out a Harrah's casino whenever and wherever they play.

In 1993, changing gaming laws allowed Harrah's to expand into new markets through the building of new properties and the acquisition of other casinos. As management thought about how it could create the greatest value for its shareholders, it was decided that a brand approach should be taken. With this approach, the various casinos would operate in an integrated manner rather than as separate properties. Critical to their strategy was the need to understand and manage relationships with their customers. Harrah's had to understand where their customers gamed, how often and what games they played, how much they gambled, their profitability, and what offers would entice them to visit a Harrah's casino. Armed with this information, Harrah's could better identify specific target customer segments, respond to customers' preferences, and maximize profitability across the various casinos.

In order to execute their business strategy, Harrah's made a substantial investment in information technology to create WINet. WINet sources data from casino, hotel, and event systems. The data is then integrated into a patron database that serves as an operational data store. The data store is used to support operations, such as facilitating the check-in of customers at Harrah's casinos. It is also used with "Total Rewards," Harrah's customer loyalty program. Customers accumulate reward credits based on their gaming and other activities at any Harrah's properties. These reward credits can be redeemed for cast of comps on hotel accommodations, meals, and shows. Data from the patron database is then loaded in the marketing workbench, which serves as Harrah's data warehouse. The marketing workbench supports analytical applications such as customer segmentation and profiling, and identifying customers to send offers to. WINet also provides the foundation for "closed loop marketing." With this data-driven approach, campaigns are designed, tested, and the results retained for future use.

Harrah's creative marketing, innovative uses of information technology, and operational excellence have resulted in many benefits, including a brand identity for Harrah's, consistent guest rewards and recognition across properties, a significant increase in the response rate to offers to customers, and great customer loyalty. Valuable lessons have been learned that can be applied by other companies embarking on a CRM initiative.

INTRODUCTION

Data warehousing is the most important development in decision support over the last decade. Virtually all large and even many medium-and small-size firms have a data warehouse in place. These warehouses provide a repository of data that is optimized for decision support. Data in the warehouse is accessed by users (e.g., analysts, managers) throughout the organization who employ a variety of data access tools (e.g., SQL queries, managed query environments) and applications (e.g., DSS/ EIS).

Data warehousing is being used to support many important organizational strategies and initiatives, such as balanced score carding and electronic commerce (both B2C and B2B). Yet another important initiative supported by data warehousing is customer relationship management (CRM). CRM is designed to attract new customers, enhance relationships with existing customers, and reduce customer attrition. It requires a data warehouse that integrates and stores data in a customer-centric manner. This data is then analyzed using advanced analytical methods for purposes such as campaign planning, market segmentation analysis, customer scoring and profiling, customer profitability analysis, and customer attrition analysis.

Harrah's Entertainment, Inc. (or simply Harrah's) has assumed a leadership position in the gaming industry through a business strategy that focuses on knowing their customers well, giving them great service, and rewarding their loyalty so that they seek out a Harrah's casino whenever and wherever they play. The execution of this strategy has involved creative marketing, innovative uses of information technology, and operational excellence. These component parts first came together in 1997 and by 2000 had resulted in many benefits, including:

- A doubling in the response rate of offers to customers;
- Consistent guest rewards and recognition across properties;
- A brand identity for Harrah's casinos;
- An increase in customer retention worth several million dollars;
- A 72% increase in the number of customers who play at more than one Harrah's property, increasing profitability by more than $50 million; and
- A 62% internal rate of return on the information technology investments.

Harrah's has received considerable recognition for their efforts. In 2000, Harrah's received the prestigious Leadership Award from The Data Warehousing Institute.

In the following sections, Bill Harrah's entry into the gaming industry and the customer-oriented values that he held are discussed. These values continue today and are experienced by customers in Harrah's properties across the country. Harrah's business strategy is described, focusing on the branding of the Harrah's name and customer relationship management. In order to execute their business strategy, substantial investments in information technology (IT) were required in order to integrate data from a variety of sources for use in Harrah's patron database (an operational data store) and the marketing workbench (a data warehouse). This infrastructure supports operations, offers, Total Rewards (a customer loyalty program), and analytical applications. Special attention is given to the use of IT to support "closed-loop marketing." The impacts of Harrah's initiatives are discussed.

The descriptions presented in this chapter are based on interviews that were conducted in the spring of 2000 and documents that were available at that time. Since then, Harrah's has continued to extend and enhance its data warehousing, business intelligence, and CRM efforts.

COMPANY BACKGROUND

In October 1937, Bill Harrah opened a bingo parlor in Reno, NV. He focused on customer comfort, running fair games, and ensuring that customers had a good time. In 1946, Harrah purchased The Mint Club, which took him from the bingo parlor business to full-scale casinos. After renovating the club, it was reopened as Harrah's Club and began the Harrah's style of casino entertainment. Harrah's was the "friendly casino," where employees knew the customers' names. In 1955, Harrah opened another renovated casino, this time on the south shores of Lake Tahoe. The gaming clubs at Harrah's Reno and Lake Tahoe were prosperous throughout the 1960s and 70s as Harrah continued to expand and improve these properties. By 1971, Harrah recognized that the practice of going to local bankers or competing gamblers to borrow money for supporting growth was limiting. He took his company public and became the first purely gaming company to be listed on the New York Stock Exchange.

Bill Harrah's vision for growth was continued by Philip Satre, who led Harrah's entry into the Atlantic City market and was named president in 1984. In 1993, legislation was passed that allowed gambling on Indian reservations and riverboats. Seizing the opportunity, Harrah's quickly expanded into these new markets, through the building of new properties and the acquisition of Showboat casinos, the Rio All-Suite Casino, and Players International. Entering the new millennium, Harrah's had casinos in every major U.S. market where gambling is allowed, making it one of the world's largest gaming companies.

HARRAH'S BUSINESS STRATEGY

The decision to expand into additional gaming markets was a critical part of Harrah's business strategy. The growth of these markets was considered to be inevitable and helpful to Harrah's and the industry. As management thought about how it could create the greatest value for its shareholders, it was decided that a brand approach should be taken. With this approach, the various casinos would operate in an integrated manner rather than as separate properties. This was a radical paradigm shift in the gaming industry where casino managers historically ran their properties as independent fiefdoms and marketing was done on a property by property basis. With the new approach, there would be commonalties in the gambling experience for customers across the various casinos. Advertising and offers would promote the Harrah's brand. There would be recognition and reward programs for customers who cross-played at more than one of Harrah's properties. Harrah's mission was to build lasting relationships with its customers.

Also motivating the strategy were the experiences of some of the new Las Vegas hotels and casinos (e.g., the Bellagio and Paris) that had invested vast sums of money in lavish hotels, shopping malls, and attractions such as massive dancing water shows and a replica of the Eiffel Tower. While these malls and attractions have been highly popular, their great costs have cut investment returns in half. Harrah's wanted to take a different, more cost-effective route that not only attracted customers, but also maintained and enhanced customer relationships.

Critical to their strategy was the need to understand and manage relationships with their customers. They believed that strong customer service relationships build on a foundation of customer knowledge. To build this foundation, Harrah's had to learn about their customers' behaviors and preferences. They had to understand where their customers gambled, how often they gambled, what games they played, how much they gambled, and what offers would entice them to visit a Harrah's casino. Armed with this information, Harrah's could better identify specific target customer segments, respond to customers' preferences, and maximize profitability across the various casinos.

A key addition to the Harrah's management team was Gary Loveman, who was named chief operations officer (COO). This former Harvard professor had the understanding and skills needed to analyze customer behavior and preference data and to put programs in place to capitalize on this knowledge. He helped make Harrah's customer relationship management strategy a reality.

To generate the necessary data, Harrah's had to make a substantial investment in information technology. It had to capture data from customer touch points, integrate it around the customer, and store it for later analysis. In order to understand customers' preferences, Harrah's had to mine the data, run experiments using different marketing interventions (i.e., special offerings), and learn what best met customers' needs at the various casinos. From these requirements, Harrah's Winners Information Network (WINet) emerged.

WINET: CREATING A SINGLE CUSTOMER VIEW

In 1994, Harrah's began work on WINet under the leadership of John Boushy, who at the time served as Harrah's CIO and director of strategic marketing. The purpose of WINet was to collect customer data from various source systems, integrate the data around the customer, identify market segments and customer profiles, create appealing offers for customers to visit Harrah's casinos, and make the data available for operational and other analytical purposes. The repository for this data uses a patron database (PDB) that served as an operational data store. It provided a cross-property view of Harrah's customers. In 1997, Total Gold, a patented customer loyalty program through which customers could earn points for their gambling activities (e.g., playing slot machines) and redeem their points for free retail products, rooms, food, and cash, was put in place. The marketing workbench (MWB) was also implemented to serve as a data warehouse for analytical applications.

The development of WINet was not without problems. For example, some complicated queries on MWB, originally an Informix database, took so long to run that they never finished within the computing window that was available. NCR, which had been providing benchmarking services for Harrah's, offered to run the queries on their Teradata database software and hardware. The performance improvement was so dramatic that NCR was brought in to redesign the system on NCR Teradata and NCR WorldMark 4700 UNIX System.

By 1999, PDB had increased in size to 195 GB and stored data on over 15 million customers, while MWB stored 110 GB of data. The MWB was smaller than PDB because performance problems on the data warehouse limited the amount of

Figure 1: Timeline for the development of WINet

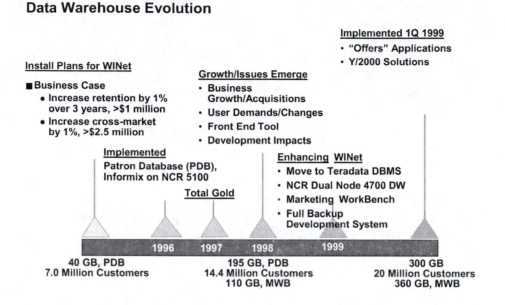

Data Warehouse Evolution

historical data that could be stored. At the same time that Harrah's was considering moving to NCR, a decision was made to review the data access tools that marketing used. The outcome was a switch to Cognos Impromtu and SAS. Marketing analysts at the corporate and individual property levels use Impromtu to run predefined reports and queries and to execute ad hoc queries. Analysts use SAS for market segmentation analysis and customer profiling.

Figure 1 shows the timeline for the development of WINet and Figure 2 presents its architecture. The component parts of WINet are described in the following sections.

Data and Source Systems

Data is captured and collected from a variety of source systems. The hotel system records the details of a customer's stay, demographic data (e.g., home address), and preference data (e.g., smoking or nonsmoking room). Data recorded from tournaments and special events (e.g., wine tasting weekend, slot machine tournaments) are included. Most players obtain a loyalty card (e.g., Total Gold) which they use to obtain points that can be redeemed for rewards (e.g., free meals, tickets to shows). In the case of slot machine play, the customer inserts the loyalty card into the machine and every play is recorded. With table games (e.g., blackjack), the player gives the card to the dealer and the pit boss enters into a PC networked to PDB the game played and the minimum, average, and maximum amount bet over a period of time (e.g., typically every 2 hours). After a customer visits a casino and

Figure 2: WINet Architecture

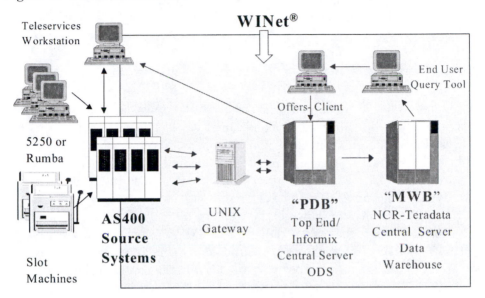

is in Harrah's system, he or she is a candidate for special offers (e.g., $50 in free chips if the customer returns within the next two weeks and plays for at least 3 hours). Data on the offers made and redeemed are recorded for each customer.

A variety of source systems is involved. Some of them are very specific to the gaming industry, such as the slot data system, which captures data automatically from slot machine play. Others such as the hotel reservation system are more generic and involve human data entry. The systems that require human input use IBM 5250s or Rumba terminal emulation for data access or entry. All of the transactional systems run on IBM AS400s. Harrah's has no mainframe.

Patron Database

At the end of the day for each source system (the definition of "end of day" varies with the system), relevant data is extracted for loading into the PDB. First, however, validity and "saneness" checks are performed. Checking for a valid address is an example of a validity check. A saneness test checks whether the data is reasonable, such as the "drop" from a 25-cent slot machine (e.g., a $1000 drop in a hour is not reasonable). Data that fail a test are placed in a suspended file and manually reviewed. At 7:00 a.m., the data is loaded into PDB from the casino, hotel, and event management systems. The load is completed and available for use by noon. In terms of source systems, no matter which casino a customer goes to, the details of every visit are captured and ultimately find their way into PDB. The data is available by customer, casino, hotel, event, gaming product, and tracked play.

Every customer is assigned an identification number, and the data about the customer are joined using the ID as the primary key. Unless needed (e.g., such as with a promotional offer), customer names and address are not used with Harrah's applications.

Marketing Workbench

Marketing workbench (MWB) was created to serve as Harrah's data warehouse. It is sourced from the patron database. MWB stores daily detail data for 90 days, monthly information for 24 months, and yearly information back to 1994. Whereas PDB supports online lookup of customers, MWB is where analytics are performed. Marketing analysts can analyze hundreds of customer attributes to determine each customer's preferences and predict what future services and rewards they will want. For example, Harrah's might award hotel vouchers to out-of-state guests, while free show tickets would be more appropriate for customers who make day trips to the casino. A major use of MWB is to generate the lists (i.e., "list pulls" in Harrah's terminology) of customers to send offers to. These lists are the result of market segmentation analysis and customer scoring using MWB.

Operational Applications

The patron database supports a variety of operational applications. For example, a valued customer may be a first time visitor to a particular Harrah's property. When the customer checks in to the hotel, the service representative can look up their profile and make decisions about how to treat the customer, such as offering free event tickets or meals. Another example is a pit boss who notes that a valued customer has been gambling heavily for a long period of time relative to the customer's profile and gives the customer a coupon for a free show.

WINET OFFERS

WINet Offers is Harrah's in-house developed application for generating offers to Harrah's customers. To create an offer, a marketing analyst works with customer segments and profile data in MWB to create a list of IDs of customers who are in the targeted segment and fit the desired profile. These IDs are then fed into PDB, and then a program generates a customized mailing and offer for the customers. PDB also records whether the offers are accepted or not. The offers are also connected to hotel systems so that rooms can be reserved for customers who accept offers. Some campaigns are run on a scheduled basis while others are ad hoc. The offers can be generated at the corporate level to support the Harrah's brand or be created by an individual property (i.e., to support a mid-week slot machine tournament). There are more than 20 million customer offers annually, and Harrah's tracks each offer to determine when and how offers are redeemed and how marketing activities influence customer behavior at a detailed segment level.

Figure 3: Customer view of the total Gold™ program

TOTAL REWARDS

Total Rewards is Harrah's customer loyalty program. It tracks, retains, and rewards Harrah's millions of customers regardless of which casinos they visit over time. Total Rewards was originally introduced as Total Gold in 1997, but it was renamed in July 1999 when a three-tiered card program—Total Gold, Total Platinum, and Total Diamond—was introduced to give more recognition to Harrah's most active and profitable customers. Customers accumulate Reward Credits (points) based on their gaming and other activities at any of Harrah's properties. These Reward Credits can be redeemed for comps on hotel accommodations, meals, and shows, and cash can be redeemed at any property. At specified Reward Credit thresholds, customers move to the next card level (e.g., from gold to platinum) and qualify for the privileges associated with that level (e.g., preferred restaurant reservations and seating, priority check-in at hotels). Customers can check their Reward Credits at any time by entering their card into a slot machine or kiosk or by logging in to harrahs.com. Total Rewards members are also sent offers of cash and comps for use at local Harrah's casinos and destination resorts such as Las Vegas and Lake Tahoe. Figure 3 shows a customer's view of the Total Rewards program.

CLOSED-LOOP MARKETING

Like other casinos, Harrah's previously extended offers to customers based primarily on observed gaming worth. Over the years, intuition-based beliefs—called *Harrahisms*—developed for what did and did not work with their marketing

Figure 4: The closed-loop marketing process

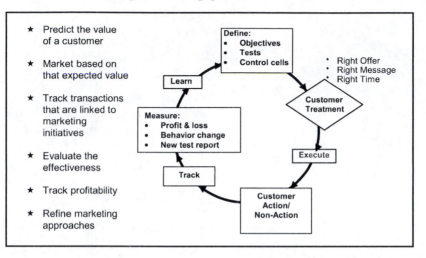

campaigns. *Harrahisms* were never tested. With WINet, the foundation was in place for a new, more scientific approach. Campaigns could be designed and tested, and the results retained for future use. This data-driven testing and learning approach is called "closed-loop marketing" and is shown in Figure 4. Its goal is to learn how to influence positive changes in customer behavior. Harrah's can learn what types of campaigns or treatments provide the highest net value.

Figure 5: Harrah's customer relationship lifecycle model

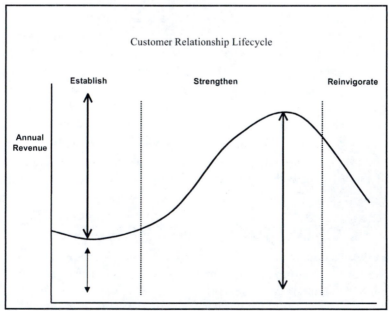

Closed-loop marketing begins with a definition of quantifiable marketing objectives, characteristics of the test procedure, and expected values of the customers selected for the test, who are divided into experimental and control groups. Based on what is already known about their gaming customers, the test campaign (customer treatment) is designed to provide the right offer and message at the right time. The selection of the customers and their treatments are based, in part, on Harrah's customer relationship lifecycle model, which is shown in Figure 5. Customers are offered customized incentives designed to establish, strengthen, or reinvigorate the relationship depending on their positions on the customer lifecycle and the time since their last visit. For example, a new customer might have characteristics that suggest that the customer has high lifetime potential value. Harrah's is likely to make an exceptionally generous offer to this customer in order to build a relationship. Or, an analysis of the customer data may reveal that a customer is "past due" to visit a Harrah's casino based on their previous gambling history. This kind of customer is also likely to receive a targeted message and offer in order to reinvigorate the relationship.

Each customer's response to the campaign is tracked and analyzed in detail. Not only are response rates measured, but other metrics as well, such as revenues generated by the incentive and whether the incentive induced a positive behavior change (e.g., increased frequency of visit, profitability of the visit, or cross-play). Based on the net value of the campaign and its profitability relative to other campaigns, Harrah's learns which incentives have the most effective influence on customer behavior or provide the best profitability improvement opportunities. This knowledge is used for continuous refinement of marketing approaches. Literally thousands of experiments of this kind have been conducted.

Figure 6: Technologies enabling closed-loop marketing

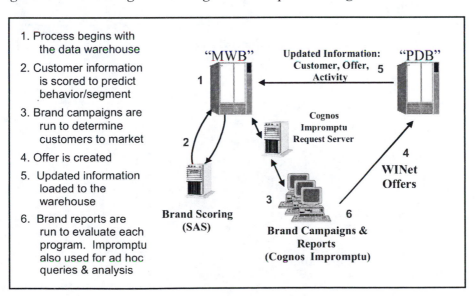

Several examples illustrate the use and value of closed-loop marketing. Two similar groups of frequent slot machine players from Jackson, MS, were identified for an experiment. Members of the first group were offered a marketing package of a free room, two steak dinners, and $30 in free chips at the Tunica casino. Members of the second group were offered $60 in chips. The second, more modest offer generated far more gambling, suggesting that Harrah's was wasting money offering Jackson customers free rooms and meals. Subsequent offers in this market focused on free chips, and profits nearly doubled to $60 per person per trip.

Another test focused on a group of monthly players who Harrah's thought could be induced to play more frequently because they lived nearby and displayed traits such as hitting slot machine buttons quickly (i.e., "high velocity" players). To entice them to return, Harrah's sent them free cash and food offers that expired in 2 weeks. The group's number of visits per month rose from 1.1 to 1.4.

The process and technologies that enable closed-loop marketing are shown in Figure 6.

THE IMPACT

Harrah's business strategy and the use of information technology are unique in the gaming industry and are more like the approaches taken in retail and financial services. Harrah's stock price has risen in response to a doubling of the company's earnings over the past year. The creation of the Harrah's brand, Total Rewards, and cross-marketing have resulted in a 72% internal rate of return on investments in information technology.

The effectiveness of Harrah's closed-loop marketing approach can be seen by how it has affected "same-store sales" (i.e., gambling revenues at a single existing

Figure 7: Increase in frequency of visits

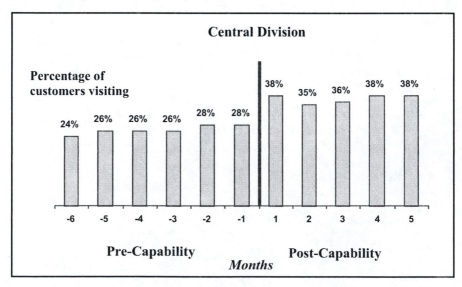

Figure 8: Impact of direct mail program on profitability in Tunica, MS

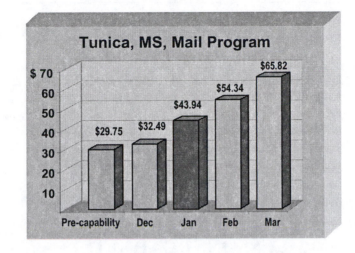

casino). In 1999, Harrah's experienced truly significant "same-store sales" revenue growth of 14%, which corresponds to an increase of $242 million over 1998. Harrah's grew revenues faster than their competition almost everywhere they do business—in some cases doubling and even tripling the market average of "same-store" sales.

Same-store sales growth is a manifestation of increased customer loyalty, which is driven by three key contributors to business value: (1) frequency of visits, (2) profitability per visit, and (3) cross-market play. Consider some specific examples of improvements in these areas.

Harrah's is successfully increasing trip frequency from a segment of customers who have historically visited its properties infrequently. Before the marketing campaign, customers visited Harrah's casinos in the central region of the country (i.e., the central division) 1.2 times per month. After customizing the offer and tailoring the message, Harrah's was receiving 1.9 trips per month from these same customers. And, more customers were visiting as represented by the percent of customers visiting; see Figure 7.

The effectiveness of Harrah's direct mail program has been significantly enhanced. This is illustrated by a campaign for Harrah's property in Tunica, where Harrah's more than doubled the profitability per customer visit; see Figure 8.

Figure 9 demonstrates Harrah's success at getting customers to play at more than one Harrah's casino. Over a two-year period, the percentage of total revenues generated from cross-market play went from 13% to more than 22%. At the Harrah's Las Vegas property, the contribution to revenues from cross-market play more than doubled, growing from $23 million in 1997 to $48 million in 1999. This increase came during a time when room supply nearly doubled in Las Vegas with the development of new luxury casinos (e.g., the Bellagio, Venetian, and Mandalay Bay) at a capital investment of over $3.5 billion.

Figure 9: Cross-market play (aggregate)

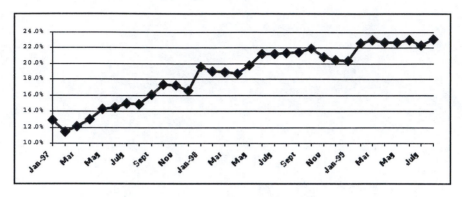

LESSONS LEARNED

The experiences at Harrah's provide several lessons that can benefit other companies embarking on a customer relationship management initiative.

- **Link the business and warehouse strategies.** Throughout its history, Harrah's has focused on building relationships with customers. The coming together of advances in information technology and the expansion of gaming markets gave Harrah's the opportunity to use data warehousing to implement a brand strategy. A business strategy supported by data warehousing has led to fundamental changes in how the company is run and a leadership position in the gaming industry.

- **Focus on business change management and link that to the success of the project.** Because Harrah's was moving from a property- to a brand-centric view of customers, there was a need for business change, not just technical changes. Strong senior executive support was key to the overall success. Also important were changes in incentive systems at the property level to reward cross-property play.

- **Have strong involvement from the business units.** Harrah's was fortunate that in the beginning of its data warehousing initiative that the same person was both the CIO and director of strategic marketing. This heavy involvement by the business units has continued throughout the project. They have taken on tasks such as planning for warehouse usage, helping develop training and certification programs for new users, and developing reports for the properties to use.

- **Have a scalable architecture.** While Harrah's initial architecture was satisfactory for the patron database, it proved to be inadequate for the marketing workbench. After considerable effort to work with what was already in place, Harrah's ultimately turned to NCR to provide an architecture that would provide satisfactory response times to users' queries. Companies often fail to create a data warehousing architecture that scales to meet future needs.

- **Include short-term milestones and prototyping.** Initially, Harrah's did not use short-term milestones and prototypes. This was a mistake and contributed to problems, such as with performance on users' queries. After this experience, future phases of the project included proofs of concepts, prototypes, and quicker deliverables.

- **Manage the consulting relationship.** Since Harrah's did not have data warehousing experience, it sought external assistance. Harrah's used NCR's Professional Services group to augment internal staff. Harrah's did not "outsource" the project, but rather, "co-sourced" it by identifying internal IT management responsible for the project and the relationship with NCR.

- **Plan for knowledge transfer and in-house expertise.** It is common for companies to hire consultants to help with their data warehousing projects. Most companies initially have little in-house data warehousing experience and consultants can move the organization more quickly up the learning curve. However, it is important to ultimately have internal data warehousing expertise. This can be achieved by hiring experienced data warehousing professionals and having a formal plan for knowledge transfer from the consultants to internal personnel. Harrah's used both of these approaches successfully. They also utilized considerable in-house training on data warehousing.

CONCLUSION

Harrah's has left little to chance. It has invested more than $100 million in computers and software to develop what is widely regarded as the industry's most sophisticated "frequent bettor" program. With the Total Rewards program, which contains the world's largest database of casino customers, they have been able to create sustainable loyalty, a dominant competitive advantage, and insulate the business from local market volatility.

Their innovative idea was to grow by getting more business from Harrah's existing customer base. This approach was in contrast to the prevalent strategy of building ever more elaborate and splashy new casinos. Gary W. Loveman refers to their success as "the triumph of software over hardware in gaming."

Harrah's has transformed how it does business. Decision making is based on analysis and information rather than intuition. Customers' behaviors, preferences, and profitability are better understood, resulting in enhanced customer service and company revenues and profits. These results have been noted by other gaming companies and they are trying to copy some of the more discernible methods.

The Total Rewards program has increased traffic in Harrah's casinos, and marketing programs driven by data from the warehouse are increasing retention.

Keeping customers goes right to the bottom line. An increase in retention of just 1% is worth $2 million in net profit annually. So far, Harrah's is enjoying an increase in retention of a couple of percentage points, thanks in large part to its data warehouse.

Closed-loop marketing is contributing to Harrah's competitive advantage. According to Tracy Austin, vice president of information technology development, by combining product information with customer behavior, "no one can touch us." Overall, the data warehouse is turning up nothing but aces for Harrah's. Harrah's "gamble" on technology is paying off.

ACKNOWLEDGMENTS

The authors would like to thank the many people at Harrah's who contributed their time for the interviews and especially Monica Tyson, who was our primary contact person and answered many of our follow-on questions.

SECTION III

ADVANCED IT
FOR
DMSS

Chapter XI

Innovative Features in a Distributed Decision Support System Based on Intelligent Agent Technology

Nicholas V. Findler
Arizona State University, USA

ABSTRACT

The author and his students were engaged in a multi-year project, SENTINEL, aimed at computerizing the strategic and tactical planning processes of the U.S. Coast Guard (USCG). In the course of this activity, we were also creating a decision support system for the human participants acting at the different levels of the USCG hierarchy. The chapter will describe the objectives, the problems and constraints of the task environment, as well as the solution to some problems that are fundamental and ubiquitous in many real-time, spatially and temporally distributed multi-agent systems.

The fundamental and overall task of a Decision Support System (DDS) implemented was to allocate moving resources to moving tasks in an optimum manner over space and time while considering numerous constraints. We have introduced three significant innovations necessary to accomplish our goals.

1.   Dynamic Scoping refers to a need-driven change in the size of the domain from which moving resources are called upon to accomplish moving tasks. The size of the domain has a limitation prescribed by the dynamic task environment, the technical capabilities of the resources, and the relationship between the expected gains and expenses.

2.   The second innovation concerns "resource scheduling under time constraints." We have introduced a method for the proper ordering of operating attributes and constraints in terms of a utility function.

$$PRIORITY = IMPORTANCE*URGENCY$$

Here, Importance is a measure of the relative static importance of an attribute in the decision making process. Urgency characterizes its gradually changing (usually increasing) relative importance over time. The constraints are arranged according to the priorities. More and more details are taken into account with each time-slice and more and more knowledge is used in the inference mechanism. A time-slice is the minimum time required for performing a unit of meaningful decision making. The ordering of constraints according to priorities guarantees that the result of planning is as good as time has permitted "so far."

3.   We have studied interagent communication and optimum message routing. Agents communicate at different levels—requesting and providing information, ordering/suggesting/accepting solutions to sub-problems, asking for and offering help, etc. The total knowledge about the environment and agent capabilities is too large to be stored by every agent, and the continual updating about the changes only aggravates the situation. The usual hierarchical organization structure for communication is inflexible, inefficient and error-prone. We have introduced the constrained lattice-like communication structure that permits direct interaction between functionally related agents at any level. The hierarchical and the lattice-like organizational structures may coexist: A transfer of temporary control over resources can be negotiated between the relevant agents directly while higher-level authorities will learn about the decisions, and can also modify or completely reject their implementation.

INTRODUCTION

The author and his coworkers have been engaged in a number of studies on distributed systems, such as algorithms for distributed air traffic control (Findler & Lo, 1986, 1993a, 1993b), distributed planning and control for manufacturing (Findler, 1989; Findler & Gao, 1987; Findler & Ge, 1989, 1994), task and resource allocation in dynamic distributed domains (Findler & Elder, 1994; Findler & Sengupta, 1993, 1994), adaptive distributed control of street traffic signals (Findler, 1993, 1999; Findler, Surender, & Catrava, 1997a, 1997b), emergent phenomena in multiagent societies (Findler & Malyankar, 1994, 1995; Malyankar & Findler, 1995), and automatic generation of an empirically based coordination theory for distributed intelligent agent societies (Findler & Malyankar, 2000; Malyankar & Findler, 1998; Malyankar, Findler, & Heck, 1998). A general overview of some characteristic properties of such systems is described in Findler (1990).

Many of the above projects also incorporated a decision support system. In this chapter, some features of a multiyear project, *SENTINEL*, are briefly described. It was designed to computerize the strategic and tactical planning processes of the US Coast Guard (USCG). In the course of this activity, we were also creating a distributed decision support system (DDSS) for the human participants acting at different levels of the USCG hierarchy. The chapter will describe the objectives, the peculiarities and the constraints of the task environment, as well as the solution to some problems that are fundamental and ubiquitous in many real-time, spatially and temporally distributed multiagent systems.

We introduce the concept of *dynamic scoping*, a protocol for *negotiation* in multiagent problem solving. When an agent fails to find a resource from its own pool, it initiates communication with its geographically nearest neighbors and requests assistance for the task at hand. If these first-level neighbors fail to locate the needed resources, they in turn communicate with their nearest neighbors. This expansion of *scope* continues until either a resource is found or else a preset limit on the expansion level (*envelope of effectiveness*) is reached. The resources are returned to their actual "owners" after the tasks at hand are accomplished.

This concept of *communication on demand* reduces interagent communication and the need for a substantial overhead in maintaining *coherency* between the agents' worlds. We also compare and contrast different message routing strategies among a set of agents in a hierarchical setup. Typically, many organizations require the message routing to conform to the pecking order in the hierarchy. There is often an obvious justification for such a setup (e.g., unambiguous assignment of responsibility). However, in some domains, a *constrained, lattice-like* strategy would allow concerned agents to bypass the hierarchy and interact directly without ignoring the required acts of control and information transmission.

Another aspect of the real world we address is the issue of resource scheduling and problem solving under the *constraints of time*. To facilitate this process, we use a utility function that is composed of two attributes, *importance* and *urgency,* to prioritize the operating attributes of the environment. These attributes are incrementally introduced into the decision making cycle, based upon their utility value. This permits the process of decision making to be terminated at any obligatory point, resulting in a solution whose quality is commensurate with the time spent.

THE SENTINEL SYSTEM

Let us consider a *task environment* with the following basic characteristics:

- There is a *hierarchy of decision making entities*—the higher the level of such an entity, the more global and abstract its knowledge is about the current state of the environment.
- Each of the decision making entities at the lowest level of the hierarchy (to be called "Stations") has a *set of resources* with given characteristics and an area of *basic jurisdiction* for task accomplishment.
- Scheduled and unscheduled *tasks* become known to the station in whose jurisdiction they occur. These tasks have to be accomplished with varying amounts and types of resources and within given, task-dependent time periods.
- The resources needed for a given task may not be available at a given Station

at the right time — they are either currently assigned to other tasks, are under repair or just are not owned in sufficient number by the Station in question. In such cases, resources assigned to lower priority tasks may have to be *reassigned* to higher priority ones or resources owned by other Stations must be *turned over* to the jurisdiction of the Station responsible for the task.

- Tasks are usually *nonstationary* and they may also move across the boundaries of Station jurisdiction. The resources assigned to such a task at a given time need not stay with the task but can be replaced by others whose location or other characteristics are better suited to the requirements.
- In turn, as tasks become accomplished, the resources assigned to them become available.
- The properties of the environment change: new Stations may be established; boundaries of Station jurisdiction may change; additional and/or new types of resources can be acquired; new types of tasks may occur; the "resource management style" of the decision making entities can be modified; and physical, legal, fiscal, organizational and other constraints are subject to change.

The following *objectives* must be considered in the environment described:

- The resources must be *allocated* in an optimum manner, over space and time, to scheduled (regular) and unscheduled (unexpected and emergency) tasks. This means that each task is completed by the most appropriate *resource-mix* (at a minimum overall cost) and within a satisfactory time period. Further, the load on the resources must be well-balanced, human resources are not to be overutilized, and repair requirements must also be satisfied.
- Relevant *past events* (tasks, plans, solutions, performance results) are recorded and made use of for a *learning program* aimed at improving performance as more experience is obtained.

Figure 1: The command hierarchy in the US Coast Guard

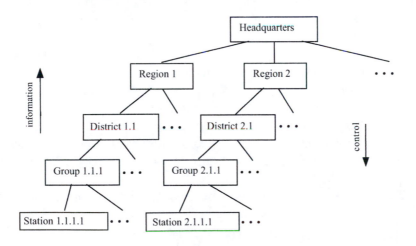

- Available resources are distributed among the Stations based on prior *task distributions*.

- The *acquisition of new resources* is done in an optimum manner. In other words, the best resource-mix has to be purchased either within a given budget or for a given set of predicted task-mix scenarios.

- The *problem-solving environment* assumes a close man-machine interaction and provides for the user high-level input and monitoring facilities.

- All *system recommendations* for action must be self-explicatory and are accompanied by a quantitative and qualitative analysis of the trade-off between cost and accomplishment.

- The human operator can *accept* any system recommendation or *override* all with a "manual" solution.

- The system must be able to *support both day-to-day and longer-term operations* (e.g., maintenance of resources, accomplishment of scheduled tasks and responding to emergency tasks versus locating Stations strategically, acquiring new resources and allocating them to individual Stations).

- In case of a partial failure with some communication or computation units, the system must not crash but undergo a *graceful degradation*; that is, it must still provide satisfactory solutions but possibly of lower quality and at a slower pace.

- It should be easy to *expand the environment* and to provide support for new Stations, resources, conditions and constraints.

Let us now characterize in a schematic manner the *command hierarchy* of the USCG. Figure 1 shows the flow of control and information in it. *Stations* (established along the coastline) are at the bottom level. A set of resources and an area of jurisdiction are associated with each Station. Several adjoining Stations operate under a group whereas districts, regions and the USCG headquarters are gradually higher up in the hierarchy. The major tasks at the *Station level* are:

- Aids to navigation — ranging from navigational charts to lighted buoys.

- Search and rescue — helping individuals and vessels in distress.

- Enforcement of laws and treaties — making sure that the citizens of the United States and other countries abide by rules and regulations as prescribed by the laws of the country and international agreements.

The Station activities can be either scheduled (e.g., buoy tending, harbor patrolling) or unscheduled (e.g., search and rescue, interception, urgent repair).

At the *Group level and higher*, the following activities are performed:

- The existing resources have to be assigned to individual Stations based on historical records and anticipated future needs.

- Complex and resource-intensive tasks, requiring high-level coordination between several Stations and possibly also political decisions, have to be managed in a timely fashion.

- Relevant historical data have to be collected and evaluated for long-term planning, report generation and internal management.

- The messages between different decision making entities have to be recorded and managed (concerning destination, pathway selection, level of secrecy, level of detail, level of urgency, etc.).
- A proper information base has to be maintained about navigational details, current resources and manpower, organizational units, task types, expected scenarios, legal procedures, and the like.

A partial list of the activities performed at the *Headquarters level* contains the following:

- To represent the interests, needs and concerns of the Coast Guard toward the Administration and the Congress.
- To request and justify budget allocations.
- To manage the vehicle acquisition problem — that is, to spend the budget of the CG in the most cost-effective manner.
- To manage individual CG programs, such as aids to navigation, search and rescue, enforcement of laws and treaties, etc.

The fundamental and overall task of a decision support system (DSS) is to allocate moving resources to moving tasks in an optimum manner over space and time while considering numerous constraints. We describe three significant innovations that were necessary to accomplish our goals.

Dynamic Scoping

The concept of dynamic scoping is a mechanism for interagent negotiation in the course of resource sharing. Figure 2 shows a hypothetical coastline along which there are several Stations. When an agent does not have the resources of the appropriate type and in sufficient number to service the task within the desired time period, it contacts adjacent nodes and gives them the specification of the task at hand. (*Adjacency* in our domain refers to neighbor locations along the one-dimensional

Figure 2: The idea of dynamic scoping

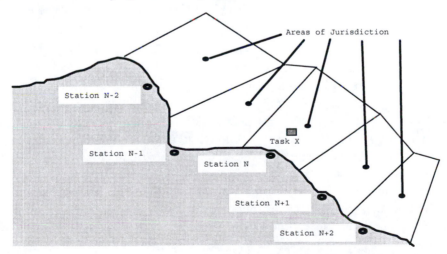

coastline. In other domains, two- or three-dimensional adjacency must be considered — for example, in ground-based air defense and in air-to-air combat, respectively.) Several possible scenarios may then arise: (i) An adjacent node has all or some of the needed resources available for the new task. It transfers the control of these to the requesting node on a temporary basis. (ii) The node has the resources but they are engaged in tasks that have a lower priority than the task at hand. These resources are preempted, again on a temporary basis, and loaned to the requesting node. (iii) The adjacent nodes jointly cannot provide all the needed resources. They must then communicate with *their* adjacent nodes, farther away from the first node with the original task, and ask for their help. This process goes on until enough resources are reassigned to the requesting agent. In turn, as tasks become accomplished, resources from other nodes return to their original "owner"—hence the name *dynamic scoping*.

We define the *level of expansion* to refer to the number of nodes involved in the resource assignment process. Level-1 means that a node asks and may get resources from the directly adjacent nodes "on loan," whereas Level-2 means that additional, once-removed nodes' resources are also involved in a multiphase dynamic scoping process. This process goes on iteratively until either all needed resources have been acquired or a so-called *envelope of effectiveness* has been reached. The latter is defined by the fact that the time and expense necessary for reaching from the task can no longer be justified by the benefit obtained from the accomplished objective—in other words, when the trade-off between the overall cost and the expected success of the operation is no longer favorable. It should also be noted that the concept of Dynamic Scoping is valid and useful also in higher dimensions.

One can say that a central control mechanism may have an advantage over a distributed regime in that its resource utilization is more efficient as it can assign its resources in a more balanced manner. It often suffers, however, from a lack of robustness, high vulnerability, sluggish responsiveness, inadequate computational power, obsolete knowledge base and unsatisfactory compromises. We have shown that Dynamic Scoping extends the efficiency of centrally controlled systems to the distributed ones without adversely affecting the superior qualities of the latter.

Interagent Communication and Optimum Message Routing

Agents have to communicate with one another at different levels — requesting and providing information, asking for and offering help, ordering/suggesting/accepting solution methods to subproblems, etc. Although it is true in general that computation is cheaper, less error-prone and faster then communication, agents cannot function in a cooperative mode without some basic communication going on. Further, the *total knowledge* available about the environment and the individual agents' capabilities is too large to be stored by every agent, and the necessary continual updating of such information about the changes only aggravates the situation. A potentially satisfactory but very difficult solution is to assign some well-defined, general and basic "knowledge package" to every agent, which is to be augmented by some node-specific information needed for its operation. Only empirical ad hoc solutions to this problem have been found for given domains with given characteristics, which of course is neither an effective nor an aesthetically pleasing situation.

Although a hierarchical organizational structure of the participating agents, as in Figure 1, is appropriate and can supply up-to-date information and control on a need-to-know basis, information (for example, sensory input about changes in the environment) usually flows from the lower-level agents upward to the higher-level ones, whereas control instructions (to perform certain planned actions) percolate downwards. At each level, this flow goes through nodes, which usually modify the contents of the messages. The reason is twofold: Higher level agents need more abstract and summarized information for their decision making activity, while increasingly detailed commands are given in the downward direction as to how a particular objective is to be achieved. However, the inflexible and lengthy pathways render the communication processes less than efficient and error-prone. Further, the limited bandwidth and possible breakdowns of the communication channels represent a high risk to the *whole operation* of any organization operating under such conditions. (Note that, for example, siblings, cousins, niece-uncle pairs and more remote relatives cannot talk to each other directly in a strict hierarchical organization — messages must travel up and down on the tree to reach their destination.)

We have introduced the notion of *constrained lattice-like communication structure* that permits direct interaction between functionally related agents at any level and enhances cooperative problem solving, plan generation and execution. The "constraints" refer to domain- and application-specific requirements that the routing strategy must abide by. For example, the transfer of control over certain resources by Dynamic Scoping may require the knowledge and even the approval by a higher-level entity. With our approach, the two routing strategies, the hierarchical and the lattice-like structures, coexist—messages are sent along the two patterns quasi simultaneously, and a higher authority can accept, modify or even override a decision when necessary (assuming appropriate timescale of the relevant domain events).

Resource Scheduling Under Time Constraints

The third innovative component of the SENTINEL system concerns *resource scheduling under time constraints*. Computation in the world of limited resources is often associated with cost/benefit trade-offs. A trade-off is defined as a relationship between two attributes of utility (for example, the immediacy and the precision of a computational result), each having a positive influence on the perceived total value of computer performance while adversely affecting the level attainable by the other (Horvitz, 1989). Based on such a need, we introduce a measure that allows the proper ordering of operating attributes and constraints used in decision making. We define a utility function

$$PRIORITY = IMPORTANCE * URGENCY$$

where IMPORTANCE is a measure that describes the relative *static* importance at a given knowledge level of an attribute in the decision making process. URGENCY characterizes its gradually *changing* (usually increasing) relative importance on the timescale. Decisions made solely on only one of the above factors would skew the scale of objectives in decision making. The constraints are arranged according to the hierarchy of priorities so that more and more details are taken into account with each *time-slice* and, correspondingly, more and more knowledge is used in the inference mechanism. A time-slice is the minimum time required for performing a single unit of *meaningful* decision making (for example, a single inference cycle). The ordering of constraints based on their priority also guarantees that the result of the planning process is as good as time has permitted "so far." We note another category of time-constrained tasks, called *deadline jobs*. Each task in it must be accomplished by a given time point, the deadline, according to which tasks are ranked in linear order.

The Need for a Distributed Decision Support System

The problem-solving task at hand is characteristic of those whose size and certain other characteristics do not allow them to be processed effectively and efficiently by a single computer system and the decisions are the joint product of humans and computers. Such tasks are characterized by one or several of the following properties:

* Spatially distributed input/output (or sensor/effector) operations.
* A need for extensive communication over long distances.
* Time-stressed demands for solution.
* A large degree of functional specialization between quasi-simultaneous processes.
* A need for reliable computation under uncertainty—that is, in relying on incomplete and inconsistent data and knowledge.
* A need for graceful degradation—the results are acceptable (although possibly of lower quality and obtained more slowly) even when some of the computational and communicational facilities have become disabled.
* A limited amount of shared resources must work on common objectives, without (outside) competition and conflict of interests.

Advances in computer and communication technology have made studies in *distributed artificial intelligence* (DAI) possible. This domain can be divided into two classes: (i) *distributed planning and problem solving system* (DPPSS) assumes that the participating agents have identical goal structures, do not compete with one another and interact with the others to accomplish the overall common goal. (ii) In *multi-agent systems*, on the other hand, the agents may have conflicting goals and are not fully or at all cooperative with one another but can form temporary alliances if it is in their interest.

It should be parenthetically noted that the above areas of activity are to be distinguished from *distributed processing* (DP), characterized by the following:

* Several dissimilar tasks are being solved simultaneously by a network of processors.

- The management of common access by the individual processors to a set of resources is the main reason for the interaction between processors.
- Resource distribution and conflicts between tasks may or may not be hidden from the user.
- From the user's point of view, each task is performed by a system dedicated to that task only.

One can conclude that our work on DDSS within the SENTINEL project had to combine the characteristics of both DP and DPPSS. It was necessary to establish a reliable, realistic and rich simulated environment in which human and machine decision makers can collaborate to accomplish the goals of day-to-day operation as well as to perform tactical and strategic planning processes.

Application Domain Description

Some C3 operations of the Coast Guard (USCG) provide an ideal environment to test the SENTINEL system. The two main responsibilities of the USCG are to perform search and rescue (SAR) and the enforcement of laws and treaties (ELT) missions. The USCG divides its maritime jurisdiction into a hierarchically organized set of subdivisions called areas, districts and groups and stations, as shown in Figure 1, which also follow the allocation of responsibilities. SAR and ELT cases represent unscheduled tasks of medium-to-high priority and require *reactive* resource scheduling. The role of a decision maker at a C3 center is to determine how to allocate the resources under its jurisdiction so that all tasks are attended to as soon as possible and in the order of their merit. (Here we have used the generic term *merit* to reference importance, urgency, deadlines, practicality, etc.) There are various constraints to be satisfied due to scheduled and unscheduled vehicle maintenance, crew endurance, different degrees of resource and fuel availability, weather and sea conditions, vehicle capabilities, etc. All this leads to an information overload for human decision making in a time-stressed environment.

ELT tasks become known when a vessel is observed that either behaves "suspiciously" or is on a *lookout list* (generated by intelligence reports). ELT cases include drug and migrant traffic and violators of fishing and other maritime treaties. SAR cases are generated by incoming distress signals and/or reports of overdue vessels. The types of USCG resources are boats of various types and sizes and aircraft (fixed-wing and helicopters). Normally, most of the resources are engaged in patrolling both coastal waters and high seas. A *plan* consists of a resource or resource-mix selection and an ordered set of actions or mission steps (e.g., interdicting, boarding, searching, etc.) to be carried out at designated locations. After the selected resource reaches the interdiction point, it performs an on-site appraisal (this may involve boarding and examining the cargo with ELT cases, and checking the need for medical or other help with SAR cases). Some cases require airlifting, towing or escorting to the nearest USCG facilities — actions collectively referred to as the *hand-off phase*. SENTINEL performs reactive planning by selecting the primary resources for interception and the secondary resources to complete the task of hand-off (escorting, towing, etc.)

Overview of the SENTINEL Architecture

The SENTINEL system is comprised of two major components: the scenario generator and the planning agents, as shown in Figure 3. The scenario generator module is comprised of three submodules: the simulation model, the task analyzer and distributor and the scenario generator message handler. The simulation module reproduces the task environment and handles details of resource movement and performance, task generation and movement, and dynamic weather conditions (sea states and visibility). The task analyzer and distributor accepts a scenario from the simulation module and performs an initial evaluation to select a suitable site for resource planning. The task and site selected are transmitted to a planning agent by the scenario generator message handler. The planning agents model the activities of a node within the distributed domain. The planning agents are distributed geographically and functionally in the model to match the organizational structure of a real-life environment. Each planning agent contains three modules: the planning agent message handler, the plan generator, and the communication and coordination module. The planning agent message handler deals with the routing of all messages, both incoming and outgoing. The plan generator is a rule-based planner that models the role of a decision maker at a site, operating under the constraints of time. The communication and coordination module is invoked for the temporary acquisition of resources from neighboring sites.

Modeling the Environment

The simulation model is a discrete-event simulator that models the task environment and the operational procedures of the USCG. It is an integral part of the scenario generator subsystem and interacts with the planning agent module to provide it with the environment in which the USCG resources carry out their tasks. The simulation model handles the following facets of the task environment:

- Traffic generation and movement—Traffic includes legal as well as illegal sea-borne or airborne traffic in the region. The vessel characteristics include size, type, suspicion level (if any), violation type (if any), flag, destination, location, and speed.
- Resources, their activities and movement—The USCG resources belong to seagoing and airborne vessel categories. Some of the attributes used in modeling resources are type, operational capabilities (such as speed and endurance), and patrol routes. Dynamically changing attributes of the vessels (such as current mission, location, speed, route, fuel level and crew mission times) are also tracked. The ELT task components include patrolling, spotting, intercepting, boarding, searching, and towing.
- Sea and visibility state changes—Weather needs to be modeled as it affects wave height and visibility. Wave height influences boat speed, while visibility

Figure 3: A high-level view of the SENTINEL system modules

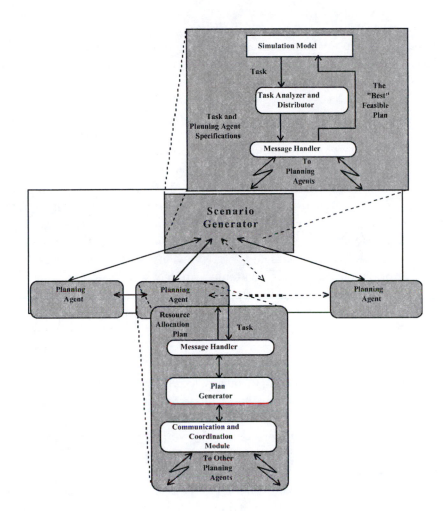

has an effect on airborne vessels and on the handling of SAR tasks. These phenomena are modeled through Markov processes (Sengupta, Bozsahin, Klesczewski, Findler, & Smith, 1990).

- Accounting for unavailable resources – Scheduled maintenance operations on boats and aircraft as well as SAR cases may take resources away from the ELT.

The primary function of the task analyzer and distributor is to evaluate an incident reported by the simulation model and to select a suitable site for appropriate action. The task and the associated world information concerning a particular site are converted to a message. The scenario generator message handler then transmits this message directly to the site selected by the task analyzer and distributor. The scenario generator message handler then waits for a response containing details of resource plans, interdiction paths, etc.

The simulation model provides the environment in which the resource plans are executed. Once a decision is made (e.g., concerning an interdiction) on the planning agent side, the simulation model simulates and monitors the execution of the mission with the assigned resources and designated targets. It also collects and prints statistics (interdiction rate, time spent in missions, etc.). Global and detailed individual statistics (e.g., by each vessel) are generated periodically during a simulation model run.

The planning agent message handler receives tasks' specifications as a message from the scenario generator or other planning agents. Information is maintained at each node about the planning agent hierarchy. This includes the planning agents' command levels (e.g., group, district, area), the names of the hardware nodes on which they reside, designated communication channels and the types of resources available. From the incoming message, details of the suspect (e.g., its profile and current activities), current location and activities of the USCG vessels, and weather conditions are extracted. The knowledge-based plan generator analyzes the information and selects a suitable resource. The responses generated by the planning agent are composed into appropriate messages and transmitted back to the scenario generator (or the requesting planning agents).

The plan generator uses a three-phase planning process for resource selection. First, the requirement phase is used to select the resource types needed. In the second phase, resource types are mapped onto resource instances. However, due to a potentially large set of resource instances, a series of heuristics are used to filter out less likely cases. Finally, in the refinement phase, each of the resource instances filtered from the preceding stage undergo an in-depth quantitative evaluation. These measurements include the exact distance of a given USCG resource from the task (invoking the path finder process) and the current status of USCG resources, fuel levels and crew endurance.

The communication and coordination module is invoked to model interagent communication. When the site selected for resource planning fails to find a suitable resource plan, it attempts to "borrow" a resource from a neighboring site, based on dynamic scoping. The flexible experimental environment permits the choice of various interagent communication protocols. In particular, two schemes have been evaluated: One protocol adheres strictly to the hierarchical chain of command while the other uses a more flexible discipline, the constrained lattice-like routing strategy.

Dynamic scoping is performed at the group level of the planning agents. A group, being unable to generate a resource plan for lack of sufficient resources, would communicate with its two nearest neighbors to acquire the needed resources from them on "loan."

In closing, a final test of the SENTINEL system has been its use as a distributed decision support system in an operational environment. In such an arrangement, the simulation model is replaced by the events of the real world, and real-time inputs are provided automatically as well as by humans.

RELATED WORK

The task of the Phoenix system is to simulate the control of forest fires by deploying bulldozers, crews, airplanes and other objects (Cohen, Greenberg, Hart, & Howe, 1989). In response to a situation, such as a new fire, an appropriate plan skeleton is retrieved from the plan library and placed in the *time line* (a temporal blackboard). *State memory* stores information, such as weather, resource conditions and sensory input, that helps the cognitive agent select appropriate plans and instantiate the variables of the chosen plan for the current situation. At any time during plan execution, sensory data can trigger reflexive actions. The reaction happens very fast relative to the cycle time of the cognitive component.

In a sense, dynamic scoping appears similar to CNet in regards to negotiation for resources from neighboring nodes (Davis & Smith, 1983). However, dynamic scoping does not use a "free-for-all" bidding process; requests are based on geographical proximity, and the requesting node resolves any conflicts and over-commitment of resources. Multistage negotiations (Conry, Meyer, & Lesser, 1986; Lesser & Corkill, 1981) have extended the basic CNet protocol by incorporating an exchange of agents' inferences iteratively to evaluate the impact of the agents' local plans on the global plan. Durfee and Montgomery (1990) provide a hierarchical protocol for interagent negotiation. For the chosen problem domain, the authors provide a mechanism for a hierarchy of agents to plan actions incrementally with the highest ranked agent planning first. Subordinate agents defer to their superior's plans and make local adjustments. Endless loops of refinement are not expected due to the nature of this hierarchy. In contrast to SENTINEL, negotiation and detailed action plans are produced up front. In Multi-Fireboss Phoenix (Moehlman & Lesser, 1990), a three-phase negotiation is used by the fireboss in acquiring resources from other neighboring firebosses. Temporal conflicts on resource usage are resolved by delaying the handling of lower priority tasks. This strategy is similar to the one used by SENTINEL where higher priority tasks can preempt resources from lower ones.

We note that a central control mechanism has, in principle, the advantage over a distributed regime in that its resource utilization is more efficient as it can assign its resources in a more balanced manner (King, 1983). One drawback of this conservative scheme is that the decision making process becomes relatively more time-consuming, especially in emergency cases. A complete relaxation of this strict organizational structure may be counterproductive as the agents' behavior would be difficult to predict. The agents' goals could become unfocused, the communication overheads may become too high, and destructive interference could degrade system response times. We feel that the facility of dynamic scoping and constrained lattice-like message routing strategies extends the efficiency of centrally controlled systems to distributed ones without adversely affecting the superior qualities of the latter.

Dean and Wellman (1991) have provided the conceptual framework for a class of reactive systems. These systems use algorithms that are characterized by linear improvement of solution quality with time. In other words, such algorithms can be suspended, the current answers checked "anytime," and the procedure continued (or resumed) from where it was interrupted. In SENTINEL, we have taken this concept and prioritized the attributes of the operating environment in the order of their utility. We have then used this in a system with an "anytime" termination feature (instead of the suspend/resume feature). We have also provided empirical results of all these implementations. The model of time-critical planning suggested here is adequate for unscheduled tasks of low-to-medium priority. However, for high priority tasks (such as a computer-controlled intensive care unit in a hospital), specialized plans need to be pre-compiled and stored in the system for fast retrieval and utilization.

Some reactive planning systems use strategies that guarantee the search process used for planning is *swapped* out so that other processes are given a chance to react to real-time inputs (Kaebling, 1986). Other systems use the strategy of delaying commitment to a particular plan till the very end or revise an initial plan reactively during execution (Ambros–Ingerson & Steel, 1988; Georgeff & Lansky, 1987). SENTINEL uses some domain-specific plan revision techniques for certain instances of plan failure during execution. Sycara, Roth, Sadeh, and Fox (1990) present the case for a multiagent resource allocation system for time-constrained applications, such as job-shop scheduling. The authors suggest a hetararchical arrangement of the agents with the use of sophisticated local control for achieving overall system goals.

It seems appropriate to list here some basic references about distributed artificial intelligence and multiagent systems. A relevant sample of the vast literature is Avouris and Gasser (1992), Bond and Gasser (1988), Cohen (1995), Forrest (1991), Gasser and Huhns (1989), Huhns (1987), Martial von (1992), O'Hare and Jennings (1996), Rosenschein and Zlotkin (1994), Schwartz (1995), Smith (1981), Weiss (1999), Werner and Demazeau (1992), and Wooldridge and Jennings (1995).

CONCLUSIONS

Dynamic scoping has been shown to be an effective negotiation mechanism for interagent cooperation and to lead to increased resource utilization in terms of higher "suspect interdictions" (a Coast Guard terminology). The simulation results also confirmed that the number of interdictions went up when dynamic scoping was extended from Level-1 to Level-2 expansion. (Level-1 means that a node asks and may get resources from the directly adjacent nodes "on loan," whereas Level-2 means that additional, once-removed nodes' resources are also involved in a multi-phase dynamic scoping process.). Similarly, the lattice-like message routing strategy fared better than the strictly hierarchical arrangement. The results from the studies of time-critical planning indicate the effectiveness of the prioritized rule base and the controlled inference mechanism.

The implementation of the time-critical planning mechanism was not com-pletely satisfactory in the SENTINEL system at first. The simulation model and the planning agents operate in lockstep fashion—the simulation model momentarily stops for the Planning Agent to provide a resource and then resumes its operation. This implies that the time taken for the actual planning process is ignored. In real life, the world does not stop during the planning process (even if it is only of a very short duration). We were able to fix this problem by slowing the simulation clock to the real-time clock during the planning/scheduling phase. Similarly, the communications between the simulation model and the planning agents and between the planning agents is now asynchronous. Such a setup is ideal in modeling the *preemption* of an ongoing planning process. Furthermore, the planning agents were made to take into account the changes in the environment during the planning phases and the time taken for planning.

The concept of the *envelope of effectiveness* can be investigated further. When resources are acquired for interdiction purposes from a distant site (as the result of dynamic scoping), the suspect is usually out of the radar spotting range of the resource. Consequently, the Coast Guard resource is unable to continue the interdiction process when the suspect uses evasive tactics. Therefore, the farther we obtain the resource from, the higher the likelihood of the case being abandoned is. This phenomenon needs to be investigated and analyzed both quantitatively and qualitatively. Similarly, the trade-offs of dynamic scoping need to be evaluated further. A quantitative analysis of costs and global success rates would help in deciding whether to preempt a local resource or to preempt a resource from a neighboring site.

In closing, the final test of a somewhat modified version of SENTINEL was its use as a distributed decision-support system in an operational environment. In such an arrangement, the simulation model was replaced by the events of the real world, and real-time inputs were provided automatically as well as by humans.

ACKNOWLEDGMENTS

This research has been supported in part by the US Coast Guard, Contract Nos. DTCG-88-C-80630 and DTCG-39-90-C-E9222, and by Digital Equipment Corporation, External Research Grant Nos. 158 and 774. We are indebted to CACI Products Company for providing SIMSCRIPT II.5. I would like to thank all the members in the Artificial Intelligence Laboratory, particularly Cem Bozsahin, Raphael Malyankar, Qing Ge, and Glen Reece for their help and support. Ken Klesczewski (USCG R & D Center) was instrumental in developing the first version of the simulation model and provided data for the later versions.

REFERENCES

Ambros-Ingerson, J. A., & Steel, S. (1988). Integrating planning, execution and monitoring. In *Proceedings of the National Conference on Artificial Intelligence* (pp. 83-88).

Avouris, N., & Gasser, L. (Eds.). (1992). *Distributed artificial intelligence: Theory and praxis*. Boston: Kluwer Academic.

Bond, A. H., & Gasser, L. (1988). *Readings in distributed artificial intelligence.* San Francisco: Morgan Kaufmann.

Cohen, P. (1995). *Empirical methods for artificial intelligence.* Cambridge, MA: MIT Press.

Cohen, P. R., Greenberg, M. L., Hart, D. M., & Howe, A. (1989). A trial by fire: Understanding the design requirements for agents in complex environments. *AI Magazine,* 32–48.

Conry, S. E., Meyer, R. A., & Lesser, V. R. (1986). Multistage negotiation in distributed computing. *Coins Tech. Rep.,* 86-67.

Davis, R., & Smith, R. G. (1983). Negotiation as a metaphor for distributed problem solving. *Artificial Intelligence, 20*(1), 63-109.

Dean, T., & Wellman, M. P. (1991). *Planning and control.* San Mateo, CA: Morgan Kaufmann.

Durfee, E., & Montgomery, T. A. (1990). A hierarchical protocol for coordinating multiagent behaviors. In *Proceedings of the 1990 National Conference on Artificial Intelligence* (pp. 86-93).

Ferber, J. (1999). *Multi-agent systems.* New York: Addison-Wesley.

Findler, N. V. (1989). Distributed knowledge-based systems in manufacturing. In G. Rzevski (Ed.). *Artificial Intelligence in Manufacturing* (pp. 17-33), New York: Springer-Verlag.

Findler, N. V. (1990). *Computer-based theory of strategies.* Berlin, Heidelberg, and New York: Springer-Verlag.

Findler, N. V. (1993). A knowledge-based approach to urban traffic control. In *Proceedings of the Conference on Applications of Artificial Intelligence in Engineering,* (Vol. 2, pp. 235-248) Toulouse.

Findler, N. V. (1999). Harmonization for omnidirectional progression in urban traffic control. *Computer-Aided Civil and Infrastructure Engineering,* 14, 369-377.

Findler, N. V., & Elder, G. D. (1994). Multi-agent coordination and cooperation in a dynamic environment with limited resources. *Artificial Intelligence in Engineering,* 9, 229-238.

Findler, N. V., & Gao, J. (1987). Dynamic hierarchical control for distributed problem solving. *Data and Knowledge Engineering,* 2, 285-301.

Findler, N. V., & Ge, Q. (1989). Perceiving and planning before acting—An approach to enhance global network coherence. *International Journal of Intelligent Systems,* 4, 459-470.

Findler, N. V., & Ge, Q. (1994). Distributed goal-directed dynamic plan revision. *International Journal of Intelligent Systems,* 9, 183-210.

Findler, N. V., & Lo, R. (1986). An examination of distributed planning in the world of air traffic control. *Journal of Parallel and Distributed Processing,* 3, 411-431.

Findler, N. V., & Lo, R. (1993a). Empirical studies on distributed planning for air traffic control. Part I: A dynamic hierarchical structure for concurrent distributed control and the location-centered cooperative planning system. *Journal of Transportation Engineering*, 119, 681-692.

Findler, N. V., & Lo, R. (1993b). Empirical studies on distributed planning for air traffic control. Part II: Experimental results. *Journal of Transportation Engineering*, 119, 693-704.

Findler, N. V., & Malyankar, R. M. (1994). Procedure-oriented studies of collective phenomena in multi-agent systems. In *Proceedings of the 1994 IEEE Conference on Systems, Man, and Cybernetics* (pp. 97-102), San Antonio, TX.

Findler, N. V., & Malyankar, R. M. (1995). Emergent behavior in societies of heterogeneous, interacting agents: Alliances and norms. In R. Conte and N. Gilbert (Eds.). *Artificial societies: The computer simulation of social life* (pp. 212-237), London: University College Press.

Findler, N. V., & Malyankar, R. M. (2000). Social structures and the problem of coordination in intelligent agent societies. CD on the Special Session on Agent-Based Simulation, Planning and Control. IMACS World Congress 2000, Lausanne, Switzerland.

Findler, N. V., & Sengupta, U. K. (1993). On some innovative concepts in distributed systems for planning and collaboration. In *Proceedings of the Operational Research Society*, 35th Annual Conference (pp. 79-93), United Kingdom: University of York.

Findler, N. V., & Sengupta, U. K. (1994). Multi-agent collaboration in time-constrained domains. *Artificial Intelligence in Engineering*, 9, 39-52.

Findler, N. V., Surender, S., & Catrava, S. (1997a). A note concerning on-line decisions about permitted/protected left-turn phases. *Engineering Applications of Artificial Intelligence*, 10, 315-320.

Findler, N. V., Surender, S., Ma, Z., & Catrava, S. (1997b). A distributed knowledge-based system for reactive and predictive control of street traffic signals: A macroscopic model in the steady-state domain. *Engineering Applications of Artificial Intelligence*, 10, 281-292.

Forrest, S. (Ed.). (1991). *Emergent computation*. Cambridge, MA: MIT Press.

Gasser, L., & Huhns, M. N. (Eds.). (1989). *Distributed artificial intelligence, Vol. II*. Los Altos, CA: Morgan Kaufmann.

Georgeff, M. P., & Lansky, A. L. (1987). Reactive Reasoning and Planning. In *Proceedings of the National Conference on Artificial Intelligence*, (pp. 677–682).

Horvitz, E. J. (1989). Reasoning about Beliefs and Actions under Computational Resource Constraints. In L. N. Kanal, T. S. Levitt, and J. F. Lemmer (Eds.). *Uncertainty in Artificial Intelligence* (pp. 301-324), Amsterdam: Elsevier Science (North–Holland).

Huhns, M. N. (Ed.). (1987). *Distributed artificial intelligence*. Los Altos, CA: Morgan Kaufmann.

Kaebling, L. P. (1986). An architecture for intelligent reactive systems. In *Proceed-*

ings of the National Conference on Artificial Intelligence.

King, J. L. (1983). Centralized versus decentralized computing: Organizational considerations and management options. *ACM Computing Surveys*, *15*(4), 319-349.

Lesser, V. R., & Corkill, D. D. (1981). Functionally accurate, cooperative distributed systems. *IEEE Trans. on System Man and Cybernetics*, *SMC*, *11*(1), 81-96.

Malyankar, R. M., & Findler, N. V. (1995). Agent modelling in distributed intelligent systems. *Systems Analysis-Modelling-Simulation*, 22, 53-74.

Malyankar, R. M., & Findler, N. V. (1998). A methodology for modeling coordination in intelligent agent societies. *Computational and Mathematical Organization Theory,* 4, 317-345.

Malyankar, R. M., Findler, N. V., & Heck, P. S. (1998). The effects of satisficing models on coordination. In Satisficing Models: Papers from the 1998 AAAI Spring Symposium, TR SS-98-05, pp. 39-45, Palo Alto, CA: AAAI Press; 1998.

Martial von F. (1992). Coordinating plans of autonomous agents. Berlin: Springer-Verlag; 1992.

Moehlman T., and Lesser, V. (1990). Cooperative planning and decentralized negotiation in multi-fireboss. Phoenix, DARPA Workshop on Innovative Approaches to Planning, Scheduling and Control, 144-159.

O'Hare G., & Jennings, N. (1996). *Foundations of distributed artificial intelligence.* New York: Wiley.

Rosenschein, J. S., & Zlotkin, G. (1994). *Rules of encounter.* Cambridge, MA: MIT Press.

Schwartz, D. G. (1995). *Cooperating heterogeneous systems.* Boston: Kluwer Academic.

Sengupta, U. K., Bozsahin, H. C., Klesczewski, K., Findler, N. V., & Smith, J. (1990). PGMULES: An approach to supplementing simulation models with knowledge–based planning systems. Workshop on Simulation and Artificial Intelligence, National Conference on Artificial Intelligence, Boston, MA.

Smith, R. G. (1981). A framework for distributed problem solving. Ann Arbor, MI: UMI Research Press.

Sycara, K., Roth, S., Sadeh, N., & Fox, M. (1990). Managing resource allocation in multi-agent time-constrained domains. DARPA Workshop on Innovative Approaches to Planning, Scheduling and Control, 240-250.

Weiss, G. (Ed.). (1999). *Multiagent systems.* Cambridge, MA: MIT Press.

Werner, E., & Demazeau, Y. (Eds.). (1992). *Decentralized artificial intelligence.* Amsterdam: Elsevier (North-Holland).

Wooldridge, M. J., & Jennings, N. R. (1995). *Intelligent agents.* Berlin: Springer-Verlag.

Chapter XII

Knowledge Warehouse: An Intelligent Analysis Platform for Enhancing Management Decision Process

Hamid Nemati
University of North Carolina at Greensboro, USA

Natalie Steiger and David Steiger
University of Maine, USA

Richard T. Herschel
St. Joseph's University, USA

ABSTRACT

This paper proposes a knowledge warehouse architecture to enhance both DSS and knowledge management efforts. First, differences in data, information, and knowledge are discussed. Then, tacit and explicit knowledge, their relationship within the knowledge spiral, and their criticality to organizational knowledge creation and decision making are explored. Finally, a knowledge warehouse architecture is proposed which enhances all aspects of the knowledge spiral and the associated decision making processes.

INTRODUCTION

Knowledge management focuses on the harnessing of intellectual capital within an organization. The concept recognizes that knowledge, not simply information, is the greatest asset to an institution. Knowledge as a concept is seen as something distinguishable from data and information. For example, Earl and Scott (1998) distinguish knowledge from data and information, arguing that knowledge is more complex, subtle, and multivariate than information.

Davenport and Prusak (1998) also distinguish between data, information, and knowledge. In an organizational context, they state that data is most usefully described as structured records of transactions and the management of data focuses on issues of cost, speed and capacity. Information, however, is described as a message, usually in the form of a document or an audible or visible communication, that has an impact on the receiver's judgment or behavior; i.e., information is derived from data because the sender of the data adds value to it in one of several ways. Knowledge is broader, richer, and deeper than data or information; i.e., knowledge is:

> a fluid mix of framed experience, values, contextual information, and expert insight that provides a framework for evaluating and incorporating new experiences and information. It originates and is applied in the minds of knowers. In organizations, it often becomes embedded not only in documents or repositories but also in organizational routines, processes, practices, and norms. (Davenport & Prusak, 1998, p. 5)

Choo (1998) states that organizations create knowledge from information via three vital knowledge creation activities. First, organizations use information to make sense of changes and developments in the external environments—a process called sense making. This is a vital activity wherein managers discern the most significant changes, interpret their meaning, and develop appropriate responses. Secondly, organizations create, organize, and process information to generate new knowledge through organizational learning. This knowledge creation activity enables the organization to develop new capabilities, design new products and services, enhance existing offerings, and improve organizational processes. Third, organizations search for and evaluate information in order to make decisions. This information is critical since all organizational actions are initiated by decisions and all decisions are commitments to actions, the consequences of which will, in turn, lead to the creation of new information.

EXPLICIT AND TACIT KNOWLEDGE

There are two forms of knowledge: explicit knowledge and tacit (implicit) knowledge. Explicit knowledge is defined as knowledge that can be expressed formally and can, therefore, be easily communicated or diffused throughout an organization. Tacit knowledge is knowledge that is uncodified and difficult to diffuse. It is hard to verbalize because it is learned and expressed through action-based skills and cannot easily be reduced to rules and recipes. It frequently involves knowledge about how to do things. The ability to effectively act on knowledge coupled with the inability to articulate an explanation is exemplary of tacit knowledge.

The interaction of tacit knowledge and explicit knowledge is seen by many knowledge management and decision support experts as critically important to a firm's knowledge creation activity. For example, Nonaka and Takeuchi (1995) view tacit knowledge and explicit knowledge as complementary entities. They claim that organizational knowledge creation is a process that amplifies the knowledge created by individuals and crystallizes it as a part of the knowledge network of the organization. Further, they state that there are two sets of dynamics that drive the process of knowledge amplification:

1.   Converting tacit knowledge into explicit knowledge; and
2.   Moving knowledge from the individual level to the group, organizational, and interorganizational levels.

Nonaka and Takeuchi (1995) suggest that there is an organizational knowledge spiral, beginning and ending with the knowledge worker (Figure 1). This knowledge spiral is based on their view that implicit (tacit) knowledge and explicit knowledge are complementary entities, and that there are four modes in which organizational knowledge is created through the interaction and conversion between implicit and explicit knowledge:

1.   Socialization: sharing experiences creates implicit knowledge such as shared mental models and technical skills. In the decision making process, socialization works to indoctrinate everyone into the "ways of doing things around here." Information technologies that can enhance socialization include digitized filming of an applicable experience, kinematics to enhance the study of a physical demonstration or experience, the Internet (to provide anytime/anyplace viewing of experiences or demonstrations), etc.

2.   Externalization: triggered by dialogue, implicit knowledge becomes explicit during a period of collective reflection through the sharing of metaphors, analogies, models, or stories. These exchanges become carriers of knowledge, carriers that can transfer general principles through the telling about particular situations. In the decision making process, externalization may include one or more of the following: 1) generating ideas or amplifying other's ideas, such as in electronic brainstorming, 2) extracting an expert's production rules for an expert system, 3) articulating parameters, objective functions, price-volume relationships, etc., in a DSS mathematical model, 4) specifying "what-if" model cases that reflect potential and realistic decision making situations, and 5) evaluating the decision alternatives, given the uncertainties in a decision making environment. Appropriate tools and technologies that enhance externalization include mathematical modeling, minimum cost network flow modeling (especially its pictorial representation), expert systems, special purpose interfaces that enhance what-if case specification, etc.

3.   Combination: the process of combining or reconfiguring disparate bodies of explicit knowledge that leads to the production of new explicit knowledge. This is a common form of knowledge transfer that typifies the learning in schools and instructional programs. In organizations, members combine their explicit knowledge by sharing reports, memos, and a variety of other documents. In the

Figure 1: The knowledge spiral

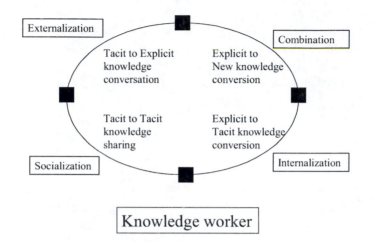

decision making process, knowledge combination is the process of combining several types or pieces of explicit knowledge into new patterns and new relations. The Gestalt theory of learning literature states that "all problems with which we may be confronted, and also the solutions of such problems, are matters of relations; not only does our understanding of the problem demand our awareness of certain relations, we cannot solve the problem without discovering certain new relations" (Kohler, 1969, pp.143-144). One potentially productive integration of explicit knowledge is the analysis of multiple, related "what-if" cases of a mathematical model to find new relationships, or metamodels, that determine the key factors of the model and show how these key factors interact to influence the decision (Sharda & Steiger, 1996; Steiger, 1998). Other forms of integration include the use of data warehousing and data mining to discover patterns and trends among otherwise seemingly disparate data. Appropriate tools and technologies that may be used to enhance combination include data mining software, artificial neural networks, GMDH (a cross between neural networks and statistics), fuzzy logic, expert systems, genetic algorithms, case-based reasoning, etc.

4.   Internalization: the process of learning and changing one's mental models so that new and explicit knowledge becomes absorbed as the implicit knowledge of the individual's style and habit. In the decision making process, internalization equates to understanding, which, from the theory of learning literature, involves the knowledge of three things: the purpose of the analysis (i.e., what the decision maker wants to understand), a set of relations or models of the process or system to be understood, and arguments about why the relations or models serve the purpose (Perkins, 1986). Internalization includes the process of using the new patterns and relations, together with the arguments of why

they fit the purpose, to update and/or extend the decision maker's own tacit knowledge base (i.e., his mental model of the process), thus creating a spiral of knowledge and learning that begins and ends with the individual (Nonaka & Takeuchi, 1995). Appropriate tools and technologies for enhancing internalization include inductive rule generation, expert systems (especially their trace and explanation capabilities), data visualization, case-based reasoning, etc.

As can be seen from the above description of the knowledge spiral, organizational knowledge can be enabled and enhanced in several ways: 1) by using mathematical modeling and expert systems to extract tacit knowledge (mental models, rules-of-thumb, etc.), 2) by using various artificial intelligence technologies to generate new and novel patterns from this explicit knowledge, as well as knowledge about knowledge (i.e., metaknowledge), 3) by using various artificial intelligence technologies to aid in the internalization/understanding of explicit knowledge via changing the users' mental models, and 4) by providing observation, storage, replay and analysis of tacit knowledge.

Thus, to enable the knowledge spiral and enhance organizational knowledge, what is needed is an integrated platform on which to store, analyze, and understand knowledge, metaknowledge, and the technologies that are used to enhance it; i.e., a knowledge warehouse that will do for knowledge what the data warehouse does for data. The architecture for such a knowledge warehouse is discussed below.

A KNOWLEDGE WAREHOUSE ARCHITECTURE

The goal of a knowledge warehouse (KW) is to provide the decision maker with an intelligent analysis platform that enhances all phases of the knowledge management process. Several comments can be made to further amplify and explain the KW goal.

First, this goal assumes that the user of the KW is the decision maker. That is, we assume that the user is not an expert in mathematical modeling, statistics, artificial intelligence, or the various technologies used to enhance knowledge management, but rather is an expert in the decision making field.

Second, an intelligent analysis platform is defined as a PC-based platform that makes available to the decision maker an array of analytical tools, each of which utilizes various technologies to aid the socialization, externalization, combination, and internalization of knowledge management. The purpose of including artificial intelligence is to amplify the cognitive capabilities of the decision maker in each phase of the knowledge spiral. The analysis platform also provides for the management of technology in knowledge management.

This goal suggests four functional requirements for KW: 1) an ability to efficiently generate, store, retrieve and, in general, manage explicit knowledge in the form of mathematical models, solved model instances (what-if cases), decision rules-of-thumb, basic principles of the business, etc., 2) an ability to store, execute and manage the tools and technologies used in knowledge externalization, combination and internalization, 3) a computer-assisted ability to generate natural language arguments concerning the comparable validity of the models, metamodels and relations produced by analysis technologies, and how this new knowledge relates to the decision maker's purpose, and 4) an effective human-machine interface that enhances the decision maker's ability to specify what-if cases, initiate analysis tasks and develop insightful understanding from the analysis results. These goals and requirements of a KW can be implemented via an extension of the data warehouse architecture. The proposed extension, shown in Figure 2, consists of six major components: 1) the knowledge acquisition/extraction module, 2) the two feedback loops, 3) the knowledge transformation and loading module, 4) a knowledge warehouse (storage) module, 5) the analysis workbench, and 6) a communication manager/user interface module. Each of these components is described below.

Knowledge Acquisition/Extraction Module

The knowledge acquisition/extraction module is primarily responsible for the tacit to explicit knowledge conversion; i.e., directly acquiring tacit knowledge from the decision maker/user. This acquisition module includes a specialized user interface to aid in one or more of the following processes: 1) idea generation in a GSS brainstorming environment, 2) mathematical model specification in a model-based environment, 3) what-if case specification in a model-based environment, 4) production rule elicitation in an expert-system-based environment, 5) purpose and fundamental knowledge elicitation in any analysis process (Steiger, 1998), and 6) kinematic analysis in a physical process demonstration.

Figure 2: Knowledge warehouse architecture

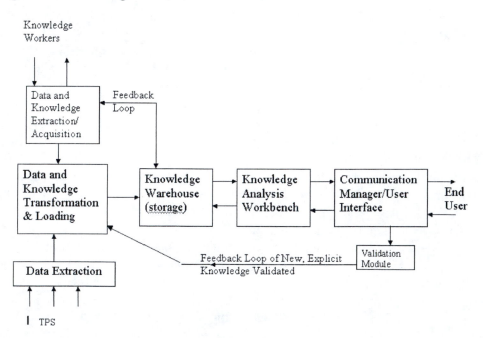

Feedback Loops

Note that there is one feedback loop between the knowledge acquisition module and the KW storage module (via the knowledge loading module). The knowledge/ warehouse feedback loop provides the capability of not only storing the explicit knowledge elicited from the decision maker(s), but also of immediately broadcasting knowledge from one user to other users (for example, in a DSS brainstorming session), displaying up-to-date lists of specified what-if cases (in a model-based DSS), or displaying current rules (in ES-based systems). The new knowledge feedback loop that exists between the extraction, transformation and loading module and the communication manager module provides for the validation of new validated explicit knowledge that has been generated in the system, especially from the knowledge analysis workbench.

Knowledge Transformation and Loading Module

The knowledge transformation and loading module is similar to that in the data warehouse in that it is responsible for reformatting, cleansing and loading data from external databases into the KW storage area (see Gray & Watson, 1998).

Knowledge Warehouse Storage Module

One of the primary components of the KW architecture is an object-oriented knowledge base management system (KBMS) that integrates the knowledge base, model base, and analysis tasks. A KBMS is a system that manages the integration of a wide variety of knowledge objects into a functioning whole. These knowledge objects include numerical data, text streams, validated models, metamodels, movie clips, animation sequences, as well as the software used for manipulating them. The KBMS is implemented in an object-oriented environment. The KBMS must not only manage data, but all of the objects, object models, process models, case models, object interaction models and dynamic models used to process the knowledge and to interpret it to produce the knowledge base.

Object-specific knowledge is stored as part of the appropriate object. The specific form of the knowledge storage mechanism may include frames, semantic nets, rules, etc. Stores of knowledge include, but are not limited to, metadata, metamodels and instances of metamodels. For example, a model's purpose is stored as part of the associated model whereas the basic underlying principles may be stored with a more general model class.

Messages sent to the objects are generic in form, independent of the method's technology. If additional information is required to execute a specified method, a message is sent to other appropriate object(s).

The object-oriented database technology provides several advantages for this application. One advantage is that existing knowledge is integrated with 1) its own metaknowledge, 2) examples or instances of the knowledge, and 3) various methods, including the analysis tasks. This enhances storage efficiency; e.g., if the knowledge is in the form of a model and its instances, related instances may differ from a base case by only one or two parameter values and the solution vector, and all common parameter values can be inherited from the base case or other parent instance for storage efficiency. A second advantage is that some analysis tasks can be logically tied to a specific class of models, whereas other analysis tasks can be tied to a super-class of all models and be independent of the specific modeling paradigms. A third advantage is that method overloading allows a single user-specified command to call several different implementations of a given task and apply the appropriate technology to different forms of knowledge; this reduces the cognitive burden on the decision maker by providing him/her with independent execution calls (i.e., messages) for all analysis tasks. It also provides a primary prerequisite for effective management of technology; i.e., overloading, in conjunction with encapsulation, makes the changing of implementation technologies transparent to the user.

Knowledge Analysis Workbench

The analysis workbench handles all interaction with the analysis tasks, including task control, and argument generation, and management of technology. The task controller handles all requests for data and runtime interactions (e.g., complexity factors in GMDH algorithms, step sizes in neural networks) required by the analysis technologies. That is, the task controller acts as an AI-based surrogate decision maker for task interactions, shielding the real decision maker from the requirements of knowing the technologies, their nuances, interactions, etc.

The argument generation sub-module evaluates the outputs of the various analysis tasks, especially the causation task, filtering out implausible or inconsistent results based on relative measures of accuracy, simplicity, conceptual validity, sufficiency, necessity, and consistency. It then generates simple and deep explanatory arguments that (hopefully) enhance the decision maker's understanding of the modeled environment. In generating these arguments, the argument generation module interfaces with the knowledge base, the instance base and model base, applying deductive knowledge, analogical reasoning, and other technologies, as appropriate.

The management of technology module manages the repository of analysis technologies. Specifically, it provides for the encapsulation of new analysis algorithms into object model classes, integration of legacy data mining applications, incorporation of new analytical models and metamodels into the object model repository, etc.

Communication Manager

This module, which handles all analysis communication between KBMS and the user interface, includes six functional sub-modules: a knowledge engineer, what-if interface, query processor, results representation manager, online help, and user interface.

The knowledge engineer sub-module is an expert-system-based subsystem responsible for interacting with the decision-maker to develop the purpose of the analysis and the basic underlying principles of the modeled environment. Both types of knowledge are used in the development of arguments. This knowledge may be stored in the knowledge base in the form of frames, rules, semantic nets, etc.

The what-if interface is designed to efficiently and effectively help the decision maker specify one or more what-if cases to be investigated. It includes an analogical component that is used to suggest pertinent instances by varying one or more parameter values. It also includes one or more interactive graphical displays, or summaries, of instances already available, so that the decision maker can see at a glance what has already been tried and what instance(s) might lead to additional insights. The what-if interface also includes a capability to suggest potentially valuable cases based on the planning analysis task.

The query processor provides the interface between the decision maker and the analysis task. It translates natural language, QBE or SQL-like queries specified by the decision maker into machine executable queries.

The result representation manager selects the most appropriate presentation view for each analysis result; e.g., graphics, natural language production rules, polynomials, decision trees, etc. The selection is based on a combination of the analysis task output and the decision maker's preference which, in turn, is based on an adaptable machine learning algorithm which analyzes previous uses of models and analysis tasks by the current decision maker (Dolk & Konsynski, 1984; Liang, 1988).

The help sub-module provides the user with information concerning the model (e.g., assumptions, parameter ranges, units of measurement, internal model structure), instances (differences from base case, key decision variable values), pertinent knowledge (e.g., metamodels, metadata, basic principles, analysis purpose), and analysis tasks (e.g., applicable technology, technology description, explanatory traces of results, technical parameters used, advantages and limitations of technologies).

The knowledge spiral proposed by Nonaka and Takeuchi (1995) along with the knowledge warehouse proposed herein suggest a different direction for DSS in the next decade. This new direction is based on an expanded purpose of DSS; specifically, the purpose of DSS should be to enhance all four aspects of the knowledge spiral (tacit to tacit knowledge sharing, tacit to explicit knowledge conversion, new knowledge generation, and explicit to tacit knowledge internalization). That is, the purpose of DSS is knowledge enhancement.

EXAMPLE APPLICATION

To illustrate the use of a knowledge warehouse, consider the following situation. A crude oil refiner is faced with an inventory control problem in their refined products. In general, product inventories include those in bulk storage at the refinery, in-transit pipeline inventories (it takes up to 21 days to ship products from their southern Louisiana refinery to their most distant markets), terminal bulk storage inventories, and retail tank inventories. While in inventory, this product is subject to drastic price swings and significant working capital costs. The vice president in charge of product inventories has decided to hire a business professor from the local university to analyze the situation and recommend a solution that would track inventories and minimize the associated costs and price risks. The professor suggested a three-step approach: 1) build a simulation model that includes all types of the existing inventories, 2) generate alternative flow options by brainstorming with the company employees, including these options in subsequent simulation models, and 3) select the best alternative based on multiple criteria of short-term shipping and holding costs, price risk, flexibility, probability of stock-outs, etc.

Prior to the initial model-building phase, the professor extracts all the pertinent tacit knowledge from the company personnel via an iterative set of interviews, and the pertinent explicit data from corporate databases, storing the knowledge in her knowledge warehouse (part of the knowledge warehouse implemented at the university). She then builds, using her knowledge analysis workbench, a suitable simulation model of the current situation based on that data and knowledge and invites seven of the company's most involved and knowledgeable employees to a knowledge management session at the university.

The purpose of the knowledge management session is threefold: 1) to demonstrate, analyze, and learn from the simulation model and the current situation it represents, especially the existing bottlenecks and excess product stores (taking full advantage of the simulation model's visual animation to enhance understanding and insight), 2) to develop and simulate alternative supply and shipping scenarios that might prove advantageous with respect to one or more of the evaluation criteria, and 3) to evaluate those scenarios.

The session is begun with a review of the knowledge and data used in the model, a demonstration of the model's results, and an interactive discussion concerning the validity of the model. This is part of the new knowledge feedback loop in which the decision makers validate and learn the current bottlenecks and excess inventory stores from the model's output.

This leads to a group brainstorming session to determine possible alternatives of operation that might reduce the inventories but maintain the target service levels. The brainstorming session is implemented with each member typing original ideas and building onto the others' ideas in a PC and having those and the ideas of others grouped and displayed anonymously upon demand. This is the essence of the feedback loop between the knowledge acquisition module and the KW storage module. When the generation of ideas slows, the leader selects one of the ideas, asks for the group to type in what they like and dislike about the idea, and then brainstorms for modification of the idea that keeps the idea's good points and addresses/solves the concerns about the idea, trying to iterate to an idea that can be implemented. Once several viable alternatives have been proposed, they are included as part of one or more simulation models and each model is run. In most simulation modeling environments, a change to the model can be made "on the fly" to see its effect visually on the critical variables (e.g., queue length, inventory levels, service levels, etc.). In addition, each simulation run and its associated statistics can be saved individually as a member of a group of related models. The entire group can then be "mined" for critical parameters and relationships between those parameters. For example, overall inventory levels may be inversely proportional to overall demand (a nonintuitive conclusion) if significant volumes of product are sourced through exchange agreements with other refiners.

At any rate, the alternatives are evaluated with respect to the evaluation criteria. Each participant in the brainstorming session may have one vote on which alternative to select. Once again, the voting is anonymous, but in some cases, the voting may be weighted with respect to the relative decision responsibility of the voter.

This process is repeated until the best, or at least a better, alternative is found and agreed upon. At this point, the model and resulting decision is filed in the knowledge warehouse storage for future review and evaluation. Further, since the model and associated decision represent a piece of corporate knowledge, it may be analyzed with other similar decisions in a case-based reasoning analysis or mined for additional metaknowledge; i.e., it might subsequently become input to other studies conducted in the knowledge analysis workbench module, using different tools and technologies and generating additional and insightful new knowledge.

IMPACT OF KW ON THE FUTURE OF DSS

A knowledge base management system (KBMS) will, in the future, be measured on one or more of the following three criteria: 1) how well it promotes and enhances knowledge and understanding within the firm, 2) the quality and growth of the knowledge contained in and produced by the KBMS, and 3) the integration and use of the KBMS in various decision making environments. One research area concerns the development of metrics and experimental designs for testing the benefits of the various components of a KBMS; e.g., applying the lens model (Brunswick, 1952). Such measures and testing would be instrumental in justifying the expense of developing a fully integrated KBMS.

In addition, the knowledge warehouse architecture proposed in this article shows several major areas in which DSS could/should foster future research and development. One such area is in providing the motivation, tools, techniques and demonstrated benefits associated with the development and use of the knowledge analysis workbench. In the DSS literature, especially the management science aspects of it, the focus of research has historically been on model specification and model solution. In the future, it seems that the analysis of solutions will be the more important aspect of modeling, along with providing the decision maker with an understanding of the analysis results. Several DSS researchers have developed some theory in this vein (Kimbrough et al, 1993; Sharda & Steiger, 1996; Steiger,

1998), but the area still needs further refinement. For example, in model-based DSS, we need to identify a "minimal spanning set" of analysis tasks that leads to successful model analysis, and to validate these tasks through experimentation.

Another research area could explore and evaluate technologies that are potentially applicable to analysis and understanding. Initial evaluation could match the input, processing, output, and feedback characteristics of various technologies against the corresponding requirements of the minimal spanning set of analysis tasks mentioned above. The results would provide a research agenda for the application of the technologies to the analysis tasks, along with empirical testing of their effectiveness.

A fourth research area would utilize artificial intelligence techniques to develop deep explanatory arguments based on basic principles and organizational goals to show why one suggested decision is "better" than comparable alternatives in a given decision making environment. Such deep explanations could improve the decision maker's confidence in the DSS, as well as enhance his/her insight into the decision making environment and foster better decisions in the future. It should be noted, however, that this research area assumes the existence of a knowledge warehouse containing the basic business principles and the organizational goals, as well as an indexing scheme and search algorithms to extract appropriate principles and goals for specific arguments.

A fifth area in the knowledge warehouse architecture that could benefit from future DSS research is in the validation process of knowledge prior to being fed back into the knowledge warehouse. Such questions that should be addressed include: 1) How much filtering of potential new knowledge should be allowed, 2) Who should be responsible for this filtering (CKO, leaders in GSS/GDSS, etc.), 3) What the filtering criteria should be, and 4) What are the trade-offs of artificial intelligence versus human intelligence in this filtering process. The answers to these questions could significantly impact the implementation and eventual overall quality of the knowledge warehouse and the decisions it supports.

SUMMARY AND CONCLUSIONS

This paper has proposed a knowledge warehouse architecture for the extraction, storage, analysis and understanding of explicit knowledge. As with the data warehouses, a knowledge warehouse could provide knowledge and support to the entire enterprise. Alternatively, a company could have several smaller knowledge marts, smaller versions of knowledge warehouses primarily applicable to a single department or function. And finally, a company might set up several operational knowledge stores, miniature versions applicable to single decisions. In general, it is envisioned that all knowledge marts and knowledge stores should be at least loosely connected to the overall corporate knowledge warehouse so that global information within the corporation would be available without duplication or temporal problems. For example, a single, interdepartmental forecast of sales should form the bases of all knowledge warehouses/marts/stores to ensure consistency and accuracy of results; few things are worse than for each department in a company to have a different sales forecast driving their departmental knowledge mart.

The proposed KW architecture consists of an object-oriented knowledge base management system module (OO-KBMS), a knowledge analysis workbench, and a communication manager. The OO-KBMS module integrates a wide variety of knowledge objects and analysis tasks. The knowledge analysis workbench handles the interaction with the analysis tasks, including task control, argument generation, and encapsulation of new analysis algorithms into object models. The communication manager handles all analysis communication between the OO-KBMS and the user interface. The communication manager accomplishes this effectively through the use of five functional sub-modules: a knowledge engineer, what-if interface, query processor, results presentation manager, and online help.

The KW will also include a feedback loop to enhance its own knowledge base with the passage of time, as the tested and approved results of knowledge analysis are fed back into the KW as an additional source of knowledge. The primary role of the feedback loop is to provide the capability of both storing the explicit knowledge elicited from the decision maker(s) and also immediately making it available for other users in the system.

The proposed KW architecture is unique in that it proposes support of all four phases of the knowledge spiral in a decision support system, especially in model-based decision support. Historical decision support system architecture focuses primarily on building, instantiating (with a database), storing (in a model base) manipulating models, and interfacing with those models (Sprague & Watson, 1996). Another has included a knowledge system (Holsapple & Whinston, 1996). And a third has included an intelligent analysis toolkit with which to analyze multiple instances of a model to generate new knowledge (Sharda & Steiger, 1996). The proposed architecture included in this paper expands on these to include not only model building components and model analysis tools, but also components that enhance the internalization/understanding of new knowledge, as well as other aspects of the tacit to explicit knowledge conversion. The proposed architecture presented herein also assumes the storage in the KB of organizational goals and basic principles of business, both as initially specified and as feedback of new knowledge generated as brainstorming sessions are held, as models are instantiated and built, as new knowledge generated through analysis, and as additional decisions are made.

REFERENCES

Choo, C. W. (1998). *The knowing organization: How organizations use information to construct meaning, create knowledge, and make decisions*. New York: Oxford.

Davenport, T., & Prusak, L. (1998). *Working knowledge*. Boston: Harvard Business School.

Devlin, B. (1997). *Data Warehouse: From architecture to implementation.* Menlo Park, CA: Addison Wesley Longman.

Dolk, D. R., & Konsynski, B. (1984). Knowledge representation for model management systems. *IEEE Transactions of Software Engineering, 10*(6), 619-628

Earl, M., & Scott, I. (1998). *What on earth is a CKO?* London: London Business School.

Gray, P., & Watson, H. (1998). *Decision support in the data warehouse.* NJ: Prentice Hall.

Holsapple, C. W., & Whinston, A. B. (1996). Decision support systems—A knowledge-based approach. NY: West.

Kimbrough, S. O., & Oliver, J. R. (1994). On automating candle-lighting analysis. Proceedings of the 27th Annual Hawaii International Conference on System Sciences (536-544).

Kohler, W. (1969). The task of Gestalt psychology. Princeton, NJ: Princeton University Press.

Liang, T. P. (1988). Model management for group decision support. *MIS Quarterly,* (667-680).

Meredith, J. R. (1981, October). The implementation of computer based systems. *Journal of Operational Management.*

Newell, A., & Simon, H. A. (1972). *Human problem solving.* Englewood Cliffs, NJ: Prentice-Hall.

Nonaka, I., & Takeuchi, H. (1995). *The knowledge creating company.* New York, NY: Oxford University Press.

Patel, V., Arocha, J., & Kaufman, D. (1999). Expertise and tacit knowledge in medicine. In R. Sternberg & J. Horvath (Eds.). *Tacit knowledge in professional practice* (pp. 75-99) Mahwah, NJ: Lawrence Erlbaum.

Perkins, D. N. (1986). *Knowledge as design.* Hillsdale, NJ: Lawrence Erlbaum.

Sharda, R., & Steiger, D. M. (1996). Inductive model analysis systems: Enhancing model analysis in decision support systems. *Information Systems Research, 7*(3), 328-341.

Sprague, Jr., R. H., & Watson, H. J. (1996). *Decision support for management.* Upper Saddle River, NJ: Prentice Hall.

Steiger, D. M. (1998). Enhancing user understanding in a decision support system: A theoretical basis and framework. *Journal of Management Information Systems, 15*(2), 199-221.

Steiger, D. M., & Sharda, R. (1993). LP modeling languages for personal computers: A comparison. *Annals of Operations Research, 43,* 195-216.

Steiger, D. M., Sharda, R., & LeClaire, B. (1993). Graphical interfaces for network modeling: A model management system perspective. *ORSA Journal on Computing, 5*(3), 275-291.

Chapter XIII

Ripple Down Rules: A Technique for Acquiring Knowledge

Debbie Richards
Macquarie University, Australia

ABSTRACT

Knowledge is becoming increasingly recognized as a valuable resource. Given its importance it is surprising that expert systems technology has not become a more common means of utilizing knowledge. In this chapter we review some of the history of expert systems, the shortcomings of first generation expert systems, current approaches and future decisions. In particular we consider a knowledge acquisition and representation technique known as Ripple Down Rules (RDR) that avoids many of the limitations of earlier systems by providing a simple, user-driven knowledge acquisition approach based on the combined use of rules and cases and which support online validation and easy maintenance. RDR has found particular commercial success as a clinical decision support system and we review what features of RDR make it so suited to this domain.

INTRODUCTION

Knowledge, in particular tacit knowledge, has been recognised as a key factor in gaining a competitive advantage (van Daal, de Haas & Weggeman, 1998). The soft and intangible nature of knowledge has led to increased utilisation of techniques such as mentoring and group activities. However, many organisations are looking for technology-based solutions to help them with knowledge management (KM). It is therefore surprising that expert systems, which are concerned with the acquisition and application of knowledge, are less commonly used than techniques such as data warehousing and data mining to assist KM. The very mention of the term expert systems (ES) can bring responses such as: research in that area is dead, they didn't deliver, and don't use that word when you speak to industry. Despite negative perceptions held by many, the reality is that while ES had shortcomings, there are successes and ES research is alive. Current research now uses the term knowledge-based systems (KBS), primarily to cover past stigmas, and includes research into knowledge management, modeling and acquisition.

Some of the problems suffered by first-generation ES include: difficult knowledge capture, brittleness, unnatural dialogues and explanations, unmaintainability, and inability to scale-up or reflect on their knowledge. To address these problems second-generation ES research is focused on modeling knowledge above its symbolic representation and at the knowledge level (Newell, 1982). The use of methodologies and extensive a priori analysis and modeling required by these approaches has achieved some industrial success by ensuring that products are systematically developed through to completion. However, due to the situated nature of knowledge (Clancey, 1997) and the unreliability of models (Gaines & Shaw, 1989) such structure has resulted in approaches that have done little to alleviate the original knowledge acquisition (KA) bottleneck or maintenance problems. In most approaches the user has become a third party which has exacerbated what we believe to have been the fundamental reasons for the lack of acceptance of early ES.

This chapter offers an alternative KBS paradigm. The purpose of this chapter is to describe a knowledge representation and acquisition technique, known as ripple-down rules (RDR), that tackles head-on the limitations of first-generation ES while avoiding some of the new problems introduced in second-generation ES. RDR are based on the view that knowledge evolves and is highly dependent on its context. To support this, RDR uses a rule-based exception structure for knowledge representation (KR) and an incremental, rapid and user-driven KA and maintenance technique that combines the use of cases and rules. RDR has found commercial success since the early 90s in the area of pathology report interpretation (Edwards, Compton, Malor, Srinivasan, & Lazarus, 1993; Lazarus, 2000) and more recently in help-desk applications (Kang, Yoshida, Motoda, & Compton, 1997). In this chapter we will consider the features and limitations of first- and second-generation ES and look at how RDR addresses these issues. We will then consider the emerging trends and future directions of KBS research.

EXPERT SYSTEMS—THEIR PAST AND PRESENT

The proliferation of the personal computer began in the 1980s. While advancements in hardware were a major factor in the massive uptake of the technology, acceptance by users can be summed up in "123," that is, Lotus123. For the first time users were given control and ownership of systems. Database packages, such as DbaseIV, together with the spreadsheet changed the relationship between the computer system and the computer user. Essentially what we were seeing was a widespread "YES" to decision support style systems. On the other hand, also during the 80s we witnessed the rise and fall of many companies involved with ES software. Instead of user satisfaction, ES were found to be unacceptable by many organizations. First-generation ES suffered from such problems as giving poor or wrong advice when queried outside their very narrow domain (the brittleness problem) or exponential growth in the time taken to maintain the system (the maintenance problem). However, while these were real problems, we believe it was the fundamental goals of ES that resulted in their lack of credibility. It had been hoped that an organization could overcome the problems of costly and limited supply of human experts through the purchase of an ES shell. This view was founded on the physical symbol system hypothesis (Newell & Simons, 1976) which relied on symbols for the representation and manipulation of knowledge. Using an ES shell, a general purpose inference engine would execute over the customized knowledge base (KB) to offer recommendations to novices and experts. The assumption that an ES could replace a human expert was unrealistic and perhaps unethical.

Whilst some classify ES as a type of decision support systems (DSS), the features of many implementations make them very strongly one or the other. Table 1, adapted from Turban (1993), summarises the two technologies. It can be seen that there is more than just the application that divides ES and DSS. The only shared feature is the development method. Many of the features which differentiate ES from DSS such as the objective, major query direction and developer can be seen as reasons why ES were not accepted by users and DSS were. Young (1989, p. 358) describes DSS as open systems which address unstructured problems that involve the use of models and the user's knowledge. Alternatively, ES are closed, inflexible systems that are internally controlled by the computer and contain prescribed/built-in knowledge. The role of DSS is to support the user who asks the questions and interprets the output. ES were typically offered in a consultative mode where the system asks the questions and gives a recommendation to the user. Even where knowledge was found to be reliable, ES became a wasted or underutilised resource because the consultative system style was not compatible with the way users saw themselves and their activities (Kidd & Sharpe 1987; Langlotz & Shortliffe, 1983) and did not allow the user to build a mental model that they can manipulate (Clancey, 1992). Lack of attention to human-computer interaction (HCI) issues in knowledge-based systems can be seen as a major reason for the limited acceptance of first-generation KBS by end users (Langlotz & Shortliffe, 1983; Salle & Hunter, 1990). RDR however completely blurs the distinction between ES and DSS. The system is truly aimed at decision support while using an ES architecture.

The notion of knowledge transfer embodied in first-generation ES was replaced in the early 90s with model-based KBS approaches founded on Newell's (1982) knowledge-level concept. The KBS community came to realize that knowledge was not simply an artifact to be extracted. A better approach to KA became the focus

Table 1: Differences between DSS and ES

	DSS	ES
Objective	Assist human decision maker	Replicate human advisers and replace them
Who advises (decides ?)	The human and/or system	The system
Major orientation	Decision making	Transfer of expertise and advice-rendering
Major query direction	Human queries the machine	Machine queries human
Nature of support	Personal, groups, and institutional	Personal (mainly) and groups
Manipulation method	Numerical	Symbolic
Characteristics of problem area	Complex, integrated, wide	Narrow, fixed domain
Type of problems	Ad hoc, unique	Repetitive
Content of database	Factual knowledge	Procedural and factual knowledge
Developer	User	Knowledge Engineer, Expert
Development method	Prototyping	Prototyping
Reasoning capability	No	Yes, limited
Explanation capability	Limited	Yes

Adapted from: Decision Support and Expert Systems. *Turban 1993.*

of most KBS research. The model-based approaches included the use of general problem solving methods (e.g., Chandrasekaran & Johnson, 1993; Puerta, Egar, Tu, & Musen, 1992; Schreiber, Weilinga, & Breuker, 1993) or ontologies (e.g., Cohen et al., 1998; Grosso, Eriksson, Fergerson, Gennari, Tu, & Musen, 1999; Guarino, 1996; Guha & Lenat, 1990; Kamori & Yamaguchi, 1999; Uschold & Gruninger, 1996). However HCI issues took even more of a backseat since the added structure and complexity increased the need for a knowledge engineer to act as a mediator between the ES and the domain expert. The KBS paradigm offered in this chapter is designed for development, maintenance and use by domain experts and other end users. The approach is incremental, simple, reliable and rapid, which makes the development of KB tailored to preferred practice in individual laboratories, departments or organizations feasible.

The focus on complex modeling as a prerequisite to knowledge capture not only alienates the end user further from the system, it also ignores some of the inherent problems associated with models. Ontological engineering provides a way of designing, maintaining and applying ontologies. Ontologies are currently seen as a means of reducing the KA bottleneck by supporting the reuse and sharing of knowledge and providing a framework within which the knowledge can be elicited in the first place. However it should be remembered that an ontology is a conceptual model of a domain or task structure. Models are not precise. Conceptual models are hard to elicit and harder to validate. A model can been seen as "a description and generator of behaviour patterns over time, not a mechanism equivalent to human capacity" (Clancey, 1992, p. 89). Furthermore, models have been shown to vary between experts in the same domain and even over time for the same individual

(Gaines & Shaw, 1989). In many model-based KA approaches it is implicitly assumed that modeling occurs before action in human behaviour. There is no evidence for this; instead "we see that experts do not need to have formalised representations in order to act" (Winograd & Flores, 1986, p. 99) and "reflection and abstraction are important phenomena, but are not the basis for everyday action" (Winograd & Flores, p. 97). The RDR approach does not attempt to capture or describe an expert's thought processes but captures the expert's behaviour. From a situated view of cognition, we cannot extract human thought from action and the context in which they occur (Clancey, 1992).

The social nature of expertise requires that an ontology represents a shared conceptualization. This involves agreement over the structure, representation, terms and the meaning of the terms. Interoperability of ontologies (or even databases for that matter) is seen "as a challenging task" (Noy & Hafner, 1997, p. 53). With the exception of Falquet and Mottaz Jiang (2000) and our approach (Richards, 2000a), differences between concepts need to be reconciled before the concept can be entered into the concept base. Standards have been offered to make sharing and reuse a technical possibility, but often require compromise and some loss of expressivity or functionality (as found in the collaborative work in Noy, Fergerson, & Musen, 2000; Schrieber, Crubezy, & Musen, 2000). Russ, Valente, MacGregor, and Swartout (1999) offer a discussion of the trade-offs between reusability and usability of ontologies and conclude that current tools do not provide a practical solution. These approaches are founded on the basic assumptions that the cost of knowledge acquisition is higher than the cost of building the ontology and that KA will more easily follow once the ontology is available. The case for this is not yet clear. As an alternative, RDR offers low cost KA. As briefly mentioned later we use formal concept analysis (FCA) (Wille, 1982, 1992) to automatically generate an ontology based directly on the RDR (Richards & Compton, 1997). Let's look at the RDR approach.

USER-CENTRED KNOWLEDGE-BASED DECISION SUPPORT

RDR were developed in the late 80s in answer to the problems associated with maintaining a large medical ES. It was evident that the knowledge provided by experts was situated and dependent on the context in which it was given. It was observed that experts did not give explanations of why they had chosen a particular recommendation but rather they tended to justify their conclusion (Compton & Jansen, 1990). The applicability of the knowledge depended on the context, consisting of the case and the person receiving the knowledge. This observation resulted in an emphasis on capturing knowledge in context by storage of the case that prompted a new rule to be added. The unwanted side effects associated with typical rule-based systems (Soloway, Bachant, & Jensen, 1987) were also avoided by developing an exception structure for knowledge representation which localized the effect of adding knowledge. In conventional KA there is an attempt to specify global knowledge or to prespecify the contexts in which the knowledge applies. This is not the case in RDR. Since knowledge is only ever patched locally, the time taken to add a rule to an RDR KB is constant at approximately 1 minute per rule. The emphasis on maintenance has resulted in a KA technique that is failure-driven (rules are only added in response to a wrong conclusion) and which not only supports but expects incremental system development and online validation of knowledge.

Single Classification RDR

RDR were first developed to handle single classification tasks. An exception structure in the form of a binary tree is used to provide rule pathways. When the expert determines that a conclusion is incorrect a new rule is added to the rule that incorrectly fired. If the new rule results in the incorrect rule remaining true then it is attached to the true path of the incorrect rule; otherwise the new rule is attached to the false branch. The case that caused the misclassification to be identified is stored in association with the new rule and is referred to as the cornerstone case. The purpose of storing the case is to assist the user with KA and to provide validation of the new rule. The new rule must distinguish between the new case and the case associated with the rule that gave the wrong conclusion (Compton & Jansen 1990).

Using the grammar developed by Scheffer (1996), a single-classification RDR can be defined as a triple <rule,X,N>, where X are the exception rules and N are the if-not rules as shown in Figure 1. When a rule is satisfied the exception rules are evaluated and none of the lower rules are tested. The major success for this approach has been the Pathology Expert Interpretative Reporting System (PEIRS) (Edwards et al., 1993), a large medical expert system for pathology laboratory report interpretation built by experts with minimal intervention of a knowledge engineer. PEIRS was one of the few medical ES actually in routine use in the early 90s. It went

Figure 1: A single classification RDR KBS

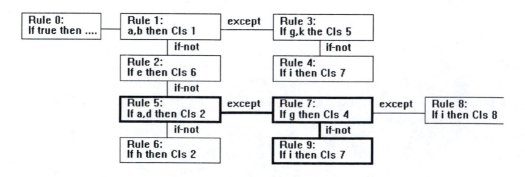

Each rule can be seen as a pathway that leads from itself back to the top node, which is rule 0. The highlighted boxes represent rules that are satisfied for the case {a,d,i}.

into operation with 198 rules and grew over 4 years to over 2,000 rules, covering 12 different tests. A total of approximately 100 hours was spent on KA. The industry standard was 2 or 3 rules per day (Edwards, 1996). Despite the random order in which knowledge is added, simulation studies have shown that the RDR approach of correcting errors as they occur produces KBs that are at least as compact and accurate as those produced by induction (Compton, Preston, & Kang, 1994, 1995). Others have used exception structures for knowledge representation but RDR are "the most general for attribute-value based representations and most strongly structured" (Scheffer, 1996, p. 279).

Multiple Classification RDR

Multiple classification RDR (MCRDR) have more recently been developed to handle classification tasks where multiple independent classifications are required (Kang, Compton, & Preston, 1995). This method builds n-ary trees and consists only of exception branches. A better description may be sets of decision lists joined by exceptions. In contrast to single classification RDR all rules attached to true parents are evaluated against the data. Figure 2 shows an example MCRDR with two levels of decision lists. An MCRDR is defined as the quadruple <rule,P,C,S>, where P is the parent rule, C are the children/exception rules and S are the sibling rules within the same level of decision list. Every rule in the first list is evaluated. If a rule evaluates to false then no further lists attached to that rule are examined. If a rule evaluates to true all rules in the next list are tested. The list of every true rule is processed in this way. The last true rule on each path constitutes the conclusions given.

Figure 2: An MCRDR KBS for the contact lens prescription domain

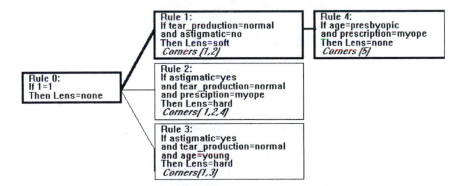

The highlighted boxes represent rules that are satisfied for the case {age=presbyopic, prescription=myope, astigmatic=no, tear_production=normal}. The classification given is Lens=none. 1=1 is the condition of the default rule which is always true. As this domain only deals with mutually exclusive conclusions we only get one conclusion, but if the domain was extended to cover spectacles and bifocals then this case could lead to multiple conclusions being given. The cornerstone case numbers associated with a rule are shown as Corners().

In single classification RDR only one case is associated with each rule. In MCRDR there may be multiple cases that must be distinguished from the current case. In the KA approach developed, the expert is presented with one cornerstone case at a time. The expert constructs a rule to distinguish the new case from the first case presented and then each case in the cornerstone list is evaluated to see if it is also distinguished by the new rule. If a case is satisfied by the rule the expert must add extra conditions to the rule to distinguish this case. This continues until all related cornerstone cases are distinguished. The KA process for MCRDR is shown in Figure 3. Remarkably the expert provides a sufficiently precise rule after two or three cases have been seen (Kang, Compton & Preston, 1995). Rules are always added, never removed or changed. To change a rule an exception rule is added. To stop an incorrect conclusion a stopping rule which has a null conclusion is added as an exception. Simulation studies (Kang, Compton & Preston, 1995) have shown MCRDR to be a superior representation to the original RDR structure by producing

Figure 3: The KA process for the development of an MCRDR

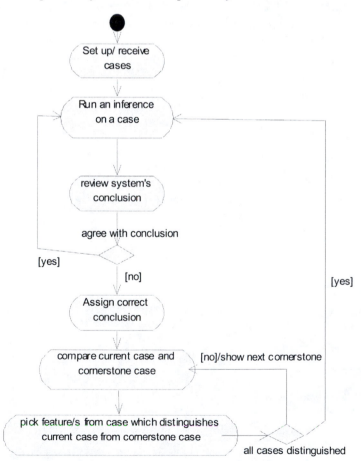

knowledge bases that mature more quickly and are more compact even for single classification domains. It is conjectured that this occurs because more use is made of expertise rather than depending on the KB structure (Kang, 1996).

RDR does not distinguish between initial KA and system maintenance. RDR develops the whole system on a case-by-case basis and automatically structures the KBS in such a way to ensure changes are incremental. Validation is designed to be performed online by the expert. The approaches offered to KA by FCA (Wille, 1989) and repertory grids (Shaw & Gaines, 1994) also minimize the role of the knowledge engineer and make use of differences but as with most KA techniques require some consideration of the whole domain each time knowledge is entered and do not consider incremental maintenance. With FCA and repertory grids, incremental maintenance is often addressed by regenerating implications associated with the revised data set. In the case of repertory grids this is not a major problem as the rules are automatically generated. The PROTÉGÉ family of systems (Grosso et al., 1999) also grew from a focus on the role of the domain expert and a desire to reduce reliance on a knowledge engineer. However, PROTÉGÉ's approach follows mainstream research by emphasizing modeling using ontologies and methods to provide mappings between the KB and problem-solving method. Also from Stanford is the KNAVE system, which facilitates acquisition, maintenance, sharing and reuse of temporal-abstraction knowledge in a visual environment (Shahar & Cheng, 1998). The use of visualisation and multiple views is similar to our work in Richards (2000b).

At a research level, RDR have been applied to numerous classification tasks such as crop management (Hochman, Compton, Blumenthal, & Preston, 1996), fraud detection (Wang, Boland, Graco, & He, 1996) and igneous rock classification (Richards & Menzies, 1998). RDR have been successfully extended to acquire complex control knowledge needed for a flight simulator (Shiraz & Sammut, 1998). Another RDR extension is nested ripple down rules (NRDR) (Beydoun & Hoffmann, 1998), which has incorporated a conceptual hierarchy into the RDR KA process. This work is concerned with capturing search knowledge and allows concepts and rules at various levels of abstraction to be defined and reused. Construction-type problems have been considered in the work on configuring an ion chromatographer (Ramadan, Mulholland, Hibbert, Preston, Compton, & Haddad 1997), room allocation (Richards & Compton, 1999) and building design (Richards & Simoff, 2001). An ontological approach to KA using RDR has been developed known as ripple down rule-oriented conceptual hierarchies (ROCH) (Martinez-Bejar, Benjamins, Compton, Preston, & Martin-Rubio, 1998). Using ROCH the expert defines a conceptual hierarchy of the domain from which cases are first developed followed by rules to cover those cases. ROCH has been extended to cover fuzzy domains with the development of fuzzy ROCH (FROCH) (Martinez-Bejar, Shiraz, & Compton, 1998). However, our approach using FCA (Richards & Compton, 1997) is more in keeping with the RDR philosophy of a simple approach that users can manage and which does not rely on a priori specification of complex models. Using FCA we start with interpretation of the MCRDR rules as a *formal context* (Wille, 1982). The rules in Figure 3 are represented as a formal context in Figure 4. The formal context is used to generate concepts based on the philosophical notion of a concept as a set of attributes and the set of objects which share those attributes. In our usage of FCA, we simply find intersections of shared rule conditions in the primitive concepts (the original rules) to generate higher-level concepts. The generated concepts are ordered and displayed as a complete lattice. Figure 5 shows the lattice generated from the formal context in Figure 4. Although we don't want to rely on experts to provide the abstractions and we do not need the abstractions for inferencing, the retrospective discovery of concepts and their structure is useful for explanation purposes. The concept hierarchy produced can be viewed as a domain ontology. We have developed a process model which compares the FCA ontologies and develops a merged conceptualization (Richards, 2000a).

Over the past decade there have been numerous implementations of RDR. Generally, each variation still used:

- cases to provide context and assist in forming rules and for validation;
- the exception structure;

Figure 4: Context of "MCRDR contact lens rules" shown in Figure 3

	1=1	astigmatic = no	tear_production = normal	age = presbyopic	prescripton = myope	astigmatic = yes	age = young
1-%LENSN	X						
2-%LENSS	X	X	X				
3-%LENSN	X	X	X	X	X		
4-%LENSH	X		X		X	X	
5-%LENSH	X		X			X	X

Figure 5: The diagram screen in MCRDR/FCA which shows the concept lattice for the formal context of "MCRDR contact lens rules" given in Figure 4

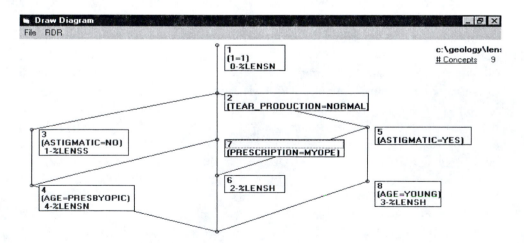

- the use of some form of preprocessor of the raw data;
- incremental KA and maintenance; and
- the development of a simple model in terms of A-V pairs and conclusions.

The differences tended to concern how the knowledge was being presented and manipulated and the inferencing strategy. The common features offer the following benefits:

1. A solution to a number of the problems associated with KBS, namely, the KA, maintenance and validation problems.
2. A direct involvement system that gives the user control and ownership of the system, which is important for the acceptance of computer systems.
3. The context in which the knowledge applies is captured, which is important in allowing knowledge reuse.

A Closer Look at RDR as a Clinical Decision Support System (CDSS)

Clinical decision support systems (CDSS) can offer a range of clinical services including: alerting, reminding, critiquing, interpreting, esoteric reports, focused reports, assisting and advising (Lazarus, 2000). While RDR's greatest success-to-date has been in the area of pathology report interpretation, the potential benefits of RDR are great for any domain where structured cases are present and there is an expert available to review the system recommendations. We believe it is only our lack of resources (not a lack of interest) that has impeded more widespread usage of RDR.

The reasons for the success of RDR in CDSS can be contrasted with reasons for the failure of traditional ES. Lazarus (2000) gives a number of reasons why the notion of a Greek oracle in medical diagnostic systems was rejected (Miller & Masarie, 1990):

- the clinician must play a subsidiary role but accept responsibility for that decision;
- the reasoning of the system is not transparent; and
- the advice is not given in real time.

In contrast, we attribute the success RDR has found to:

- The combined use of rules and cases in RDR fits with the clinician's tendency to consider the context of the current case and use heuristics based on their past experience with similar cases. Some ES use probilistic approaches which are less natural.
- The manner in which knowledge is acquired and maintained is close to the way that the human performs that task without a computer, that is, see case, assign conclusion and pick features in case to justify conclusion.
- The incremental acquisition of knowledge allows the approach to be part of the daily routine of the expert.

- The system is not designed to replace but to support the pathologist by saving considerable time in both deciding on the wording and writing the comment. The interpretation is included to assist the referring doctor in advising the patient.
- The system becomes a second expert with whom the pathologist can confer.
- The fact that maintenance does not increase as the number of cases or rules grow is a substantial benefit over typical rule-based systems, which tend to encourage abandonment after a critical point is reached (e.g., Mittal, Bobrow, & De Kleer, 1988).
- The ability to provide patient-specific and laboratory-customized comments has been found to be a highly attractive feature of the RDR approach.
- Finally, exception structures have been found to be comprehensible structures (Gaines, 1996) that act as useful mediating representations between humans and machines (Catlett, 1992).

In support of these claims we offer the following scenario which demonstrates how the KA process given in Figure 3 applies to our CDSS for pathology report interpretation. Once a pathology specimen is received the pathology laboratory performs the requested tests. The results of these tests and the patient and doctor

Figure 6: The Make Rules screen in MCRDR/FCA which shows the concept lattice for the formal context of "MCRDR contact lens rules" given in Figure 4

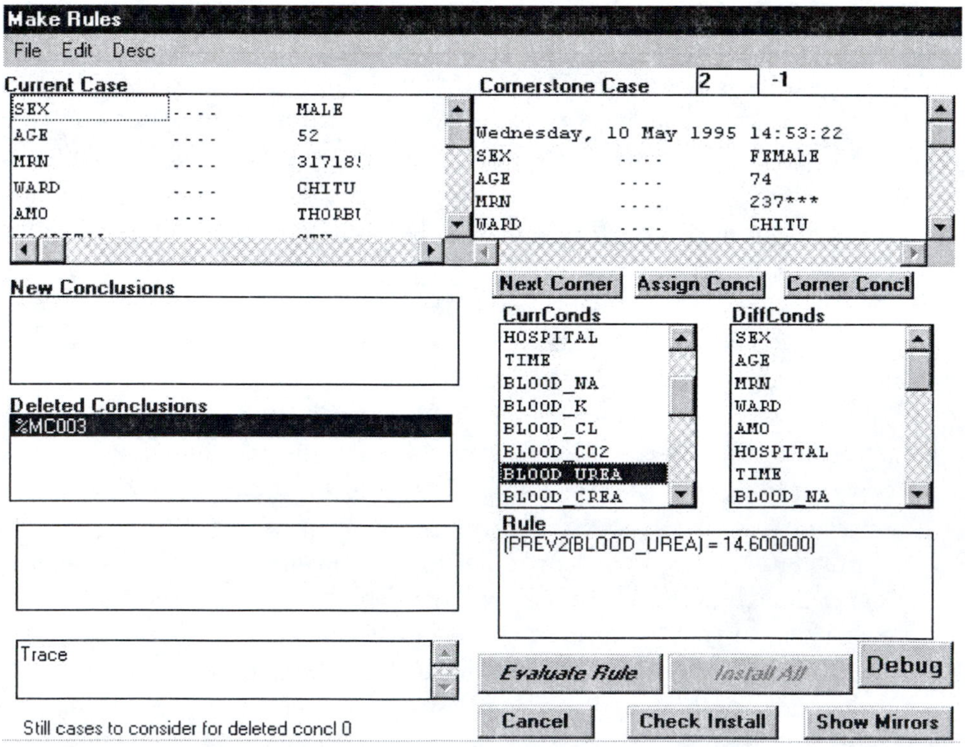

information are recorded in the computer. The patient results are used to perform an inference on the pathology knowledge base using RDR. The CDSS produces a printed report to be sent to the referring clinician. Before dispatch of the report and at a convenient time, the pathologist reviews a pile of reports for signing. If the pathologist does not agree with the comments supplied by the expert system, the report is put into a separate pile. To handle the reports in error, the pathologist can add handwritten comments to an uncommented report and perform system maintenance later or perform the modification immediately. To perform an update the pathologist will use the CDSS to retrieve the case in error, assign the correct conclusion/s to the case and select the salient features that warrant that conclusion. The tasks of reviewing, accepting or modifying an interpretation are similar to receiving an opinion from another human expert, then agreeing or disagreeing with them and stating what you believe to be the correct conclusion and why.

As shown in Figure 6, the system assists the user in selecting the conditions to form the new rule by showing the cornerstone case (the case associated with the rule that fired) and a list of differences. The naturalness and the simplicity of interacting with this CDSS are not readily apparent in the research version shown in Figure 6. The user interface of the commercial version of MCRDR has been engineered for usability but cannot be shown here due to current copyright/patent restrictions. In addition to receiving a second opinion, the CDSS saves the pathologist considerable time in writing comments and produces more consistent comments. In return the pathologist spends about 15 minutes per day performing system maintenance.

EXPERT SYSTEM TRENDS AND DIRECTIONS

CDSS have the potential to change current clinical and patient practice. Within the emerging fields of online healthcare and health informatics, CDSS can offer benefits to the various direct and indirect users such as patients, specialists, referring clinicians and laboratory administrators. For these benefits to be realized the needs of these different groups of users must to be understood and included in the system. The focus must be on how technology can assist the user rather than how the user needs to adapt to utilize the technology. Clancey (1997) and Collins (1997) argue that what we do and say only makes sense in our social context. An awareness is needed of the context-dependent and socially situated nature of expertise, which brings with it recognition of the importance of HCI issues. A social view of knowledge prompts the question "how can we embed our concepts into a computer and use them when computers don't share our social view ?" Collins (1997) suggests treating the KBS as a valuable assistant, where the expert takes advantage of the machine's ability to store and process more information and heuristics than a human mind but the inputs and outputs are blended by the expert to fit the social context. The lessons learned from the lack of acceptance of first-generation ES should be heeded. Otherwise current KBS will find history repeating itself.

DSS played a significant part in changing the role of the computer from a sophisticated calculator or filing cabinet to a machine that drives much of the modern organisation. Knowledge technologies have a major future role particularly when combined with advances in natural language technology. While the field of KM is expanding and to a large extent subsuming KBS research, it is interesting that much of the work done under the KM banner is essentially applying artificial intelligence (AI)/ES ideas to databases. An interesting phenomena of AI research, of which ES is a part, is that when a problem becomes solved it no longer holds any mystery and moves from being called AI to being just another part of information processing. This phenomena was first noted by Donald Michie and is thus known as the *Michie effect* (Gaines, 2000). A classic example of the demystification of AI can be found in the Deep Blue chess games. The ability to beat (or even play) a grand chessmaster can be considered intelligent behaviour. However, when it was discovered that Deep Blue won by brute force the achievement was not even seen as an AI technique. Examples of the assimilation of AI/ES concepts into mainstream data processing are the use of machine learning techniques in knowledge discovery from databases, the inclusion of business rules in database technologies and the use of ontologies for information systems development and Web searching. As ES concepts are taken up in other areas and as they are integrated and imbedded more and more, the perception within industry is that they don't really exist. So while there are many challenges remaining for ES research and we can expect much of the research to become practice, it may not be recognized as coming from the efforts of ES researchers.

Current work into the reuse and sharing of ontologies will be beneficial in data warehousing, B2B applications, e-commerce and Internet applications requiring knowledge-level interoperability of information systems and intelligent processing by agents. Once standards become more widely adopted, many of the current impediments to sharing will be overcome at least at a representation level. Advances in natural language technology research will benefit ES research by allowing knowledge to be acquired in natural language. The current trend towards interoperability of systems and integration of technologies will continue. Only the applications and domains will differ. Individual research communities will exist but the need for cross-fertilization of ideas and collaboration between research groups will become even more important. Continuing the trend in the 90s, stand-alone ES will become nonexistent. Just as we see moves towards a global economy and global village, it is becoming inappropriate to describe a system as either an ES or a DSS. Intelligent decision support systems (IDSS) will become more sophisticated, incorporating a range of technologies such as Web technology, natural language interfaces, machine learning and neural net techniques as well as more traditional database processing and statistical analysis. While these systems become more complex underneath, user interfaces will need to become more transparent and user-driven.

Part of the reason for the *Michie effect* is that achievements within AI/ES to date have done little to describe or replicate the nature of human expertise and knowledge. We are beginning to define and develop methods to identify tacit knowledge (e.g., Busch, Dampney, & Richards, 2001) but we are still a long way from knowing how to capture and transfer it within an organization. The RDR approach does offer a way of capturing tacit knowledge without the need for the expert to perform the codification. If our goal is to use computers as a support to human endeavours then we are achieving our goal. If our focus is on replication or replacement then we have a long way to go. Before we can begin this journey we need to answer some basic questions such as "What is knowledge or expertise?" or "How does a human reason?" A lesson to be learned from ES history is that we are doomed to failure if our expectations are unrealistic or even undesirable. I have no problem sending in a computer to disarm a land mine or fix a satellite. I am also happy to have my specialist consult an ES containing a body of up-to-date findings to verify his own decision. When it comes to deciding if these tasks should be done and what the final decision will be, then I prefer to keep a human expert in the loop.

The future for RDR is to further develop the range of tasks to which RDR can be applied. We continue to review the RDR structure and inferencing mechanism to develop a truly general purpose inference engine that can reason over many different problem types rather than seeking to develop a suite of PSMs, one for each type of task such as design, diagnosis, etc. As mentioned, at a research level we have used RDR to solve a wide range of problems, but the simplicity and novelty of RDR has meant that we have always had to provide real-world proof through evaluation, experimentation and particularly industrial application in order to gain acceptance. The integration of RDR with other technologies is also seen as an important step forward. We are excited about a current project in Europe to use RDR in an approach to manage the semantic Web.

CONCLUSION

RDR allows the user to capture a simple observable model of their world using attribute-value pairs and conclusions. The user has ownership of the KB developed. Using FCA, the user is able to retrospectively view and explore their underlying conceptual models. The simplicity of the approach and the range of activities and views supported in the RDR KA technique are applicable to a wide range of decision styles and situations with the user in control of the way they interact with their knowledge. The focus is on intelligent decision support. If we are willing to give up the Greek oracle notion and let the computer take over routine work and act as a second opinion then (intelligent) decision support systems will be with us for a long time.

REFERENCES

Beydoun, G., & Hoffmann, A. (1998, April) Building Problem Solvers Based on Search Control Knowledge. In B. Gaines & M. Musen (Eds.). *Eleventh*

Workshop on Knowledge Acquisition, Modeling and Management (KAW'98), (Vol. 1:SHARE.3, pp. 18-23) Banff, Alberta, Canada.

Busch, P., Dampney, C.N.G., & Richards, D. (2001, September). Formalising tacit knowledge within organisation X European. *CSCW 2001 Workshop on Managing Tacit Knowledge* (pp. 15-21) Bonn, Germany.

Catlett, J. (1992, November). Ripple-Down-Rules as a Mediating Representation. In *Interactive Induction Proceedings of the Second Japanese Knowledge Acquisition for Knowledge-Based Systems Workshop* (pp. 155-170) Kobe, Japan.

Chandrasekaran, B., & Johnson, T. (1993). Generic tasks and task structures. In J.M. David, J.-P. Krivine, & R. Simmons (Eds.). *Second Generation Expert Systems Springer* (pp. 232-272) Berlin.

Clancey, W. (1997). The conceptual nature of knowledge, situations and activity. In P.J. Feltovich, Ford, M. Kenneth, & R. R. Hoffman (Eds.). *Expertise in Context: Human and Machine* (pp. 248-291) Cambridge, MA: AAI Press/MIT Press.

Clancey, W. J. (1992). Model construction operators. *Artificial Intelligence*, 53,1-115.

Cohen, P., Schrag, R., Jones, E., Pease, A., Lin, A., Starr, B., Gunning, D., & Burke, M. (1998). The DARPA high-performance knowledge bases project. *AI Magazine, 19*(4), 25-49.

Collins, H. M. (1997). RAT-Tale: Sociology's contribution to understanding human and machine cognition. In P.J. Feltovich, Ford, M. Kenneth, & R. R. Hoffman (Eds.). *Expertise in Context: Human and Machine* (pp. 293-311) Cambridge, MA: AAAI Press/MIT Press.

Compton, P., & Jansen, R. (1990). A philosophical basis for KA. *Knowledge Acquisition, 2*, 241-257.

Compton, P., Preston, P., & Kang, B. (1994). Local patching produces compact knowledge bases. In L. Steels, G. Schreiber, & W. Van de Velde (Eds.). *A future in knowledge acquisition* (pp. 104-117) Berlin: Springer-Verlag.

Compton, P., Preston, P,. & Kang, B. (1995). The use of simulated experts in evaluating knowledge acquisition. *Proceedings 9th Banff Knowledge Acquisition for Knowledge Based Systems Workshop Banff.* (February 26–March 3, Vol. 1, 12.1-12.18).

Edwards, G. (1996). *Reflective expert systems in clinical pathology*. Unpublished doctoral thesis, University of New South Wales.

Edwards, G., Compton, P., Malor, R., Srinivasan, A., & Lazarus, L. (1993). PEIRS: A pathologist maintained expert system for the interpretation of chemical pathology. *Reports Pathology*, 25, 27-34.

Falquet, G., & Mottaz Jiang, C-L. (2000). Conflict resolution in the collaborative design of terminological knowledge bases. In R. Dieng & O. Corby (Eds.). *Proceedings of the 12th European Knowledge Acquisition Workshop (EKAW 2000), Lecture Notes in Artificial Intelligence 1937* (pp. 156-171) Berlin: Springer-Verlag.

Gaines, B. (2000). Knowledge science and technology: Operationalizing the Enlightenment. In P. Compton, A. Hoffmann, H. Motoda, & T. Yamaguchi (Eds.). *Proceedings of the 6th Pacific Knowledge Acquisition Workshop* (December 11–13, pp. 97-124) Sydney.

Gaines, B. R. (1996). Transforming rules and trees into comprehensible knowledge structures. In U. M. Fayyad, G. Piatetsky-Shapiro, P. Smyth, & R. Uthurusamy (Eds.). *Advances in Knowledge Discovery and Data Mining* (pp. 205-226) Cambridge, Massachusetts: MIT Press.

Gaines, B. R., & Shaw, M. L. G. (1989). Comparing the conceptual systems of experts. The 11th International Joint Conference on Artificial Intelligence, 633-638.

Grosso, W. E, Eriksson, H., Fergerson, R. W., Gennari, H., Tu, S.W., & Musen, M. (1999, October). Knowledge modelling at the millennium (The design and evolution of Protégé-2000). In *Proceedings of the 12th Workshop on Knowledge Acquisition, Modeling and Management (KAW'99)* Banff.

Guarino, N. (1996). Understanding, building and using ontologies. In N. Gaines & M. Musen (Eds.). *Proceedings of the 10th Knowledge Acquisition Workshop (KAW'96)* Banff.

Guha, T.V., & Lenat, D. B. (1990). CYC: A Mid-term report. *AI Magazine, 11*(3), 32-59.

Hochman, Z., Compton, P., Blumenthal, M., & Preston, P. (1996). Ripple-down rules: A potential tool for documenting agricultural knowledge as it emerges. *In Proceedings of the 8th Australian Agronomy Conference* (pp. 313-316) Toowoomba.

Kamori, S.. & Yamaguchi, T. (1998). Interactive composition of software engineering process using ontologies. In H. Motoda, R. Mizoguchi, P. Compton, & H. Liu (Eds.). *Proceedings of the Pacific Knowledge Acquisition Workshop (PKAW'98),* (November 22-23, 1-12).

Kang, B., Compton, P., & Preston, P. (1995). Multiple classification ripple down rules: Evaluation and possibilities. Proceedings 9th Banff Knowledge Acquisition for Knowledge Based Systems Workshop Banff (February 26–March 3, Vol 1, 17.1-17.20).

Kang, B., Yoshida, K., Motoda, H., & Compton, P. (1997). Help desk with intelligent interface. *Applied Artificial Intelligence, 11,* 611-631.

Kidd, A. L., & Sharpe, W. P. (1987). Goals for expert system research: An analysis of tasks and domains. In *Expert System IV* (pp. 146-152) Cambridge University Press.

Langlotz, C. P., & Shortliffe, E. E. (1983). Adapting a consultation system to critique user plans. *International Journal of Man-Machine Studies, 19,* 479-496.

Lazarus, L. (2000) Clinical decision support systems: Background and role. In *Clinical Support.* Retrieved from http://www.pks.com.au/CDSS_White_Paper_doc.pdf.

Martinez-Bejar, R., Benjamins, R., Compton, P., Preston, P., & Martin-Rubio, F. (1998). A formal framework to build domain knowledge ontologies for ripple-down rules-based systems. In B. Gaines & M. Musen (Eds.). *Eleventh Workshop on Knowledge Acquisition, Modeling and Management (KAW'98)*, (April 18-23, Vol. 2:SHARE.13) Banff, Alberta, Canada.

Martinez-Bejar R., Shiraz, G. M., & Compton, P. (1998). Using ripple down rules-based systems for acquiring fuzzy domain knowledge. In B. Gaines & M. Musen (Eds.). *Eleventh Workshop on Knowledge Acquisition, Modeling and Management (KAW'98),* (April 18-23, Vol. 1:KAT.2) Banff, Alberta, Canada.

Miller, R. A., & Masarie, F. E. (1990). The demise of the Greek oracle for medical diagnosis systems. *Meth Inform Med*, 29, 1-2.

Mittal, S., Bobrow, D.G., & de Kleer, J. (1988). DARN: Toward a community memory for diagnosis and repair tasks. In J. A. Hendler (Ed.). E*xpert Systems: The User Interface* (pp. 57-63) Ablex Publishing.

Newell, A. (1982). The knowledge level. *Artificial Intelligence,* 18, 87-127.

Newell, A., & Simon, H. A. (1976). Computer science as empirical inquiry: Symbols and search. *Communications of the ACM, 19*(3), 113-126.

Noy, F., Fergerson, R., & Musen, M. (2000). The knowledge model of Protégé-2000: Combining interoperability and flexibility. In R. Dieng & O. Corby (Eds.). *Proceedings of the 12th European Knowledge Acquisition Workshop (EKAW 2000), Lecture Notes in Artificial Intelligence 1937* (pp. 17-32) Springer-Verlag, Berlin.

Noy, N. F., & Hafner, C. D. (1997). The state of the art in ontology design: A survey and comparative review. *AI Magazine Fall 1997 18*(3), 53-74.

Puerta, A. R, Egar, J. W., Tu, S. W., & Musen, M. A. (1992). A multiple method knowledge acquisition shell for automatic generation of knowledge acquisition tools. *Knowledge Acquisition 4*(2), 171-196.

Ramadan, Z., Mulholland, M. Z., Hibbert, D. B., Preston, P., Compton, P., & Haddad, P. R. (1997). *Towards an expert system in ion chromatography using multiple classification ripple down rules* (MCRDR). Poster presented at International Ion Chromatography Symposium, Santa Clara, CA.

Richards, D. (2000a). Reconciling conflicting sources of expertise: A framework and illustration. In P. Compton, A. Hoffman, H. Motoda, & T. Yamaguchi (Eds.). *Proceedings of the 6th Pacific Knowledge Acquisition Workshop* (December 11-13, pp. 275-296) Sydney.

Richards, D. (2000b). The visualisation of multiple views to support knowledge reuse. *Intelligent Information Processing Conference (IIP'2000)* In conjunction with the 16th IFIP World Computer Congress WCC2000 (August 21-25, pp. 47-54) Beijing, China.

Richards, D., & Compton, P. (1997). Uncovering the conceptual modes in ripple down rules. In D. Lukose., H. Delugach, M. Keeler, L. Searle, & J. F. Sowa (Eds.). *Conceptual Structures: Fulfilling Peirce's Dream, Proc. of the 5th Int. Conf. on Conceptual Structures (ICCS'97)*, (August 3-8, University of Washington, Seattle, USA, LNAI 1257, pp. 198-212) Springer-Verlag, Berlin.

Richards, D., & Compton, P. (1999). Sisyphus I revisited: An incremental approach to resource allocation using ripple down rules. In B. Gaines & M. Musen (Eds.). *12th Workshop on Knowledge Acquisition, Modeling and Management (KAW'99),* Banff, Canada, SRDG Publications, Departments of Computer Science, University of Calgary, Calgary, Canada.

Richards, D., & Menzies, T. (1998). Extending the SISYPHUS III experiment from a knowledge engineering to a requirements engineering task. In B. Gaines & M. Musen (Eds.). *11th Workshop on Knowledge Acquisition, Modeling and Management (KAW'98),* Banff, Canada, SRDG Publications, Departments of Computer Science, University of Calgary, Calgary, Canada, Vol 1:SIS-6.

Richards, D., & Simoff, S. (2001). Design ontology in context: A situated cognition approach to conceptual modelling. *Special Issue on Conceptual Modelling in Design Computing in the International Journal of Artificial Intelligence in Engineering* 15, 121–136.

Russ, T., Valente, A., MacGregor, R., & Swartout, W. (1999) Practical experiences in trading off ontology usability and reusability. In *Proceedings of the 12th Workshop on Knowledge Acquisition, Modeling and Management (KAW'99),* (October 16-21) Banff.

Salle, J. M., & Hunter, J. (1990). *Computer/user cooperation issues for knowledge-based systems: A review.* Tech. Rep. AUCS/TR9003. Aberdeen University.

Scheffer, T. (1996). Algebraic foundation and improved methods of induction of ripple down rules repetition. In P. Compton, R. Mizoguchi, H. Motoda, & T. Menzies (Eds.). *Proceedings of Pacific Knowledge Acquisition Workshop PKAW'96,* (October 23-25, pp. 279-292) Coogee, Australia.

Schrieber, F., Crubezy, M., & Musen, M. (2000). A case study in using Protégé-2000 as a tool for CommonKADS. In R. Dieng & O. Corby (Eds.). Proceedings of the 12th European Knowledge Acquisition Workshop (EKAW 2000), Lecture Notes in Artificial Intelligence 1937, Springer-Verlag, Berlin, 33-48.

Schreiber, G., Weilinga, B., & Breuker, J. (Eds.). (1993). KADS: A principled approach to knowledge-based system development. *Knowledge-Based Systems,* London: Academic Press.

Shahar, Y., & Cheng, C. (1998). Model-based visualisation of temporal abstractions proceedings. *Fifth International workshop on Temporal Representation and Reasoning (TIME'98),* Sanibel Island, Florida.

Shaw, M.L.G., & Gaines, B.R. (1994). Personal construct psychology foundations for knowledge acquisition. In L. Steels, G. Schreiber, & W. Van de Velde (Eds.). A Future for Knowledge Acquisition Proceedings of the 8th European Knowledge Acquisition Workshop, EKAW'94, Lecture Notes in Artificial Intelligence 867, Springer Verlag, Berlin, 256-276.

Shiraz, G.M., & Sammut, C. (1998). Acquiring control knowledge from examples using ripple-down rules and machine learning. 11th Workshop on Knowledge

Acquisition, Modeling and Management, Banff, Canada, SRDG Publications, Departments of Computer Science, University of Calgary, Calgary, Canada, Vol 1:KAT-5.

Soloway, E, Bachant, J., & Jensen, K. (1987). Assessing the maintainability of XCON-in-RIME: Coping with problems of a very large rule base. *Proceedings of the Sixth International Conference on Artificial Intelligence* (Vol 2, pp. 824-829) Seattle, WA: Morgan Kaufman.

Turban, E. (1993) Decision support and expert systems: Management support systems. (4th ed.). New York: MacMillan.

Uschold, M., & Gruninger, M. (1996). Ontologies: Principles, methods and applications. *Knowledge Engineering Review, 11*(2), 93-155.

Van Daal, B., de Haas, M., & Weggeman, M. (1998). The knowledge matrix: A participatory method for individual knowledge gap determination. In *Knowledge and process management, 5*(4), 255-263.

Wang, J. C., Boland, M., Graco, W., & He, H. (1996). Use of ripple-down rules for classifying medical general practitioner practice profiles repetition. In P. Compton, R. Mizoguchi, H. Motoda, & T. Menzies (Eds.). *Proceedings of Pacific Knowledge Acquisition Workshop PKAW'96*, (October 23-25, pp. 333-345) Coogee, Australia.

Wille, R. (1982). Restructuring lattice theory: An approach based on hierarchies of concepts. In *Ordered Sets* (pp. 445-470) Boston: Reidel, Dordrecht.

Wille, R. (1989). Knowledge acquisition by methods of formal concept analysis. In E. Diday (Ed.). *Data Analysis, Learning Symbolic and Numeric Knowledge* (pp. 365-380) New York: Nova Science.

Wille, R. (1992). Concept lattices and conceptual knowledge systems. *Computers Math. Applic., 23*(6-9), 493-515.

Winograd, T., & Flores, F. (1986). U*nderstanding computers and cognition: A new foundation for design.* Ablex Norwood, NJ.

Young, L. F. (1989). *Decision support and idea processing systems.* Iowa: Win C. Brown Publishers.

Chapter XIV

Intelligent Support Framework of Group Decision Making for Complex Business Systems

Charu Chandra
University of Michigan-Dearborn, USA

Alexander V. Smirnov
St. Petersburg Institute for Informatics and Automation of the Russian
Academy of Sciences, Russia

ABSTRACT

As firms compete in global markets, they design and implement complex business systems, such as Supply Chain, Virtual Enterprise, Web-Based Enterprise, Production Network, e-Business, and e-Manufacturing. Common traits of these systems are (i) co-operation to implement shared goals, (ii) global distributed product development and manufacturing, and (iii) co-ordination of strategies and communication of information, among enterprise partners.

Information in this complex business system can be shared via the Internet, Intranet, and Extranet. One of the goals of Internet-Based Management (e-management) is to facilitate transfer and sharing of data and knowledge in the context of business collaborations. It offers the platform for design and modeling of diverse implementation strategies related to the type of agreement, optimisation criteria, decision mode, organisation structures, information sharing mechanisms, and business policies for this system.

"A General Framework of E-Management" that integrates (i) intelligent information support, (ii) group-decision making, and (iii) agreement modeling for a complex business system is proposed. A generic methodology of e-management information support based on "Ontology-Driven Knowledge Management" and "Multi and Intelligent Agents Technologies" for distributed decision making in scalable business systems is described. It is based on the premise that knowledge management should emphasize synergistic use of knowledge from multiple sources.

INTRODUCTION

As firms compete in global markets, they assume complex business system forms, such as supply chain, virtual enterprise, Web-based enterprise, production network, e-business, and e-manufacturing. Common traits of these systems are (i) cooperation to implement shared goals, (ii) global distributed product development and manufacturing, and (iii) coordination of strategies and communication of information, among enterprise partners. These traits have led the trend of transformation from a *capital*-to an *intelligence*-intensive business environment and from product-push to consumer-pull strategies.

The purpose of this type of system is to transform incomplete information about customer orders and available resources into coordinated plans for production and replenishment of goods and services in the *temporal network* formed by collaborating units. Information in this complex business system can be shared via Internet, intranet, and extranet for business-to-consumer, business-to-business service, and business-to-business goods transactions. One of the goals of Internet-based management (e-management) is to facilitate transfer and sharing of data and knowledge in the context of scalable business collaboration. It offers the platform for design and modeling of diverse implementation strategies related to the type of agreement, optimization criteria, decision mode, organization structures, information sharing mechanisms, and business policies for this system.

A general framework of e-management that integrates *(i) intelligent information support and (ii) group decision making* for a complex business system is proposed. Implementation of e-management methodology would fundamentally change the global business environment by enabling collaboration among its network units to achieve shared objectives. This approach satisfies the need for increasingly complex business relationships and underlying technology infrastructure being implemented in business systems by firms to support their global strategies.

A generic methodology of e-management information support based on *ontology-driven knowledge management* and *multiagents and intelligent agent technologies* for distributed decision making in *scalable* business systems is described. It is based on the premise that knowledge management should emphasize synergistic use of knowledge from multiple sources. Knowledge must be relevant to business system goals and processes and be accessible in the right form, place, and time. This is accomplished via design and development of knowledge at various levels and in different forms, such as (i) system knowledge, (ii) facilitator knowledge, (iii) unit (plant, department, etc.) knowledge, and (iv) user knowledge. Ontology is a form of knowledge representation applied in various problem domains. The ontology-driven knowledge management approach is implemented by translation and mapping between different types of ontologies. It utilizes reusable components and knowledge is configured as needed, in order to assist the business system's units and/or users (agents) in group decision making.

This chapter offers insights into a supply chain management problem-solving approach that enables implementing e-management philosophy by integrating capabilities for intelligent information support and knowledge interface through shared ontologies. First, current concepts, trends and requirements of a complex business system are discussed. This is followed by an overview of published research in decision support system (DSS) frameworks. Next, a general information framework that lays the blueprint of integrating information support to decision making activities in an enterprise is described. Then, we discuss major requirements for an intelligent enterprise information support. Following this, ontology-driven knowledge integration as a knowledge management technology is described. Finally conclusions and directions for future research in this field are highlighted.

COMPLEX BUSINESS SYSTEMS: CURRENT CONCEPTS, TRENDS AND REQUIREMENTS

Figure 1 depicts the evolution of enterprise organization from traditional forms to an "intelligent enterprise" (IE) (Olin, Greis, & Kasarda, 1999).

Figure 1: Evolution of the enterprise organization form (adapted from Olin et al., 1999)

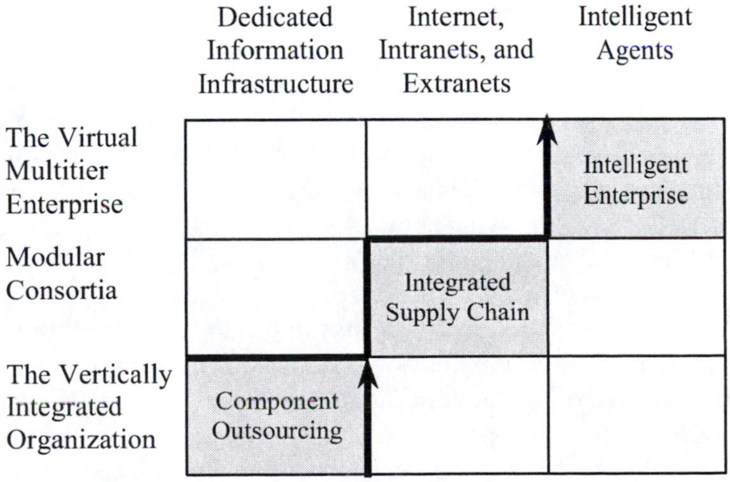

Knowledge is a critical resource for an IE. System integration deals with achieving common interface "within" and "between" various components at different levels of hierarchies, architectures and methodologies (Hirsch, 1995; Sousa, Heikkila, Kollingbaum, & Valckenaers, 1999) using distributed artificial intelligence and intelligent agents (Fischer, Miller, Heimig, & Scheer, 1996; Gasser, 1991; Jennings, 1994; Jennings, Faratin, Johnson, Brien, & Wiegand, 1994; Lesser, 1999; Sandholm, 1998; Smirnov, 1999; Wooldridge and Jennings, 1995). Knowledge modeling and ontologies describe unique system descriptions that are relevant to specific application domains (Fikes & Farquhar, 1999; Gruber, 1995; Gruninger, 1997; Smirnov & Chandra, 2000).

Supply chain (SC) is a special class of IE. In this form of complex business system, the key is to coordinate information and material flows, plant operations, and logistics (Lee & Billington, 1993).

Management of above information technologies requires capabilities for real-time decision support. The challenge is to accommodate interaction of various units with competing objectives as they share information with each other, and provide decision making capabilities towards achieving their shared goals. Therefore, e-management has come to symbolize a management philosophy that reflects important traits of the global digital economy, namely, dynamic real-time decision making, customer orientation, and speed in responding to market demands. This topic has evinced interest among academics and researchers on various aspects of the problem, based on Internet technologies, such as e-commerce, e-business, and e-manufacturing.

DECISION SUPPORT SYSTEM – PAST AND PRESENT

Gorry and Scott-Morton (1989) have proposed a DSS framework based on the research of Simon (1977) and Anthony (1965). The first part of the framework identifies three decision making phases, viz., intelligence, design, and choice. Decisions are classified as structured, semi-structured (Keen & Scott-Morton, 1978), and unstructured. Examples of these decision types are computerized clerical assistance, data processing, and model to support decision making, respectively. The second part is based upon the taxonomy suggested by Anthony (1965), which defines three major categories of user activities—strategic planning, management control, and operational control. A growing number of studies in DSS have been reported in the paper by Elam, Huber and Hurt (1986).

A further improvement in the development of decision support techniques witnessed the embodiment of knowledge and abilities of human experts in knowledge-based systems, labeled as expert systems, which enable the computer to offer advice to the user. As a result, the concept of knowledge-based model management systems was introduced to support the task of formulating a new decision model, choosing a model from the model base, analyzing the model, and interpreting the model's result (Blanning, 1993). Expert systems embedded into group decision support system (GDSS) have made these systems user-friendly, relevant to specific problems, and efficient problem-solving tools (Aiken, Sheng, & Vogel, 1991).

In Angehrn (1993), the conversational framework for decision support was introduced as the basis of a new generation of active, intelligent DSS and executive information systems. The modern distributed DSS and GDSS are based on agent and constraint satisfaction technologies (Durfee, 2001; Weiss, 1999; Wooldridge & Jennings, 1995). Based on the knowledge integration trend, an advanced DSS structure was proposed which includes the following components—data management, user interface, model management, and knowledge management (Turban, McLean, & Wetherbe, 1999). Here, knowledge management (Tsui, Garner, & Staab, 2000) is a new component, usually based on ontology as a knowledge representation model (Chandrasekaran, Josephson, & Benjamins, 1999; Fikes & Farquhar, 1999; Guarino, 1997).

The framework proposed in this chapter integrates decision making approaches and technologies for intelligent information support and problem solving. Its main components are knowledge, ontology, and agents and a unifying e-management decision making environment.

GENERAL INFORMATION FRAMEWORK OF E-MANAGEMENT FOR COMPLEX BUSINESS SYSTEMS

For efficient management of an SC, it is essential that its design be properly configured. An important facet of configuration is to understand the relationship between the SC system components defining its structure, which are products,

Figure 2: Interconnectedness of approaches and technologies

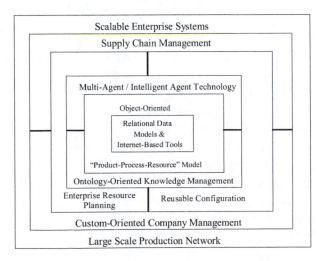

associated processes and resources. The primary goal of *e-management* is to facilitate transfer and sharing of knowledge in the context of new forms of enterprise configurations, such as supply chains; and virtual, extended and Web-based enterprises.

Figure 2 depicts a template used for describing interconnectedness between problem-solving approaches and technologies for the enterprise information environment. The proposed e-management technologies are categorized into two groups, (i) problem solving and (ii) information support.

For the first group, these are (1) custom-ordered (mass customization) management, (2) configuration management, and (3) constraint satisfaction and propagation. For the second group, these are (1) data and knowledge management, (2) ontological representation of knowledge, (3) multiagent and intelligent agent, and (4) conceptual and information modeling.

INFORMATION FRAMEWORK OF AN INTELLIGENT ENTERPRISE: MAJOR REQUIREMENTS AND TECHNOLOGIES

Major functions of knowledge integration for an IE could be determined as (i) communication, (ii) coordination, (iii) collaboration, and (iv) common or shared memory. The general structure of a multiagent system for e-management of an IE would allow distributed application domain knowledge description on dynamic constraint networks and cooperative decision making by means of local, delegated and shared problem solving. The local problem is a domain-specific problem that is applied for one agent (unit or user) and may have a unique solution. The delegated problem has two types of agents. One agent type is autonomous which may generate several solutions, while the other agent type acts as an arbiter that selects Pareto-optimal solution(s) from the solution set. The shared problem is common among agents (units or users) and may have a common solution.

The information support architecture for an SC builds on an agent classification implementation of e-management technologies, namely, custom-ordered management, configuration management, constraint satisfaction and propagation, and data and knowledge management (Fischer et al., 1996). The agent classification of this approach is described in Figure 3.

- *Problem-solving agent* (PSA) is designed for problem solving of different e-management processes, such as sourcing, forecasting, and inventory management in an SC. PSA is based on constraint satisfaction and propagation techniques and incorporates common beliefs and agreements of network members in order to facilitate problem solving (Smirnov & Sheremetov, 1998).
- *System information agent* (SIA) is oriented for consistency checking, controls of constraints for integration between units of an SC and its management and maintenance.

Figure 3: General framework for e-management information support for a supply chain

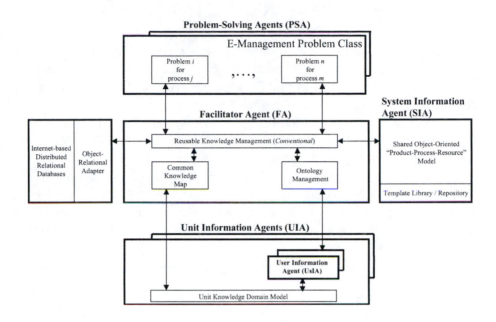

- *Facilitator agent* (FA) is oriented for distribution of knowledge and identification of access level in sharing data and knowledge base. It has three major components—(i) conventional reusable knowledge management techniques (Livelink, 1998), (ii) common knowledge map that describes distribution of knowledge sources for an SC, and (iii) ontology management.
- *Unit information agent* (UIA) is oriented towards application of reusable methods, techniques and solutions for problem solving at the unit level. It also includes the *user information agent* (UsIA).
- *Object-relational adapter* maps relational models to object-oriented data models and vice versa.

In order to solve a problem, the PSA through the FA deploys reusable knowledge management to communicate with the shared object-oriented data model (based on template libraries and repositories) in SIA and ontology-based/user-oriented knowledge domain models of UIA. The unit knowledge domain model describes the environment at the unit level, such as objectives, constraints and resources. The FA utilises the shared object-oriented data model for consistency checks of the unit's data and knowledge for problem solving. The FA communicates through the object-relational adapter with Internet-based distributed relational databases that describe the dynamic environment of an SC.

ONTOLOGY-DRIVEN KNOWLEDGE INTEGRATION AS A KNOWLEDGE MANAGEMENT TECHNOLOGY

An important requirement for a collaborative system is the ability to capture knowledge from multiple domains and store it in a form that facilitates reuse and sharing (Sousa et al., 1999). The methodology suggested in this chapter is limited to designing SC configurations for "product-process-resource" (PPR) systems and focused on utilizing *reusable knowledge* through ontological descriptions. It is based on GERAM, the Generalized Enterprise Reference Architecture and Methodology (ISO TC 184/SC 5/WG 1, 1997) at the domain level and MES (MESA, 1998), MEIP (1999), NIIIP (1994) and WFM (1996) methodologies at the application level.

Applying the above methodologies enables forming the conceptual model of the SC system. This is accomplished by knowledge modeling its product, process, and resource components to satisfy manufacturing constraints in its environment. The implementation of the e-management approach is based on the shared information

Figure 4: Links of users to knowledge and data in supply chain

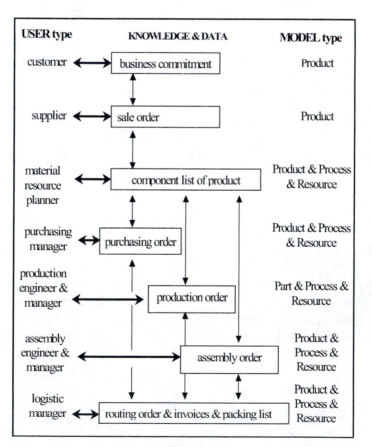

environment that supports the PPR model, used for integration and coordination of user's (unit's) activity. This model is studied from various viewpoints of user (unit) groups, as depicted in Figure 4.

Reusable knowledge management is a concept of knowledge management to organize "knowledge clusters" by their inherently common characteristics, as observed in various problem domains, and utilizing these as templates to describe unique conceptual models of an enterprise or its components.

Ontology is useful in creating unique models of an SC by developing knowledge bases specific to various e-management problem domains. Ontological translation of an SC, such as a virtual SC, is necessary because networks are multi-ontology classes of entities.

Ontology design is based on an ontology hierarchy. The top-level ontology is the "shared ontology" for domain-independent representation of the problem set. This type of ontology is needed to describe an abstract model using common knowledge model representation. The lower-level ontology is an "application ontology" and is a combination of the "domain-specific ontology" and the "problem-specific ontology." This type of ontology is needed to describe special knowledge about an application or a problem for unit and user. The top-level ontology is oriented for dynamic constraints network, while the lower-level ontology is for ontology-based constraints network (Smirnov & Chandra, 2000).

An *ontology management agent's (OMA)* function includes the possibility to convert the product-process-resource model employed in the problem-solving module from one problem-solving ontology to another. The system is supported by a number of ontologies:

- Service ontologies (forecasting, inventory, capacity and production planning)
- Domain ontologies (textile and automobile industry SC cases)
- Ontology of administration and management (FIPA management; FIPA, 1998)
- Ontology of roles (supplier, consumer, producer, negotiator, and bidder)

Knowledge management tools support the conversion of the PPR model from ontology to ontology. An abstract PPR model is based on the concept of ontology-based dynamic constraint networks. The above ontology management approach is based on two mechanisms (Smirnov & Chandra, 2000): (i) object class inheritance mechanism supported by inheritance of class ontologies (attributes inheritance) and by inheritance of constraints on class attribute values, and (ii) constraint inheritance mechanism for inter-ontology conversion supported by constraint inheritance for general model (constraints strengthening for "top-down" or "begin-end" processes).

CONCLUSIONS

A consumer-focused supply chain network approach offers various alternatives for enterprise integration through shared information infrastructure for decision making. The motivation in proposing this approach is to incorporate elements of scalability, reconfigurability and reusability of enterprise components. A *general information framework of e-management* utilizing the above methodologies offers an integrated approach to knowledge-based modeling of customer responsive systems. The proposed framework offers a mechanism to experiment with various types of behavior patterns that may emerge through interaction of virtual enterprise members and apply lessons learned in developing robust e-management models. Implementation of e-management methodology would fundamentally change the global business environment by enabling constructive collaboration among its network units to achieve shared objectives. This approach satisfies the need for increasingly complex business relationships and underlying technology infrastructure that firms are implementing to support their global strategies.

ACKNOWLEDGMENTS

This chapter documents results of research by authors on intelligent decision making frameworks. For the first author, it is supported by grants from Department of Energy, Los Alamos National Laboratory, including subcontract # H1757-0019-2G, 11/9/98; SAP America, Inc. during the year 2000 under the University Alliance Program; and Ford Motor Company during the years 1999-2001. For the second author, support is provided by grants during the year 1999-2001 from Ford Motor Company. The Russian Academy of Sciences has also provided partial support for this research through project # 4.4 of the research program "Intelligent Computer Systems."

REFERENCES

Aiken, M., Sheng, L., & Vogel, D. (1991). Integrating expert systems with group decision support systems. *ACM Transactions on Information Systems*, *9*(1), 75-95.

Angehrn, A. (1993). Computers that criticize you: Stimulus-based decision support system. *Interface*, *23*(3), 3-16.

Anthony, R. N. (1965). *Planning and control systems: A framework for analysis.* Cambridge, MA: Harvard University Graduate School of Business Administration.

Blanning, R. (1993). Model management systems: An overview. *Decision Support Systems*, *9*(1), 9-18.

Chandrasekaran, B., Josephson, J. R., & Benjamins, V. R. (1999). What are ontologies, and why do we need them? *IEEE Intelligent Systems and Their Applications*, 20-26.

Durfee, E. (2001). Distributed problem solving and planning. In M. Luch, V. Marik, O. Stepankova, & R. Trappl (Eds.). *Multi-agent systems and applications: Lecture notes in artificial intelligence #2086* (pp. 118-149) Springer.

Elam, J., Huber, G., & Hurt, M. (1986). An examination of the DSS literature (1975-

1985). In *Decision Support Systems: A Decade in Perspective* (pp. 239-251) Amsterdam: Elsevier Science.

Fikes, R., & Farquhar, A. (1999). Distributed repositories of highly expressive reusable ontologies. *IEEE Intelligent Systems*, (March/April), pp. 73-79.

Fischer, K., Müller, J. P., Heimig, H., & Scheer, A.-W. (1996). Intelligent agents in virtual enterprises. Proceedings of the First International Conference and Exhibition on the Practical Application of Intelligent Agents and Multi-Agent Technology (pp. 205-223) London: The Westminister Central Hall.

Foundation for Intelligent Physical Agents. (1998). *FIPA 98 Specification*, Part 12—Ontology Service. http://www.fipa.org.

Gasser, L. (1991). Social conceptions of knowledge and action: DAI foundations and open systems semantics. *Artificial Intelligence*, 47, 107-138.

Gorry, G. A., & Scott-Morton, M. (1989). A framework for management information systems. *Sloan Management Review*, 30, 49-61.

Gruber, T. (1995). Toward principles for the design of ontologies used for knowledge sharing. *International Journal of Human and Computer Studies*, 43(5/6), 907-928.

Gruninger, M. (1997). Integrated ontologies for enterprise modeling: Enterprise engineering and integration. In K. Kosanke & J. B. Nell (Eds.). *International Consensus* (pp. 368-377) Springer.

Guarino, N. (1997). Understanding, building, and using ontologies. A Commentary to *Using Explicit Ontologies in KBS Development* (by van Heijst, Schreiber, and Wielinga). *International Journal of Human and Computer Studies*, 46(2/3), 293-310.

Hirsch, B. (1995). Information system concept for the management of distributed production. *Computers in Industry*, 26, 229-241.

ISO TC 184/SC 5/WG 1 (1997) Requirements for enterprise reference architectures and methodologies. http://www.mel.nist.gov/sc5wg1/gera-std/ger-anxs.html

Jennings, N., Faratin, P., Johnson, M., Brien, P., & Wiegand, M. (1996). Using intelligent agents to manage business processes. In *Proceedings of the International Conference "The Practical Application of Intelligents and Multi-Agent Technology"* (pp. 345-360) London.

Jennings, R. (1994). Cooperation in industrial multi-agent systems. *World Scientific Series in Computer Science*, (Vol. 43) World Scientific.

Keen, P., & Scott-Morton, M. (1978). *Decision support systems: An organizational perspective*. MA: Addison-Wesley.

Lee, H. L., & Billington, C. (1993). Material management in decentralized supply chains. *Operations Research*, 41(5), 835-847.

Lesser, V. R. (1999). Cooperative multi-agent systems: A personal view of the state of the art. *IEEE Transactions on Knowledge and Data Engineering*, 11(1), 133-142.

Livelink: Collaborative Knowledge Management. (1998). http://www.opentext.com/livelink/knowledge_management.html

Manufacturing Enterprise Integration Program (MEIP). (1999). *National Institute of Standards and Technology (NIST)*. Gaithersburg, Maryland. http://www.atp.nist.gov

MESA International White Paper # 6. (1998). *MES Explained: A High Level Vision*. http://www.mesa.org

National Industrial Information Infrastructure Protocol (NIIIP). (1994). www.niiip.org

Olin, J. G., Greis, N. P., & Kasarda, J. D. (1999). Knowledge management across multi-tier enterprises: The problem of intelligent software in the auto industry. *European Management Journal, 17*(4), 335-347.

Sandholm, T. (1998). Agents in electronic commerce: Component technologies for automated negotiation and coalition formation. In *Proceedings of the International Conference on Multi Agent Systems* (pp. 10-11) Paris, France.

Simon, H. (1977). The new science of management decision. Englewood Cliffs, NJ: Prentice Hall.

Smirnov, A. (1999). Agent-based knowledge management for concurrent enterprise configuring. In *Proceedings of the First International Workshop of Central and Eastern Europe on Multi-agent Systems (CEEMAS'99)*, (pp. 256-269) St. Petersburg, Russia.

Smirnov, A., & Chandra, C. (2000). Ontology-based knowledge management for co-operative supply chain configuration. In *Proceedings of the 2000 AAAI Spring Symposium "Bringing knowledge to business Processes"* (pp. 85-92) California: Stanford: *AAAI Press*.

Smirnov, A.V., & Sheremetov, L. B. (1998). Agent & object-based manufacturing systems re-engineering: A case study. In N. Martensson et al. (Eds.). *Advances in Design and Manufacturing: Changing the Ways We Work* (Vol. 8, pp. 369-378) IOS Press.

Sousa, P., Heikkila, T., Kollingbaum, M., & Valckenaers, P. (1999). Aspects of co-operation in distributed manufacturing systems. In *Proceedings of the Second International Workshop on Intelligent Manufacturing Systems* (pp. 685-717) Leuven, Belgium.

Tsui, E., Garner, B. J., & Staab, S. (2000). The role of artificial intelligence in knowledge management. *Knowledge-Based Systems, 13*, 235-239.

Turban, E., McLean, E., & Wetherbe, J. (1999). *Information technology for management.* New York: John Wiley & Sons, Inc.

Weiss, G. (Ed.). (1999). *Multiagent systems: A modern approach to distributed artificial intelligence.* (p. 619) London: MIT Press.

Wooldridge, M., & Jennings, N. R. (1995). Intelligent agents—Theories, architectures, and languages. In M. Wooldridge & N.R. Jennings (Eds.). *Lecture Notes in Artificial Intelligence* (Vol. 890, No. 403) Springer-Verlag.

Work Flow Management (WFM) (1996). www.wfmc.org

Chapter XV

How Synthetic Characters Can Help Decision Making

Giuliano Pistolesi
ThinkinGolem, Italy

ABSTRACT

Synthetic characters are intelligent agents able to show typical human-like cognitive behavior and an artificially-made perceived personality by means of complex natural language interaction and artificial reasoning and emotional skills. They are mainly spreading on the web as highly interactive digital assistants and tutoring agents on online database systems, e-commerce sites, web-based communities, online psychotherapy, and in several consulting situations where humans need assistance from intelligent software. Until now, synthetic characters, equipped with data, models, and simulation skills, have never been thought as the building blocks for natural language interaction-based intelligent DMSS. This chapter illustrates the first research and development attempt in this sense by an Open Source project in progress centred on the design of a synthetic character-based DMSS.

INTRODUCTION

Synthetic characters are intelligent agents able to show typical human-like behavior by means of natural language interaction (Cheong, 1996; Mauldin, 1994). They are applied successfully in consulting situations, where the human user needs help to solve a problem, e.g., buy a product, choose an article, decide among two or more options in a business, understand or frame an ill-defined problem, and so on (Maes, 1998). Those kind of intelligent agents are common both as support systems on e-commerce Web sites or in Web-based communities (Lesnick & Moore, 1997; Norman, 1998) and as consultants on psychotherapy programs (Weizenbaum, 1976). All those applications of synthetic characters are framed within a typical consulting process in a problem-solving situation involving humans (Turkle, 1996).

Up to now, synthetic characters have never been thought of as building blocks for natural language interaction-based DMSS. The power of such models as support systems to help human decision making is being explored in our open-source research project currently under development by our information technology company.

The process inside this DMSS of new conception is quite simple. First, the synthetic character enables a sort of brainstorming between it and the human decision maker by a questions-and-answers natural language interaction, e.g., a conversation. This interaction helps the user to frame the problem and assign variables, decision factors, weights and scores to a hybrid multifactorial decision model which integrates features of decision tree models and Bayesian networks. Second, the synthetic character instances a decision making model or recovers a similar example previously stored in its knowledge base for that decision problem and designs scenarios for simulations through the interaction with the user. Finally, simulations are performed and the decision making process can be modified after an analysis of results by the user and the synthetic character together, redefining elements either of the scenarios or of the model designed with a new brainstorming phase.

The main purpose of this chapter is to describe a new kind of DMSS based on synthetic characters, which represent an interesting and promising research field within the intelligent agents domain. We will briefly discuss how decision making can be supported by a particular highly interactive kind of intelligent agent, namely, synthetic characters. We will introduce an overview from intelligent agents toward synthetic characters in agent-based support systems. We will also discuss general characteristics of decision making modeling and the architecture and processing flow of DEMON (DEcision Making OrgaNizer), the decision support agent we are developing. Finally, we will draw some concluding remarks.

AGENT-BASED SUPPORT SYSTEMS

Autonomous agents are computational systems that inhabit some complex, dynamic environment, sense and act autonomously in this environment, and by doing so realize a set of goals or tasks for which they are designed (Maes, 1994; Wooldridge, 2000). Autonomous agents can take many different forms, depending on the nature of the environment they inhabit. If the environment is the real physical environment, then the agent takes the form of an autonomous robot. Alternatively, one can build 2-D or 3-D animated agents that inhabit simulated physical environments. Finally, so-called *bots*, software agents or interface agents, are disembodied entities that inhabit the digital world of computers and computer networks (Maes, 1994).

There are obvious applications for all these types of agents. For example, autonomous robots have been built for surveillance, exploration, and other tasks in environments that are unaccessible or dangerous for human beings. There is also a long tradition of building simulated agents for training purposes. Finally, more recently, software agents have been proposed as one mechanism to help computer users deal with work and information overload (Maes, 1998; Norman, 1998).

To the extent that such a system understands how a particular user's needs differ from what the standard interface presents, it builds a private interface between the computer and the user. In this interface, the agent will "understand" the user's needs to perform formerly complex or unknown tasks with computer-created simplifying macros: This is what we often see on modern portal Web sites, where the Web interface can be adapted to the user's needs by an assistant agent. An interface agent is defined as an autonomous agent which mediates between a human user and computer environment. An interface agent differs from an ordinary interface since it is expected to change its behaviors and actions autonomously according to the human user's behaviors and the situations as the interaction progresses. At the same time, the agent is expected to maintain a consistent, defined personality even though it displays various behaviors in different situations depending on the context (Mase, 1997).

Chatterbots, which are an implementation of anthropomorphic systems equipped with natural language interaction skills (Maes, 1995), can be very successful in this task: Weizenbaum's (1976) program ELIZA could convince users briefly that they were conversing with a real person. MICKIE (an ELIZA derivative of Bevan, Pobgee, & Somerville, 1981) was used successfully to obtain information from medical patients. JULIA is another example of anthropomorphic systems living in a multi-user domain (MUD) and interacting with human users via natural language processing (Mauldin, 1994; Turkle, 1996).

A chatterbot has several different modules for dealing with the different functions required to interact with a human user in natural language. Typically, the conversation module is implemented as a network of mini-experts, which are collections of input patterns (i.e., words and phrases) and associated potential responses. Chatterbots go beyond the ELIZA system in that they use more smart tricks to analyse language and answer and have more sophisticated memories of past events or conversations.

Though no one seems to agree on exactly what is meant by the term agent, there are a growing number of them on the market. They are known as "chatterbots", "synthetic characters," "personal assistants," "knowbots," "softbots," "userbots," "knowledge navigators," and "guides." Thus, agents might set up schedules, reserve hotel and meeting rooms, arrange transportation, and even outline meeting topics, all without human intervention. Agents may well have numerous positive contributions to our lives. They can simplify our use of computers, allowing us to move away from the complexity of command languages or the tedium of direct manipulation toward intelligent, agent-guided interaction. Agents offer the possibility of providing friendly assistance so smoothly that users need not even be aware (Norman, 1994), on condition that they would be able to evolve their cleverness to make the human user confident in their *competence*. This is commonly referred to as the typical issue of *trust* on agents (Maes, 1998).

The selling points for these programs are that they claim to have captured the essential qualities of human intelligence. According to Bates (1994), this means reasoning, problem solving, learning via concept formation, and other qualities apparently central to the capacity we call intelligence. The agent technology is being researched to engage and help all types of end users (Riecken, 1994) with such tasks as information filtering, information retrieval, mail management, meeting scheduling, selection of books, movies, music, and so forth (Maes, 1994). Agents that can build up goals and perform tasks driven by those goals are certainly useful in several contexts. If humans identify with and accept an agent as human instead of artificial, they would be more able to trust the agent and better able to communicate with it, and for this reason, building agents requires the agent researcher to think more about the user behaviors (Norman, 1994; Trappl & Petta, 1997).

Currently, there are many signs that interest in this research and application field will continue to increase and that computer intelligence manifested through synthetic agents will grow significantly (Elliott & Brzenzinski, 1998).

DEMON: A SYNTHETIC CHARACTER-BASED DECISION MAKING SUPPORT SYSTEM

There is some empirical evidence that structuring decision problems and identifying creative decision alternatives determine the ultimate quality of decisions. DMSS aim mainly at this broadest type of decision making, and in addition to supporting choice, they aid in identifying and modeling decision opportunities and structuring decision problems (Druzdel & Flynn, 2000).

DEMON is a synthetic character-based DMSS model to make a human user able to manage complex decision problems with the help of a sophisticated intelligent agent. It is the first intelligent agent under development within the framework of the DEMONS Open Source project at *ThinkinGolem* (www.thinkingolem.com), inspired to the *Pandemonium* model of cognition (Selfridge, 1959): a set of interactive DEMONs, i.e., a multiagent system composed of DEMON decision support agents that supports both individual and group decision making. Then, the main purpose of the whole project is to develop a general-purpose, customizable, adaptive, multiagent-based DMSS at low cost that will be distributed according to the *Open Source* freelosophy (www.opensource.org).

Decision Making Modeling in DEMON

A simple view of decision making is that it is a problem of choice among several alternatives (Anderson, 1975; Lindsay & Norman, 1977). It has been rather convincingly demonstrated in numerous empirical studies that human judgment and decision making are based on intuitive strategies as opposed to theoretically sound reasoning rules (Bell, Raiffa, & Tversky, 1988; Dawes, 1988; Kahneman, Slovic, & Tversky, 1982; Kahneman & Tversky, 1972, 1973; Tversky, 1969; Tversky & Kahneman, 1973), but decision making can be improved if a rigorous process of framing the decision problem is performed.

Decision modeling is the fundamental process of decomposing and formalizing a decision problem (Druzdel & Flynn, 2000). Building a model of a decision problem allows for applying scientific knowledge that can be transferred across problems and often across domains. It allows for analyzing, explaining, and arguing about a decision problem.

While mathematically a model consists of variables and a specification of interactions among them, from the point of view of decision making a model and its variables represent the following three components: (1) a measure of preferences over decision objectives, (2) available decision options, and (3) a measure of uncertainty over variables in the decision and the outcomes.

Preference is widely viewed as the most important concept in decision making. Outcomes of a decision process are not all equally attractive and it is crucial for a decision maker to examine these outcomes in terms of their desirability. Preferences can be ordinal (e.g., more income is preferred to less income), but it is convenient and often necessary to represent them as numerical quantities, especially if the outcome of the decision process consists of multiple attributes that need to be compared on a common scale. Even when they consist of just a single attribute but the choice is made under uncertainty, expressing preferences numerically allows for trade-offs between desirability and risk.

The second component of decision problems is available decision options. Often these options can be enumerated (e.g., a list of possible suppliers), but sometimes they are continuous values of specified policy variables (e.g., the amount of raw material to be kept in stock). Listing the decision options is an important element of model structuring.

The third element of decision models is uncertainty. Uncertainty is one of the most inherent and most prevalent properties of knowledge, originating from incompleteness of information, imprecision, and model approximations made for the sake of simplicity. It would not be an exaggeration to state that real-world decisions not involving uncertainty either do not exist or belong to a truly limited class (Druzdel & Flynn, 2000).

Decision making under uncertainty can be viewed as a deliberation: *determining which alternative or action or plan should be choosen to better accomplish the decision-maker's goal*. The process rests on the assumption that a good decision is one that results from a good decision-making process that considers all important factors and is explicit about decision alternatives, preferences, and uncertainty.

The decision making model adopted by DEMON is an hybrid model in which features of different decision models are integrated to perform the choice for an alternative in a decision problem (Figure 1).

Figure 1: An example of the hybrid decision making model adopted by DEMON; decision trees characteristics are integrated with some of a multi-factorial decision model to build a decision making model whose features meet some desirable qualities of Bayesian networks

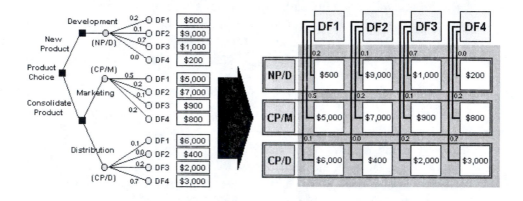

DEMON uses a multifactorial decision model (Keeney & Raiffa, 1976; Montgomery & Svenson, 1976) integrated with a decision tree model to represent the features of the decision problem, namely, variables (e.g., alternatives), decision factors, constraints, weights and scores (Behn & Vaupel, 1982). For what concerns weights (and possibly scores, in case of a qualitative decision problem), DEMON considers them like subjective probabilities (as in the decision tree model), according to a Bayesian view (Raiffa, 1968; von Winterfeldt & Edwards, 1988), since Bayesian networks (Pearl, 1988) offer a compact representation of joint probability distributions and can be easily extended with decision and value variables for modeling decision problems.

The hybrid decision making model used by DEMON is an excellent tool for making both qualitative and quantitative decisions where a lot of complex information needs to be taken into account. It provides an effective structure in which alternative decisions and the implications of taking those decisions can be laid down and evaluated. It also helps both the user and the synthetic character to form an accurate, balanced picture of the risks and rewards that can result from a particular choice. Therefore, this hybrid model provides an effective method of decision making because it (Bazerman, 1990): (1) clearly frames the problem so that all choices can be viewed, discussed and challenged; (2) provides a framework to quantify the values of outcomes and the probabilities of achieving them; (3) helps both the user and the synthetic character to make the best decisions on the basis of the existing information and best guesses.

Anyway, the DEMON model-base system can be improved anytime by direct programming or uploading new decision making model scripts.

Architecture of DEMON

DMSSs are interactive, computer-based systems that aid users in judgment and choice activities (Alter, 1991; Er, 1988; Finlay, 1989; Gorry & Scott-Morton, 1971; Laudon & Laudon, 2000; Pinsonneault & Kraemer, 1993; Sprague, 1980; Turban & Aronson, 1998; Turban, McLean & Wetherbe, 1996; Wysocki & Young, 1989; Zwass, 1998). They provide data storage and retrieval and support framing, modeling, and problem solving. Typical application areas of DMSS are management and planning in business, health care, the military, and any area in which management will encounter complex decision situations. Typically, there are three fundamental components of DMSS (Sage, 1991).

The first component is the data-base management system (DBMS). A DBMS serves as a data bank for the DMSS. It stores large quantities of data that are relevant to the class of problems for which the DMSS has been designed and provides logical data structures (as opposed to the physical data structures) with which the users interact. A DBMS separates the users from the physical aspects of the database structure and processing. It should also be capable of informing the user of the types of data that are available and how to gain access to them.

The second component is the model-base management system (MBMS). The role of MBMS is analogous to that of a DBMS. Its primary function is providing independence between specific models that are used in a DMSS from the applications that use them. The purpose of an MBMS is to transform data from the DBMS into information that is useful in decision making. Since many problems that the user of a DMSS will cope with may be unstructured, the MBMS should also be capable of assisting the user in model building.

Finally, the third component is the dialog generation and management system (DGMS). The main product of an interaction with a DMSS is insight. As their users are often managers who are not computer-trained, DMSS need to be equipped with intuitive and easy-to-use interfaces. These interfaces aid in model building, but also in interaction with the model, such as gaining insight and recommendations from it. Like any other interface, the primary responsibility of a DGMS is to enhance the ability of the system user to utilize and benefit from the system support (Card, Moran, & Newell, 1983; Newman & Lamming, 1995; Preece, 1994).

While a variety of DMSS exists, the above three components can be found in most parts of DMSS architectures, and DEMON is not an exception (Figure 2).

While the quality and reliability of modeling tools and the internal architectures of DSS are important, the most crucial aspect of DMSS (and, therefore, of DEMON) is, by far, their user interface (Angehrn, 1993). Current issues of DMSS can provide several interface facilities using friendly concepts and properties of a graphical user interface (GUI), following the *direct manipulation* metaphor (Schneiderman, 1988), but this can be a somewhat hit-and-miss affair in practice, requiring significant management skills on the part of the user, which, on the contrary, should be confident with a more reliable intelligent supporting system, according to the metaphor of a *personal assistant* (Chin, 1998; Maes, 1998).

Figure 2: The main processing flow of DEMON

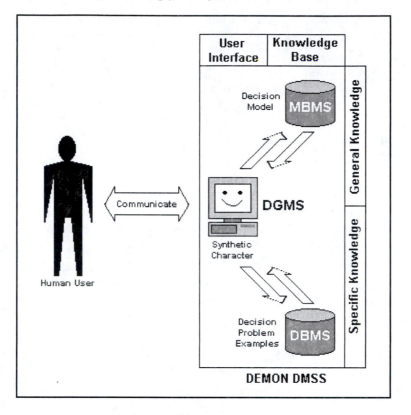

DEMON is able to perform all tasks required for a good DMSS user interface and more, thanks to the synthetic character who performs natural language interaction (e.g., conversation; Bobrow, 1968) with the user, extracting and providing information by well-formed sentences (Cheong, 1996; Mauldin, 1994).

Gorry and Scott-Morton (1971) proposed that the attributes of information (e.g., accuracy, source, aggregation level, currency) vary depending on the level of managerial activities (Anthony, 1965) and relative degree of structure in the decision making (Simon, 1960). Many other researches suggested that information processing requirements depend on task uncertainty, mechanism for control and coordination, nature of decision making, and level of management activities (Alloway & Quillard, 1983; Cooper, 1985; Daft & Lengel, 1986; Daft & Macintosh, 1978; Davis & Olson, 1985; Gordon, Larker, & Tuggle, 1978; Gorry & Scott-Morton, 1971; Zmud, 1983). In general, what those researchers emphasized is that a DMSS should be designed to provide an appropriate amount and quality of information according to task variety and analyzability, in order that users may clarify ambiguities and define problems (Daft & Lengel, 1986; Daft & Macintosh, 1978; Ito & Peterson, 1986; Rice, 1992). Since the most important result of a session with a DMSS is insight into the decision problem, to accomplish this goal a good user interface to DMSS supports model construction and model analysis, reasoning about the problem structure in addition to numerical calculations and both choice and optimization of decision variables. Not only DEMON is able to vary the amount and quality of information provided through sophisticated natural language interaction strategies employed to adapt to the human user's needs (Barnard, 1987; Barnard, Hammond, Morton, Long, & Clark, 1981), but it is also able to manage individual differences and styles in problem solving and decision making (Cowan, 1991; Haley & Stumpf, 1989; Hayes & Allinson, 1994; Huitt, 1992; Nutt, 1990; Taggart & Valenzi, 1990).

DEMON learns about the user and adapts to him/her, and, on the other hand, the user learns about the DMSS and adapts his behavior accordingly, since a truly adaptive system should support the user's learning of the system (Sasse, 1992; Vassileva, 1996). Thanks to cognitive and behavior scripts, the synthetic character is able to decide whether to adapt to the user at all or when it is better to teach him something instead (i.e., to make the user adapt to the system), that is, whether to be *reactive* or *proactive*. Then, the agent is an active participant in the interaction (Carroll & Campbell, 1989), which can decide and manage the course of interaction and not just follow embedded decisions made at design time, i.e., normative decisions. However, such a support system is able to negotiate its decisions with the learner and not just impose them on him, since in pursuing its decision making supporting goals, DEMON relies explicitly on its relationship with the user (Sasse, 1992; Vassileva, 1995).

Processing Flow of DEMON

The main processing flow of DEMON is shown in Figure 3.

The model is based on the explicit representation of goals, choices, relationships, and strategies, and the use of natural language to receive information and produce explanations (Slade, 1994).

Through a continuous natural language interaction, the synthetic character extracts knowledge, that is, information about the decision problem, actions to perform, and evaluations and suggestions about the DMSS's performance on that problem. It also provides information to the human user, that is, information about the decision problem and operations performed, results about that problem and actions performed, and suggestions on operations to perform with the agreement of the user.

As decision problem information is gathered, the decision model script (the hybrid multifactorial decisionmaking model) is recalled from memory and it is progressively filled with knowledge acquired.

During this script fullfillment process, a case-based reasoning upon memory for decision problem examples is performed to find a similar case.

If a similar decision problem case is found then features and solutions of that case are recalled.

If a similar case is not found, the DMSS builds and simulates decision scenarios on the basis of information gathered and searches for stable solutions through scenarios.

Figure 3: Component architecture of DEMON

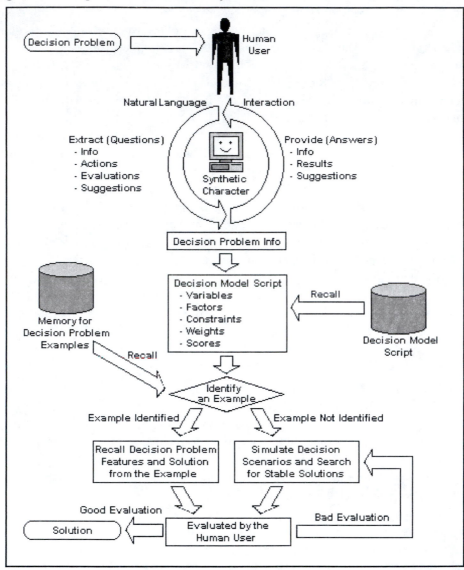

Finally, results from both branches are shown to the human user for evaluation and refining of the decision problem currently framed or to end the decision making process with the acceptance of solution (e.g., alternative, choice) proposed by the DMSS.

Then, the DEMON processing flow traces those phases of a typical decision making process (Simon, 1960): intelligence (i.e., searching for information), design (i.e., developing alternatives), choice (i.e., selecting an alternative), and review (i.e., assessing past choices).

Moreover, DEMON is able to acquire and evolve its knowledge base by learning from several sources (Figure 4).

Figure 4: Learning sources for DEMON

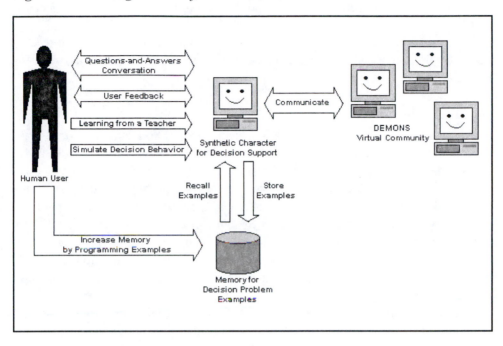

First, the synthetic character learns rules and preferences directly by natural language interaction with the user through a questions-and-answers conversation, like typical chatterbots (Cheong, 1996; Lesnick & Moore, 1997; Mauldin, 1994; Turkle, 1996; Weizenbaum, 1966). By a sophisticated pattern recognition our agent extracts information from natural language sentences provided by the user. Extracted information fills in slots of the decision problem knowledge script (Minsky, 1975; Schank, 1975; Schank & Abelson, 1977), which, in turn, motivate the synthetic character (Toates, 1986) to acquire more knowledge by driving conversation (e.g., by choosing successive conversation functions properly) with the user on the decision problem.

Second, the synthetic character learns to refine its performance by direct and indirect user feedback (Thorisson & Cassel, 1997), that is, by a kind of social reinforcement learning (Russell & Norvig, 1995). Indirect feedback occurs when the user decides to ignore or accepts suggestions of the agent about the decision problem matter, while direct feedback occurs when the user gives explicit negative or positive reinforcement through appropriate natural language patterns.

Third, the agent can learn from correlational analysis between the current decision problem and examples stored in its memory, like in case-based reasoning decision aiding systems (Kolodner, 1991). Examples can be given explicitly by the user through programming of new decision problem scripts (*direct programming of examples* mode), which will increase the synthetic character's memory on which base decision problem case-based reasoning is performed. Moreover, the user can train the synthetic character by giving it hypothetical examples of decision problems and either telling it exactly what to do in those cases (*learning from a teacher* mode) or asking it how the agent would face those decision problems (*simulate decision behavior* mode).

Fourth, the agent can ask for advice from other agents of the same kind (DEMONS) that assist other human users with the same (or similar) decision problems.

Future Trends

The main aspect of the DEMONS project that will be further explored is the development of the virtual community of synthetic-character-based DMSS. Through the World Wide Web it is possible for agents to communicate to each other experiences and suggestions about decision problem scripts like a virtual community (of virtual lifelike agents) to increase the knowledge base of the synthetic character. Group decision-making support systems, or GDMSS, are a hybrid type of DMSS that allows multiple users to work collaboratively in groupwork using various software tools typical of groupware, emphasizing communications, collaboration and shared decision making support among participants (De Sanctis & Gallupe, 1987; Dennis, Quek & Pootheri, 1996).

It is no longer necessary that the DMSS is an almighty information system knowing the answer to any question that may arise during the interaction session with a human user. Networking provides a possibility to find somewhere else another DEMON who can provide help and information for that question. This trend can be seen in the increasing work on collaborative learning systems, which are able to find appropriate partners for help or collaboration and to form teams and support goal-based group activities (Collins et al., 1997; Hoppe, 1995). For this purpose, it is needed that DEMONS are able to communicate the information about their users (user models) about their available resources and goals and in order to find an appropriate partner with the desired answers. These agents can communicate and negotiate among themselves for achieving their decision making support goals.

The DEMONS virtual community of agents devoted to performing decision making support is a practical application of these conceptions which integrates the two perspectives of intelligent decision support and group decision support, like in other similar agent-based systems (Rachlin et al., 1998).

CONCLUSIONS

Intelligent agents radically change the style of human-computer interaction. Actually, a lot of software systems make use of them to assist the user in using the software itself. The user delegates a range of tasks to personalized agents that can act on the user's behalf, according to the metaphor of *personal assistants*. Also DMSS can benefit from a particular kind of intelligent agents, namely, synthetic characters, which summarize significant features both of personal digital assistants and of chatterbots. DEMON is the first implementation of a synthetic-character-based DMSS and the first building block for an extensive multiagent-base DMSS available to the whole information community.

DEMON gradually learns how to better assist the user in decision making by: (1) interacting with the user in natural language, asking him/her for information and knowledge about the features of the decision problem under management (e.g., variables, decision factors, constraints, and any other significant characteristic of the situation); (2) receiving positive and negative feedback from the user through natural language interaction; (3) analysing correlations between the current decision problem and those examples stored in its memory (the user can increase the memory for examples through his/her direct programming of decision making scripts); (4) receiving explicit instructions from the user about that kind of decision problem (i.e., *learning from a teacher* mode); and (5) simulating decision behavior in imaginary decision problem examples proposed by the user (i.e., *simulate decision behavior* mode).

This DMSS of new conception tackles two of the hardest problems deriving from the implementation of agents-based systems: *competence* and *trust* (Maes, 1998). Competence is met through adaptive behavior of the synthetic character, who becomes more and more helpful as it accumulates knowledge about both decision problems and the user's style in facing those problems. Increasing competence, the DEMON increases the user's trust in its capabilities and decision making support effectiveness.

The perspective to build a virtual community of DEMONS to put in practice an integration between the intelligent decision support and the group decision support systems is one of the main future trends of our project, currently under development at the Open Source community of ThinkinGolem (www.thinkingolem.com).

REFERENCES

Alloway, R. M., & Quillard, J. A. (1983). *User manager's systems needs. Management Information Science Quarterly*, 6, 27-41.

Alter, S. (1991). *Information systems: A management perspective*. Reading, MA: Addison-Wesley.

Anderson, B. F. (1975). *Cognitive psychology: The study of knowing, learning, and thinking*. New York: Academic Press.

Angehrn, A. A. (1993). Computers that criticize you: Stimulus-based decision support systems. *Interfaces, 23*(3), 3-16.

Anthony, R. N. (1965). *Planning and control systems: A framework for analysis*. Cambridge, MA: Harvard University Press.

Barnard, P. J. (1987). Cognitive resources and the learning of human-computer dialogs. In J. M. Carroll (Ed.). *Interfacing Thought: Cognitive Aspects of Human-Computer Interaction*. Cambridge, MA: MIT Press.

Barnard, P. J., Hammond, N. V., Morton, J., Long, B. J., & Clark, I. A. (1981).

Consistency and compatibility in human-computer dialogue. *International Journal of Man-Machine Studies*, 15, 87-134.

Bazerman, M. H. (1990). *Judgment in managerial decision making.* (2nd ed.) New York: Wiley & Sons.

Behn, R. D., & Vaupel, J. W. (1982). Quick Analysis for Busy Decision Makers. New York: Basic Books.

Bell, D., Raiffa, H., & Tversky, A. (Eds.). (1988). *Decision making.* New York: Cambridge University Press.

Bevan, N., Pobgee, P., & Somerville, S. (1981). MICKIE: A microcomputer for medical interviewing. *International Journal of Man-Machine Studies*, 14, 39-47.

Bobrow, D. (1968). Natural language input for a computer problem-solving system. In M. Minsky (Ed.). *Semantic Information Processing.* Cambridge, MA: MIT Press.

Card, S., Moran, T. P., & Newell, A. (1983). *The psychology of human-computer interaction.* Hillsdale, NJ: Lawrence Erlbaum.

Carroll, J. M., & Campbell, R. L. (1989). Artifacts as psychological theories: The case of human-computer interaction. *Behaviour and Information Technology,* 8, 247-256.

Cheong, F. C. (1996). Internet agents: Spiders, wanderers, brokers and bots. Indianapolis, IN: New Riders.

Chin, D. N. (1998). Intelligent interfaces as agents. In M. T. Maybury & W. Wahlster (Eds.). *Readings in Intelligent User Interfaces.* San Francisco: Morgan Kaufmann.

Cohen, P. R. (1992). The role of natural language in a multimodal interface. *ACM Symposium on User Interface Software and Technology.* Monterey, CA.

Collins, J., Greer, J., Kumar, V., McCalla, G., Meagher, P., & Tkatch, R. (1997). Inspectable user models for just-in-time workplace training. *Proceedings of User Modeling '97* (pp. 327-338) Berlin: Springer.

Cooper, R. B. (1985). Identifying appropriate MIS/DSS support: A cost analysis approach. *Proceedings of the 6th International Conference on Information Systems,* Vol. 89-104.

Cowan, D. A. (1991). The effect of decision making styles and contextual experience on executives' descriptions of organizational problem formulation. *Journal of Management Studies, 28*(5), 463-483.

Daft, R. L., & Lengel, R. H. (1986). Organizational information requirement, media richness and structural design. *Management Science*, 32, 554-571.

Daft, R. L., & Macintosh, N. B. (1978). A new approach to the design and use of management information. *California Management Review*, 21, 82-92.

Davis, G. B., & Olson, M. H. (1985). *Management information systems.* New York: McGraw-Hill.

Dawes, R. M. (1988). Rational choice in an uncertain world. San Diego: Hartcourt Brace Jovanovich.

De Sanctis, G., & Gallupe, R. B. (1987). A foundation for the study of group decision support systems. *Management Science, 23*(5).

Dennis, A. R., Quek, F., & Pootheri, S. K. (1996). Using the Internet to implement support for distributed decision making. In P. Humphreys, L. Bannon, A. McCosh, P. Migliarese & J. C. Pomerol (Eds.). *Implementing Systems for Supporting Management Decisions: Concepts, Methods, and Experiences.* London: Chapman & Hall.

Druzdel, M. J., & Flynn, R. R. (2000). Decision support systems. In A. Kent (Ed.). *Encyclopedia of Library and Information Science.* New York: Marcel Dekker.

Elliott, C., & Brzezinski, J. (1998). Autonomous agents as synthetic characters. *AI Magazine, 2*, 13-30.

Er, M. C. (1988). Decision support systems: A summary, problems and future trends. *Decision Support Systems, 4*(4), 355-363.

Finlay, P. N. (1989). *Introducing DSS.* Oxford: NCC & Blackwell.

Gordon, L. A., Larcker, D. F., & Tuggle, F. D. (1978). Strategic decision processes and the design of accounting information systems: Conceptual linkages. *Accounting, Organization and Society*, 3, 203-213.

Gorry, G. A., & Scott-Morton, M. (1971). A framework for management information systems. *Sloan Management Review, 13*(1), 55-70.

Haley, U. C. V., & Stumpf, S. A. (1989). Cognitive trails in strategic decision making: Linking theories of personalities and cognitions. *Journal of Management Studies, 26*(5), 477-497.

Hayes, J., & Allinson, C. W. (1994). Cognitive style and its relevance for management practice. *British Journal of Management*, 5, 53-71.

Hoppe, H. U. (1995). The use of multiple student modeling to parameterize group learning. *Proceedings of Artificial Intelligence and Education '95*, Charlottesville, VA: AACE, 234-241.

Huitt, W. (1992). Problem solving and decision making: Consideration of individual differences using Myers Briggs type indicator. *Journal of Psychological Type*, 24, 33-44.

Ito, J. K., & Peterson, R. B. (1986). Effects of task difficulty and interunit interdependence on information processing systems. *Academy of Management Journal, 29*(1), 139-149.

Kahneman, D., Slovic, P., & Tversky, A. (Eds.). (1982). *Judgment under uncertainty: Heuristics and biases.* New York: Cambridge University Press.

Kahneman, D., & Tversky, A. (1972). Subjective probability: A judgment of representativeness. *Cognitive Psychology, 2*, 430-454.

Kahneman, D., & Tversky, A. (1973). On the psychology of prediction. *Psychological Review, 80*, 236-251.

Kay, A. (1990). User interface: A personal view. In B. Laurel (Ed.). *The Art of Human-Computer Interface Design.* Reading, MA: Addison-Wesley.

Keeney, R. L., & Raiffa, H. (1976). *Decisions with multiple objectives, preferences and value tradeoffs.* New York: Wiley.

Kolodner, J. L. (1991, Summer). Improving human decision making through case-based decision aiding. *AI Magazine*, 52-68.

Laudon, K. C., & Laudon, J. P. (2000). *Management information systems.* New York: Prentice Hall.

Lesnick, L. L., & Moore, R. E. (1997). *Creating cool intelligent agents for the Net.* New York: McGraw-Hill.

Lesser, V., Horling, B., Klassner, F., Raja, A., Wagner, T., & Zhang, S.X.Q. (2000). BIG: An agent for resource-bounded information gathering and decision making. *Artificial Intelligence*, 118, 197-244.

Lindsay, P. H., & Norman, D. A. (1977). *Human information processing: An introduction to psychology.* New York: Academic Press.

Maes, P. (1994). Modeling adaptive autonomous agents. *Journal of Artificial Life*, 1.

Maes, P. (1995). Artificial life meets entertainment: Lifelike autonomous agents. *Communications of the ACM,* 38, 108-114.

Maes, P. (1998). Agents that reduce work and information overload. In M. T. Maybury & W. Wahlster (Eds.). *Readings in Intelligent User Interfaces* (pp. 525-535) San Francisco: Morgan Kaufmann.

Mase, K. (1997). Aspects of interface agents: Avatar, assistant and actor. *Workshop on Animated Interface Agents: Making Them Intelligent* (August 25) Nagoya, Japan.

Mauldin, M. (1994). ChatterBots, tinyMUDs, and the turing test: Entering the Loebner prize competition. In *Proceedings of the Twelfth National Conference on Artificial Intelligence* (pp. 16-21). Cambridge, MA: MIT Press.

Minsky, M. (1975). A framework for representing knowledge. In *P. H. Winston (Ed.). The Psychology of Computer Vision* (pp. 211-277). New York: McGraw-Hill.

Montgomery, H., & Svenson, O. (1976). On decision rules and information processing strategies for choices among multiattribute alternatives. *Scandinavian Journal of Psychology,* 17, 283-291.

Newman, W., & Lamming, M. (1995). Interactive systems design. Reading, MA: Addison-Wesley.

Norman, D. A. (1994). How might people interact with agents. *Communications of the ACM*, 37, 68-71.

Norman, D. A. (1998). *The invisible computer.* Cambridge, MA: MIT Press.

Nutt, P. C. (1990). Strategic decisions made by top executives and middle managers with data and process dominant styles. *Journal of Management Studies,* 27(2), 173-194.

Pearl, J. (1988). *Probabilistic reasoning in intelligent systems: Networks of plausible inference.* San Francisco: Morgan Kaufmann.

Pinsonneault, A., & Kraemer, K. L. (1993). Survey research in management information systems: An assessement. *Journal of Management Information System.*

Preece, J. (1994). *Human-computer interaction*. Reading, MA: Addison-Wesley.

Rachlin, J. et al. (1998). A-teams: An agent architecture for optimization and decision-support. In J. P. Miller, M. P. Single, & A. S. Rao (Eds.). *Intelligent Agents V: Agents Theories, Architectures, and Languages* (pp. 261-276) Berlin: Springer-Verlag.

Raiffa, E. (1968). Decision analysis: Introductory lectures on choices under uncertainty. Reading, MA: Addison-Wesley.

Rice, R. (1992). Task analyzability, use of new media, and effectiveness: A multisite exploration of media richness. *Organization Science, 3*(4), 475-500.

Rickel, J., & Johnson, W. L. (1997). Steve: An animated pedagogical agent for procedural training in virtual environments. Workshop on Animated Interface Agents: Making Them Intelligent (August 25) Nagoya, Japan.

Riecken, D. (1994). Intelligent agents. *Communications of the ACM, 37*, 18-21.

Russell, S. J., & Norvig, P. (1995). *Artificial intelligence: A modern approach*. Englewood Cliffs, NJ: Prentice-Hall.

Sage, A. P. (1991). *Decision support systems engineering*. New York: John Wiley & Sons.

Sasse, M. A. (1992). Users' models of computer systems. In Y. Rogers & A. Rutherford (Eds.). *Models in the Mind*. London: Academic Press.

Schank, R. C. (1975). The structure of episodes in memory. In D.G. Bobrow & A. M. Collins (Eds.). *Representation and Understanding: Studies in Cognitive Science*. New York: Academic Press.

Schank, R. C., & Abelson, R. P. (1977). *Scripts, plans, goals, and understanding*. Hillsdale, NJ: Lawrence Erlbaum.

Schneiderman, B. (1988). Direct manipulation: A step beyond programming languages. *IEEE: Transactions on Computation, 16*(8), 57-69.

Selfridge, O. (1959). Pandemonium: A paradigm for learning. In *Symposium on the Mechanization of Thought Processes*. London: HM Stationery Office.

Simon, H. A. (1960). *The new science of management decision*. New York: Harper and Row.

Slade, S. B. (1994). *Goal-based decision making: An interpersonal model*. Hillsdale, NJ: Lawrence Erlbaum.

Sprague, R. H. Jr. (1980). A framework for the development of decision support systems. *Management Information Science Quarterly, 4*(4).

Taggart, W., & Valenzi, E. (1990). Assessing rational and intuitive styles: A human information processing metaphor. *Journal of Management Studies, 27*(2), 149-172.

Thorisson, K. R., & Cassel, J. (1997). Communicative feedback in human-humanoid dialogue. Workshop on Animated Interface Agents: Making Them Intelligent (August 25) Nagoya, Japan.

Toates, F. (1986). *Motivational systems*. New York: Cambridge University Press.

Trappl, R., & Petta, P. (Eds.). (1997). *Creating personalities for synthetic actors*. Berlin: Springer-Verlag.

Turban, E., & Aronson, J. E. (1998). *Decision support systems and intelligent systems.* Upper Saddle River, NJ: Prentice Hall.

Turban, E., McLean, E., Wetherbe, J. (1996). *Information technology for management.* New York: Wiley.

Turkle, S. (1996). *Life on the screen.* Cambridge (Ma.): MIT Press.

Tversky, A. (1969). Intransitivity of preferences. *Psychological Review,* 76, 31-48.

Tversky, A., & Kahneman, D. (1973). Availability: A heuristic for judging frequency and probability. *Cognitive Psychology,* 5, 207-232.

Vassileva, J. (1995). Reactive instructional planning to support interacting teaching strategies. *Proceedings of the 7th World Conference on Artificial Intelligence and Education* (pp. 334-342) Charlottesville, VA: AACE.

Vassileva, J. (1996). A task-centered approach for user modeling in a hypermedia office documentation system. *User Modeling and User Adapted Interaction,* 6, 185-223.

von Winterfeldt, D., & Edwards, W. (1988). *Decision analysis and behavioral research.* New York: Cambridge University Press.

Weizenbaum, J. (1966). ELIZA: A computer program for the study of natural language communication between man and machine. *Communication of the ACM,* 9, 36-45.

Weizenbaum, J. (1976). *Computer power and human reason.* San Francisco: Freeman.

Wooldridge, M. (2000). *Reasoning about rational agents.* Cambridge, MA: MIT Press.

Wysocki, R. K., & Young, J. (1989). *Information systems: Management principles in action.* New York: Wiley.

Zmud, R. W. (1983). *Information systems in organization.* Palo Alto, CA: Scott, Foresman & Co.

Zwass, V. (1998). *Foundations of information systems.* New York: McGraw-Hill.

Chapter XVI

Using Narratives To Convey Knowledge in Decision Making Support Systems

Lee A. Freeman
University of Michigan-Dearborn, USA

ABSTRACT

Information systems, and specifically decision making support systems, present information to users in a variety of modes—raw data, tables, graphs, and others. Rarely, if ever, does an information system present information to users in a narrative or story-based format. The last three decades have seen a variety of research articles that have presented an argument, an example, or a reference to what can be termed narrative-based information systems (NBIS). This chapter traces this history as they contribute to the development of NBIS. This chapter traces this history as they contribute to the development of NBIS. Previous work has come from multiple disciplines and multiple streams within Information Systems. To date, there has been very little work done in this area, and it is hypothesized that the reason is in part due to the multi-disciplinary approach and the lack of a unified effort. In order to further the efforts of this area of research, a conceptual model of the history is developed. The paper concludes with areas for future research.

INTRODUCTION

Information systems present information to the user in a wide variety of modes. Rarely does an information system present information to the user in a narrative or story-based format. However, every one of us uses stories and anecdotes when we speak with our colleagues and friends. These stories allow us to explain or talk about an event in greater detail and with more personal meaning to the listener. Instead of merely providing someone with a few facts, we tie them together with a story that provides meaning.

We use examples and asides to provide details and necessary explanations of the main point that we are trying to bring forth. Our listeners can relate to these examples and small stories in a way that gives them more information. For example, if a person were to tell us about her trip to Europe by stating the names of the cities she visited, followed by the names of the museums she visited, and then the names of the hotels at which she stayed, we would have the necessary data to know what she did on her trip. However, there is no meaning to this data. Traveling in Europe is an event that occurs over time and it can be better represented through the use of one or more stories that tie the relevant pieces of data together to create meaning and context. So, if she were to describe her three days in Copenhagen, followed by her four days in Paris, and then her two days in Rome, we would have a much better understanding of her trip. This would be in part due to an increase in our interest level as a result of her descriptions, but also due to an increase in meaning as we are able to visualize her experiences and relate to the details and events. The story provides much more than sequencing logic; it provides details and the meaning to the data.

Another example, and one more appropriate to that of decision making in a managerial setting, may be as follows. A sales manager must reallocate his sales personnel in a changing customer market. Through the use of charts, graphs, and tables filled with sales data, comparisons, trends, and projections, he is able to gain an understanding of the nature of the market and determine where to put his sales personnel for the upcoming year. Many, if not most, sales managers make these and similar decisions in just this manner. However, if the same sales manager were to receive a written, prose-like report that describes the current market, the historical market, and the projected market, taking into account the data, comparisons, trends, and projections previously shown via other presentation formats, deeper explanations and meaning could be conveyed in order to give him the ability to make the best decision possible. The data can all be assimilated and organized into a very clear description of the entire situation, without the need for the sales manager to read and interpret numerous charts and tables, as well as compare them to each other.

The question then arises of why information systems do not present information to the user through the use of stories, narratives, or anecdotes. Information systems have been around for decades and technological capabilities are growing almost by the day. Information Technology (IT) is the backbone of today's economy, and the availability of and access to information is a necessity in business. It follows, then, that organizations desire accurate and useful information, for inaccurate information can be very costly and useless information wastes valuable resources. This is particularly the case with information systems being utilized for decision support— decision support systems, expert systems, executive information systems, etc. If greater meaning can be conveyed through stories in normal conversations, shouldn't they be used in these information systems?

To be sure that an understanding of the decision support system (DSS) exists, a brief introduction follows. Decision support systems are designed, built, and used to assist and support the decision making process. They are focused on the effectiveness of this process and the accuracy of the resulting information. The presentation language of a DSS, a part of the user interface, is where the output is presented to the user. It is here that narratives and stories could be incorporated to achieve greater meaning and understanding.

The purpose of this chapter is to summarize and coalesce research from the last three decades as it relates to narrative-based information systems (NBIS) in order to introduce a method for information presentation to be used for decision making. Several key areas will be introduced in the following sections to aid in the understanding and development of narrative-based information systems. The remainder of this chapter is organized as follows: narrative-based information systems will be explained and defined in the next section. The history of NBIS will then be presented as it has progressed over the last three decades. A conceptual model will be examined and used to outline areas for further research, and theoretical and practical implications will be discussed. The final section will provide some concluding comments.

DEFINING NARRATIVE-BASED INFORMATION SYSTEMS

There are several aspects of narrative-based information systems that warrant further clarification before proceeding with the history of the literature. These aspects deal with presentation mode, human-computer interaction, and narratives. Each is presented in turn and then integrated into a working definition of an NBIS.

Presentation Mode

The notion of using stories is not new, as it was first presented almost 30 years ago.

> An information system consists of at least one PERSON of a certain PSYCHO-LOGICAL TYPE who faces a PROBLEM within some OR-GANIZATIONAL CONTEXT for which he needs EVIDENCE to arrive at a solution (i.e., to select some course of action) and that the evidence is made available to him through some MODE OF PRESENTATION.
> (Mason & Mitroff, 1973, p. 475)

This definition has been the cornerstone of numerous research efforts on nearly every aspect and variable since its publication. Though mentioned last in their definition of an information system, the mode of presentation (or presentation mode) is a key component. Mason and Mitroff (1973, p. 484) put forth the argument that "stories, drama, role plays, art, graphics, one-to-one contact and group discussions may be more effective in some information contexts ... [over] the language of abstract symbols and 'hard' data." They do not attempt to describe how such an information system would be built, though they do admit that the technology may be "radically different" from the current technology. It would be a safe argument to state that today's technologies are indeed radically different from those in 1973.

Human-Computer Interaction

Human-computer interaction (HCI) is the study of the human response to information technology, with particular emphasis on how we can learn from this in terms of shaping future information technology. HCI is a relatively new field (Baecker, Grudin, Buxton, & Greenberg, 1995), and it draws its intellect from multiple disciplines—computer science, human factors, cognitive psychology, sociology, organizational psychology, and software engineering, to name a few. Each discipline brings a particular perspective or insight onto the problems and questions of the field of HCI.

Some of the major focus points within HCI concern the usability, design, and impact of information technologies with respect to humans. A narrative-based computer system is clearly a topic that draws on HCI issues. The presentation of information (used loosely in this context) from the computer to the user through an interface is a primary area of focus for HCI researchers. The type of information presented through the NBIS interface is also an HCI issue, as it will affect the interaction of the user with the system. The question of whether such a system is feasible must be asked. Usability concerns must be addressed and tested, again a major HCI issue.

Narratives and Stories

A story is "the narrating or relating of an event or series of events, either true or fictitious, intended to INTEREST [emphasis added] or amuse the hearer or reader." A narrative is "a story or description of actual or fictional events; a narrated account" (American Heritage Dictionary of the English Language, 1981). These two terms are synonymous with each other and will be used as such throughout. The word "interest" has been emphasized in order to point out that this interest is what provides the ability to convey greater detail and meaning through stories. If the hearer or reader is not interested in the story, then she will not benefit from the story.

Stories and narratives are important for several reasons. First, as previously mentioned, they provide more personal meaning to the information being presented. Second, as mentioned above, they are more interesting to the hearer or reader. Third, the interpretation of the information provided via a story can be compared with other interpretations (either provided or already in memory) more easily. Finally, stories and narratives capture an entirely different type of information than the traditional, "hard" information of most information systems (Schultze & Boland, 1997).

Narrative-Based Information Systems

The above background allows for the defining of narrative-based information systems. They can be divided into two categories: those systems that present information from the system to the user in a narrative format and those systems that present information between users (sharing information) in a narrative format. It is not required that ALL information in either of these systems be presented in a narrative format; other presentation modes may be present as well.

Narrative-based information systems in the first category are concerned with the output from the system as it is presented to the user. Narratives will replace other presentation modes that may have been used in the past with similar systems. These systems require very sophisticated programming in order to create a meaningful story for the user. Narrative-based information systems in the second category are different in that they do not require the same level of sophisticated programming to be effective. In these systems, knowledge is shared among the users; however, the users have an additional method at their disposal for presenting their contributions to the system. Both categories of narrative-based information systems will be discussed in greater detail in the next section.

HISTORY OF NBIS

To fully understand the historical and theoretical development of narrative-based information systems, major contributing research articles will be summarized in a chronological order. Due to a break in the literature in the mid-1980s, the history of NBIS can be broken down into early (1972-1987) and recent (1987-present).

Early History

Winograd (1972) describes an artificial intelligence system that answers user questions, executes commands, and accepts user input in an interactive English dialog—using natural language for all of its functions. All knowledge within the system is represented as procedures that work as steps in a process (as opposed to tables of rules or lists of patterns), and each procedure could theoretically call on any other procedure within the system. These procedures cover the essence of human language understanding—syntax, semantics, and reasoning (Winograd, 1972).

The book is extremely detailed about the programming code, the relationships between the different programs within the system, and the many tests and experiments conducted throughout the project. While this information is relevant to someone wishing to design and build such a system, the mere fact that this was accomplished and recognized as an optimal method of presentation is the most relevant for this chapter. In fact, the use of procedures to represent knowledge will surface again in the 1990s with expert systems. Therefore, the incorporation of natural language into information systems was jump-started by Winograd and is seen as the initial step towards Narrative-based information systems.

As previously stated, the Mason and Mitroff (1973) article set the stage for the interpretation of and research on information systems. Their very specific definition provided a starting point for many researchers, including those concerned with presentation mode. In addition, their mention of stories as being a possible presentation mode previously unconsidered substantiated its place in IS. However, a mention was all that was done. The article did not call for any specific research or exploration of stories or what this chapter is calling Narrative-based information systems. However, as far as the history of NBIS, Mason and Mitroff set the stage for others to follow.

Not surprisingly, it was not long before the issue of stories and narratives in information systems was revisited by Mason and Mitroff. Mitroff, Nelson, and Mason (1974) take the idea of stories as a presentation mode to the fullest. They introduce what they call management myth-information systems (MMIS) that present information from the system to the user through stories. They present their definition of MMIS as a system wherein "data becomes information if and only if it is tied to an appropriate story that has personal meaning to the individual who needs the information, the organization in which he is located, and the type of problem that he faces" (Mitroff et al., 1974, pp. 1-2), a similar notion to moving up the information hierarchy of data, information, intelligence, knowledge, and wisdom (Haeckel & Nolan, 1993-1994). They state that this personal meaning will be created when the story properly addresses the person's psychological type, the problem, the organization, and the nature of the evidence. This is a direct adaptation of Mason and Mitroff (1973).

The authors use myth as a great epic story, one that carries significant meaning through anecdotes and symbols. They go into very little detail regarding the supporting theories of mythology and storytelling as a basis for their MMIS. However, they do make the key point that myths are understood by many cultures and there are underlying similarities with all of the great myths in both form and structure. Mitroff et al. (1974) use this support to contend that stories in the MMIS can be designed in similar ways. This article does not focus on the results of their experiments with an MMIS. Rather, it focuses on the creation of such a system and the interactions with the human user. Therefore, while showing their audience that such a system can be built and used, they do not attempt to apply it to other situations beyond their experiment.

When Winograd (1972), Mason and Mitroff (1973), and Mitroff et al. (1974) are viewed together, the initial attempts at narrative-based information systems can be seen. Winograd's and Mitroff et al.'s systems use stories, narratives, or natural language as the sole Presentation Mode between the system and the user. Mitroff et al.'s work seemed the most promising in that it was coming from IS researchers. However, the article was published by the US Department of Health, Education, and Welfare's National Institute of Education and many researchers never read it. Still, these three articles set the foundation for narrative-based information systems.

Hayes and Reddy (1983) write about narrative-based information systems as interactive systems. They compare these interactive systems with regular human communication and conversation. They argue that the major difference between the two forms of interaction is the "robustness," or gracefulness, of the interaction. This "robustness" refers to the ability of the participants to react and respond to unanticipated situations and to effectively fix other problems with the communication. Their "robustness" is broken down into a number of independent conversational and communicative skills that provide "a good working basis from which to build gracefully interacting systems" (Hayes & Reddy, 1983, p. 233). They find that a number of contemporary systems do possess some of these "robustness" skills, but no one system comes close to possessing all of them. However, they do feel that such a "robust" system is possible, given the right parameters.

Whereas the articles previous to Hayes and Reddy (1983) have all had very positive outlooks on the general issue of a narrative-based information system, Suchman (1987) shows the truc value of Hayes and Reddy's article. Suchman shows how they provide us the opportunity to take a step back and look at what it will take to make such a system really work. Their "robustness" skills for communication—parsing input; ensuring that the intended meaning has been conveyed; explaining abilities and limitations; and describing things in the appropriate context—are difficult to create in a computer system. When they are not done correctly and completely, the communication will break down. However, in normal human conversation, when the communication breaks down, the two participants will attempt to resolve the problem and then continue with their conversation. With a computer system, a Narrative-Based Information System, this corrective procedure is not possible and not only will the particular conversation come to an end, but possibly all communication and interaction with the system.

Recent History

Daft and Lengel's (1986) and Trevino, Lengel, and Daft's (1987) works on media richness bring forth several issues that contribute to the development of Narrative-based information systems. Daft and Lengel found that a major problem for managers is a lack of clarity with their information, not a lack of data. Dillon (1987, p. 378) also notes "clear, explicit information best facilitates the acquisition of user knowledge." In addition, Dillon found that the ability of a user to form such knowledge is greatly influenced by the interface as "the provider of information." A major advantage of narrative-based information systems is the better understanding and meaning generated by the presentation of information. Trevino et al. found that when content was important in communication, managers selected face-to-face communication or other very rich media. This finding supports narrative-based information systems in that the narratives and stories are intended to reproduce communication that typically occurs between people in a rich format such as face-to-face. The media richness research found that organizations attempt to reduce uncertainty (the absence of information) and reduce equivocality (the existence of multiple interpretations; ambiguity). Narrative-based information systems are an example of an information system designed to do just that for the users and ultimately the organization.

Returning to a more applied approach to narratives, the expert systems literature has made important contributions to Narrative-based information systems. Lamberti and Wallace (1990) studied the interface and its design within expert systems. For the purposes of this chapter, their study of knowledge presentation formats is highly relevant. They tested two knowledge presentation formats on users' problem-solving performance. The first, declarative presentation, involves the system providing "a static collection of facts about objects, events, and situations … [and] lacking a built-in procedural interpretation of how to carry out the steps or when to apply the rules needed to solve a problem" (Lamberti & Wallace, 1990, p. 281). This is very much like traditional information systems that provide information without meaning or context.

The second knowledge presentation format, procedural presentation, involves an IF…THEN format of premise and action pairs which "specify the sequence of actions used to solve a problem" (Lamberti & Wallace, 1990, p. 281). This is very similar, though never stated as such, to the narrative approach seen in Winograd (1972) and Mitroff et al. (1974). It is similar in the sense that the procedural presentation format provides context and direction for solving a problem. It is more than just a listing of facts or hard data.

Lamberti and Wallace found that for low uncertainty tasks, procedural presentations and explanations gave rise to greater successes in problem solving than declarative presentations. Under high uncertainty, the procedural system was likely unable to create the necessary interpretations in the given explanations, causing the users to perform better with declarative presentations (Lamberti & Wallace, 1990).

Unlike the Winograd (1972) and Mitroff et al. (1974) systems, this system is not solely reliant on narratives for information presentation. Expert systems, including the one tested by Lamberti and Wallace (1990), combine a variety of presentation modes dependent on the information presented and the needs of the users. Still, expert systems have begun to incorporate narratives among the more traditional formats. In fact, Lamberti and Wallace (1990, p. 304) even suggest that additional research be done that examines "the impact of multiple representations of the same knowledge using procedural AND [emphasis added] declarative formatting."

One of Huber's (1991) constructs associated with organizational learning is organizational memory and the subconstructs of storing and retrieving information and computer-based organizational memory. Taken together, these two subconstructs allow organizations to store and retrieve, either electronically or otherwise, relevant data, rules, procedures, memos, processes, etc., that are a part of the operations of the organization. Most of these types of information are considered "hard" in that they are definitive and set. Huber points out that expert systems are increasingly being used for the storage of "soft" information. Some of this soft information may be in the form of narrative procedures. This assertion that human memory is story-based is supported by Schank (1990) and Stein and Zwass (1995).

As this journey through the literature nears an end, there are only a few pieces remaining in the history of narrative-based information systems—a practical piece, an application piece, and a theoretical piece. Daft (1995) wrote a nonresearch article, though it is based on his experiences as a researcher and author. This article suggested that the best way to write research articles so they have the best chance of being published is to tell a story. "Storytelling explains the 'why' of the data and gives meaning to observed relationships" (Daft, 1995, p. 178). This is the same argument made for stories and narratives within information systems.

The application piece deals again with expert systems. Yetim (1996) calls for the use of natural language, bringing the discussion of narrative-based information systems full circle to Winograd (1972). Yetim's approach to natural language (like Winograd's) is different from its traditional use as a form of input (e.g., Adam & Gangopadhyay, 1994; Capidale & Crawford, 1990; Chan & Lim, 1998; Ein-Dor & Spiegler, 1995; McQuire & Eastman, 1998).

Yetim examines the use of Natural Language explanations as opposed to rule-based or declarative explanations. The system that he has tested uses an algorithm to change the declarative explanations to "a representation more understandable for the final user … in a more abstract and natural language form" (Yetim, 1996, p. 10). While Yetim does not refer to these explanations as narratives, he is using Natural Language in much the same way as Winograd (1972) and procedural presentations in much the same way as Lamberti and Wallace (1990).

The final piece of the history of narrative-based information systems involves a more detailed definition and exploration by Schultze and Boland (1997) of Yates and Orlikowski's (1992) and Orlikowski and Yates' (1994) papers on communication genres. Schultze & Boland propose that genres can be further divided into either hard or soft information. Soft information genres include "stories, tidbits of news and know-how" and are typically much harder to incorporate into systems. Most times, soft information genres rely on numerous details and a sequential ordering in order to convey the necessary meaning and understanding. The authors wanted to see if discussion databases (via Lotus Notes) could handle softer information effectively. Based on two experiments, they concluded that discussion databases (an example of the second category of NBIS—sharing between users) could indeed handle softer information genres. In fact, the databases were able to incorporate both hard and soft information genres. It was left to the users to determine the course of action and which genre to use. Over time, norms were created and accepted by the user-population.

Schultze and Boland (1997), in combination with Huber (1991) and Stein and Zwass (1995), link knowledge management to narrative-based information systems. They provide examples of how Narrative-based information systems can be used for the presentation of knowledge between two users via an information system.

Whether it is an expert system (Huber, 1991) or a discussion database (Schultze & Boland, 1997), narratives are an effective way of communicating organizational memory and there are systems in place to handle this presentation format. Narratives, therefore, expand the toolbox of knowledge management to incorporate softer information without losing the knowledge.

CONCEPTUAL MODEL OF NBIS

One way of viewing narrative-based information systems is through a conceptual model showing the disciplines in which Narrative-based information systems are based in the literature, the theories that are most relevant, and the current state of narrative-based information systems as they have been applied. This conceptual model is seen in Figure 1.

Narrative-based information systems are clearly multidisciplinary. While there is a fair amount of literature in the information systems discipline, a large portion of the relevant literature stems from education, cognition/cognitive psychology, human-computer interaction, and communication. These five disciplines contribute theories that determine the design of a narrative-based information system. First, genres of communication and genres of information must be determined for the particular system. These decisions will in part determine the level of media richness and in part the choices regarding interface design. Next, issues of presentation mode and natural language must be addressed before the use of narratives will exist. At this

Figure 1: Conceptual model of narrative-based information systems

Conceptual Model of NBIS

Applications
- Expert Systems
- Discussion Databases
- MMIS

Design Theories
- Narratives
- Presentation Mode
- Natural Language
- Media Richness
- Interface Design
- Genres of Communication
- Genres of Information

Disciplines
- Education
- Information Systems
- Cognition
- Human-Computer Interaction
- Communication

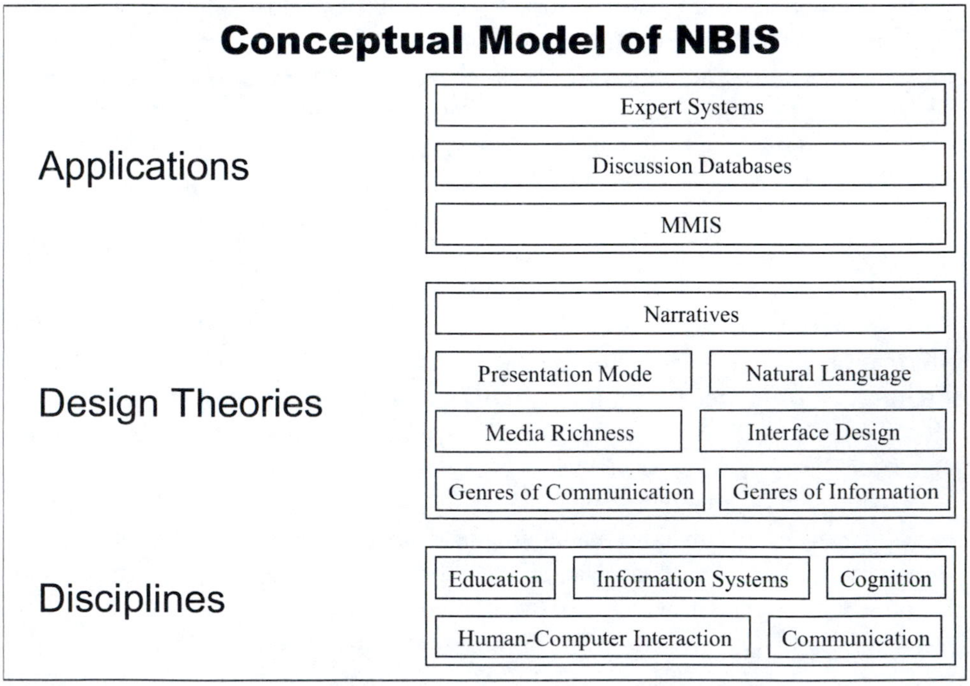

point, a narrative-based information system exists that can be applied to one of the three application areas that has been previously developed, or to a new application area yet to be developed.

As mentioned earlier, there are two categories of NBIS—those that allow for narrative presentations between the system and the user, and those that allow for narrative presentations between users. Of the three application areas currently developed, expert systems and MMIS development both fall into the first category; discussion databases fall into the second. Much of the work described in the previous section has been concerned with the first category, though this does not necessarily indicate a higher level of importance for these types of systems.

The conceptual model in Figure 1 serves two main purposes. First, it provides a concrete way to view and categorize the past research in the area of NBIS. Second, it serves as a starting point for all future research in NBIS. As will be discussed in the next section, the future of NBIS is full of challenges and opportunities.

IMPLICATIONS

This chapter has outlined an area with enormous implications for the book's theme, "Achievements, Trends and Challenges for the New Decade." There are great challenges ahead if decision making support systems are to take advantage of the use of narratives and stories for information presentation.

Theoretical

The theoretical contribution is the identification of an area of research that contains many opportunities for future research. Using the conceptual model from Figure 1 as a starting point, there are a number of issues that warrant attention in future research. The first question that should be raised is why has so little been done in this area previously. The answer to this question will determine the fate of this stream of research. It may be that the technology is not yet available to adequately and successfully build the types of systems that are described, relating back to the "robustness" issues of Hayes and Reddy (1983). Therefore, only a few researchers have been able to do much work at all.

Perhaps the reason that so little has been done is due to the fact that this is truly a multidisciplinary topic. No one discipline has taken the lead, though if any leader had to be named it seems that information systems would be it, though human-computer interaction is right there as well. Still, this scattering of knowledge and research has not done well to inform the academic and research communities. I would venture to say that most people who read this are hearing of many of these issues for the first time. As a result, there is no research stream or body of work, rather individual pieces of research that prior to now have not been associated with each other.

Assuming that this is relevant and worthwhile research and that the technology is available to create these systems, there are some additional areas for future research. Narrative-based information systems need to continually (and initially, in some cases) be tested against more traditional information systems, specifically decision making support systems, in terms of their usability, following guidelines presented by Eberts (1994), Nielsen (1993), and Sweeney, Maguire, and Shackel (1993), among others. Measures should include user understanding of the information, user satisfaction with the system, successful decision making, etc. Only then will we know if these systems are beneficial, for perhaps the narratives will not be properly conveyed by the information system, thereby causing poor decisions and lower satisfaction.

Second, there must be additional categories of information systems that can benefit from narratives in some way or another. It is hard to believe that expert systems, discussion databases, and the Mitroff et al. (1974) MMIS model are the only application areas. System constraints, time constraints, and budget constraints are likely the current barriers to answering this question.

Practical

Though research in this area has been disparate in the past, there are a number of existing, practical examples of narrative-based information systems being utilized today—the discussion databases described by Schultze and Boland (1997) and the expert system developed by Yetim (1996). An awareness of these uses and possibilities can be extremely beneficial to practitioners wishing to add value to their decision making processes. Therefore, the practical contribution will be the introduction of a new mode of information presentation that can, in certain types of information systems, be implemented immediately. A combined theoretical and practical contribution will be the increased awareness and interest created in industry R&D divisions and IS/IT departments to address these issues and improve organizational decision making.

CONCLUSION

This chapter has attempted to "label" a new area of research that has existed previously as a multitude of disparate fields. In order to justify this research stream, the history of the research and the applications of narrative-based information systems were traced from their initial onset nearly 30 years ago. A conceptual model of narrative-based information systems was developed in order to create continuity within the field and a starting point for further research.

As a result of this review, it seems clear that Narrative-based information systems are not a pipe dream; however, they are definitely not a piece of cake. There are many factors prohibiting the advancement of this research, the most foreboding being technology itself. Yet, the future remains bright and full of opportunity.

Narrative-based information systems should enhance the existing architectures of DSS and DMSS through their presentation of the information via stories and anecdotes. This presentation format will increase the accuracy and effectiveness of the communication between the system and the user(s) and therefore lead to greater decision making accuracy by the user(s).

REFERENCES

Adam, N. R., & Gangopadhyay, A. (1994). A form-based approach to natural language query processing. *Journal of Management Information Systems, 11(2), 109-145.*

American heritage dictionary of the English language. (1981). Boston: Houghton Mifflin.

Baecker, R. M., Grudin, J., Buxton, W. A. S., & Greenberg, S. (Eds.). (1995). *Readings in human-computer interaction: Toward the year 2000.* San Francisco: Morgan Kaufmann.

Capidale, R. A., & Crawford, R. G. (1990). Using a natural language interface with casual users. *International Journal of Man-Machine Studies, 32,* 341-361.

Chan, H. C., & Lim, L. H. (1998). Database interfaces: A conceptual framework and a meta-analysis on natural language studies. *Journal of Database Management, 9*(3), 25-32.

Daft, R. L. (1995). Why I recommend your manuscript be rejected and what you can do about it. In L. L. Cummings & P. J. Frost (Eds.), *Publishing in the organizational sciences* (pp. 164-182) New York: Sage.

Daft, R. L., & Lengel, R. H. (1986). Organizational information requirements, media richness and structural design. *Management Science, 32,* 554-571.

Dillon, A. (1987). Knowledge acquisition and conceptual models: A cognitive analysis of the interface. In D. Diaper & R. Winder (Eds.), *People and computers III* (371-379) Cambridge, MA: Cambridge University Press.

Eberts, R. E. (1994). *User interface design.* Englewood Cliffs, NJ: Prentice Hall.

Ein-Dor, P., & Spiegler, I. (1995). Natural language access to multiple databases: A model and a prototype. *Journal of Management Information Systems, 12*(1), 171-197.

Haeckel, S. H., & Nolan, R. L. (1993-1994). The role of technology in an information age: Transforming symbols into action. Annual Review of Institute for Information Studies, T*he Knowledge Economy: The Nature of Information in the 21st Century*.

Hayes, P., & Reddy, D. R. (1983). Steps toward graceful interaction in spoken and written man-machine communication. *International Journal of Man-Machine Studies, 19,* 231-284.

Huber, G. P. (1991). Organizational learning: The contributing processes and the literatures. *Organizational Science, 2*(1), 88-115.

Lamberti, D. M., & Wallace, W. A. (1990). Intelligent interface design: An empirical assessment of knowledge presentation in expert systems. *MIS Quarterly, 14*(3), 279-311.

Mason, R. O., & Mitroff, I. I. (1973). A program for research on management information systems. Management Science, 19, 475-487.

McQuire, A. R., & Eastman, C. M. (1998). The ambiguity of negation in natural language queries to information retrieval systems. *Journal of the American Society for Information Science,* 49, 686-692.

Mitroff, I. I., Nelson, J., & Mason, R. O. (1974). *On management myth-information systems.* U.S. Department of Health, Education, and Welfare's National Institute of Education Publication.

Nielsen, J. (1993). *Usability Engineering.* New York: Academic Press.

Orlikowski, W. J., & Yates, J. (1994). Genre repertoire: The structuring of communicative practices in organizations. *Administrative Science Quarterly,* 39, 541-574.

Schank, R. C. (1990). *Tell me a story: A new look at real and artificial memory.* New York: Charles Scribner & Sons.

Schultze, U., & Boland, R. J., Jr. (1997). Hard and soft information genres: An analysis of two Notes databases. *Proceedings of the Thirtieth Annual Hawaii International Conference on System Sciences.*

Stein, E. W., & Zwass, V. (1995). Actualizing organizational memory with information systems. *Information Systems Research, 6*(2), 85-117.

Suchman, L. A. (1987). *Plans and situated actions.* New York: Cambridge University Press.

Sweeney, M., Maguire, M., & Shackel, B. (1993). Evaluating user-computer interaction: A framework. *International Journal of Man-Machine Studies,* 38, 689-711.

Trevino, L. K., Lengel, R. H., & Daft, R. L. (1987). Media symbolism, media richness, and media choice in organizations. *Communication Research,* 14, 553-574.

Winograd, T. (1972). *Understanding natural language.* New York: Academic Press.

Yates, J., & Orlikowski, W. J. (1992). Genres of organizational communication: A structurational approach to studying communication and media. *Academy of Management Review, 17*(2), 299-326.

Yetim, F. (1996). An approach to the flexible and user-oriented structuring of answers for explanation dialogues. *Research in Information Systems, 1*(1), 1-16.

SECTION IV

EVALUATION AND MANAGEMENT OF DMSS

Chapter XVII

Quality Factors for DMSS Assessment: An Application of Research Frameworks

Harold W. Webb
University of South Florida, USA

Surya B. Yadav
Texas Tech University, USA

ABSTRACT

The objective of this chapter is to demonstrate the use of a decision support systems research (DSSR) framework to improve decision making support systems (DMSS) quality. The DSSR Framework, which was developed to integrate theoretical constructs from various information systems areas into a coherent theme, can serve as a tool for DMSS developers. Developed to provide a unified reference to theoretical constructs used in theory building and testing, the DSSR framework can also be used as the basis for the identification and selection of a hierarchy of factors potentially affecting the quality of DMSS development. The chapter proposes that a unified set of quality factors derived from the DSSR framework be used in tandem with the generic software quality metrics framework specified in IEEE Standard 1061-1992. The integration of these two frameworks has the potential to improve the process of developing high-quality decision making support systems and system components. The usage of these frameworks to identify system quality factors is demonstrated in the context of a military research and development project.

This work was supported in part by The National Institute for System Testing and Productivity at the University of South Florida under the USA Space and Naval Warfare Systems Command, Grant No. N00039-01-1-2248.

INTRODUCTION

As information technology advances, organizations, individuals, and supporting information systems become increasingly interrelated. Within this environment exists the need for high quality systems or system components that support decision making. Evolving from stand-alone systems used primarily by staff specialists, decision making support systems can be found embedded as components of larger integrated systems and range from personal financial planning aids to complex decision-making components integrated into advanced military systems. Underpinning this need is a body of research applicable to decision-making support systems (DMSS) that describes, to various degrees, factors relevant to the development of high quality systems.

Factors affecting the development, use, and operation of DMSS can be identified in over three decades of theoretical and empirical research from the fields of decision support systems (DSS), management information systems (MIS), and their referent disciplines. Included in this body of research are several proposed frameworks influencing both DMSS research as well as systems development. Some of these frameworks offer breadth without specification of well-defined research constructs while other frameworks are much narrower, focusing on a subset of a field. This set of frameworks has been useful in establishing the credibility of these research fields; however, most lack depth and do not represent a cumulation of theoretical knowledge. Their usefulness for theory building and the identification of quality factors needed by systems developers has been limited.

Most MIS and DSS frameworks have been developed from a particular viewpoint that highlights a set of concepts as well as a particular level of analysis. Several early DSS-specific frameworks have guided research in the field of DSS. Alter (1977) developed an early taxonomy of DSS organized into seven DSS types lying along a single dimension ranging from extremely data-oriented to extremely model-oriented. Bonczek, Holsapple, and Whinston (1981) present a number of conceptual and operational frameworks, strategies, and techniques primarily focused on system construction. Sprague (1980) developed a research framework focusing on a developmental approach for creating a DSS and the roles of key players. While the impact of emerging information technologies on DSS remains an issue, the specific technologies of interest have changed from office automation systems (Blanning, 1983) to data warehousing (Gray & Watson, 1998), Web technologies, and integration of legacy systems.

Beyond the early DSS-specific frameworks, there are a number of more general frameworks for MIS research. The Mason and Mitroff (1973) model is one of the first comprehensive MIS research frameworks. This model views an information system as consisting of the following key variables: an individual's psychological type, the class of problem, the method of evidence, the organizational context, and the mode of presentation. The Ives, Hamilton, and Davis (1980) model of an information system, the most comprehensive of these early frameworks, consists of five environmental variables, three process variables, and the IS subsystem itself.

Recent research frameworks point out the continued need for an integrated approach in developing a comprehensive DSS research framework. Each of these frameworks presents a research agenda based on a particular point of view of the field of DSS or a subset of DSS. A descriptive theory of DSS (Eierman, Niederman, & Adams, 1995) identifies a model of eight broad constructs containing 17 relationships among those constructs. Pearson and Shim (1995) extend the work of Alter (1977), investigating five classes of DSS structures based on the degree of support for DSS subsystems and environments. Adam, Fahy, and Murphy (1998) offer a framework, based on the Gorry and Scott-Morton (1971) framework, for the classification of DSS usage across organizations. Tung and Turban (1998) present a framework for analyzing the impacts of group support systems on distributed group processes.

The existing frameworks have described DSS research along a number of overlapping dimensions. Newer frameworks have extended selected existing research frameworks, but with the exception of Tung and Turban (1998) have not integrated the various research dimensions identified in the family of published frameworks during the past 30 years.

A mechanism is needed that provides a view of the entire discipline yet also provides the level of detail necessary to identify common factors, interrelationships, and research findings. These commonalties are required to achieve precision and consistency in theory development and theory testing as well as providing DMSS development teams with an array of factors useful for assessing system quality.

The decision support system research (DSSR) framework (Yadav & Webb, 2001) is a tool developed to bridge this gap. The DSSR framework, which focuses on theoretical construct definition and classification, is useful in directing the efforts of researchers. As an extension the DSSR framework can also be used to identify quality factors affecting DMSS system development efforts needed by users and developers.

Our overall objective of this chapter is to show how the DSSR framework can be used to identify factors affecting the quality of decision-making support systems and components. The framework, when applied to the context of system development:

- defines major areas affecting DMSS system development so they are easier to identify and understand;
- provides a comprehensive list of potential DMSS research constructs in a uniform and systematic manner that may be applied to the context of system development; and
- complements the quality metrics framework (IEEE, 1993) by identifying potential quality factors that may be used to assess DMSS throughout the system development cycle.

In the next section, we provide a summary of the DSSR Framework. We then discuss the use of the DSSR Framework as an aid in systems development. This is followed by an illustration of the use of the framework in the context of the development of an advanced military system having a critical decision-making support system component.

DSSR FRAMEWORK

The DSSR Framework (Yadav & Webb, 2001) represents a synthesis of previous research and presents a taxonomy of constructs affecting DMSS (Figure 1). Constructs have been defined as "terms, which though not observational either directly or indirectly, may be applied or even defined on the basis of the observable" (Kaplan, 1964). They are related to, but distinct from variables, which are observable units that can assume two or more values and can be operationalized empirically (Schwab, 1980). Constructs may be defined in a hierarchical fashion in terms of other constructs, which then may be operationalized by variables.

The purpose of the framework is to draw attention to the wide range of constructs at various levels of aggregation that are potentially of interest to DSS researchers, developers and users. The framework also provides a common vocabulary for identification of constructs, development of theoretical propositions, and testing hypotheses. An extended use of this framework is as a tool to identify quality factors potentially affecting the development, operation, and use of DMSS.

Figure 1: The decision support system research framework; adapted from Yadav and Webb (2001)

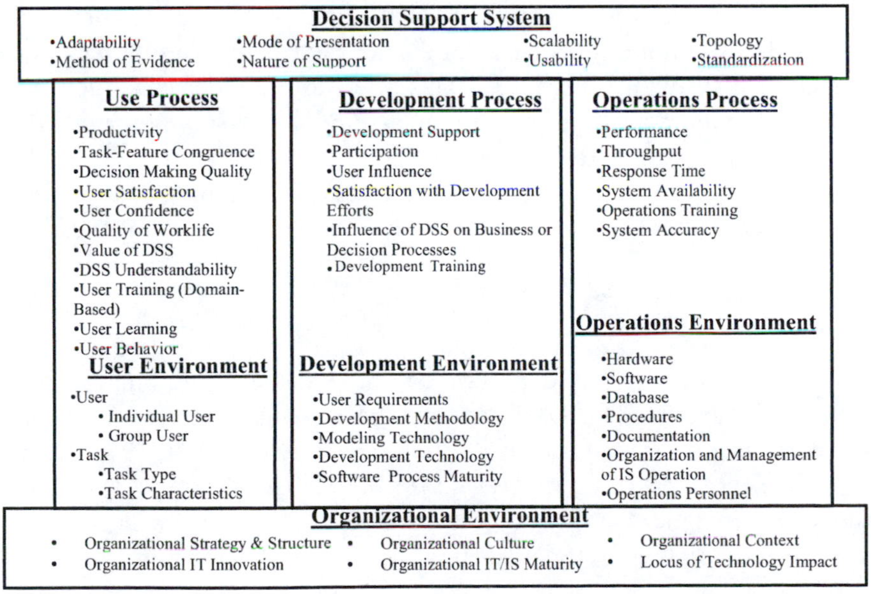

Decision Support System

•Adaptability	•Mode of Presentation	•Scalability	•Topology
•Method of Evidence	•Nature of Support	•Usability	•Standardization

Use Process

- •Productivity
- •Task-Feature Congruence
- •Decision Making Quality
- •User Satisfaction
- •User Confidence
- •Quality of Worklife
- •Value of DSS
- •DSS Understandability
- •User Training (Domain-Based)
- •User Learning
- •User Behavior

Development Process

- •Development Support
- •Participation
- •User Influence
- •Satisfaction with Development Efforts
- •Influence of DSS on Business or Decision Processes
- •Development Training

Operations Process

- •Performance
- •Throughput
- •Response Time
- •System Availability
- •Operations Training
- •System Accuracy

User Environment

- •User
  - • Individual User
  - • Group User
- •Task
  - •Task Type
  - •Task Characteristics

Development Environment

- •User Requirements
- •Development Methodology
- •Modeling Technology
- •Development Technology
- •Software Process Maturity

Operations Environment

- •Hardware
- •Software
- •Database
- •Procedures
- •Documentation
- •Organization and Management of IS Operation
- •Operations Personnel

Organizational Environment

- Organizational Strategy & Structure
- Organizational IT Innovation
- Organizational Culture
- Organizational IT/IS Maturity
- Organizational Context
- Locus of Technology Impact

The DSSR Framework, an extension of the model for information system research (Ives et al., 1980), provides a common DSS terminology and classification scheme facilitating construct identification within the general research areas of: 1) content, which refers to the system itself; 2) process, which refers to various processes affecting the system; and 3) context, referring to various types of external influences on the system. This framework does not include the external environment as defined by Ives et al. (1980). For decision-making support systems and system components, high-level factors such as legal, social, and political considerations provide indirect effects through the organizational environment, which is included in the framework. This framework also does not address group support systems and their relationship with group processes; rather the reader is referred to the Tung and Turban (1998) research framework. We now provide a summary of the research constructs addressed by the DSSR Framework.

Content: The Decision Support System

Central to an examination of research issues concerning decision-making support systems and system components is the system or component itself. The DSSR Framework includes dimensions of DSS that have been consistently identified in existing research frameworks such as the method of evidence and the mode of presentation (Alter, 1977; Barron, Chiang, & Storey, 1998; Blanning, 1983; Bonczek et al., 1981; Mason & Mitroff, 1973; Nolan & Wetherbe, 1980; Sprague, 1980). It also includes system adaptability (Bonczek et al., 1981; Finlay & Wilson, 2000; Pearson & Shim, 1995; Sprague, 1980), nature of support (Alter, 1977), usability (Sprague, 1980), scalability (Pearson & Shim, 1995), topology (Bonczek et al., 1981), and standardization of the system (Bonczek et al., 1981; Pearson & Shim, 1995; Sprague, 1980).

Beyond these high-level constructs that relate to general features of DSS content, the DSSR Framework addresses the need to establish a set of lower-order constructs for investigative purposes. This set of lower-order constructs enables researchers to more consistently operationalize content features for use in DSS research as well as system development (Yadav & Webb, 2001). These lower-order constructs, derived from a review of the DSS literature, may be used as potential DMSS factors and sub-factors by developers and users to assess system quality.

DSS Processes

DSS Use Process: The use process of a DSS is the focal point at which the decision maker (user) and the DSS interact. The most consistently referred to use-process construct in existing frameworks is user behavior (Alter, 1977; Blanning, 1983; Bonczek et al., 1981; Eierman et al., 1995; Nolan & Wetherbe, 1980; Pearson & Shim, 1995; Sprague, 1980). User behavior includes the decision-making process of the manager (Mintzberg, Raisinghani, & Theoret, 1976; Simon, 1960). Other constructs include productivity (Alter, 1977; Bonczek et al., 1981; Gorry & Scott-Morton, 1971; Mason & Mitroff, 1973), user satisfaction (Alter, 1977; Eierman et al., 1995; Ives et al., 1980; Pearson & Shim, 1995), user confidence, understandability, learning (Alter, 1977), decision-making quality (Eierman et al., 1995; Ives et al., 1980), value of DSS (Blanning, 1983) and user training (Alter 1977; Bonczek et al., 1979; Finlay & Wilson, 2000; Sprague, 1980). Quality sub-factors that may be used to determine DMSS success can be derived from the lower-order constructs and may also be derived from the DSSR Framework (Yadav & Webb, 2001).

DSS Development Process: The construct most frequently included in existing frameworks is participation in the development process (Alter, 1977; Blanning, 1983; Finlay & Wilson, 2000; Ives et al., 1980; Pearson & Shim, 1995; Sprague, 1980). Other constructs of interest include development support (Alter, 1977; Ives et al., 1980), user influence (Alter, 1977), satisfaction with development efforts (Ives et al., 1980), user influence (Franz & Robey, 1984), influence on business processes (Fedorowicz & Konsynski, 1992), and development training (Metzger, 1991).

DSS Operations Process: The operations process (Ives et al., 1980) clusters constructs potentially affecting DMSS quality including performance, throughput (Goslar, Green & Hughes, 1986), response time, system availability (Goslar et al., 1986), operations training, and system accuracy.

Context of the DSS

The decision-making environment may be partitioned into four levels: user, development, operations, and organizational, each having the potential to affect a DMSS.

User Environment: The user environment is a broad category that includes a large group of constructs encompassing primary users and intermediaries who filter or interpret the output of information systems for decision-makers (Ives et al., 1980). Major constructs within the user environment are the task and the user. Users may be individual users or group users (Tung & Tuban, 1998). The individual user construct includes the individual user characteristics as well as the role or type of individual user. Lower-order constructs having the potential to affect DMSS quality within the user environment may be identified (Yadav & Webb, 2001).

Development Environment: The development environment is frequently cited in research frameworks. Constructs within the development environment include modeling tools (Muhanna, 1993; Muhanna & Pick, 1994), development methodology (Yadav, Mukesh & Rohatgi, 1991), user requirements (Ross & Schoman, 1977; Yadav, Bravoco, Chatfield & Rajkumar, 1988), development tools (Alter, 1977; Ives et al. 1980; Nolan & Wetherbe, 1980), and software process maturity (Herbsleb, Zubrow, Goldenson, Hayes, & Paulk, 1997; Ives et al., 1980).

Operations Environment: The operations environment in which an information system exists includes the hardware, software, databases, procedures, documentation, management, and personnel (Ives et al., 1980).

Organizational Environment: The last major environmental construct is the organizational environment, which includes organizational context (Alter, 1977; Anthony, 1965; Bonczek et al., 1981; Mitroff, 1973), organizational culture (Schein, 1990), strategy (Mata, Fuerst & Barney, 1995; Porter, 1985), structure (Mason & Mitroff, 1973; Zmud, 1982), organizational IT innovation (Grover & Gosler, 1993; Rogers, 1985), organizational IS maturity (Grover & Gosler, 1993), and the locus of technology impact (Prescott & Conger, 1995).

The DSSR Framework was compared to 14 other DSS and MIS research frameworks published over the past three decades on the criteria of comprehensiveness; the ability to address both micro and macro issues; the ability to generate relevant, testable hypotheses; the ability to group critical dependent variables; and the ability to map existing research constructs to the framework. This comparison examined constructs across frameworks and demonstrated that even recent frameworks are incomplete, often not including constructs previously identified. The DSSR Framework fills this gap by including over 50% more constructs than the next most comprehensive research framework as well as meeting the four other comparison criteria (Yadav & Webb, 2001). While the DSSR Framework was developed primarily to support theory building and testing, it may also be used as a tool to identify and select DMSS quality factors. The impact of the framework on the development of successful systems and the use of this tool as a complement to an existing software quality methodology are discussed in the next section.

USE OF THE DSSR FRAMEWORK FOR SYSTEMS DEVELOPMENT

Organizations should be aware of factors that impact upon the success of a DMSS. A DMSS must be developed and implemented successfully in order to have a positive impact on the organization. There are several factors that affect the overall DMSS success. DMSS success, among other things, depends upon the DMSS project success, DMSS use success, and the quality of the system or system components. A system's project success, in turn, depends upon the success of its analysis, design, implementation, and project development processes. An organization should be aware of the effects of these factors. This awareness may allow proper attention to be paid to the situation-relevant factors needed for a successful DMSS.

A methodology addressing software quality is provided by IEEE Standard 1061-1992 (1993). We have applied this methodology to the assessment of DMSS quality. Software quality is defined as the degree to which a desired combination of attributes is possessed. The standard, however, does not offer a list of mandatory attributes, nor does it specify typical quality attributes by type of system. The standard calls for a methodology that utilizes a generic software quality metrics framework, a hierarchy that begins with the establishment of quality requirements by developers and users. Quality is defined in terms of quality factors, which may be measured by either direct metrics or through a hierarchy of sub-factors that are measured by validated metrics (IEEE, 1993). The purpose of the software quality metrics framework is to facilitate the early establishment of quality requirements, communicate factors in terms of quality sub-factors, and identify related metrics in software development. This process mirrors the process researchers must use in identifying research constructs, variables, and measures. There is not a unified set of factors to aid developers and users in implementation of the quality metrics methodology. Developers are left to search through an array of literature for potential factors and sub-factors that must ultimately be measured to assess the quality of a DMSS. As with research constructs, the DSSR Framework fills this gap in identifying potential quality factors.

The next section demonstrates the potential use of the DSSR Framework in the context of an advanced military systems project having support for improved decision-making as a major required operational capability.

ILLUSTRATION OF DSSR USE IN SYSTEMS DEVELOPMENT

The 1990 Gulf War presented a situation in which lightly armed forces were initially deployed to Saudi Arabia to aid Allied forces in defending against a large Iraqi armored force. The risk to these contingency forces highlighted by this event presented the US Department of Defense with a complex problem. A broad solution to this problem was to provide advanced technologies to future forces. While a number of alternatives were available, one alternative selected for experimentation took advantage of a variety of developmental sensor and weapons systems. These systems would be linked and controlled using an advanced information system. One required capability of this information system was to provide contingency units operating in austere environments a sophisticated level of decision-making support.

The Rapid Force Projection Initiative (RFPI) was conceived after the war and designed as a Department of Defense (DoD) Advanced Concept and Technology Demonstration (ACTD) in 1994 . A major goal of the RPFI was to demonstrate the capability to link a suite of advanced sensor systems with an array of advanced weapons systems using a system-of-systems approach. This linkage centered on the use of electronic data, provided almost exclusively in a wireless mode, to an automated command and control center. The command and control center would utilize decision-making support technologies to coordinate advanced systems in battles involving light forces against a large tank-supported threat. Key decision-making tasks were to identify potential targets, select and prioritize targets, assign targets to appropriate weapons systems, and assess damage. The concept for the development of the system called for joint user-developer management; a series of increasingly complex simulations; the integration of those technologies in both simulated and live environments; and the fielding of new units equipped with operational prototypes by the early 2000s.

One of the early tasks of the user-developer management team was to identify required operational capabilities and assessment measures. These capabilities and measures were established using a dendritic hierarchy focused on high-level operational issues such as 1) increased situational awareness and 2) increased control of battle tempo. The idea behind the use of dendritic hierarchy was to establish and identify issues, criteria, measures of effectiveness, and measures of performance. From these measures, data requirements and specific data elements for collection during the evaluation and testing process would be identified (Tackett, 2001). These requirements would drive the planning for 24 studies, assessments, experiments, and tests conducted during the 1990s. This approach was consistent with the US Army Test and Evaluation Command regulations (1999) and IEEE Standard 1061-1992 (1993). However, neither these documents nor existing research frameworks provided a detailed unified hierarchy of constructs, factors, or criteria tailored to decision-making support systems. As a result of these limitations, the user-developer team was unable to locate a comprehensive source for quality factors and was forced to rely on factors derived from the past experiences of team members and available literature. This gap created the potential for incomplete test and evaluation planning.

Applying the constructs from the DSSR Framework, we demonstrate in Tables 1 and 2 how a hierarchy of detailed quality factors could have been derived for two required RFPI capabilities. The required capability and criterion depicted in the two leftmost columns in these tables were used as the basis for actual test and evaluation planning (Tackett, 2001). The three rightmost columns are derived from the DSSR Framework, depicting a hierarchy of quality factors that, with user and developer knowledge of the framework, could have been used as early as 1993 during project planning as the basis for data collection efforts during testing and evaluation of the system.

The majority of RFPI assessment events culminated in 1998 with a large-scale field experiment. A number of concerns were expressed by the joint user-developer management team after analysis of data collected during the field experiment (US Army Infantry School, 2001). Key areas of concern have been used in the following examples to demonstrate the potential effects that the lack of a comprehensive construct or factor framework may have on the development of high quality DMSS.

The RFPI criterion of increased situational awareness could be affected by numerous factors that are identifiable from the DSSR Framework (Table 1). For example, the factors usability, topology, and standardization potentially affect user situational awareness. Problems reported from field experiments included network configuration, interoperability with other systems, and user interventions required during system use (US Army, 2001). A separate high-level DSSR Framework factor, use process, may also affect increased situational awareness. The behavior of the user includes specific actions to identify and process data received from the

Table 1: Use of the DSSR framework to derive potential quality factors affecting target acquisition

Required Capability	Criterion	Example DSSR framework constructs/factors for measuring system quality		
Increased target acquisition capabilities (Tackett, 2001)	Increased situational awareness of threat force by 90-100% of the baseline system (Tackett, 2001)	•DSS	•Usability •Topology •Standardization	
		•Use Process	•User behavior	•Identify data •Summarize information •Categorize information •Compare information
		•Operations Process	•Performance •Throughput •Response time •System availability •System accuracy •Operations training	

suite of sensors. Information overload during system use was reported as an issue from field experiments (US Army, 2001). The operations process, as defined by performance, throughput, etc., is a third high-level factor potentially affecting situational awareness. System performance and availability were reported as issues in the field experiment (US Army, 2001).

Table 2 demonstrates the use of DSSR constructs to define factors potentially affecting the required capability to control battle tempo and the associated criterion of decreased decision cycle time. In this example the DSS, use process, and user environment are the high-level factors affecting the criterion. The nature of support potentially affects decision-making cycle time. Early in RFPI program planning, one of the most contentious issues was the nature of support the system would provide. Technologists initially began developing the system with the notion that the system would operate in an automatic decision-making mode. In this mode, targets were acquired and identified by remote sensors, some of which were unmanned, and weapon systems were directed to fire. This was not acceptable to the user because of the high operational risk of attacking friendly, neutral, or incorrect targets. This issue would drive not only the design of the system, but also the process of system use. Specific lower-order quality factors affecting this capability were not identified for assessment early in the planning process. However, the need for a higher-level

Table 2: Use of the DSSR framework to derive potential quality factors affecting control of battle tempo

Required Capability	Criterion	Example DSSR Framework constructs/factors for measuring system quality		
Increased control of battle tempo (Tackett, 2001)	Decrease command decision cycle time by 25-50% of the baseline system (Tackett, 2001)	• DSS	•Nature of support •Method of evidence •Mode of presentation •Usability	
		• Use Process	•User behavior	•Analyze situation •Recognize decision need •Diagnose problem •Conduct selection •Authorize action •Communication decision •Control decision
			•Productivity	•Effectiveness •Efficiency
			•Decision making quality •Task-feature congruence •User satisfaction •User training	
		• User Environment	•User characteristics	•Cognitive ability •User attitude •User perception •User expectations •User background
			•Task characteristics	•Judgment tasks •Decision tasks •Fuzzy tasks

of decision-making support was noted after field experiments. The behavior of the user supported by the system, originally defined as a cycle of detect, decide, deliver and assess, was questioned as the optimal behavior. Further experimentation and assessment was recommended based on a revised decision making cycle described as detect, decide, track, re-decide, deliver, and assess (US Army, 2001).

Use process factors affecting decision cycle time were user training and user satisfaction. Training on digital systems was reported to be a highly perishable skill (US Army, 2001). User satisfaction with the command and control component of the RFPI system of systems was marginal, with this system, including decision-making support components, retained for experimentation and further development but not for operational use (US Army, 2001). Factors within the user environment affecting decision cycle time included both user and task characteristics. Operator workload within a constrained organizational structure and during continuous operations affected overall system performance (US Army, 2001).

The availability of a comprehensive framework of constructs or factors in the early 1990s could have been a significant aid in the identification and selection of system quality factors. This affected the detailed planning supporting the numerous system assessments and ultimately the quality of the DMSS delivered for field experimentation.

CONCLUSIONS

The DSSR Framework advances research into DMSS by helping to build a cumulative research tradition as well as supporting the development of high quality systems in several important ways.

- First, the framework has practical use in identifying factors and sub-factors affecting the design, use, and operation of quality DMSS in organizational settings.
- Second, the framework, when used in conjunction with the software quality metrics framework and methodology, serves as a tool for developers and users to plan for and assess the quality of DMSS early in the development cycle.
- Third, it provides a lens through which to view a unified set of theoretical constructs that are conducive to forming the propositions and hypotheses needed to drive scholarly research.
- Finally, the framework realizes the synergy between IS fields by providing a mechanism for classification of existing empirical research, categorization of contributions of each subdiscipline, and identification of areas for future research.

Future research is needed in a number of areas to further extend the DSSR Framework. The DSSR Framework was developed using selected articles specifically from the area of decision support systems from 1971 through 2000. Additional research is needed to expand the empirical studies contributing to factors identified by the framework to systems affecting decision-making such as adaptive decision support systems, executive information systems, executive support systems, management information systems, and expert systems. Another research area that will add significantly to both researchers and developers of quality DMSS systems is defining how best to operationalize and measure quality factors. The development of validated metrics, instruments, and scales for measuring the factors having either weak or nonexistent measurement tools is another research area needed to further the development of quality DMSS.

Research in DSS is young in comparison to other disciplines within the social sciences. This chapter synthesizes several frameworks from academics and industry and demonstrates their practical application in system development. The DSSR Framework is intended to be used as a living framework, with future research findings enabling its refinement as knowledge of factors and associated metrics accumulates.

REFERENCES

Adam, F., Fahy, M., & Murphy, C. (1998). A framework for the classification of DSS usage across organizations. *Decision Support Systems*, 22, 1-13.

Alter, S. (1977). A taxonomy of decision support systems. *Sloan Management Review, 19*(1), 39-56.

Anthony, R. A. (1965). *Planning and control systems: A framework for analysis.* Boston: Graduate School of Business Administration, Harvard University, Division of Research.

Barron, T. M., Chiang, R. H. L., & Storey, V. (1999). A semiotics framework for information systems classification and development. *Decision Support Systems*, 25, 1-17.

Blanning, R. W. (1983). What is happening in DSS? *Interfaces, 13*(5), 71-80.

Bonczek, R. H., Holsapple, C. W., & Whinston, A. B. (1981). *Foundations of decision support systems.* New York: Academic Press.

Eierman, M. A., Niederman, F., & Adams, C. (1995). DSS theory: A model of constructs and relationships. *Decision Support Systems*, 14, 1-26.

Fedorowicz, J., & Konsynski, B. (1992). Organization support systems: bridging business and decision processes. *Journal of Management Information Systems, 8*(4), 5-25.

Finlay, P. N., & Wilson, J. M. (2000). A survey of contingency factors affecting the validation of end-use spreadsheet-based decision support systems. *Journal of the Operational Research Society*, 51, 949-958.

Franz, C. R., & Robey, D. (1984). An investigation of user-led system design: rational and political perspectives. *Communications of the ACM, 27*(12), 1202-1209.

Gorry, G. A., & Scott-Morton, M. S. (1971). A framework for management information systems. *Sloan Management Review, 13*(1), 55-70.

Goslar, M. D., Green, G. I., & Hughes, T.H. (1986). Decision support systems: An empirical assessment for decision making. *Decision Sciences, 17*, 79-91.

Gray, P., & Watson, H. J. (1998). *Decision support in the data warehouse*. Upper Saddle River, NJ: Prentice Hall.

Grover, V., & Goslar, M. D. (1993). The initiation, adoption, and implementation of telecommunications technologies in U.S. organizations. *Journal of Management Information Systems, 10*(1), 141-163.

Herbsleb, J., Zubrow, D., Goldenson, D., Hayes, W., & Paulk, M. (1997). Software quality and the capability maturity model. *Communications of the ACM, 40*(6), 30-40.

IEEE Standard 1061-1992. (1993). *IEEE standard for a software quality metrics methodology*. New York: IEEE.

Ives, B., Hamilton, S., & Davis, G. B. (1980). A framework for research in computer-based management information systems. *Management Science, 26*(4), 910-934.

Kaplan, A. (1964). *The conduct of inquiry*. San Francisco: Chandler.

Mason, R. O., & Mitroff, I. I. (1973). A program for research on management information systems. *Management Science, 19*(5), 475-487.

Mata, F. J., Fuerst, W. L., & Barney, J. B. (1995). Information technology and sustained competitive advantage: A resource-based analysis. *MIS Quarterly, 19*(4), 487-505.

Metzger, P.W. (1991). *Managing a programming project*. Englewood Cliffs, NJ: Prentice Hall.

Mintzberg, H., Raisinghani, D., & Theoret, A. (1976). The structure of 'unstructured' decision processes. *Administrative Science Quarterly, 21*(2), 246-275.

Muhanna, W. (1993). An object-oriented framework for model management and DSS development. *Decision Support Systems, 9*(2), 217-229.

Muhanna, W. A., & Pick, R.A. (1994). Meta-modeling concepts and tools for model management: a systems approach. *Management Science, 40*(9), 1093-1123.

Nolan, R.L., & Wetherbe, J.C. (1980). *Toward a comprehensive framework for MIS research*. MIS Quarterly, 4(2), 1-19.

Pearson J. M., & Shim, J. P. (1995). An empirical investigation into DSS structures and environments. *Decision Support Systems, 13*(2), 141-158.

Porter, M. E. (1985). *Competitive strategy: Techniques for analyzing industries and competitors*. New York: Free Press.

Prescott, M. B., & Conger, S. A. (1995). Information technology innovations: A classification by IT locus of impact and research approach. *DATABASE, 26*(2 and 3), 20-41.

Rogers, E. M. (1983). *Diffusion of innovations*. New York: Free Press.

Ross, D. T., & Schoman, K.E., Jr. (1977). Structured analysis for requirement definition. *IEEE Transactions on Software Engineering*, Se-3.

Schein, E. (1990). Organizational culture. *American Psychologist, 45*(2), 109-119.

Schwab, D. P. (1980). Construct validity in organizational behavior. In B.M. Staw and L.L. Cummings (Eds.), *Research in organizational behavior* (pp. 3-43) Greenwich, CT: JAI Press.

Simon, H. (1960). *The new science of management decision*. New York: Harper and Row.

Sprague, R. H. Jr. (1980). A framework for the development of decision support systems. *MIS Quarterly, 4*(4), 1-25.

Tackett, G. B. (2001). Field experimentation design for multi-threaded analysis. Redstone Arsenal, AL: U.S. Army Aviation and Missile Research, Development and Engineering Center. (NTIS No. ADA392039INZ).

Tung, L., & Turban, E. (1998). A proposed research framework for distributed group support systems. *Decision Support Systems, 23*(2), 175-188.

United States Army Infantry School, Dismounted Battlespace Battle Lab. (2001). Rapid force projection initiative (RFPI) advanced concept technology demonstration (ACTD): Field experiment final report, executive summary. Retrieved August 31, 2001, from http://www-benning.army.mil/dbbl/bcd/rfpiactd.htm.

United States Army Test and Evaluation Command. (1999). ATEC regulation 73-1: System test and evaluation policy, Alexandria, VA. Retrieved August 31, 2001, from http://www.atec.army.mil/inside/731.htm.

Yadav, S. B., Bravoco, R. R., Chatfield, A. T., & Rajkumar, T. M. (1988). Comparison of analysis techniques for information requirements determination. *Communications of the ACM, 31*(9), 1090-1097.

Yadav, S. B. & Mukesh R. (1991). *A framework for comparative analysis of software design methods.* Tech. Rep., Texas Tech University, College of Business Administration, Information Systems and Quantitative Science Area.

Yadav, S. B., & Webb, H. W. (2001). *Specification of theoretical constructs through an integrative decision support systems research framework.* Manuscript in preparation. Texas Tech University.

Zmud, R. W. (1982). Diffusion of modern software practices: influence of centralization and formalization. *Management Science, 28*(12), 1421-1431.

Chapter XVIII

Executive Information Systems in Spain: A Study of Current Practices and Comparative Analysis[1]

José L. Roldán and Antonio Leal
University of Seville, Spain

ABSTRACT

Executive Information Systems (EIS) began to become popular in Spain in the 1990s. This chapter offers a primary descriptive study of EIS in Spain, bearing in mind two aims: to study the EIS usage in Spain and undertake a comparative analysis with reference to previous research. In this way, starting from the recognized EIS development framework of Watson, Rainer and Koh (1991), the authors focus on the structural perspective of the EIS elements and the development process. The study is based on a survey involving 70 organizations. The results show both parallelisms with preceding studies and new contributions to the current knowledge in the EIS field. Finally, the chapter identifies future trends in the executive information system concept.

INTRODUCTION

Ten years ago, Watson, Rainer, and Koh (1991) set a landmark in the study of executive information systems (EIS) practices. Their work described a useful framework for EIS development which encompasses three elements: a structural perspective of the elements and their interaction, the development process, and the dialogue between the user and the system. They cast light on EIS research because previous literature was mainly based on case studies or had an anecdotal character. Indeed, based on their framework, they offer the first important descriptive study of EIS practices.

Starting from this milestone, several contributions that show a general view on EIS usage in different countries can be found in the literature (Allison, 1996; Fitzgerald, G., 1992; Kirlidog, 1997; Liang & Hung, 1997; Nord & Nord, 1995, 1996; Park, Min, Lim, & Chun, 1997; Pervan, 1992; Pervan & Phua, 1997; Thodenius, 1995, 1996; Watson, Rainer, & Frolick, 1992; Watson, Watson, Singh, & Holmes, 1995). However, there has been little interest in EIS among Spanish researchers because of the nonexistence of any empirical research on EIS usage in Spain. Given this picture and following the trend manifested in the preceding research lines, this chapter is aimed at the following objectives: (1) to study the EIS usage in Spain and (2) to undertake a comparative analysis between the Spanish situation of EIS and the results obtained in several descriptive studies.

Based upon EIS literature, a questionnaire was constructed. The questionnaires were distributed to 136 Spanish organizations that were using EIS. As a result, 70 usable surveys were attained. This figure is higher than any previous work.

BACKGROUND

There are two terms which are equally used to describe those information systems developed to support top managers (Watson et al., 1991): executive information systems (EIS) and executive support systems (ESS). Rockart and DeLong (1988) suggest that while the first term makes reference to an information supply system, the second refers to a broader scope information system (IS), covering, among others, electronic communications, data analysis and office automation tasks. Although both terms are nowadays considered as synonymous, in practice the first name has prevailed (EIS), absorbing all the above features that used to characterize ESS (Partanen & Savolainen, 1995).

An executive information system can be defined as a computer-based information system designed to provide executives with easy access to internal and external information relevant to their management activities.

EIS differ considerably in scope and purpose. These systems can be developed with a corporation, division or functional action field. On the other hand, the primary purpose of the system will change from one organization to another, and this will also occur with the information it may include. From this perspective, an executive information system should be considered as something as unique as the organization it serves (Watson, Houdeshel, & Rainer, 1997).

Among the main characteristics of such systems the following can be highlighted: (a) focus on the information needs of each executive; (b) extract, filter, organize, compress, and deliver data; (c) access and integrate a broad range of internal and external data; (d) provide current status access to performance data; (e) trend analysis; (f) drill down capabilities to examine supporting detail; (g) exception reporting to highlight variances; (h) tracking critical success factors and key performance indicators; (i) integration into other organizational information systems (DSS, GSS, ES) and provide access to other software applications the user may need.

Although at the beginning the target public for this type of IS was top management, nowadays this system has often spread to other nonexecutive users such as middle managers, support staff, analysts, and knowledge workers (Frolick, 1994). Because of this widespread use, it has been suggested that the EIS acronym should currently stand for everyone information system or enterprise intelligence system (Wheeler, Chang, & Thomas, 1993). This wider presence among a larger user base has led to changes both in the information distributed among them and in the capabilities offered by such systems (Kennedy-Davies, 1995).

MAIN THRUST OF THE CHAPTER

Executive information systems have experienced a great expansion since the 1980s (Rockart & DeLong, 1988) as a consequence of facilitating and pressuring (internal and external) factors. Likewise, an important literature has been produced since the first paper on this type of system was published by Nash (1977). On the other hand, there are several studies which show the use of EIS in different countries (USA, UK, Sweden, Australia, Korea, etc.). However, in Spain the following scenario is presented. Despite the existence of data from vendors and consultants denoting the 1990s as the starting date of the EIS expansion, there is an absence of empirical research work on the use of these systems in Spain (Roldán, 2000).

Considering this situation, a descriptive study to find out the characteristics of the use of executive information systems in Spain has been conducted. At the same time, a comparative study of the results achieved in Spain and those obtained in other countries has been also undertaken, enabling the understanding of the evolution experienced by this type of system.

The Study

Keeping in mind the chapter's objectives, the study follows the EIS development framework put forward by Watson et al. (1991). In accordance with Sprague (1987), a framework "is helpful in organizing a complex subject, identifying the relationships between the parts, and revealing the areas in which further developments will be required" (p. 130). With regards to the area of executive information systems, a number of frameworks have been identified, such as the works by Byun and Suh (1994), Srivihok and Whymark (1996), and Watson et al. (1991). This study has followed the framework developed by Watson et al. (1991) since this is the one most disseminated among the EIS community. This EIS development framework encompasses three elements: a structural perspective of the elements and their interaction, the development process, and the dialogue between the user and the system. This study will focus on the first two components.

Methodology

A survey instrument was used to gather data to develop the study. The questionnaire was built based upon EIS literature. We mainly analyzed the works of Fitzgerald, G., (1992), Thodenius (1995, 1996), Watson and Frolick (1993), Watson et al. (1991), and Watson et al. (1995). Questions and items were translated and adapted to the Spanish EIS context.

The survey was carried out in Spain from January to June 1998. A pilot test of the survey was conducted in order to assess content validity (Straub, 1989). The instrument was pretested with EIS consultants (n = 4) and business and IS professors (n = 3). Suggestions were incorporated into a second version that was then tested by two other management professors. No additional suggestions were made. Thus, bias in response from misinterpretation of the instrument should be reduced.

The sample was selected following the method called snowball sampling (Biernacki & Waldorf, 1981), obtaining an initial list of 178 organizations based on the contributions of seven software development and distribution firms and four consulting firms.

Between March and June 1998, the manager in charge of the EIS implementation was contacted via telephone. In these interviews the existence of an operative EIS or at least an EIS under implementation was confirmed, and, after explaining the study's objectives to the persons responsible for EIS implementation, they were asked for their collaboration. Following this communication process, the cooperation of 136 organizations was achieved.

Finally, valid responses from 75 organizations were obtained, which represents a participation percentage of 55.15%. After analyzing the EIS situation in this group of entities, 70 questionnaires which could be analyzed were selected. These represented organizations with EIS, operative or in an implementation stage suffi-ciently advanced as to enable the answering of the questions asked. This number of valid questionnaires is higher than any obtained in previous EIS descriptive studies.

Results

Demographics

The organizations participating in the study belonged primarily to the manufac-turing (37.1%) and banking/financial services (24.3%) sectors. Other sectors present in the study were retailers (8.6%), logistics (8.6%) and government (8.6%). According to the European Union classification, most of the participating entities are large enterprises, with 71% of them with more than 500 employees, while 62% have gross revenues exceeding US $139 million.

Of the respondents, almost 50% belong to the IS department, followed by planning/management control department (17.6%) and finance (10.3%). Respondents average 7 years of work experience. The EIS included in the survey have an average age of 33 months and range in age from 1 month to 8 years. Most of the EIS have a corporative scope (69.6%), followed at a distance by systems specifically developed for a division or strategic business unit (23.2%). Notwithstanding, there is a small percentage of cases in which the scope of the IS is functional (7.2%), having been developed for the marketing/sales, finances and management control areas.

Structural Perspective

According to the framework developed by Watson et al. (1991), the structural approach shows the key elements which are critical for the development of an EIS as well as the interactions taking place among them (Figure 1).

The first stage is to analyze the motivations leading Spanish organizations to implement such systems. Based on the contributions listed in the literature, the following classification can be made: (1) factors facilitating the introduction of an EIS in the firm and (2) factors pressuring the organization, leading it to take the step for the implementation of this type of systems differentiating between internal and external pressures.

The participants in the research study were provided with a list of 14 factors, asking them to grade the relevance of each factor for the introduction of an EIS in their organization in a 1-5 scale (1 = low importance; 5 = high importance; see Table 1). From examining their responses, the three main motivations for the development of an EIS are internal ones. This agrees with the motivations listed in the studies made

Figure 1: The structural perspective of an EIS; adapted from Watson et al. (1991) and Frolick (1994)

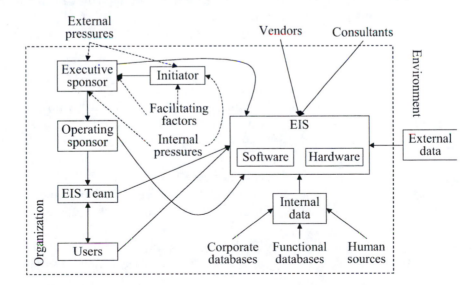

Table 1: Motivations leading to EIS development

	M	SD
[IP] To have quick and easy access to organizational information	4.7391	0.5045
[IP] To have more consistent, accurate, pertinent and timely information	4.5507	0.6539
[IP] To improve organizational performance monitoring	3.8406	0.9795
[EP] To be more proactive in dealing with external environment	3.6571	1.034
[IP] To improve communication	3.5714	1.0296
[IP] To improve the efficiency and effectiveness of executives	3.5143	0.9592
[IP] To extract and integrate data from incompatible sources	3.4857	1.2825
[EP] Increasingly competitive environment	3.3134	1.0329
[FF] Availability of adequate technology	3.1304	1.3163
[FF] A better executive attitude to use computers	3.1143	1.1862
[FF] A better executive knowledge about IT potential	3.1014	1.1395
[IP] To change or improve executives' mental model	3.087	1.0395
[EP] Increasingly turbulent environment	2.7857	1.1019
[IP] To downsize the organization	1.4783	0.7972

[EP]: external pressure, [FF]: facilitating factor, [IP]: internal pressure.

by Pervan and Phua (1997), Thodenius (1995, 1996), Watson et al. (1991), and Watson et al. (1995). It is also agreed that external pressures do not have an important weight.

The initiator is the person originally responsible for the idea of introducing an EIS in the organization. This figure is usually a top manager who perceives the need for this type of system and promotes its development and implementation (Houdeshel & Watson, 1987; Rockart & DeLong, 1988). However, in a growing number of cases this role is performed by a manager or a member of the IS department (Fitzgerald, B., & Murphy, 1994; Fitzgerald, G., 1992; Kirlidog, 1997).

This study confirms both these situations (Table 2), although the role of the IS/ information technology (IT) department manager is highlighted, since his/her presence is pointed out by 37.7% of participating organizations. The managing director is revealed in almost 25% of cases, while there is a slightly higher presence of a top manager in the functional area (26.1%). This is usually the financial manager or a manager belonging to the planning and management control area.

An executive sponsor is usually a quite empowered top manager who assesses the EIS potential and is willing to invest the time, efforts and resources required for the system's development (Mayne, 1992). The role of executive sponsor can be identified with the figure of the initiator. However, if the source of the idea is a manager of a technical unit, i.e., the IS/IT department, this person will have to start a process to identify, convince and attract a top manager of the organization to assume the role of committed executive sponsor (Burkan, 1991; Paller & Laska, 1990).

Based on the data of this study (Table 2), the following conclusions can be drawn: (1) As in Allison's study (1996) a predominance of a top functional manager

Table 2: Key agents in EIS development (multiple answer questions)

	EIS initiator		Executive sponsor		Operating sponsor	
	Freq.	% of firms	Freq.	% of firms	Freq.	% of firms
Chair	2	2.9%	0	0.0%	--	--
CEO	7	10.1%	9	13.0%	--	--
Managing director	17	24.6%	11	15.9%	--	--
IS/IT manager	26	37.7%	21	30.4%	26	37.7%
Top functional manager	18	26.1%	25	36.2%	23	33.3%
Middle managers	--	--	--	--	8	11.6%
Support staff	--	--	--	--	7	10.1%
Other	8	11.6%	10	14.5%	10	14.5%

(36.2%) as executive sponsor compared to poorer figures for the CEO (13%) and the managing director (15.9%) has been found. (2) There is a significant presence of the IS/IT department manager, who is mentioned by 30.4% of the entities. This high level attained by technical department managers has not been confirmed by the early studies (Fitzgerald, G., 1992; Watson et al., 1992; Watson et al., 1991). However, this situation started to be confirmed from the appearance of the works of B. Fitzgerald (1998) and Watson et al. (1995), which already started to outline the members of the IS/IT departments as predominant agents in many of the process stages of EIS development.

Due to the difficulties in finding the time required to promote the project, the executive sponsor usually tends to appoint an operating sponsor to manage the everyday work of EIS development (Rockart & DeLong, 1988). With this purpose, the operating sponsor works with managers, analysts, functional area staff, IS staff, consultants and software vendors to create the EIS (Watson et al., 1992).

This research points out two positions in the organization as the most common ones to perform such a role (Table 2). On the one hand, the IS/IT manager is mentioned as operating sponsor in 37.7% of firms, which is in line with the results obtained by G. Fitzgerald (1992), Watson et al. (1992) and Watson et al. (1991). On the other hand, the operating sponsor is a top manager of a functional area (33.3%), with this role corresponding mainly to the planning/management control manager or the financial manager, which supports the results of G. Fitzgerald (1992).

The EIS team is made up of all the people responsible for creating and maintaining an EIS (Watson et al., 1991). This definition comprises two different missions corresponding to two stages of the IS life cycle (Watson & Frolick, 1993): first, the design and introduction of the EIS; second, its maintenance once it is operative. Following this line, two types of teams can be differentiated in this research: (1) the development team and (2) the support and maintenance team.

With reference to the first, it can be seen that its size ranges from 1 to 20 persons, with an average of 4.37, which is a figure similar to those presented in the studies of Watson et al. (1991; 4 members), and Watson et al. (1992; 4.1 persons). In relation to its composition, we can observe that 72.5% of organizations include staff from the

IS/IT departments while there are lower percentages for other managers contributing a business perspective, such as top managers of functional areas (33.3%) and middle managers (26.1%). What is different from the results of other research studies is the greater presence of consultants (49.3%) and software vendors (34.8%). These greater percentages may result from the sample selection technique used.

As far as the maintenance team is concerned, it is usually in smaller size, with an average number of members of 2.3. This figure is lower than that obtained by Watson et al. (1992), which stated an average size of 3.5 persons. With regards to its make-up, there is also a high presence of members from the IS/IT department (70.1%), with lower responses for the other members proposed in the survey.

The average number of users in all the organizations studied is 75.93 persons. This figure is significantly higher than that shown in the study performed by G. Fitzgerald (1992) among British firms (13 users). However, it must be mentioned that this high average number includes three firms with more than 400 users, with one of them reaching a total number of 1,800 users. Therefore, it would be more appropriate to take into account the mode and median values, which suggest the number of 20 users as a measure of the central trend.

In this research (Table 3), top functional managers show higher use levels (88.6%) than top managers, which confirms the results of the previous studies by Basu, Poindexter, Drosen, and Addo (2000), Liang and Hung (1997), and Nord and Nord (1995). The close similarity in the percentage of organizations which have middle managers as users (68.6%) as compared to the levels achieved by the managing director (70%) is also significant. It is also worth mentioning that 21.4% of organizations declare that they have other users, which, after analyzing the responses to this question, can be clearly classified as knowledge workers and analysts. Thus, considering their degree of dissemination among the different organizational levels and areas, and the high number of users they are reaching, it is no surprise that in many cases the EIS acronym has been relabeled as enterprise intelligence systems.

With regards to the different types of information included in an EIS (Table 4), commercial and sales information (82.9% of responses) appears as the most important item. A second level of financial information (65.7%) and production information (55.7%) is found. Other previous research studies agree in presenting these three types of information as the most relevant ones (Allison, 1996; Kirlidog, 1997; Thodenius, 1996).

Although some authors have defended the inclusion in the EIS of further reaching information with multiple perspectives and including a set of financial and nonfinancial, external and internal indicators (Taylor, Gray, & Graham, 1992), it can be observed that the information that appears predominantly in these systems has an internal character (Preedy, 1990). External information obtains lower response levels: competitors (22.9%), market (20%), suppliers (17.2%), strategic planning (14.3%), and external news services (12.9%).

Table 3: EIS users (multiple answer question)

	Frequency	% of firms
Chair	14	20.0%
CEO	20	28.6%
Managing director	49	70.0%
Top functional manager	62	88.6%
Middle managers	48	68.6%
Other	15	21.4%

Information is usually presented (Table 5) according to functional areas (62.9%) and products (61.4%). In turn, information according to processes ranks quite low, existing in only 20% of participating entities. This situation was already criticized by Wetherbe (1991) as one of the traditional problems of the information systems for top managers, i.e., that they are considered as functional systems rather than being considered as systems crossing functions. Nevertheless, the study's results are understandable since the most important user group is that of top functional managers.

One of the features present in an EIS is the mining, filtering, organization and consolidation of multiple data sources. Table 6 shows that the greatest part of the information comes from internal sources, mostly of a quantitative character: corporate databases (87.1%) and functional area databases (41.4%). Related to what has been previously stated about the low percentage of presence of external information, a low presence of the use of external sources can be appreciated in line with this: external databases (27.1%) and Internet (2.9%). This trend towards internal sources is a repetition of the results obtained by other research studies (Basu, et al., 2000; Fitzgerald, G., 1992; Kirlidog, 1997; Watson et al., 1992; Watson et al., 1991).

Table 4: Types of information included in EIS (multiple answer question)

	Frequency	% of firms
Commercial/Sales	58	82.9%
Financial	46	65.7%
Production	39	55.7%
Human resources	31	44.3%
Quality	22	31.4%
Competitors	16	22.9%
Inventory control	14	20.0%
Market	14	20.0%
Suppliers	12	17.1%
Strategic planning	10	14.3%
External news services	9	12.9%
Stock market	5	7.1%
Other	7	10.0%

Table 5: Information presentation (multiple answer question)

	Frequency	% of firms
By functional areas	44	62.9%
By products	43	61.4%
By geographical areas	37	52.9%
By strategic business units	37	52.9%
By key performance indicators	33	47.1%
By processes	14	20.0%
By projects	11	15.7%
Other	4	5.7%

With regards to the hardware platform selected, the client-server configuration (C/S) appears as the most preferred option among the hardware structures supporting EIS with the 2-tier C/S architecture as the most prevalent one (38.2%), followed by the 3-tier C/S architecture (27.9%), which confirms the evolutive trend towards multitier C/S architectures.

On the other hand, one of the components of the C/S configuration which has become more popular since the late 1990s will be analyzed. This is the data warehouse (DW) concept. From a C/S structure perspective, two basic types of architecture in this type of configuration can be distinguished: 2-tier DW and 3-tier DW. Based on the set of responses obtained, we can verify that this configuration is starting to become a true reality, with these two types (2- and 3-tier) accounting for more than 50% of cases. There is a strong presence of 2-tier DW architecture (32.3%), though the 3-tier architecture is gaining ground with 20% of cases.

With respect to the software configuration used, there are two predominant patterns. On the one hand, 47.1% of the organizations developed their executive information system with commercial software provided by vendors. On the other hand, 47.1% of them performed a combination task of in-house software and commercial software acquired from vendors. In both cases, the presence of commercial software for the system's development is found. On the other hand, what is blatantly clear is the low number of cases in which the system has been developed with software produced by the organization itself (5.7%), which used to be the most common scenario in the creation of the first EIS systems.

Table 6: Data sources (multiple answer question)

	Frequency	% of firms
Corporate databases	61	87.1%
Functional area databases	29	41.4%
Documents	24	34.3%
Human	23	32.9%
External databases	19	27.1%
Internet	2	2.9%

The most frequently mentioned commercial software products were: Commander from Comshare (39.1%), DSS Agents from MicroStrategy (21.9%), Forest & Trees from Platinum Technology (15.6%), and Focus/EIS from Information Builders (10.9%).

Development Process

The development process describes how an EIS is developed, implemented and evolved over time. In this section, those factors which are more relevant to understand how organizations undertake this process are focused on.

The first fact that must be highlighted is that in 78.3% of cases the development process is performed with the help of external support, either from software vendors (27.5%), or from external consultants (26.1%), or from both (24.6%). This panorama shows a parallelism with the results of G. Fitzgerald (1992) for the United Kingdom, where 85% of firms have developed their systems with the support of vendors and consulting firms.

The average time to develop the first EIS version was 8.53 months, which should be considered as a long term compared with previous studies (Park et al., 1997; Watson et al., 1992; Watson et al., 1991), which could negatively affect the users' acceptation of the system (Young & Watson, 1995).

With reference to the development methodology, participants were asked to rank the approach they had used in a 1-5 scale, in which level 1 represented the so-called linear approach, i.e., a highly structured linear process with sequential stages (similar to the traditional SDLC), while level 5 represented an evolving approach, that is an ongoing growing EIS development and delivery cycle process. The mean reached 3.55 while the mode and median attained a value of 4. This represents a slight bias towards the iterative approach, close to the results obtained by Watson et al. (1995; average 4 points). The trend towards this methodology can be confirmed in the studies by Allison (1996), G. Fitzgerald (1992), Kirlidog (1997), Park et al. (1997), and Watson et al. (1991). On the other hand, participants ranked their satisfaction level with the approach used via a 1-5 scale, resulting in a 3.59 average. When conducting a bi-variant correlation analysis (Pearson's coefficient) between the approach used and the degree of satisfaction, a 0.463 index significant at 0.01 (bilateral) was obtained. This level shows the evidence of a moderate relation (Kinnear & Taylor, 1999) and is statistically significant between the methodology used and the satisfaction with it perceived, which renders an additional support to the literature supporting the application of the evolving approach in EIS development.

Taking into account the difficulties associated with the identification of the information requirements of managers, organizations have opted for using a set of methods to determine the information requirements of EIS users. According to this study the methodologies most frequently used are (Table 7): dialogue with managers (97.1%), examination of the computer-generated information currently received by managers (92.9%), and recommendations currently made by the manager on a voluntary basis (81.4%). However, as the work of Kirlidog (1997) shows, a fact to be underlined is the low use level of a technique traditionally linked to the implementation of these IS: the critical success factors method (CSF) (Rockart, 1979; 48.6%). The increasing use of new management approaches such as the balanced scorecard (BS) (Kaplan & Norton, 1996; 37.1%) in the determination of information needs has also been confirmed.

The perceived usefulness of these methods was measured on a 5-point anchored scale (1 = low level, 5 = high level). Table 7 describes a close correspondence with the frequency of use. Besides, the low reached levels of structured methods, such as BS (2.9615) and CSF (2.7941) should be highlighted. A tentative explanation of these results is the lack of an adequate training among EIS builders for the application of these methods.

On the basis of a list of existing problems in the development of EIS included in the study of Watson et al. (1995), participants were asked to rank in a 1-5 scale the importance of such items in the development of the IS (Table 8). By far the most frequent problem detected was getting accurate data (4.31). This problem is not a specific feature of Spanish organizations since it was already highlighted in the works of Pervan (1992) and Watson et al. (1995). The comparison with USA data shows a similar classification, though the Spanish organizations have a higher intensity in the perception of the problems, probably due to a shorter experience in developing information systems for executives.

FUTURE TRENDS

To develop this section, the opinion of people included in the ISWorld Net Faculty Directory who had shown their interest in research on EIS/ESS systems were consulted via e-mail. Based on their contributions the following trends are identified.

Table 7: Summary of frequency of use and perceived usefulness of the methods for determining information requirements of an EIS

	Percentage using the method	Mean perceived usefulness
Discussions with executives	97.1%	4.0746
Examinations of computer-generated information	92.9%	3.6769
Volunteered information	81.4%	3.8596
EIS planning meetings	80.0%	3.4643
Discussions with support personnel	77.1%	3.7407
Examinations of non-computer-generated information	62.9%	2.7955
Attendance at executive meetings	57.1%	3.2051
Strategic business objectives method	52.9%	3.2703
Tracking executive activity	52.9%	3.3243
Examination of the strategic plan	50.0%	3.0556
Critical success factors (CSF) method	48.6%	2.7941
Balanced scorecard (BS) method	37.1%	2.9615

It is an evident fact that EIS have spread throughout the organization. As Friend (1992) suggested, the EIS acronym should be understood as everybody's information systems or enterprise intelligence systems. The idea is to make EIS available to all organizational levels and not just for the top management. Therefore, currently and in the future, it will be difficult to find organizations developing IS just for managers (Basu et al., 2000).

EIS products as a separated application are already disappearing. Nowadays, they tend to be included in larger software systems, becoming a module integrated in quite a few ERP systems such as SAP. Furthermore, ongoing progress is being made in the integration of EIS into DSS systems, which is generally known through the business intelligence systems (BIS) label as an umbrella term introduced by the Gartner Group in 1989. According to Challener (1999), business intelligence systems "provide a mechanism for supplying individuals within an organization with the data they need in an easy-to-use format in combination with real-time analysis capabilities" (p. 37). BIS solutions usually present the following components: data mining, knowledge management, analytical applications, reporting systems, data warehousing, OLAP, etc.

Table 8: Problems in developing an EIS

	Spain $\underline{M}$	USA $\underline{M}$ [1]
Getting accurate data	4.3143	3.44
Getting executives to use the system	3.8358	2.98
Defining objectives for the system	3.7	3.27
Identifying initial information requirements	3.6471	2.92
Maintaining executives' interest	3.5714	3.20
Keeping abreast of executives' changing information requirements	3.3768	3.43
Linking the system to business objectives	3.3433	2.64
Learning to use the technology required to develop the system	3.2029	2.77
Having sufficient staff and computer resources	3.1343	3.20
Managing the spread of system	3.1286	3.18
Finding an initial application with high impact	2.9706	2.29
Getting committed executive sponsorship	2.9697	2.68
Identifying technical system requirements	2.9552	2.35
Deciding what hardware and software to use	2.7647	2.26
Maintaining sponsorship	2.7077	2.69
Justifying the cost of developing and maintaining the system	2.7015	2.30
Getting support from the IS department	2.6269	2.25
Avoiding political resistance	2.3636	2.93
Surviving sponsor turnover	2.3438	1.85

[1] Watson et al. (1995)

From a technical perspective, the use of Web technologies in the distribution of information is becoming widespread (Basu et al., 2000). Hereto, the availability of this technology together with the need to build something similar to an EIS but focused on all members of the organization has led to the development of the enterprise information portal (EIP) concept, which, to some extent, represents the latest incarnation of EIS. This term has been popularized by a report made by Merill Lynch in 1999. There are very different definitions of the term, but in accordance with the results of the EIP survey at Survey.com (Trowbridge, 2000), two elements can characterize these systems according to the respondents: EIP "acts as a single point of access to internal and external information" and "gives users access to disparate enterprise information systems" (p. 20). Furthermore, this survey points out that what is expected from such systems is: (1) enabling access to relevant information; (2) faster, better decision making; and (3) saving end users' time. Certainly, both the definition and the expectations are very close to the purposes proposed for the EIS in the literature of the early 1990s, with the particular feature of extending their influence to all members of the organization.

And, just to finish, according to Hugh Watson (personal communication, April 9, 2001), a lot of what an EIS is can be found reborn in the information systems supporting the management approach called balanced scorecard (Kaplan & Norton, 1996).

CONCLUSION

In this section, the main results achieved in this study are presented, differentiating between those results that confirm the conclusions reached in previous studies and those that contribute new facts to the current knowledge in the field of executive information systems.

The parallelisms found with previous studies are as follows: (1) EIS are mainly developed in order to provide easy and quick access to internal information. (2) The main motivations for the development of an EIS respond to internal pressures. (3) External information has a low presence within the contents of these systems. (4) The types of information most frequently contained in EIS are: commercial/sales, financial and production. (5) During the development process, organizations look for the support of software vendors, external consultants or both. (6) EIS are usually built with the use of a development methodology focusing on the evolving approach. (7) The main problem encountered by EIS builders is related to data management.

On the other hand, this work presents new contributions to the current knowledge in the field of executive information systems: (1) Their use is slowly spreading among small and medium-sized enterprises, as well as in the public sector. (2) The role of initiator is mainly performed by the manager of the IS/IT department. (3) The role of executive sponsor is usually performed by either a top functional manager or the IS/IT manager. (4) There is evidence of a larger number of users than in previous studies. (5) There is a predominance of the client/server architecture and, in more than half of the cases, these have data warehouse configurations. (6) There is a moderate but significant correlation between the use of an evolving development approach and the level of satisfaction of EIS managers with the development methodology. (7) There is a small use and a low level of usefulness of traditional methodologies to identify the information requirements, such as the critical success factors (CSF) method.

To finish this chapter, the opinion of the Swedish professor Björn Thodenius (1996; personal communication, July 16, 2001) is quoted. He differentiates between the EIS system (product or system itself) and the IS intended to support senior executives in their work. The question to be considered is the design and use of computer-based information systems which meet the special and specific information needs of top managers and adapt to their specific management styles. Whether this is achieved with one technology or another is of no importance. What is really crucial is that it will always be necessary to define an IS that meets the specific manager information requirements.

ENDNOTE

[1]An earlier version of this chapter was presented at the I Encuentro Iberoamericano de Finanzas y Sistemas de Información [First Ibero-American Meeting on Finance and Information Systems] (2000; November 29-December 1; Jerez de la Frontera, Spain). Financial support for this work was provided by the Andalusian Research Plan (Research Group SEJ-115).

REFERENCES

Allison, I. K. (1996). Executive information systems: An evaluation of current UK practice. *International Journal of Information Management, 16*(1), 27-36.

Basu, C., Poindexter, S., Drosen, J., & Addo, T. (2000). Diffusion of executive information systems in organizations and the shift to Web technologies. *Industrial Management & Data Systems, 6*(100), 271-276.

Biernacki, P., & Waldorf, D. (1981). Snowball sampling. Problems and techniques of chain referral sampling. *Sociological Methods & Research*, 10, 141-163.

Burkan, W. C. (1991). *Executive information systems: From proposal through implementation.* New York: Van Nostrand Reinhold.

Byun, D. H., & Suh, E. H. (1994). A builder's introduction to executive information systems. *International Journal of Information Management, 14*(5), 357-368.

Challener, C. (1999). Decision support graduates to business intelligence. *Chemical Market Reporter, 256*(17), 37.

Fitzgerald, B. (1998). Executive information systems without executives. In D. Avison & D. Edgar-Nevill (Eds.), *Proceedings of Third Conference of the UK Academy for Information Systems* (pp. 298-310). UK: Lincoln University.

Fitzgerald, B., & Murphy, C. (1994). *Factors involved in the introduction of executive information systems into organizations: An empirical study* (Paper Ref. 7/94). Cork, Ireland: University College Cork, Executive Systems Research Centre.

Fitzgerald, G. (1992). Executive information systems and their development in the UK. *International Information Systems, 1*(2), 1-35.

Friend, D. (1992). EIS and the collapse of the information pyramid. In H. J. Watson, R. K. Rainer, & G. Houdeshel (Eds.), *Executive information systems: Emergence, development, impact* (pp. 327-335). New York: John Wiley & Sons.

Frolick, M. N. (1994). Management support systems and their evolution from executive information systems. *Information Strategy: The Executive's Journal, 10*(3), 31-38.

Houdeshel, G., & Watson, H. J. (1987). The management information and decision support (MIDS) system at Lockheed-Georgia. *MIS Quarterly,* 11, 127-140.

Kaplan, R. S., & Norton, D.P. (1996). *The balanced scorecard: Translating strategy into action.* Boston: Harvard Business School Press.

Kennedy-Davies, H. (1995). Everybody's information system? *Management Accounting-London, 73*(5), 44.

Kinnear, T. C., & Taylor, J. R. (1995). *Marketing research: An applied approach* (5th ed.). New York: McGraw-Hill Higher Education.

Kirlidog, M. (1997). Information technology transfer to a developing country: Executive information systems in Turkey. *OCLC Systems & Services, 13*(3), 102-123.

Liang, T. P., & Hung, S. Y. (1997). DSS and EIS applications in Taiwan. *Information Technology & People, 10*, 303-315.

Mayne, L. (1992). *In touch on top: The business guide to executive information systems.* Melbourne: Longman Sheshire.

Nash, D. R. (1977). Building EIS, a utility for decisions. *Data Base, 8*(3), 43-45.

Nord, J. H., & Nord, G. D. (1995). Executive information systems: A study and comparative analysis. *Information & Management,* 29, 95-106.

Nord, J. H., & Nord, G. D. (1996). Why managers use executive support systems. *Information Strategy: The Executive's Journal, 12*(2), 34-38.

Paller, A., & Laska, R. (1990). *The EIS book. Information systems for top managers.* Homewood, IL: Business One Irwin.

Park, H. K., Min, J. K., Lim, J. S., & Chun, K. J. (1997). A comparative study of executive information systems between Korea and the United States. Seoul, Korea: Sangmyung University, Department of Telecommunications Systems Management.

Partanen, K., & Savolainen, V. (1995). Perspectives on executive information systems. *Systems Practice,* 8, 551-575.

Pervan, G. P. (1992). Issues in EIS: An Australian perspective. *Journal of Computer Information Systems, 32*(4), 6-10.

Pervan, G. P., & Phua, R. (1997). A survey of the state of executive information systems in large Australian oganisations. *Australian Computer Journal, 29*(2), 64-73.

Preedy, D. (1990). The theory and practical use of executive information systems. *International Journal of Information Management,* 10, 96-104.

Rockart, J. F. (1979). Chief executives define their own data needs. *Harvard Business Review, 57*(2), 81-93.

Rockart, J. F., & DeLong, D. W. (1988). *Executive support systems. The emergence of top management computer use.* Homewood, IL: Business One Irwin.

Roldán, J. L. (2000, December). Sistemas de información ejecutivos (EIS): Un estudio descriptivo sobre la situación en España [Executive information systems (EIS): A descriptive study about the Spanish situation]. In M. J. Selva (Coord.), *La empresa del siglo XXI: Finanzas, tecnologías y sistemas de información* (Vol. II, pp. 237-254). Cádiz, Spain: Diputación de Cádiz [Servicio de Publicaciones].

Sprague, R. H. (1987). A framework for the development of decision support systems. In H. J. Watson, A. B. Carroll, & R. I. Mann (Eds.), *Information systems for management. A book of readings* (4th ed., pp. 123-157) Plano, TX: Business Publications.

Srivihok, A., & Whymark, G. (1996, June). *Executive information systems framework: A new framework for implementation.* First Asia Pacific Decision Science Institute Conference (pp. 379-386), Hong Kong.

Straub, D. W. (1989). Validating instruments in MIS research. *MIS Quarterly*, 13, 147-190.

Taylor, B., Gray, A., & Graham, C. (1992). Information: The strategic essential. *Accountancy, 110*(1191), 43-45.

Thodenius, B. (1995, April). *The use of executive information systems in Sweden.* Paper presented at the CEMS Academic Conference—Recent Developments in Economics and Business Administration, Wien, Austria.

Thodenius, B. (1996). Using executive information systems. In M. Lundeberg & B. Sundgren (Eds.), A*dvancing your business: people and information systems in concert* (chap. IV). Stockholm, Sweden: EFI, Stockholm School of Economics. Retrieved from http://www.hhs.se/im/efi/ayb.htm

Trowbridge, D. (2000). EIP—More profitable for integrators than users? *Computer Technology Review, 20*(5), 20.

Watson, H. J., & Frolick, M. N. (1993). Determining information requirements for an EIS. *MIS Quarterly*, 17, 255-269.

Watson, H. J., Houdeshel, G., & Rainer, R. K., Jr. (1997). *Building executive information systems and other decision support applications.* New York: John Wiley & Sons.

Watson, H. J., Rainer, R. K., Jr., & Frolick, M. N. (1992). Executive information systems: An ongoing study of current practices. *International Information Systems, 1*(2), 37-56.

Watson, H. J., Rainer, R. K., Jr., & Koh, C. E. (1991). Executive information systems: A framework for development and a survey of current practices. *MIS Quarterly,* 15, 13-30.

Watson, H. J., Watson, R. T., Singh, S., & Holmes, D. (1995). Development practices for executive information systems: Findings of a field study. *Decision Support Systems*, 14, 171-184.

Wetherbe, J. C. (1991). Executive information requirements: Getting it right. *MIS Quarterly*, 15, 50-65.

Wheeler, F. P., Chang, S. H., & Thomas, R. J. (1993). Moving from an executive information system to everyone's information systems: Lessons from a case study. *Journal of Information Technology*, 8, 177-183.

Young, D., & Watson, H. J. (1995). Determinants of EIS acceptance. *Information & Management*, 29, 153-164.

Chapter XIX

Critical Factors in the Development of Executive Systems—Leveraging the Dashboard Approach

Frédéric Adam
University College Cork, Ireland

Jean-Charles Pomerol
Université Pierre et Marie Curie, France

ABSTRACT

Based on the Rockart's critical success factor (CSF) approach, this chapter puts forward a practical method to guide the development of executive information systems (EIS) in organizations. This method extends the current theory of EIS by using the concept of the dashboard of information to show how an enterprise-wide approach to the development of more effective decision support for managers can deliver tangible benefits without requiring the time-consuming and single-decision focus of the traditional development methods. This method also attempts to leverage the latest computing technologies now available for the development of such systems, notably graphical user inter-faces (GUI), data warehousing (DW) and OLAP. The proposed approach is illustrated by examples of dashboard developments, which show how managers should carry out the analysis and development of such a system in their own organizations, business units or functional areas.

INTRODUCTION

In this chapter, a practical method based on the critical success factor (CSF) approach proposed by John Rockart as early as 1979 is put forward to guide the development of executive information systems in organisations. This method extends the current theory of EIS by using the concept of *dashboard of information* to show how an enterprise-wide approach to the development of more effective decision support for managers can deliver tangible benefits without requiring the time-consuming and single-decision focus of the traditional development methods. This method also attempts to leverage the latest computing technologies now available for the development of such systems, notably, graphical user interfaces (GUIs), data warehousing and online analysis process (OLAP).

Based on a top-down CSF analysis, a hierarchy of indicators can be built up which covers all relevant aspects of the management of an organisation and supports the achievement of strategic goals. The outcome of this analysis can then be used as a blueprint for the development of an organisational DSS including a large database or data warehouse and a set of differentiated interfaces serving the specific needs of all managers. Each manager is given access to a dashboard containing the indicators which he or she most requires and has control over. Our approach is illustrated by examples of dashboard developments which show how managers should carry out the analysis and development of such a system in their own organisation, business unit or functional area.

The resulting organisational EIS may then become a support for the delegation and decentralisation of decision making and control in the organisation as top managers have guarantees that their subordinates have access to reliable and timely information to monitor their own performance. It also provides an incentive scheme for staff and can be used to compute performance-related bonuses in a manner which is fair and objective.

DIFFICULTIES IN DEVELOPING TOP MANAGEMENT'S INFORMATION SYSTEMS

After more than 30 years of research on how the work of managers can be supported by computers, the observation that developing computer systems that are truly useful for top management is a highly complex and uncertain task is still as valid as ever. Information systems for executives raise specific problems, which have primarily to do with the nature of managerial work itself (Mintzberg, 1973), as they are intended to tackle the needs of users whose most important role is "to create a vision of the future of the company and to lead the company towards it" (King, 1985, xi).

The major difficulty in supporting managers with computer systems comes from the very nature of management work (Mintzberg, 1973, 1975, 1976), where over 80% are concerned with communication, coordination and people management. At the time of his research, Mintzberg (1973) had noted how little time is left for reflection and for "playing" with computer systems. This has been a significant difficulty from the origins of MIS systems because their primarily "operational" focus was not central to executives' concerns (Ackoff, 1967; Keen & Scott-Morton, 1978). Twenty years later, this difficulty has also been largely responsible for the shift from decision support systems to executive information systems (EIS). EIS were intended to be very easy to use and to help users manipulate required data without the need for much training, which would be very attractive to top executives who want to have, at a glance, a very comprehensive view of their business. Specific descriptions of the differences between DSS, EIS and co-operative decision systems can be found in Pomerol and Brézillon (1998). Naturally, computer literacy amongst executives has increased to a great extent, notably, thanks to the development of electronic mail and the World Wide Web. However, whatever designs were put forward over the years, it has remained true that managers are not inclined to spend countless hours browsing computer data, such is the time pressure under which they operate.

Beyond the time pressures under which executives must operate, there are issues of trust and of credibility of the information that can be found in a computer system, which mitigate against intensive executive reliance on information systems, especially in a long-term perspective. First of all, the lack of confidence of executives in their models has been noted by many researchers (Abualsamh, Carlin, & McDaniel, 1990; Cats-Baril & Huber, 1987; e.g. Wallenius, 1975). The idea that decision makers need sophisticated models may actually be wrong. People in charge of the preparation of decisions would probably be able to understand and use smart models, but the high-level executives who most commonly make the final decisions are far too busy to train with and use involved systems. On the contrary, they appear to prefer simple systems that they trust and understand and that display very timely simple information. More often, the data required to make the best decisions will already reside in some form or another in the database of the organisation or can be captured with an online feed into a computer system, and what is really needed is a device to filter and display and to warn executives about the most important variances (Simon, 1977). As noted by Kleinmutz (1985), "the ability to select relevant variables seems to be more important than procedural sophistication in the processing of that information" (p. 696).

In EIS, the underlying models built into the system are normally very simple and easily understandable, which is a great help in increasing the acceptability of a computer system.

To conclude, the specificities of managerial decision making can be synthesised as follows:
- Most decisions are made very quickly under considerable time pressure (except some strategic decisions).
- Strategic decision making is often the result of collaborative processes.
- Most decisions are linked to individuals who have specific intentions and commitments to personal principles and ideas.

It is therefore very difficult to support managers and to analyse the decisions presenting the above complex characteristics. This is the reason why, despite many years of research, little is known about the way information systems could support such unstructured tasks. Efforts to meet the specific information requirements of managers have focused on developing systems aimed at supporting mainly the information processing activities (management information systems, or MIS), the decision making activities (decision support systems, or DSS) and the communication (groupware) of managers. As far as DSS is concerned, it has been noted that the use of DSS was pushed down towards middle managers and towards the resolution of operational problems. Decision support systems have turned out to be used more widely by middle managers (Ackoff, 1967) and for the monitoring of straightforward tasks than the literature on DSS concepts had anticipated. Some problems have also been reported with the way in which DSS applications are developed; most of them being the product of end-user approaches rather than the result of cooperation between the IS staff and managers from other functional areas (Fahy & Murphy, 1996). It must be stressed that DSS designers have often relied heavily on operational research and optimisation culture. This has led to the use of overly sophisticated models which are well suited to the optimisation of operational tasks (allocation of resources, routing, scheduling etc.) but not at all to top managers' work.

This resulted throughout the '80s in a shift from DSS including sophisticated prescriptive models to simpler systems with more attractive display and dialogue functions. For executives, a mere information filter seems more valued than high level, involved models, and quick reaction to problems is more useful than sophisticated look-ahead; at least executives seem to think so! There is ample empirical evidence that this perception is correct and that quick reaction and decision making are the most valued qualities of executives and organisations (Eisenhardt, 1990; Mintzberg, 1993); managers must be provided with tools that help them to identify signs in their environments (even the weakest ones) and to analyse key market trends rather than being flooded with sophisticated forecasts based on uncertain hypotheses. As a result, the emphasis in information systems design has shifted towards systems that provide managers with the information they require in a broader sense than for just one specific decision and that support their communication needs.

Executive information systems (EIS) and executive support systems (ESS) have been put forward as the solution to the problems of information provision to senior managers (Gulden & Ewers, 1989; Rockart & De Long, 1988). Scott-Morton (1986) has defined executive support systems as being focused on a manager's or a group of managers' information needs across a range of areas. He added the following comment:

Rather than being limited to a single recurring type of decision, ESS incorporate in one system the data and analytic tools to provide information support for many managerial processes and problems. (Scott-Morton, 1986) On the basis of a few famous examples (exceptions at the time), Rockart and

Treacy (1986) have claimed that ESS (a term they first coined in 1982) was going to allow a revolution in executives' use of computers. This did not happen and Rockart corrected his prediction in a later publication (Rockart & De Long, 1988). He suggested that no computer system, even an EIS/ESS-type computer system, would ever be the sole source of information for executives. This echoes Mintzberg's (1993) warning about strategic planning and about the true nature of strategic management.

Many researchers have pointed out the numerous benefits that will accrue to organisations which implement EIS competently (Paller & Laska, 1990): (1) an increased span of control available "from the keyboard"; (2) a saving in time enabled by the possibility to get an answer quicker not only because the data are already in the corporate database, but because new software allows managers to formulate their requests directly into a language that the machine can understand; (3) unlimited access into the corporate data resources guided by several levels of summary data authorising managers to "drill down" into layers of data to the level of detail they need; and (4) easy-to-use access to external sources of information now widely available (Economist Intelligence Unit, 1991). In addition, EIS systems have often provided non-performance-related information such as travel information and even nonmanagerial company news, such as classified sections.

A number of examples of successful EIS systems has been presented in the literature. The AIMS system developed by British Airways is interesting because it was a very early example of ESS (1982). It was originally designed for the top managers of the company, but now has a very large number of regular users and is believed to have allowed British Airways to defend its market share better than its competitors throughout the '90s. It has also been noted that EIS can play a considerable role in focussing the attention of staff and other managers on the key areas that determine the performance of the firm. Thus, if staff are aware that top managers' EIS track down certain parameters, these parameters are likely to receive far more attention than those not being monitored.

Nevertheless, at a fundamental level, there is considerable difficulty in understanding, to any significant degree, what the fundamental role of information in the decision making of a manager and in management at large might be. Information systems designers lack a theory about manager's needs and behaviour and this forces designers of executive systems to "reinvent the wheel" everytime a new system is developed. It also makes the communication between managers and developers more difficult and makes managers worry that they may not get value for money from the time they spend analysing their information needs. Thus, although the domain of executive information requirements analysis is well charted (Watson & Frolick, 1993; Wetherbe, 1993), an overall methodology for guiding the development of specific executive systems including the determination of the information content of these systems is still missing and authors have identified gaps in the range of performance measurements commonly used by developers of information systems for executives (Ballantine & Brignall, 1994). Information systems could be used to help the organisation change and learn, but little is known about how this can be achieved.

A VEHICLE FOR INFORMATION REQUIREMENTS ANALYSIS: CRITICAL SUCCESS FACTOR

In pre-EIS days, Rockart (1979) put forward a methodology called critical success factors, or CSF, to guide information systems planning. The method had its adepts though it failed to make a general impact on the planning process of organisations. Its potential in other areas, notably the development of information systems, has been explored by a number of researchers. In this chapter, we explore its usefulness as a guide for the development of executive systems as much from an information content as for the determination of the interface of these systems. This research does not rely on any specific empirical study, but is based on the experience of the authors in carrying out CSF analyses in collaboration with managers in a number of organisations.

CSF analysis assume that the performance of organisations can be improved by focusing on "the few key areas where things must go right for the business to flourish" (Rockart, 1979). In simple terms, the method seeks to isolate, using the expertise and gut feeling of managers, the factors which may make the difference between success and failure for the firm. For instance, most organisations use profit margin as a key indicator of performance, and brand awareness (expressed as a percentage of the general public who know about a certain brand) may be considered by managers to be critical to success in the household product market. CSF can be traced back to an article by Daniel (1961), which claimed (like Ackoff in 1967) that, despite the wealth of data gathered in the information systems of large corporations, very little could really be used for the purpose of decision making. A decade later, Anthony, Dearden, and Vancil (1972) attempted to apply the concept to the development of management control systems and drew some interesting lessons from their experience with CSF. They pointed out that:

> The control system must be tailored to the specific industry in which the company operates and to specific strategies that it has adopted; it must identify the critical success factors that should receive careful and continuous management attention if the company is to be successful and it must highlight performance with respect to these key variables in reports to all levels of management.

A number of key points about CSF make it a very attractive technique. First of all, while CSF is essentially a generic framework it recognises that all firms are different and operate in different markets. Thus, CSFs are different for different organisations. Secondly, the CSF theory takes into account that the needs of managers within the same organisations are also different based on their hierarchical level, but more importantly, based on their style and their specific areas of responsibility. In general, there are only a limited number of factors which each manager should monitor closely and this guarantees that managers can concentrate their limited attention to factors that really matter and that are within their control. It is actually rarely useful to ask managers to monitor factors that are not under their control. There are exceptions though, as managers may have to keep a close eye on external factors outside their control such as exchange rates or inflation rates. The attractive aspect about this breakdown of responsibility is that the CSF sets controlled by the different managers add up to a complete organisational set that covers all the key areas of the business.

Van Bullen and Rockart (1986) identified a number of primary categories of CSFs that are useful in guiding the analysis of the organisational CSF set. These generic sources of CSFs are: (1) the industry where the organisation operates (these CSFs are shared by mainstream organisations in this industry), (2) the competitive position and strategy pursued by the organisation (which are unique to its set of circumstances and objectives set by its top managers), (3) the environment factors surrounding the organisation (over which it has no control over, but which it must monitor closely to compete), (4) temporal factors (which relate to specific events or change programmes currently facing the organisation and require the temporary monitoring of additional factors) and finally (5) CSFs that are specific to each manager and their role in the company. This highlights that the nature of an organisation's CSFs may be different at each level and that a hierarchy of CSFs from different sources may feed into each other is the key to providing a complete range of observations about the firm and its environment. Other authors have added other potential sources such as CSFs related to the analysis of main competitors (especially industry leaders) and the evolution of their business (Leidecker & Bruno, 1984). Another useful classification of CSFs proposed by Van Bullen and Rockart (1986) differentiates between *building CSFs,* which are used to achieve specific objectives or implement changes in practices or performance, and *monitoring CSFs,* which are used in the long-term monitoring of key issues. These sources add up to a wealth of potential factors and measurements which are sufficient for effective monitoring of the business of most organisations so much so that the application of the CSF method may lead to an overload of indicators, which can be controlled by trial and error leading to a concentration on the preferred indicators of managers.

An alternative method, called *balanced scorecard*, has been put forward in management accounting, mot notably by Kaplan and Norton (1992, 1993, 1996a, 1996b). Instead of leaving a free hand to analysts, the balanced scorecard provides a set framework for measuring performance based on four pillars: (1) financial perspective, (2) customer perspective, (3) internal business perspective and (4) innovation and learning. Thus, each key performance indicator must be linked to one of these categories and is assigned a coefficient which describes its contribution to the overall performance at the higher level. In our experience, balanced scorecard has proven constraining in some organisations where managers had difficulties relating to the imposed top-level categories and lost interest as a result. However, the Balanced Scorecard must be regarded as a useful framework likely to force managers to ask pertinent questions about their business.

In the next stage of the development of executive systems, designers must create an interface for displaying the CSFs. The design of this interface is nearly as important as the selection of the indicators in shaping the perception of managers of the usefulness of their information systems and keeping their interest in the long run. One technique which has worked well in selecting and presenting indicators is the application of the dashboard concept to the management of organisations. The dashboard concept is explored in the next section.

THE CONCEPT OF DASHBOARD

The concept of dashboard as it relates to the development of executive systems is based on an analogy with the devices which have been used by car makers to give increasing levels of control to drivers over their vehicles. Dashboards are meant to provide drivers with real-time data about the state of their vehicle and its progression along the road. Data falls in different categories depending upon their frequency of use and the degree of urgency of the signal they provide. In understanding the concept of dashboard, it is useful to consider, for example, the difference between the use of the speedometer (which is used frequently for a quick control) and the petrol gauge (which is of more value at the start of the journey to plan for the use of available resources and may flash when it requires the driver's attention).

Fundamentally though, the concept of dashboard reflects the application of the concept of *control room* to the management of the firm and echoes the call for a warning or exception reporting functionality in EIS-type systems. The control room is a specially designed physical area of a plant where the proper operation of key equipment can be monitored. Control rooms have developed because of the need to monitor increasingly complex processes, such as petrol refining or the operation of nuclear power plants. The control room allows operators to control a process without looking at it with their own eyes and with a degree of accuracy and completeness that could not be achieved with human perception alone. Thus, control rooms provide indications of temperature, pressure, flow, and speed of rotation, which are provided by high-tech sensors placed strategically in the plant. In many cases, these sensors are located in areas where human operators could not survive or could not penetrate. Perrin (1993) has explained how the control room provides an *information mediation* between operators and the tools they control such that physical contact (as in the case of a hammer, for instance) is no longer required. Thus, a nuclear power plant can be controlled by a handful of highly specialised operators thanks to a tight set of alarm systems.

This type of analogy is attractive because it implies that a dashboard may be developed that could considerably rationalise and centralise the management of firms. This is obviously somewhat naive because many of the decisions faced by managers in the day-to-day and long-term administration of their firms are of such a nature that they do not lend themselves to the type of modelling or systematic investigation that can be performed in the case of power plants. The nature of management itself is highly dynamic and diverse (Mintzberg, 1973) and involves consideration of an infinite number of parameters in a way that is fundamentally different from the monitoring of a manufacturing process. Thus, management has significant "human interaction" component that cannot easily be supported by computer systems. Simon (1977), Gorry and Scott-Morton (1971) and others have commented comprehensively on the degree to which managerial decisions are programmable or not; however, it remains that the implementation of many of the objectives of the firm, however elusive, can be monitored using a dashboard-type interface and that the CSF method can be a powerful vehicle in selecting the indicators to be shown on each manager's dashboard.

However, the difficulty with CSF-based dashboards resides in the operationalisation of managers' key concerns and the identification of specific targets for CSF monitoring, the design of measurement logic for each indicator and the development of the interfaces that can be used by managers to easily and effectively review the performance of the firm in relation to each of the indicators.

TOWARDS A METHODOLOGY FOR DASHBOARD DEVELOPMENT

At the height of the EIS movement, King (1985) remarked that:

It is so easy to lose sight of reality—to believe that the computer model's numerical forecasts are real and that they describe future outcomes that will, in fact, come to pass. ... The computer model's forecasts are based solely on those predictions about the future that we are able to quantify. Those things that are not readily quantifiable are usually omitted, and in being omitted there is a danger that they may be ignored.

This illustrates well the dangers inherent in an approach to management that would be based solely on numbers, however obtained. Other examples can be put forward to highlight the risk there is in relying too heavily on indirect monitoring rather than direct observation, especially in the long term (Hogarth & Makridakis, 1981; Makridakis, 1985). This is confirmed by the fact that observational plant tours are still regarded as one of the most reliable methods for collecting data in manufacturing environments (Jones, Saunders, & McLeod, 1988).

Problems have occurred in environments where direct observation is not an option and no other case study better illustrates the danger of dashboards as the accident in Three Mile Island (Harrisburg, PA). In 1979, a combination of poor interface design and operator error nearly culminated in a complete meltdown at the nuclear power plant. A valve in the cooling system of the reactor malfunctioned and remained open, causing thousands of gallons of coolant to escape from the reactor, but operators misread the signals given to them by their dashboards and aggravated the problems by further draining the reactor when they should have been raising the cooling water levels. This was explained by the fact that operators on duty did not fully understand the meaning and mode of operation of some of the indicators. It was also identified in the inquiry that followed that a red alarm light went unnoticed for four hours that would have told operators what they were doing was wrong right away. This was due to the bad layout of the control room which did not allow operators to see all the indicators required for a proper interpretation of events at the same time. There was also no consistency in the use of colour and dials, such that a red light could indicate the proper operation of a device in one area of the room and the imminent explosion of the reactor in another area of the room. While this example is remote from the everyday concerns of managers, it is still very useful because it indicates that designing a dashboard must take into account the following four key issues:

(1) *Limited Attention:* Given the limited attention of managers and the costs inherent in sourcing certain data, the indicators displayed on the dashboard must be carefully selected using the CSF method described in detail in Van Bullen and Rockart (1986). This is required if designers are to avoid the "Christmas tree" effect observed in the early control rooms, where so many alarms (visual and audible) rang at the same time that determining the origin of a fault was impossible. This was a significant feature of the Three Mile Island incident and it has been reported that several hundred conflicting alarms were flashing and sounding in the control room at one point.

(2) *Performance Measurement:* The measurements used to monitor indicators or CSFs are crucial. The usefulness and effectiveness of the dashboard is totally dependent on the accuracy of the data used and the realism of the calculations presented to managers. The latest information technologies available in terms of data capture and retrieval, such as OLAP, data mining or data warehousing, should also be leveraged to maximise the accuracy and completeness of the dashboard.

(3) *Operator Training:* It is also critical that managers understand the assumptions built into the dashboard and the algorithms used to reach the results presented to them. They must also be fully aware of how data are collected and what limitations apply to the accuracy of the measurements. Thus, it is important that managers are not cut off from the underlying data and introducing some degree of drill down as described by EIS proponents (Watson, Rainer, & Koh, 1991) is very useful. Meall (1990) described how drill down can make the difference between "using information to manage more intelligently and more effectively and making the same old mistakes but with more speed." Proper understanding of the dashboard as a tool for decision making will also boost the confidence managers have in their information systems.

(4) *Dashboard Layout:* The layout of the dashboard has a direct impact on the understanding derived by managers. The relative importance of indicators must

be reflected in the way they are presented. Size, colour and location on the screen must be used consistently so that managers can visualise immediately where they should focus their attention as a matter of priority. Exception reporting and colour coding as described by EIS proponents (Watson et al., 1991) can be used to achieve this. The latest information technologies available in terms of graphical user Interface should also be leveraged to maximise the visual impact of the dashboard.

These key factors point to a collaborative approach to dashboard development where designers and managers work together in creating and maintaining the dashboard. Just like the traditional model of DSS development recommends, it is useful if managers can feed back their perception of the dashboards to developers so that the design can be improved over time and the indicators refined or replaced (as in the case of temporal CSFs). However, this collaborative process can be hard to start up. Managers may be reluctant to invest too much time in CSF analyses if they are not convinced that the finished product is going to be of use to them. Designers may be tempted to skip the required analysis stage where managers must indicate where their priorities lie. Finally, top management may be slow to encourage such a project if they fail to see how they can control the effects of the implementation of the dashboard.

One way that these concerns can be addressed is to begin the project at a high level and to use the strategic orientation given by top management to provide a backdrop for the identification of the indicators. This top-down technique is also suggested by Van Bullen and Rockart (1986) as indicated in the diagram in Figure 1.

Figure 1: Top-down approach to dashboard development

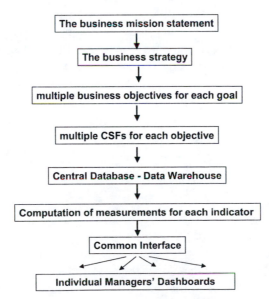

Note: Depending on how broadly or narrowly objectives are defined, each objective may be adequately captured by one or several indicators.

The novelty of the approach proposed in this paper comes from our acknowledgment of the fact that, even after a complete set of CSFs has been identified, much of the work remains to be done. Clearly, the operationalisation of the dashboard is not complete until a number of key questions has been answered. These questions pertain to each indicator and must be answered fully before a dashboard can be developed that is likely to be useful to managers. These questions and a description of why they are so important are listed below.

Question 1: *Who will use these indicators?*

This is of course an obvious question to ask, but the answer may not be so simple when not one, but a number of individuals may be interested in monitoring certain indicators. The first rule that should be applied (given that not everyone can get involved with monitoring all indicators) is that managers concentrate on monitoring the parameters most closely associated with their own performance or that of the areas directly under their control. This ensures a more effective monitoring because individuals are properly motivated to act on the signals they are getting from their dashboards. However, this is not enough and designers should also ensure that they don't put individuals under undue pressure by asking them to monitor indicators that are outside their control or that conflict with their own objectives. When conflict may arise because two indicators move in opposite directions, the overall monitoring should be left to superiors who have a more global understanding and vision and can resolve conflicts by trading off the conflicting variances. Two instances of areas where such conflicts can arise are production and quality control. In one organisation, quality control staff were commonly referred to as the *sales prevention department* because they opposed the release of substandard goods to the market even when production was unable to meet demand, thereby aggravating the pressures on production and sales. Such conflicts are likely to exist in many organisations, but they need not become disruptive and counterproductive if properly managed by superiors.

When properly designed, dashboards can become arbitration and learning tools used to show organisational actors the trade-offs involved in making key decisions such as setting high quality standards and helping staff understand the implications of these decisions. A detailed analysis of where responsibilities lie in the organisation, including potential areas of conflict will be required if a successful organisation-wide CSF-based dashboard is to be developed in an organisation.

Question 2: *Can it be mapped out to a specific objective at a higher level?*

From the perspective of a top-down CSF exercise, it will be useful if indicators can be mapped out to specific objectives pursued by top management. Thus, indicators can be merged into higher-level composite indicators presented to higher-level managers. This also helps developers because it maps out the drill down facility to be built into the dashboard so that top managers can understand the underlying causes of poor or good performance.

In practice, some indicators cannot always be mapped out to higher-level indicators, especially if they correspond to specific concerns of individual managers, but a significant proportion of CSFs used should be linked to higher-level objectives. This will ensure the support of top managers for the dashboard project and will provide much needed scope to the development effort. It may also motivate managers to actively take action to redress bad situations that are signalled on their dashboards, especially in the case of building CSFs that measure the progress of the firm in the implementation of a change plan or in the pursuit of radically new objectives.

Question 3: *How frequently will managers need to monitor it?*

One of the key issues listed in EIS literature is how designers can keep their designs evolutionary in order to keep the attention of their users. Keith Ralpey, who was head of the design team for British Airways' AIMS (Harvey & Mickeljohn, 1991), admitted to trying to add something new to the EIS every day either in the form of updated information or better features. Thus, in some organisations, it has been reported that certain key indicators (such as share values or sales performance) changed from a daily update to an hourly or up-to-the-minute update. This may be exaggerated outside a "process control" environment (where immediate measurements are useful) and may lead to frustration from the part of both developers and users; rather, it is the calibration of the frequency of update of each piece of data in the system that is important. Market share statistics are not used in the same way as sales figures or quality control parameters. Market share variations are normally useful for mid- to long-term monitoring and cannot normally be obtained in real time, whereas sales figures are examined on a weekly or even daily basis. Furthermore, quality control parameters such as calibre for machined parts or dry content for food products must be monitored on an hourly basis or even in real time. Thus, questions about how frequently indicators must be updated can only be answered on a case by case basis. There may also be issues of costs involved with frequent update and it may not make sense to purchase expensive data or carry out vast amounts of calculations on a regular basis if the variations of indicators are unlikely to be significant.

Ultimately, it is managers' perception of how frequently significant or revelatory variations are likely to occur that should be used as a guide for deciding how frequently indicators should be updated. The scope of the benefits that may arise as a result of the monitoring should also be considered if high costs are likely to be incurred (see Question 11).

Question 4: *What calculation methods are available? What unit of measurement will be used?*

Question 4 is a crucial aspect of the development of a dashboard. The choice of calculation method can actually influence the variation of the indicator greatly and also shift the burden of responsibility from one area to another. For instance, managers in charge of monitoring the output of assembly lines are often uncertain whether to use gross production figures or net production figures (that don't include goods which, for one reason or another, are not available or not good enough for commercial use). This is an important issue because it goes to measuring the performance of operators and the workshops to which they belong. There are a number of reasons why goods are not released for commercial use: Some goods are used for sampling and measuring quality; some goods are withdrawn because they fail to reach quality standards or because marketing staff needs free samples to distribute to prospective customers. Production staff will be eager to see gross production used for measures of output, but top management will be more interested in net figures. A well-designed dashboard should allow managers to visualise the breakdown of responsibilities in reducing the gross figures. This is reminiscent of the construction of the criteria set in multi-criteria decision making (MCDM) situations and constitutes a fundamental issue for DSS. Pomerol and Barba-Romero (2000) have provided insights in the construction of a family of criteria with minimal properties and such that criteria are exhaustive and nonredundant (see also Roy & Bouysson, 1993). These two characteristics clearly apply to the selection of CSFs, which must (1) describe the whole business and (2) monitor distinct aspects of the business. As in MCDM situations, the issue of the independence of the CSFs is highly problematic.

Another example of how measurement methods used can affect results is the tracking of additional time spent on operations such as packaging because of special requirements placed on production staff by other departments. Special offers, which require decorating products with stickers and adding extra manipulations to make *two-for-the-price-of-one* packages, can reduce the productivity of operators quite substantially, which a dashboard should be able to measure. Failure to measure such factors means that production will always bear the cost of marketing initiatives, which may bias decision making in this area.

The choice of the unit of measurement is normally straightforward for quantitative analysis, but can become far more complex for less tangible CSFs that involve the estimations of qualitative factors. Customer satisfaction is a perfect example of a much needed CSF which will require vision and creativity if it is to be measured properly. Some quantitative measures may be applicable such as the number of complaints received per time interval, but other measures may have to be found that can act as surrogates of customer satisfaction as is explained in Question 5.

Question 5: *What data source exists? What should be created?*

Ideally, any CSF or any indicator needed by management should be presented in the organisation's dashboard. However, it may happen that some data are missing from existing organisational databases and systems. Some data may already be captured, but reside in a proprietary system (e.g., a custom-built process control system) that does not integrate well with other systems. It may also be that some data are not captured at all and require a significant investment in equipment and special devices (such as scanners and sensors). In some cases, manufacturing organisations have had problems tracking down labour hours with great accuracy, especially in open plant environments where workers move around quite a bit. Data capture systems exist that monitor the movement of staff around the premises and record accurately in which area they spend their time. However, such equipment is very costly and, while it would be of use to have such data available, it may not always be economically viable to commit to such an investment. OLAP and ROLAP (relational OLAP) can be configured to automatically provide summary and aggregated data and to calculate CSF indicators.

In other cases, data capture can only be performed by adding an additional step in an already complex process. Staff will have to spend extra time recording production defects on the spot or the home address of customers in telesales businesses and this may disrupt the work to such an extent that the organisation is not willing to incur the cost of data collection. For instance, most newspapers need regular advertising revenues to survive and it is critical for them to understand who places ads, on what day of the week, etc. In one newspaper we visited, top management was curious as to the gender of people placing ads in the weekend issue, but line managers refused to collect the data because it slowed down phone operators and limited the number of ads that each could collect in one day. The introduction of a web interface where the burden of providing the data was borne by the people placing the ads rather than the staff of the newspaper revolutionised this side of the business and far more data was gathered as a result of customers being involved in the data collection. Generally speaking, electronic commerce companies have all noted how the use of a Web interface provides great opportunities to collect data about their customers and their patterns of sales, either that these data are provided by the customers themselves or that data collection can be automated by the addition of tracking software into the Web site.

In some cases, surrogate measures can be found for data that just cannot be captured. Food business firms spend significant resources on R&D to boost the resistance of their products and increase the shelf life. However, products are often subjected to conditions that do not respect the producers' specifications. Refrigeration equipment may break down or be turned off to reduce costs either during transportation or storage. This may then have repercussions as customers return damaged goods and the company may lose their customers through no fault of its operators. Companies that want to evaluate in which conditions their products travel use indicators based on simulated conditions created inside the factory. Products are taken in every batch and stored at different temperatures. For fresh products, goods may be kept at 4, 8 and 12 degrees to simulate various degrees of bad treatment. When damaged products are returned, they can be compared to the samples kept by the firm to visualise what conditions they seem to have been exposed to. This may serve to show the haulage firm used by the company or the managers of the stores selling the products that their equipment is below standard. When product resistance is reduced and returns increase, these data will also be of great use for the company to explain poor sales figures or even loss of market share.

Question 6: *How detailed should the analysis presented by the dashboard be? How can the indicators be broken down to be more meaningful?*

Many indicators are too broad to be suitably presented as one figure (especially when it comes to designing the dashboard of line managers) and some disaggregating may be required. Typical organisations sell multiple products in multiple markets. Thus, sales figures need to be disaggregated to present £ figures, volumes and variances for each product on each market while also presenting the aggregated data. Multidimensional modelling can be used to support the organisation and retrieval of such data. For instance, multidimensional spreadsheets use a data cube to generalise to n dimensions the two-dimensional tables commonly used by managers using Lotus 123 or MS Excel. Each cell in the model represents one item of data such as a monthly sale for a specific product in a specific market for a particular year. Users can then manipulate the data cube to display the information they want as a two- or three-dimensional table depending upon the mode of representation available, as illustrated in Figure 2.

This method of manipulation of the data is particularly useful for organisations that deal with many products in many markets because it considerably eases the tasks of consolidation of accounting results and the forecasting/planning process. Individual markets and individual products can be monitored by managers without any additional burden for the operators who prepare the dashboards presenting sales data. This type of manipulation has been a starting point for many EIS application as illustrated by the old Execu-view product sold by Comshare in the mid and late '80s. In fact, Execu-view was so successful that Comshare delayed the decision to discontinue it several times as it introduced a new generation of modelling tools. More recently Powerbuilder, Cognos, CorVu, Brio and many other third-party software and reporting tools vendors have developed multidimensional modelling and balanced scorecard based software that are mostly used as an additional layer of software by organisations trying to extract maximum benefits from their enterprise resource planning (ERP) applications.

In the example presented in Figure 2, the breakdown to products, markets and months/years is natural, but it may be more difficult to decide how to best breakdown the data to be presented to managers. In the case of manufacturing environments, a breakdown based on the layout of the plant (e.g., per workshop or work cell) may be well suited because it will accurately break down the responsibility of gains or losses of productivity between operators or groups of operators. Generally speaking, the aim of the break down should always be to help pinpoint more accurately the source of problems and bring about the improvements that will reduce the unwanted

Figure 2: Multidimensional modelling applied to a product/market matrix

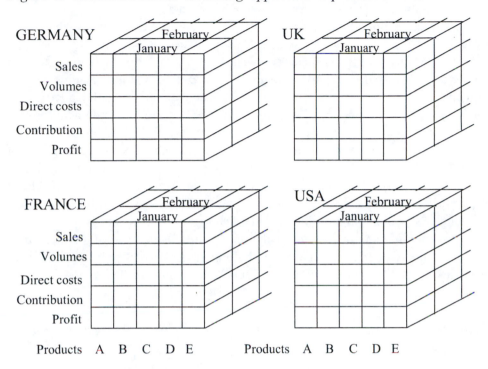

Products   A   B   C   D   E   Products   A   B   C   D   E

variances. Once more, this is reminiscent of the issue of aggregation and disaggregation in multi-criteria decision making.

Question 7: *What threshold values should be used to differentiate between adequate and inadequate performance? What comparisons can be made to assess the company's performance?*

Absolute measurement figures presented by a dashboard may not be meaningful to managers unless they can be examined in light of other data. Most companies already have a tight budget system in place and this can be used as a source of normative values. Engineering specifications often include predictive or desirable figures for productivity, material usage, rate of defect, etc. Sales budgets can also be used to compare sales performance for each product on each market. However, other key data can also be used to make sense of the values presented by a CSF-based dashboard. First of all, current performance can be compared with previous performance, either to review trends over the last few months or years or, in businesses that are characterised by strong seasonality patterns, by comparing indicators with measurements obtained at the same time the previous year. This is particularly true for sales figures which may be driven up and down by seasonal buying and show rises and falls that don't lend themselves to longitudinal analysis.

This problem also arises for alarm-based monitoring systems when it comes to setting threshold values that cause indicators to change colour.

Many indicators should also be compared to competitors' performance when available or at least to industry standards as published by government sources or industry forums. These data can be particularly useful for such indicators as employee turnover (especially if regional data can be found), average wages, percentage of overtime used or profit margin. The comparison with leaders in the industry, also known as *benchmarking,* will be a useful complement for the comparisons made with previous performance of the firm. There is an obvious danger in always comparing the firm to its own performance as productivity gaps that may exist between firms may never be measured and never be bridged resulting in the gradual erosion of the company's market share. In some cases, when firms have never measured key parameters, benchmarking is the only way to calibrate the newly implemented systems and decide on suitable targets for the business.

Dashboards can use the latest technology available in terms of graphical user interfaces and colour-coded charting to help managers visualise how far they are from desired performance or from the leaders in their industry. This is considered in the next section.

Question 8: *How can it be represented for maximum visual impact?*

One of the difficulties inherent in the concept of dashboard resides in reducing the impact of information overload and using the technology available in terms of graphical user interfaces (GUIs) to its fullest to speed up the information retrieval of managers. The Three Mile Island example indicates how bad layout can cause users to miss important signals or to misinterpret them (although in most cases, interpretation errors are more likely to be caused by inadequate representation of problems as discussed by Boy, 1991, and by poor diagnosis of the current situation as discussed in Pomerol, 1997). Thus, the use of colour coding, icons and graphs should be consistent throughout the interface. Some software toolboxes are now available to help designers create displays and objects that mirror the type of controls normally found on dashboards. Gauges with specific colour-coded threshold values can easily be created and special charts can be made clickable to build intuitive drill down into the data. These speed up and facilitate the data reading of managers. For instance, line charts are particularly suited to the illustration of trends and evolution over time. By contrast, pie charts are more suited to the illustration of breakdowns such as share of different products into overall sales figures. Bar charts can be used to illustrate specific comparisons between budget, actuals, and previous period figures.

These new dedicated software environments also enable designers to implement exception reporting on a large scale (Paller & Laska, 1990). Threshold values can be hard-coded into the dashboard so that the attention of managers is attracted to unusual or worrying variances. This may include tabular data signalled with colour-coded cells, hypertext-enabled headlines provided in the top page of the interface, special reports automatically generated or even e-mail alarms that are sent directly into managers mailboxes. Various degrees of automatic search and data mining functions may also be built into the interface to assist managers in browsing through more data than is presented in the dashboard.

Ultimately, it is useful to remember that the look and feel of the interface may be perceived as attractive or repulsive by users depending on whether it is good or bad and that, although it is in no way sufficient to have a good interface, it certainly does not help to have a bad one! However, we have observed cases in organisations where bad design (e.g., cramped and cluttered screen layouts) has not deterred managers if they perceived that they could not get similar data anywhere else. This reinforces the notion that the information content and the choice of calculation methods are probably the keys to the usefulness of an organisational dashboard. Nevertheless, given the availability of cheap software toolboxes to support the development of executive dashboards, the design of an attractive interface should be at least a secondary priority and it may be decisive in determining the perception executives have of their dashboard, especially at times of stress or when they are under time pressure (sometimes with disastrous consequences, as revealed in the Three Mile Island accident).

Question 9: *What action must be taken when good or bad performance is measured? Is there scope for corrective action to be taken based on the indicator?*

As part of the development of the dashboard, it is useful to consider the outcome of the process of consultation of the indicators presented. Whenever good or bad results are presented, managers should be aware of the avenues that can be pursued, based on the observation that there is as much to be learned from good as from bad performance. Reporting mechanisms (e.g., electronic mail) can be built into the dashboard to facilitate and accelerate the dissemination of interesting results and their discussion.

However, in the longer term, increased familiarity with the indicators and what their evolution means should have practical decision making implications for all managers and staff. Thus, users' reaction times to certain signals should be reduced and their responses should improve, especially in recurrent situations. With time, managers should be able to anticipate changes quicker and in turn fine-tune their monitoring to learn to identify new trends. This can then be used to redesign the dashboard or some of its underlying components, for instance, new, more ambitious threshold values and targets.

Question 10: *How will it be monitored/archived in the long term?*

A key element of the approach described in this paper is the learning that can be achieved when CSFs are monitored over long periods. Staff and managers learn from regularly sampling their performance and that of their areas and seeing it compared to other data, such as budgets, previous performance or industry standards. They also learn from being able to map out the rises and falls in performance with other events that occur in the company. Staff morale or motivation may be reflected in indicators and managers may be able to anticipate changes in internal relations better. Greater learning will be derived if managers and staff set time aside to review and discuss indicators on a regular basis and try to work towards a more refined understanding of the underlying causes of good and bad performance. These discussions may lead to better indicators or measurement systems that take better account of the specificity of the firm or help resolve emergent or ongoing conflicts between areas.

Thus, data storage technologies should be used to archive dashboard data on a continuous basis so that users can review the evolution of all indicators over long periods and chart indicators side by side to look for correlation between their evolutions. Again, this may lead to a better and richer understanding of the causes of bad performance. In one food processing organisation, charting of product defects against certain parameters monitoring the composition of the products led to new ideas for more resistant products with a longer, more reliable shelf life. This is a key area for many food processors as these organisations rarely control what happens to their products when they leave the factory. Despite this loss of control, it is in the producer's interest that their products retain their characteristics until expiry of the shelf life and organisations will be eager to keep a close eye on the resistance of their products, even in extreme conditions (such as the breakdown of refrigeration equipment in stores), using data capture mechanisms or simulated environments of the kind described in Question 5.

The issue of reviewing the outcome of decisions and learning from them is quite a difficult one. Simon (1977) introduced the notion of *review* as a fourth phase in his normative model of decision making. However, it must be realised that learning from past decisions is problematic because: (1) learning is not be possible without a clear representation of the causal relationships between CSFs and between the variations of the CSFs and the evolution of the environment (Hall, 1984); (2) learning is limited if managers cannot obtain clear, timely and specific feedback for their actions (Kleinmurtz, 1985, 1993; Sterman, 1989); and (3) learning requires a knowledge of all relevant parameters and possible scenarios that can be anticipated at the time a decision was made, which, in most cases, a dashboard does not give. The use of the dashboard is in helping managers react more quickly, but it may not directly improve their understanding of reality. Furthermore, it may not be very useful in developing new representations of the world, whether the current mental models of managers are wrong or not. Review of the evolution of dashboard indicators and of the decisions made by users will therefore be required to verify that decision making has not led to a "zigzag" type policy.

Question 11: *Is there any potential bias inherent in the methods and data used for calculations? What incentives are being given to organisational actors?*

The key issue for top managers when it comes to implementing proper measurement of performance in the firm is that of incentives. When decisions are made to measure performance in certain ways and to specify what constitutes appropriate or inappropriate performance, the behaviour of organisational actors will necessarily be affected. Managers may even decide that the systems measuring employee performance are sufficiently accurate and objective that they can be used to compute a pay-related portion of salaries. In any case, the issue of incentives must be considered. It has been reported that cars and trucks produced in the Soviet Union in '50s and '60s were always extremely heavy (even heavier than they should be by design) because the output of car factories was measured in weight. Given this incentive, it is quite understandable that plant managers and supervisors directed workers to use heavier materials to make wheels, chassis and other components, because their output was boosted as a result. This is an extreme case, but it illustrates that wrong incentives can be given by improperly designed measurement systems that lead to unsuitable behaviour. The rise of strict quality control in many industries has resulted in the update of many performance measurement systems away from measures of gross output towards measures of output that take quality into account. Sales representatives are also being motivated to work harder on certain products by the structure of their reward systems, which specify that they get greater commission on the sale of certain products than on others.

When managers neglect to consider the incentives given to actors by new measurement systems, there may be unintended consequences, such as sudden changes of output or rise and fall in product performance. Hammer and Champy (1993) have described how the conflict between performance assessment systems in different areas of a firm can lead to loss of overall performance. In an airline company, the maintenance department was subjected to a tight control of its expenditure, and when an aircraft was grounded by a technical fault on a remote airport, the maintenance manager refused to send a specialist before the next morning so that he would not have to spend the night and incur accommodation expenses. This decision which saved $50 in the budget of the maintenance department also cost the company several millions as the plane was grounded and a replacement aircraft had to be chartered to cater for the stranded passengers. In this simple example, the incentives given to the maintenance manager were wrong because they encouraged him to focus on a narrow measure of performance to the detriment of the greater good of the company.

Thus, the development of new performance measurement systems, such as a dashboard of indicators, should always be guided by consideration of the incentives given to actors and the behaviour likely to result from the implementation of the underlying indicators. There may also be a change management aspect to the project as managers negotiate with staff during the implementation of the system. Staff may object to certain types of measurement (which they may perceive to be threatening or invasive) or the implementation of devices dedicated to monitoring their work. Proper discussions about the sought impact of planned measurement systems and genuine efforts at empowering staff to use these systems to review their own performance so they can control their activity themselves should be part of any implementation plan (see also Question 9).

These 11 key questions provide a framework for guiding the development of the organisational dashboard. They are summarised in the framework presented in Table 1. Only when comprehensive analysis of informational needs has been carried out and the issues outlined in the framework have been addressed can a successful dashboard be developed. Failure to answer some of these key questions may lead to problems with the resulting dashboard either because staff resistance mounts or because the new system falls to disuse.

CONCLUSION

As early as 1986, Bjorn-Andersen, Eason, and Robery, remarked that managers would never be dependent on computers for their information or decision making. Indeed, the case for managing the firm solely based on numbers has already been argued and lost. At this point, it is well established that managing firms cannot and should not be compared to the administration of a power plant. This does not mean, however, that the concept of a control room does not have potential when applied to

Table 1: The 11 key questions for the design of the dashboard

Question 1	Who will use this indicator?
Question 2	Can it be mapped out to a specific objective at a higher level?
Question 3	How frequently will managers need to monitor it?
Question 4	What calculation methods are available? What unit of measurement will be used?
Question 5	What data source exists? What should be created?
Question 6	How detailed should the analysis presented by the dashboard be? How can the indicators be broken down to be more meaningful?
Question 7	What threshold values should be used to differentiate between adequate and inadequate performance? What comparisons can be made to assess the company's performance?
Question 8	How can it be represented for maximum visual impact?
Question 9	What action must be taken when good or bad performance is measured? Is there scope for corrective action to be taken based on the indicator?
Question 10	How will it be monitored/archived in the long term?
Question 11	Is there any potential bias with the methods and data used for calculations? What incentives may be given to organizational actors?

the management of organisations. Faced with increasingly complex situations and responsibility for the administration of increasingly complex business processes, managers have less and less time to spend monitoring the key factors of the business. The development of a dashboard can speed up this process and help managers catch far more information than they normally would without assistance. They still need additional sources of information, especially for the softer information they require in their job, and EIS developers have often included non-performance-related information and services (such as travel information) in their designs, but a daily look at a dashboard of information may teach managers far more than whatever time they could afford to invest in browsing through the reports circulated by their subordinates and peers.

Following the steps highlighted in this paper will also give organisations a much better idea of what parameters they should worry about and how to measure performance. Peter Swasey, one of the directors of the Bank of Boston, commented that "what you don't measure, you don't manage" (McGill, 1990). The preparatory analysis work on the CSFs of the firm will provide much confidence to organisational actors that they understand their business and have a comprehensive hold upon its vital functions, and the dashboard ultimately developed will provide flexible and speedy access to vital information, thereby freeing time for other key activities such as business or staff development. As a by-product, managers may also be able to use the analysis carried out for their dashboard as a blueprint for the incentive systems of their company.

REFERENCES

Abualsamh, R., Carlin, B., & McDaniel, R.R. Jr. (1990). Problem structuring heuristics in strategic decision making *Organisational Behaviour and Decision Process*, 45, 159-174.

Ackoff, R. L. (1967). Management MISinformation systems. *Management Science*, *14*(4), 147-156.

Anthony, D.L., Dearden, J. & Vancil, R.F. (1972). *Management Control Systems*. Homewood, IL: Irwin.

Ballantine, J, & Brignall, S. (1994). A taxonomy of performance measurement frameworks. *Warwick Business School Research Papers*, 135, Coventry.

Bjorn-Andersen, N., Eason, K., & Robery, D. (1986). *Managing Computer Impact*. Norwood, NJ: Ablex.

Boy, G. (1991). *Intelligent assistant systems*. New York: Academic Press.

Cats-Baril, W.L., & Huber, G. (1987). Decision support systems for ill-structured problems: An empirical study. *Decision Science,* 18, 350-372.

Daniel, D. R. (1961). Management information crisis. *Harvard Business Review*, September/October, 91-101.

Economist Intelligence Unit. (1991, July). *Executive information systems*. (Special Rep. No. S123.)

Eisenhardt, K. M. (1990). Speed and strategic choice: How managers accelerate decision making. *California Management Review*, 31, 39-54.

Fahy, M., & Murphy, C. (1996). From end user computing to management developed systems. In Cuehlo Dias, T. Jelassi, W. Konig, H. Krcmar, R. O'Callaghan, & M. Saarksjarvi, (Eds.), *Proceedings of the Fourth European Conference on Information Systems* (July, pp. 127-142) Lisbon, Portugal.

Gorry A., & Scott-Morton, M. (1971). A framework for management information systems. *Sloan Management Review*, Fall, 55-70.

Gorry, A., & Scott-Morton, M. (1989). Retrospective commentary on the Gorry and Scott-Morton framework. *Harvard Business Review*, Spring, 58-60.

Gulden, G., & Ewers, D. (1989). Is your ESS meeting the need? *ComputerWorld*, July 10th, 85-91.

Hall, R. (1984). The natural logic of management policy making: its implications for the survival of an organization. *Management Science,* 30, 905-927.

Hammer, M., & Champy, J. (1993) *Re-engineering the corporation: A manifesto for business revolution.* New York: Harper Business.

Harvey, J., & Mickeljohn, M. (1991). *The EIS report.* London: Business Intelligence.

Hogarth, R., & Makridakis, S. (1981). Forecasting and planning: An evaluation. *Management Science*, 27. 115-138.

Jones, J., Saunders, C., & McLeod, R. (1988). Information media and source patterns across management levels: A pilot study. *Journal of Management Information Systems*, 5(3), 71-84.

Kaplan, R., & Norton, D. (1992). The balanced scorecard: Measures that drive performance. *Harvard Business Review,* 70(1), 71-79.

Kaplan, R., & Norton, D. (1993). Putting the balanced scorecard: measures to work. *Harvard Business Review, 71*(5), 134-142.

Kaplan, R., & Norton, D. (1996a). Using the balanced scorecard as a strategic management system. *Harvard Business Review, 74*(1), 75-85.

Kaplan, R., & Norton, D. (1996b). *The balanced scorecard: Translating strategy into action.* Boston: Harvard Business School Press.

Keen, P.G., & Scott-Morton, M.S. (1978). *Decision support systems: An organisational perspective.* Reading, MA: Addison-Wesley.

King, W. R. (1985). Editors comment: CEOs and their PCs. *Management Information Systems Quarterly*, 9, xi-xii.

Kleinmutz, D. N. (1985). Cognitive heuristics and feedback in a dynamic decision environment. *Management Science*, 31, 680-702.

Kleinmutz, D. N. (1993). Information processing and misperception of the implications of feedback in dynamic decision making. *Systems Dynamics Review*, 9, 223-237.

Leidecker, J., & Bruno, A. (1984). Identifying and using critical success factors. *Long Range Planning, 17*(1), 23-32.

Makridakis, S. (1985). The art of science of forecasting: An assessment and future directions, SIAD-85, *Systemes Interactifs d'Aide à la Decision*, ENA, ADI and CXP Eds., AID: Paris.

McGill, P. (1990). Executive support systems. *Business Quarterly*, Summer 1990.

Meall, L. (1990, September). EIS: Sharpening the executives' competitive edge. *Accountancy*.

Mintzberg, H. (1973). *The nature of managerial work.* New York: Harper and Row.

Mintzberg, H. (1975). The manager's job: Folklore and fact. *Harvard Business Review*, July/August, 49-61.

Mintzberg, H. (1976). Planning on the left side and managing on the right. *Harvard Business Review*, July/August, 120-130.

Mintzberg, H. (1993) *The rise and fall of strategic planning: Reconceiving roles for planning, plans, planners.* Glencoe: Free Press.

Paller, A., & Laska, R. (1990). *The EIS book: Information systems for top managers.* New York: Business One.

Perrin, D. (1993). *L'impact des Nouvelles Technologies*, Les Editions d'Organisation, Paris.

Pomerol, J.-C. (1997). Artificial intelligence and human decision making. *European Journal of Operational Research*, 99, 3-25.

Pomerol, J. -C., & Barba-Romero, S. (2000). *Multicriterion decision making in management: Principles and practice.* New York: Kluwer.

Pomerol, J. -C., & Brézillon, P. (1998). From DSSs to cooperative systems: Some hard problems still remain. In R. Dolk (Ed.), *Proceedings HICCS 31* (Vol 5, 64-71) IEEE Pub.

Rockart, J. (1979). Chief executives define their own data needs. *Harvard Business Review*, 57(2), 81-93.

Rockart, J., & DeLong, D. (1988). *Executive support systems: The emergence of top management computer use.* New York: Business One.

Rockart, J., & Treacy, M. (1986). The CEO goes on-line. In J. Rockart & C. Van Bullen (Eds.), *The rise of managerial computing* (pp. 135-147) Homewood, IL: Dow Jones Irwin.

Rockart, J., & Van Bullen, C. (1986). *The rise of management computing.* Homewood, IL: Dow Jones Irwin.

Roy, B., & Bouysson, D. (1993). *Aide multicritère a la decision: Methods et cas*, Economica Publications, Paris.

Scott-Morton, M. (1986). The state of the art of research in management information systems. In J. Rockart & C. Van Bullen (Eds.), *The rise of management computing* (Chap. 16, pp. 325-353) Homewood, IL: Dow Jones Irwin.

Simon, H. (1977). *The new science of management decisions.* Englewood Cliff, NJ: Prentice Hall.

Sterman, J. D. (1989). Modeling managerial behaviour: Misperceptions of feedback in a dynamic decision making experiment. *Management Science*, 35, 321-339.

Van Bullen, C., & Rockart, J. (1986). A primer on critical success factors. In J.

Rockart & C. Van Bullen, *The rise of management computing*, Homewood, IL: Dow Jones Irwin.

Wallenius, J. (1975). Comparative evaluation of some interactive approaches to multicriterion optimization. *Management Science*, 21, 1387-1396.

Watson, H. J., & Frolick, M. N. (1993). Determining information requirements for an executive information system. *MIS Quarterly, 17*(3), 255-269.

Watson H. J., Rainer, K. R. Jr., & Koh, C. E. (1991). Executive information systems: A framework for development and a survey of current practices. *MIS Quarterly*, *15*(1), 13-50.

Wetherbe, J. C. (1993). Executive information requirements: Getting it right. *MIS Quarterly, 17*(1), 51-65.

Chapter XX

DMSS Implementation Research: A Conceptual Analysis of the Contributions and Limitations of the Factor-Based and Stage-Based Streams

Manuel Mora
Autonomous University of Aguascalientes, Mexico

Francisco Cervantes-Pérez
Mexico Autonomous Institute of Technology, Mexico

Ovsei Gelman-Muravchik
National Autonomous University of Mexico, Mexico

Guisseppi A. Forgionne
University of Maryland, Baltimore County, USA

Marcelo Mejía-Olvera and Alfredo Weitzenfeld-Reitel
Mexico Autonomous Institute of Technology, Mexico

ABSTRACT

The implementation process of Decision-Making Support Systems (DMSS) is a highly complex process. Frequent implementation failures have caused the number of DMSS installed and adequately used to be far less than expected. The Theory of Factors and the Theory of Stages have been used to study this problem. Both approaches have generated a rich picture about key DMSS implementation issues. However, this knowledge is fragemented and disperse, offering only partial and reduced views and finding about strategies, tactics and operational processes to avoid failures in DMSS implementations. In this chapter, we organize the previous work into a unified and complete picture of the phenomenon. First, we examine the nature of the implementation problem from these research perspectives. Secondly, we continue with a conceptual analysis of the theoretical foundations of the Factor-based and Stage-based approaches. In this analysis we discuss the main models posed in both approaches and synthesize their findings. Then, their contributions and limitations are discussed and the Systems Approach is suggested as a research methodology to alleviate the difficulties. Finally, conclusions and directions for further research are presented.

INTRODUCTION

In the last 30 years managerial literature has reported that the decision-making process (DMP) is a critical and relevant executive activity (Huber, 1990; Huber & McDaniel, 1986; Mintzberg, 1990; Simon, 1973, 1997). Nobel laureate H. A. Simon foretold that organizations of the post-industrial society would focus on the DMP more than in other managerial activities during the early 1970s. Under this perspective the management central problem is to organize effective decisions rather than efficient production (Simon, 1973, pp. 269-270). The high relevance of DMP takes root in the strong positive or negative impact on future organizational performance of the decisions realized. Consequently poor or wrong decisions have been main causes for executive removal (Rowe, Davis, & Vij, 1996; p. xi). Furthermore deciders are currently faced with more complex managerial decisions: i.e., the number of decision alternatives is increased, the certainty of data is reduced, the degree of structure of tasks is diminished, the decision framing time is shortened, the degree of critical impacts is increased, and the pressure to obtain better results from decisions is also increased (Mora & Cervantes-Perez, 2000). All of this occurs because the business environment has become more turbulent, hostile, dynamic and competitive than in the past (Huber & McDaniel, 1986; Nolan, 1991).

To assist managers in this new environment, specialized computer-based information systems, called decision-making support systems (DMSS), have emerged in response. DMSS are systems designed specifically to support any, several or all phases of the DMP, from intelligence through design, choice and implementation (Forgionne, 1991; Forgionne, Mora, Cervantes, & Kohli, 2000; Turban & Watson,

1989). DMSS can be individual (stand-alone) or integrated systems. Individual or stand-alone DMSS include executive information systems (EIS) (Rockart & Tracy, 1982), decision support systems (DSS) (Sprague & Carlson, 1982) and expert systems/knowledge-based systems (ES/KBS) (Feigenbaum, McCorduck, & Mii, 1988). Integrated DMSS are systems that incorporate the functions of two or more individual (stand-alone) systems into a single unified system. These integrated systems include executive support systems (ESS), which integrate an EIS and a DSS (Rockart & DeLong, 1988) and expert decision support systems (EDSS), which at the same time integrate an ES/KBS and a DSS (Klein & Methlie, 1990; Turban & Watkins, 1986). Full integration of the three components are called integrated decision making support systems (IDMSS); i.e., systems incorporating the functions of an EIS, a DSS and an ES/KBS (Forgionne, 1991; Forgionne & Kholi, 1995; Forgionne et al., 2000; Mora, Forgionne, & Cervantes-Perez, 2000; Turban & Watson, 1989). Studies have reported that the usage of stand-alone DSS (Eom, Lee, Kim, & Somarajan, 1998; Udo & Guimaraes, 1994), EIS (Leidner, 1996; Rockart & DeLong, 1988; Watson, Rainer and Houdeshel, 1992) and ES/KBS (Feigenbaum et al., 1988; Liebowitz, 1990; Turban, 1995; Tyran & George, 1993) have generated benefits such as improved organizational performance, improved decision quality, improved communication, enhanced mental models, amplified analytical skills of decision makers, and reduced decision time. Despite the proffered benefits, stand-alone and integrated DMSS still have many reported implementation failures. Therefore, in practice, the number of DMSS installed and adequately used has been far less than expected. A study that summarized the main literature in the field of DMSS implementation (Mora, Cervantes-Perez, & Forgionne, 2000) reported that the main general cause of failures in DMSS implementation is the inherent high complexity of the process. Using the theory of factors and the theory of stages (Cooper & Zmud, 1990; Kwon & Zmud, 1987), Mora et al. (2000) also report that previous research studies conducted on the problem during the last 20 years have generated a rich corpus of knowledge about key DMSS implementation issues. However, this knowledge is fragmented and disperse. Therefore, the available knowledge offers only partial views and findings about strategies, tactics and operational processes to avoid failures in DMSS implementations.

In this chapter, we extend the previous work by analyzing the contributions and limitations to the knowledge about DMSS implementations from both the factor-based and stage-based research streams. First of all, we examine the nature of the implementation problem from these research perspectives. Secondly we continue with a conceptual analysis of the theoretical foundations of the factor-based and stage-based approaches; in this analysis we will discuss the main models posed in both approaches and synthesize the main findings from the models. Then, the contributions and limitations of these research streams are discussed and the systems approach is suggested as a research methodology with the potential to capture the full complexity of the phenomenon of DMSS implementations. Finally, conclusions and directions for further research are given.

THE NATURE OF THE PROBLEM OF DMSS IMPLEMENTATION

In general, the implementation process of information systems (IS) is a research topic that has been widely studied in the last three decades (Lucas, 1975; Kivijarvi & Zmud, 1993; Zmud & Kwon, 1987). Based on common definitions reported in the literature (Bergeron, Raymond, Rivard, & Gara, 1995; Finlay & Forghani, 1998; Turban & Aronson, 1998; Tyran & George, 1994), IS implementation can be defined as the overall process that is performed in an organization from the acknowledgement of a potential and new IS until the institutional acceptance and usage of the system. Researchers and practitioners are interested in the topic because of the high financial and organizational efforts dedicated to implement an IS. Consequently, failures in the process can cause the project to be cancelled during its development, underutilization of the developed system, or eventual discarding of the developed system. These negative implementation results have adverse impacts on the organization. There could be a loss of financial resources, wasted organizational efforts, and organizational distrust in the system development process (Ewusi, 1997; Mohan & Bean, 1979, quoted by Hardaway & Will (1990); Poulymenakou & Holmes, 1996). In addition, it has been argued that despite the high availability of advanced information technology (IT) and development methodologies and tools, critical implementation failures are still frequent in organizations (Poulymenakou & Holmes, 1996). Yet, in traditionally technological-focused research fields, similar core ideas have been identified: (i) developing software is a complex process; (ii) problems and accidents caused by software systems faults are frequent; and (iii) the use of a specific development life-cycle or technological tool is not sufficient to guarantee the quality of the system. The software development process (SDP), which deals with "the methods and technologies used to assess, support, and improve software development activities" (Fuggetta, 2000, p. 27) is a case in point.

To alleviate this problematic situation, several initiatives of quality-based process models such as CMM, CMMi and ISO 9000 based standards (Fuggetta, 2000) have emerged for improvement of the SDP. The use of these models has effectively improved the quality of the produced software, the ability to meet budget and schedules, and the reduction of the failure rate of IS projects (Goldenson and Hersbsleb, 1995). However, the first generation of these models was focused on technical rather than organizational issues and the failure rate of IS projects was still high (Fuggetta, 2000). In the process, developers have learned that it is important to consider managerial, organizational, economic, political, legal, behavioral, psychological and social factors when developing software. From the early '90s, efforts have been made to integrate these factors into the SDP research stream (Kellner, Curtis, deMarco, Kishida, Schulumberg, & Tully, 1991). As Fuggetta (2000, p. 28) recently suggested, "rather, we (e.g., the software process community) must pay attention to the complex interrelation of a number of organizational, cultural, technological and economic factors." While achievements in the SDP field are useful, the proposed approach is incomplete from an IS perspective. That is because the software development life-cycle process is only a part of the overall implementation process. Furthermore, SDP scientists have realized that the introduction of a new process model of software development really involves the introduction of a long-term innovation (Software Engineering Institute, 2001). Therefore, the literature on the adoption of innovations, change management, and organizational behavior has become increasingly relevant to this community (Cattaneo, Fuggetta, & Lavazza, 1995; Fowler & Levine, 1993; Nishiyama, Ikeda, & Niwa, 2000). The IDEAL model from the Software Engineering Institute is a case in point (McFeely, 1996).

It must be noted that findings about failures on IS projects from IS, DMSS, and the SDP literature all note the relevance of managerial and organizational issues. For example, a recent empirical study of failures in IS projects revealed that these are unsuccessful because of management considerations rather than lack of economical or technological resources (Standish Group, 1999, p. 1). This study also found that organizational and managerial issues are the most relevant influences for successful IS projects. Among these issues are user involvement, top executive support, and clear business objectives. Project management, standard infrastructure and scope minimization of projects are also relevant success factors. In summary, quality-based models of software development can result in successful project management and result in a standardized infrastructure for the software development. While such models can ensure the technical success of the developing DMSS software as a software product, they are insufficient to guarantee the organizational success of the overall DMSS implementation as a specialized Information System for Decision-Making. As Ballantine et al. indicate (1996, p. 12): "A technically excellent system, but one in which users have not been involved, might be rejected by users and fail to result in a used information system at the deployment level." Similarly, the CHAOS report points out that (Standish Group,, 1999, p. 4): "Even when delivered on time and on budget, a project can fail if it does not meet users' need."

DMSS are IS and they are also software-based products. Therefore, DMSS projects can encounter the same, or similar, implementation problems. Furthermore, DMSS have additional characteristics that increase the level of risks and consequently reduce the probabilities of conducting a successful implementation. These characteristics include: (i) top-level management utilization, (ii) high complexity of tasks supported, and (iii) high technical knowledge and expertise required for development, among others (Mora, Cervantes-Perez, et al., 2000). DMSS implementation, then, can be influenced by social and organizational, as well as technical issues. Evidence of these potential issues has been reported for EIS by Young and Watson (1995), for ES/KBS by Bradley and Hausser (1995), for DSS by Finlay and Forghani (1998), and for DMSS in general by Turban and Aronson (1998). Table 1 summarizes the key symptoms associated with DMSSs implementation failures. The problems and symptoms have stimulated research on DMSS implementation. As in IS implementation research, two main approaches have emerged in a similar way to the research of IS implementation: the factor-based and the stage-based approach (Kwon & Zmud, 1987).

Table 1: Facts related to DMSS implementation failures

Symptoms of DMSS Implementation Failures	Evidence
A low return on investment by underutilization of DSS due to the voluntary nature of usage.	Alavi and Joachinsthaler (1992); Eom and Lee (1990), referenced in Alavi and Joachiminsthaler (1992).
An inadequate implementers' awareness of the social and technical conflicts present in the implementation process of DSS.	Finaly and Forghani (1998).
There are high risks of implementation failures due to special characteristics of EIS that are seen as technological innovations.	DeLong and Rockart (1986).
A low number of successful cases of EIS reported; a high number of implementation failures in EIS projects.	Rai and Bajwa (1997); Rainer and Watson (1995).
A low percent of successful ES/KBS implementations.	Hardaway and Will (1990); Tyran and George (1993); Keyes (1989), referenced in Tyran and George (1993); Turban (1990).
Early successful projects of ES/KBS implementations were abandoned some years later despite their high technical quality.	Gill (1995).
Failures in ES/KBS implementations cause financial losses, organizational disturbances and dissatisfaction in future potential users.	Duchessi and O'Keefe (1995).

The former is based on survey and experimental research methods, which use statistical tools such as causal or structural equation modeling to analyze the data collected from the phenomenon (Barclay, Thompson, & Higgins, 1995; Falk & Miller,1992; Lee, Barua, & Whinston, 1997). The second is based mainly on case study methods that use qualitative tools for data collection and analysis (Walsham, 1995; Yin, 1994). According to Duchessi and O'Keefe (1995), both approaches are complementary. While we accept that claim, we submit that both approaches have serious limitations in capturing the full complexity of the DMSS implementation phenomenon as a whole process. Before posing an emergent research approach, we will review both current research approaches.

A REVIEW OF KEY LITERATURE ON THE FACTOR-BASED APPROACH IN THE RESEARCH OF DMSS IMPLEMENTATIONS

The factor-based approach (FBA) involves the search for elements associated with the success or failure of a process (Kwon & Zmud, 1987). This theoretical scheme assumes that the success and failure of a process is associated with the presence or absence of a set of factors frequently called critical success factors (Rockart, 1979). With this perspective, if a process has these key elements, the project will be successful. Otherwise, the project will fail. In fact the FBA has its theoretical foundations in a strong cause-effect or mechanistic view of a phenomenon. A strict mechanistic perspective assumes that events are determined completely by their causes, and the causes are necessary and sufficient. An expression using a well-formed sentence from predicate calculus (Luger & Stubblefield, 1993, pp. 46-57), of this approach can be defined as:

$$presence(F1, P) \land presence(F2, P) \ldots \land presence(Fk, P) \Rightarrow success(P)$$

where the predicate *presence(X, Y)* stands for true if the element X is present in the Y situation and the predicate *success(Y)* stands for true if the situation Y can be assessed as successful. This FBA expression holds out a rigid perspective of the phenomenon; a problem detected by William and Ramaprasad (1996). Moreover, these researchers criticized the ambiguity involved in using critical factors. To alleviate this, they posed a taxonomy to distinguish the level of criticality. In their taxonomy, there was association, necessity, necessity and sufficiency, and causal mechanism levels. Association implies that a factor is regularly present in successful cases, but its presence does not guarantee success. Necessity implies that a factor is required for the effect, and these necessities are usually called facilitating factors (William & Ramaprasad, 1996). Necessary and sufficient factors will unavoidably generate success. According to Little (1991), single factors are rarely necessary and sufficient, but several together can acquire this property. A causal mechanism separates necessary and sufficient factors where the behavioral laws are well known from those that are of a black box nature. Studies of IS and DMSSs implementations have used the FBA extensively through use of surveys, and in some isolated cases, experimental methods. Figure 1, based on the scheme called "inventory of causes" (Blalock, 1969, p. 35), shows a generic research model for the FBA.

Figure 1: Typical model of investigation and research hypothesis used in FBA

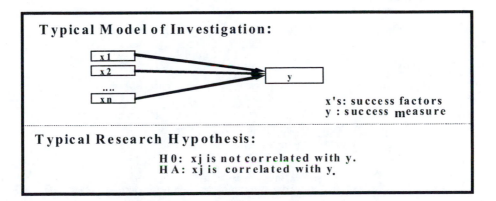

As Figure 1 illustrates, the FBA research model is relatively simple. The generic research question and hypothesis are: (a) does the presence of the factor X affect the occurrence of variable Y? and (b) the higher (higher) the value of the factor X, the higher (lower) the value of the variable Y. This model offers the advantage of parsimony and easiness to capture, through survey studies, the data required to support or reject the hypothesis posed. However, practical models are limited to a reduced number of variables, not only for statistical restrictions but also for the impossibility that real users will answer long questionnaires. For this practical reason, the main studies report that a subset of a reduced number of factors will be considered. Therefore, the whole problem is analyzed partially, with the implicit premise that by joining the part's findings we will be able to understand the whole situation. The high rate of DMSS implementation failures still present could imply that this mechanistic-based approach is not enough to understand the behavior of complex phenomena (Ackoff, 1973).

A review of the IS- and DMSS-relevant FBA literature reveals that there is not a standard framework or taxonomy of factors related with the success of IS or DMSS implementations. However, there have been several efforts to summarize them. The main DMSS frameworks have been the following: (i) a framework for EISs implementation by Watson, Rainer, and Koh (1991); (ii) a framework of DSS constructs by Eierman, Niederman, and Adams (1995); and (iii) a framework for DMSS implementation by Turban (1995) and Turban and Aronson (1998). Main contributions from the studies include a compilation of key DMSS implementation success factors at the date of the study. These factors, as reported by Watson et al. (1991) are summarized in Table 2. According to Watson et al. (1991), these factors were present in multiple EIS implementations. Individual reported factors were not present in all studies but were present in the majority of studies or were critical in some studies. Watson et al. reported that the existence of organizational external and internal pressures and the availability of a top management sponsor were always critical factors to successful implementation.

This framework organizes disperse findings reported in the literature and empirically confirmed in this study. Still the scope is limited to EIS implementations. Moreover, the framework does not link relevant individual categories of factors, such as task, technology, organization, and environment.

Table 2: Scheme of factors for EIS implementation from Watson et al. (1991)

CATEGORIES OF FACTORS	LIST OF FACTORS
Structural (Personnel and Data)	Initiator, sponsor, user, developers, staff, IS personnel, internal and external data.
User-System Dialog	User training, system documentation, user, interface, system response time, output format, colors of outputs.
Process	External organizational pressures, internal organizational pressures, cost-benefit analysis, development time frame, development methodology, system capabilities, information generated by the system, system evolution and diffusion.

Table 3 shows the categories of factors and individual factors reported by Eierman et al. (1995). These researchers focus their study on the development of a theory of constructs for DSS research. Their framework accounts for the main expected outcomes from individual successful DMSS implementations, grouped in the "performance" category. Additionally, this framework reported that only 17 of the 54 possible relationships among the eight categories have been explored. Eierman et al's work offers an extensive review of DSS implementation literature, a comprehensive framework, and explicit relevant categories for evaluation. These categories include the environment, the task, and the configuration (technology). The main limitations are the framework's narrow DSS scope and the overlapping of some categories that must be separated, such as the environmental and organizational categories.

Table 4 exhibits the categories and individual factors reported by Turban and Aronson (1998). Turban and Aronson assert that their framework organizes the large quantity of factors related with successful DMSS implementations. This framework does explicitly recognize the category of "organization" and separate such factors from the "environment" in agreement with systems theory foundations. On the other hand, they specify "user participation characteristics" as a single category instead of remarking the "user" category as a single entity relevant to the problem. As the same of Eierman et al.'s framework, Turban and Aronson's framework separates some properties of users in the "user" category itself and the "implementation process" category, and it could cause confusion by the conceptual mix of different types of hierarchical levels used in the frameworks.

Main contributions of Turban and Aronson's (1998) framework are the confirmation of the existence of previously reported common categories of factors,

Table 3: Scheme of factors for DSS implementation from Eierman et al. (1995)

CATEGORIES OF FACTORS	LIST OF FACTORS
Environment	Organizational culture, organizational goals, environment stability, organizational resources and constrains, organizational structure, top management support, sponsor.
Task	Complexity, structure, decision level, decision phase, functional area, level of relevance.
Implementation Process	Development methodology, user participation, user training, support of IS department.
System	Accuracy, timeliness, format, user interface, special capabilities.
Configuration	Hardware, software.
User	Aptitude, expectations, motivation, knowledge, cognitive style.
User Behavior	Frequency of use, strategy of use, quantity of information used, time frame of use.
Performance	Quality of decision, efficiency, economical value, user satisfaction.

the addition of new and relevant single factors, such as the relationships among the organization and IT research centers, and the separation of "organization" from the "environment" category. Limitations of this framework are the omission of relevant categories, such as "system" and "task", and the commingling of single factors with categories (for example, decision style, technological competence of the development team, and user participation).

Table 4: Scheme of factors for DMSS implementation from Turban and Aronson (1998)

CATEGORIES OF FACTORS	LIST OF FACTORS
Technology	Technological feasibility, technological available resources, technological competence of development team.
Organizational Behavior	Decision style, organizational climate, change resistance, organizational expectations.
Implementation Process	Top management support, commitment of management, user commitment, institutionalization strategies, user experience.
User Participation	User involvement, adequate communication among users and techniques.
Organization	Availability of resources, support of IS department, organizational policies, sponsor.
Ethical Values	Project goals, impact on other systems, legal issues.
Environment	Economical, political, sociocultural issues, relationships with IT suppliers and IT research centers.
Project	Cost-benefit evaluation, organizational expectations, project management, financial resources available, project scheduling, project priority.

From the review, it is apparent that there is not a consensus about the classification of categories and single factors for successful DMSS implementation. Recently, Mora, Cervantes-Perez, et al. (2000) attempted to integrate the findings of the previous FBA schemes. The summary presented in Table 5, which maps critical success categories and factors with the previous schemes, evolved from this work. The updated scheme presented in Table 5 includes six of the eight categories proposed by Eierman et al. (1995).

The category of "performance" was not added because it is equivalent to the output variable of this process, i.e., the success of the implementation process. The other category that was not considered is "user behavior," because the main user factors are already incorporated in the "user characteristics" category. It provides a better hierarchical conceptual classification where the properties of an entity can be considered as a part-of association instead of an independent association relationship (Sowa, 1984). In contrast with Turban and Aronson's (1998) scheme, the Table 5 framework explicitly recognizes the categories of "system" and "task." The original work of Mora, Cervantes-Perez, et al. (2000) then, integrates the single

Table 5: Scheme of factors for DMSS implementation updated from Mora et al. (2000)

Factors from Mora, Cervantes and Forgionne	Type of DMSS			Watson et al's Scheme	Eierman et al's Scheme	Turban and Aronson's Scheme
	DSS	EIS	ES			
1. User characteristics				•	•	•
User aptitude.	✓	✓	✓		•	≈
Norm motivation.	✓	✓			•	≈
Cognitive style.		✓			•	•
Realistic expectations.			✓		•	≈
2. Task characteristics.					•	
Task difficulty and newness	✓					
Task uncertainty degree.		✓				
Task organizational alignment (priority)		✓	✓		≈	≈
Adequate task domain and complexity.			✓		•	
3. Development team characteristics.				•		≈
Project champion	✓	✓	✓			≈
Leader business skills		✓				
Leader technical skills		✓				
Developers technicals skills.			✓			•
4. Implementation process.				•	•	•
User training.	✓			•	•	≈
User involvement.	✓				•	•
Development Methodology (Evolved)	✓	✓	✓	≈	•	•
Development frame time.	✓					≈
Cost-benefit analysis		✓	✓	•		≈
Data accessibility		✓		•		
Change and resistance management		✓	✓			•
Support for evolution and diffusion		✓		•		≈
Support of IS department		✓	✓	•	•	•
Commitment of maintenance.			✓			≈
5. Technological characteristics.				•	•	•
Software.	✓	✓	✓	•	•	≈
Hardware.	✓	✓	✓	•	•	≈
6. Organizational characteristics.				•		•
Top management support.	✓	✓	✓	≈	•	•
Top sponsor.		✓	✓	•	•	≈
Organizational climate.			✓		≈	•
7. Environment characteristics.					•	•
Hostile and uncertainty environment.		✓		≈	•	≈
Relations with IT suppliers and RC			✓			•
8. System (DMSS) characteristics.				•	•	
Accuracy and format of results.	✓	✓			•	
Management level supported.	✓				•	
Decisional phase supported	✓				•	
Relevance of results	✓				•	
Degree of system sophistication		✓			•	
Timeless information		✓		≈	•	
Easiness of usage		✓		≈	≈	
Impact in user´s work			✓			≈
Legal and ethical issues			✓			•

factors reported in the studies of stand-alone DMSSs and improves a hierarchical conceptualization of categories of factors. This framework incorporates missing categories from previous studies, and it identifies previously unstudied factors. For example, the "commitment of maintenance" was found only in ES/KBS implementation studies, although it has potential relevance for the successful implementation of other types of DMSS. Indeed, Gill (1995) reported that the lack of such a

Table 6: Technological, organizational and mixed groups of categories of factors.

Technological Factors	User-system dialogue (Watson et al.); system, configuration (Eierman et al., 1995); technology (Turban & Aronson); technology, task and system (Mora et al.).
Socio-Organizational Factors	Personnel (Watson et al.); environment, task, user, user behavior (Eierman et al.); organization, environment, organizational behavior, user participation, ethical (Turban & Aronson); organization, user, environment (Mora et al. updated).
Mixed Factors	Development process (Watson et al.); implementation process (Eierman et al.); implementation process, project (Turban & Aronson); implementation process, development team (Mora, Cervantes-Perez, et al.).

commitment was one of the main causes of ES/KBS failure. As Sprague (1989, p. 14) points out, a framework, "in absence of theory, is helpful in organizing a complex subject, identifying the relationships between the parts and revealing the areas in which further developments will be required." The Table 5 framework fulfills this purpose by providing a comprehensive framework that organizes a highly complex theme by accounting for the main findings reported in the FBA literature concerning DMSS implementation. Also, it alerts researchers of potential missing knowledge links.

An analysis of the four frameworks reveals that all account for the widely accepted technological and socio-organizational factors summarized in Table 6. In short, the four frameworks account for practically all the factors that are potentially associated with the success of DMSS implementations. They offer a rich picture of insights to understand the complexity of the DMSSs implementation process.

Nevertheless, statistical restrictions have made it difficult to prove that the summarized factors are necessary and sufficient for DMSSs implementation success (William & Ramaprasad, 1996). According to Baker (1994), causality is established statistically when: (i) the cause variable precedes the effect variable, (ii) there is a high correlation among the cause and effect variables, and (iii) there is not a spurious relationship among the cause and effect variables. The third condition is usually controlled through experimental research, while the majority of the factor studies have been executed through survey methods. Then, from a statistical perspective, association is the most common relationship established in the survey studies. Despite the availability of advanced statistical procedures, known as hard modeling techniques (Falk & Miller, 1992), rigorous data requirements make it difficult to employ such methods in practical factor studies. Fornell (1982, p. 7) suggests that "Causal laws cannot be proven; they are always assumed by the researcher." In experimental design, causality is traditionally assumed when there is enough evidence to suggest that the null hypothesis is false." Therefore, for survey studies where the conditions are more relaxed, it is not valid to infer causality from correlation or regression coefficients. In this way, causality must be assumed according to the specific theoretical context.

A REVIEW OF KEY LITERATURE ON THE STAGE-BASED APPROACH IN THE RESEARCH OF DMSS IMPLEMENTATIONS

The stage-based approach (SBA), also called the process-based research stream, is concerned with the identification of a sequence of generic phases needed for the successful implementation of DMSS projects (Kwon & Zmud, 1987). This theoretical scheme holds that the success or failure of an implementation process is affected by the activities realized in each phase or process. SBA is based on two core principles: (i) an implementation process seeks to introduce an organizational change (Kwon & Zmud, 1987; Marakas, 1998) and (ii) an implementation process deals with the introduction of a technological innovation (Keen & Scott-Morton, 1978; Kwon & Zmud, 1987). This scheme has been less used than the FBA. Yet, several authors have noted that such an approach can offer a broader view of the implementation phenomenon (Cooper & Zmud, 1990; Ginzberg, 1981; Kwon & Zmud, 1987). Furthermore, the SBA assumes a dynamic perspective of the phenomenon and can include the main findings of the FBA. In a similar situation to FBA there is not a standard SBA model. Main models reported in the literature are the: (i) change model of Lewin-Schein (1952), (ii) model of diffusion of innovations of Rogers (1983, 1995), (iii) model of IT implementation of Cooper and Zmud (1990) and Kwon and Zmud (1987), and (iv) model of DMSS implementation of Mora, Cervantes-Perez, et al. (2000). There have been far fewer reported applications of the SBA as opposed to FBA models. Some reasons are: (i) FBA is based on the traditional way of conducting scientific research; (ii) there are more researchers prepared in quantitatively based research approaches; and (iii) there are more organizational barriers for data collection. Table 7 presents Lewin-Schein's model.

This table summarizes three studies that used this model to study DSS implementations (Finlay & Forghani 1998; Palvia & Chervany, 1995; Welsch, 1986) and ideas presented in Marakas (1998). Lewin-Schein's (1952) model offers a framework to describe the adequate sequence of stages needed to implement a

Table 7: Lewin-Schein (1952) model of stages of planned change

STAGE	FOCUS
Unfreezing	To create a favorable atmosphere and create awareness of the necessity of the system and to make the positive decision.
Movement	To act through the design, building and installation of the system.
Refreezing	To reinforce the usage and acceptation of the system to get its institutionalization.

DMSS. This model suggests that an early start with technical activities, i.e., the moving phase, is highly risky and involves potential negative consequences for user acceptance. The first stage, i.e., "unfreezing," is useful to gain the trust of future users about the positive impacts of the system. Also, the last stage, i.e., "refreezing," is necessary to formalize the new user and organizational behavioral patterns and to get the institutionalization of the system (Chervany, 1995; Marakas, 1998; Palvia & Finlay & Forghani, 1998; Welsch, 1986). This model contributes to the IS implementation literature by offering generic frameworks of theory of stages and by suggesting a need to consider dynamic factors (Lewin, 1951), i.e., the interaction of driving and inhibiting forces for getting successful changes. The model's main shortcoming is the lack of specificity inherent in the approach. In IS or DMSS implementation studies, the process must be interpreted and explicitly defined by the researcher.

Table 8 presents the stages of Rogers' model of diffusion of innovations (1983, 1995). This theory has been used in several fields (Alanís, 1990), including IS (Prescott & Conger, 1995). In this model, an innovation is considered an idea, object or practice that is perceived as new by an individual or an organization. Because of the sophisticated characteristics of DSS, EIS, or ES/KBS, a DMSS is considered to be a technological innovation (Dologite & Mockler, 1989; Keen & Scott-Morton, 1978; Rockart & DeLong, 1988).

While Rogers' model can be considered a descriptive theory, it suggests also a normative perspective about how the DMSS implementation process should be conducted. This model proffers that the final acceptance of an innovation, i.e., in this case a DMSS, does not occur randomly, but it follows a process. In turn, cases of successful implementation form the descriptive basis for implementing a normative model successfully. According to Rogers' model, the first two phases, i.e., "knowledge" and "persuasion," are critical phases to create realistic expectations about the system and to create the awareness of these systems.   Internal or external organizational sources are used to create the knowledge and persuasion. In a similar way, the last phase is required to reinforce the positive and manage the negative impacts of the system. Otherwise, the organizational and financial effort invested in the system may be wasted by users rejecting or sub-utilizing the system. Rogers' model more explicitly identifies the phases involved in the implementation of an IS than Lewin-Schein's model.   Both models, however, provide only qualitative descriptions about how stage elements or factors are related. While there have been quantitative models of innovation diffusion, these models only describe how a specific

Table 8: Rogers' (1983, 1995) model of stages of diffusion of innovations.

STAGE	FOCUS
Knowledge	To know the characteristics of the innovation.
Persuasion	To sell the idea of the innovation to key deciders.
Decision	To make the decision of following or canceling the project.
Implementation	To build or acquire the innovation and install it.
Confirmation	To assess the institutional acceptance of the innovation.

innovation (e-mail, a cellular phone, and so on) are adopted by a particular population. This research is focused on reporting the complexity of the SBA relationships and the dynamics between the SBA and FBA.

Table 9 presents the stage model of IS implementation developed firstly by Kwon and Zmud (1987) and extended later by Cooper and Zmud (1990). The later researchers extended the original model by incorporating post-adoption issues reported in Zmud and Apple (1989). These organizational post-adoption behaviors are required to avoid the disuse of the innovation resulting from user misunderstandings or change resistance.

While based on Lewin-Schein's model of change, Zmud's models also consider the implementation process as a diffusion process of an innovation. For Zmud's proponents, an IS implementation deals with the adequate diffusion of the system throughout the user community. Using Lewin-Schein's model and Table 9, we can observe that Zmud's model focuses on the last stage of "refreezing." Zmud's model divides this last stage into the acceptance by the group of initial system users, then the acceptance of the innovation by these initial users as a normal tool, and finally full organizational diffusion to maximize the positive potential of the system. By highlighting the importance of the last stages of the implementation cycle, Zmud's model provides a prescription for maintaining an adequate atmosphere in the organization for the introduction of future innovations. In addition, the model identifies the need to relate stages and factors when studying the implementation phenomenon. As such this establishes the basis for a more robust and comprehensive framework to guide research in the field (Kwon & Zmud, 1987). Nevertheless, this framework has shortcomings. It offers only qualitative descriptions of how stages are performed and provides only a broad perspective of what categories of factors must be considered in the various stages. Again, DMSS implementation knowledge reported is partial.

Table 10 presents the stage model of the DMSS implementation reported recently by Mora, Cervantes, et al. (2000). This model is a conceptual framework

Table 9:   Kwon-Zmud and Cooper-Zmud's (1987) model of stages of implementation

STAGE	FOCUS
Initiation	To identify formal or informally opportunities or problems to introduce a system.
Adoption	To conduct negotiations among the stakeholders to make the decision.
Adaptation	To develop, install and maintain the system.
Acceptation	To promote system usage.
Routinization	To encourage and reinforce system usage so that it will not yet be perceived as an innovation.
Infusion	To increase the positive impacts of system usage in order to maximize its potential usefulness.

based on Lewin-Schein, Rogers, and Kwon and Zmud and Cooper and Zmud frameworks. The Mora et al. model purposes are to consider omissions in the previous frameworks and to highlight the importance of all stages in the implementation process. Rogers' model proffers three stages before an investment decision about the innovation is made, and it focuses on the early stages of the process. In turn, Zmud's model poses three stages after an investment decision is made, and it focuses on the last stages of the implementation process. Mora, Cervantes-Perez model, based also on Lewin-Schein's model, poses two stages prior to system realization and two stages after the realization. This model theorizes that the first stages involve the seeking of the innovation and the negotiation of the introduction of the system. These stages are as important as the last stages of accepting and institutionalizing the system.

Mora et al.'s model offers a reinterpretation of Rogers' first stage by noting the importance of overcoming ignorance during the implementation process. Previous models assume that innovations arrive automatically to organizations through an external or internal source, or they are already under consideration. Yet, advanced IT, such as DMSS, can be available for some time before they are recognized and adopted by organizations. For example, Fichman and Keremer (1999), in a study about diffusion of IT innovations, point out that the existence of knowledge barriers can cause organizations to defer the acquisition of an IT innovation. Nambisan, Agarwal, and Tanniru (1999), in turn, in a study about the role of users as sources of organizational IT innovations, point out the relevance of the organizational knowledge creation process to initiate the introduction of an advanced IT. Therefore, Mora et al., suggest that this organizational ignorance about the real capabilities of DMSS, or about the availability of these technologies, can create opportunity costs and other organizational losses from a lack of awareness or use. Influenced by the Zmud et al.'s models, Mora et al.'s model also considers the integration of previously reported factors and, in the process, offers a balanced framework that considers previously reported main, relevant characteristics. Nevertheless, as with the previous models, it offers only a qualitative-based description about how stages and factors interact and it implies a partial perspective of the phenomenon.

Table 10:   Mora, Cervantes-Perez, et al.'s (2000) model of stages of DMSS implementation

STAGE	FOCUS
Ignorance	To eliminate the organizational ignorance of the existence of the innovation.
Promotion	To gain the trust of key stakeholders to make a favorable decision.
Construction	To develop, install and capacitate.
Acceptation	To evaluate the degree of acceptation of the system.
Institutionalization	To disseminate the system to all potential users.

Table 11: Comparison of implementation stage-based models.

Lewin-Schein's Model (1952)	Rogers' Model (1983, 1995)	Zmud et al.'s Model (1987)	Mora, Cervantes-Perez, and Forgionne's Model (2000)
	Knowledge		Ignorance
Unfreezing	Persuasion	Initiation	Promotion
	Decision	Adoption	
Moving	Implementation	Adaptation	Construction
Refreezing	Confirmation	Acceptation	Acceptation
		Routinization	Institutionalization
		Infusion	

Table 11 presents a summary of the four models and the correspondence between stages. As this table shows, Rogers' model focuses on the early stages and Zmud et al.'s model focuses on the last stages of the implementation process. Mora et al.'s model suggests equal weight for all implementation stages. In this table, we can observe also that only Rogers' and Mora et al.'s models explicitly relate the phase with the knowledge acquisition process on the IT innovation.

Table 11 also exhibits the correspondence between stages from the different models and maps this correspondence to the three stages of Lewin-Schein's model. All these models provide alternative research mechanisms within the FBA. Two models suggest the integration of stages and factors, but they are limited to the offering of only qualitative descriptions about how this integration could be realized. Further research toward more detailed models is required.

DISCUSSION OF CONTRIBUTIONS AND LIMITATIONS OF FACTOR-BASED AND STAGE-BASED APPROACHES

In the last 30 years factor-based and stage-based approaches have generated important contributions to the knowledge of the phenomenon of IS implementation. In previous sections, we have already reported strengths and weakness of both approaches to study the phenomenon of DMSS implementation. In this section, we only highlight the key contributions and limitations in a summary format. First of all, Tables 12 and 13 present the contributions of FBA and SBA respectively.

However, none of the approaches is complete. Limitations of the FBA approach have been reported previously in the literature (Nandhakumar, 1996; Rogers, 1983, 1995; William & Ramaprasad, 1996). Nandhakumar (1996) also refers to the studies from Newman and Robey (1992), Walsham (1995), and Cottrell and Rapley (1991). Table 14 summarizes the main limitations of the FBA.

Table 15: Limitations of the stage-based approach

LIMITATIONS OF THE STAGE-BASED APPROACH
• Current frameworks have offered only a high-level perspective of the phenomenon.
• Available frameworks have not developed tests about what specific factors are relevant for each stage.
• All frameworks have described the stages in terms of general and qualitative descriptions and quantitative metrics are missing (i.e., metrics of duration, cost, quality level and success level of each stage).
• Studies using this approach are limited in scope due to the extensive research resource requirements of more complete examinations; i.e., organizations are not willing to share critical information.
• It has seldom been used in specific cases of DMSS; i.e., the complexity of DMSS implementations could be an inhibitor to using this approach.
• The analysis conducted on the dynamic perspective of the phenomenon is usually done through case study methods and it has been founded weak and incorrect for complex dynamic systems due to the counterintuitive behavior of these types of systems.

In particular, Rogers proposes (1995, pp. 188-189) that the understanding of complex phenomenon (such as implementation of innovations) must be conducted with different methods than the FBA approach. He suggests that FBA methods, called by him "variance research methods," which concentrate on a fixed point of time and on the covariances of the study variables, are limited. Therefore, studies focused on the dynamic perspective of the whole situation are encouraged. Nevertheless, the same as the FBA, the SBA has limitations. Table 15 summarizes the main of these.

Hence, we have analyzed the nature of the DMSS implementation problem and the key contributions and limitations of the main research approaches used: FBA and SBA. We claim that although the majority of the research efforts in this field have used these methods, the implementation process of advanced IT, such as DMSS, is an inherently complex process that requires a more comprehensive research approach where the reasearcher should be able to acquire an integrated vision of the phenomenon and overcome the limitations of the FBA and SBA approaches.

Some studies have suggested indirectly (Ballantine et al., 1996) that a systems approach (Ackoff, 1973; Checkland, 2000; Gelman & Garcia, 1989) can overcome the limitations of the FBA and SBA methods. The Systems Approach (Fuentes-Zenón, 1990) is a research methodology that offers several tools to study and simulate complex phenomena in field or laboratory conditions. In particular, a simulation technique called systems dynamics (Forrester, 1961, 1991, 1994) may be appropriate to account for complex nonlinear relationships among variables and to study the dynamic behavior of a system, e.g., an organization with an implementation process. Furthermore, the systems approach has been used to formalize the concept of information systems (Gelman & Garcia, 1989; Mora, Gelman, Cervantes-Perez, Mejia, & Weitzenfeld, 2002) and it could provide a robust foundation to develop models that capture the complexity inherent in the DMSS implementation process. This research approach, then, can alleviate the limitations and complement the benefits of the FBA and the SBA approaches. Despite the contributions of the

Table 12: Contributions of the factor-based approach

CONTRIBUTIONS OF THE FACTOR-BASED APPROACH
• Identification of a group of main factors with the potentiality to affect the success or failure of a DMSS implementation.
• Gathering of evidences that socio-organizational and environmental factors are also important for a successful implementation process.
• Gathering of evidences of a strong association between specific factors and implementation outcomes.
• Development of a framework to guide the research of missing relationships between factors.
• Delineation of a set of practical implementation guidelines and recommendations.

Table 13: Contributions of the stage-based approach

CONTRIBUTIONS OF STAGE-BASED APPROACH
• Awareness of the dynamic perspective of the phenomenon.
• Some findings have been useful to confirm findings from the FBA and therefore both approaches have generated consistent knowledge.
• Providing of explanations based on qualitative case studies of how and why an implementation process fails.
• Development of a more comprehensive IS implementation framework than the FBA.
• Delineation of a set of practical implementation guidelines and recommendations.

Table 14: Limitations of the factor-based approach

LIMITATIONS OF THE FACTOR-BASED APPROACH
• The majority of the relationships tested in practice are of the lowest level of criticality.
• Tests of higher levels of criticality are practically not feasible since these demand experimental research designs and the phenomenon is organizationally highly complex to let experimentation in real settings.
• The number of factors to be studied is large and survey studies used in practice usually cover a reduced set of these factors.
• Some factors reported as critical and necessary do not appear in successful implementation cases.
• Data collection assumptions have limited the ability to study factor interactions.
• It offers only a static rather than dynamic view of the phenomenon.
• The typical data collecting method is a sample survey, so that deep insights and explanations about how factors are related and why they affect the implementation process are lost.

systems approach to the IS and DSS fields that have been already reported in the literature (Eom, 2000; Xu, 2000), still it has not been used as much as a main research methodology to study the IS and DMSS implementation phenomena. Further research in this direction is required to explore the potential of the systems approach to complex phenomena, as are the IS and DMSS implementation process.

CONCLUSIONS

The decision-making process (DMP) is one of the most critical and relevant organizational activities. To support decision makers, special information systems have been developed since the 1970s. At present, they are known as decision making support systems (DMSS). Such systems can improve the quality of decisions, improve response time, and improve communication, among other things. However, despite the high interest in organizations to deploy these systems, the implementation of a DMSS is a complex process. Consequently, relatively few have been successfully implemented in practice. To understand and facilitate implementation, two main research approaches have emerged in the field of information systems: the factor-based approach and the stage-based approach. Both have generated a rich set of findings, but this knowledge is fragmented and dispersed. To overcome the lack of cohesion, several frameworks or models have been posed to organize this rich body of knowledge. These models were discussed in this chapter. Both research approaches still have inherent limitations to capture a comprehensive and detailed view of the phenomenon. For these reasons, new research approaches may be needed. The systems approach seems to offer promises in this direction.

ACKNOWLEDGMENTS

The authors thank the anonymous reviewers for the valuable suggestions to improve the content and structure of this chapter.

REFERENCES

Ackoff, R. (1973). Science in the systems age: Beyond IE, OR and MS. *Operations Research, 21*(3), 661-671.

Alanis, M. (1990). Controlling the introduction of strategic information technologies. In E. Szewczak et al. (Eds.), *Management Impacts of Information Technology: Perspectives on Organizational Change and Growth* (pp. 421-437) Hershey, PA: Idea Group Publishing.

Alavi, M. & Joachiminsthaler, E. A. (1992). Revisiting DSS implementation research: A meta-analysis of the literature and suggestions for research. *MIS Quarterly, 16*(1), 95-116.

Baker, T. (1994). *Doing social research*. New York: McGraw-Hill.

Ballantine, J., Bonner, M., Levy, M., Martin, A., Munro, I., & Powell, P.L (1996). The 3-D model of information systems success: the search for dependent variable continues. *Information Resource Management Journal*, Fall, 5-14.

Barclay, D., Thompson, R., & Higgins, C. (1995). The partial least squares (PLS) approach to causal modeling: personal computer adoption and use as an illustration. In U. Gattiker, (Ed.), *Technology studies* (pp. 285-309) New York: Walter de Gruyter.

Bergeron, F., Raymond, L., Rivard, S., & Gara, M. (1995). Determinants of EIS use: Testing a behavioral model. *Decision Support Systems, 14*(2), 131-146.

Blalock, H. (1969). *Theory construction*. Englewood Cliffs, NJ: Prentice-Hall.

Bradley, J.H. & Hausser, R.D. Jr. (1995). A framework for expert system implementation. *Expert Systems with Applications, 8*(1), 157-167.

Cattaneo, F., Fuggetta, A., & Lavazza, L. (1995). An experience in process assessment. In *Proceedings of the International Conference on Software Engineering*. ACM digital library at www.acm.org

Checkland, P (2000). Soft systems methodology: A thirty year retrospective. *Systems Research and Behavioral Science,* 17, 11-58.

Cooper, R.B. & Zmud, R.W. (1990). Information technology implementation research: A technological difussion approach. *Management Science, 36*(2), February, 123-139.

Cottrell, N. & Rapley, K. (1991). Factors critical to the success of executive information systems in Brithish Airways. *European Journal of Information Systems, 1*(1), 65-71.

DeLong, D.W. & Rockart, J.F. (1986). Identifying the attributes of successful executive support system implementation. Transactions of the 6th International Conference on Decision Support Systems.

Dologite, D.G. & Mockler, R.J. (1989). Developing effective knowledge-based systems: Overcoming organizational and individual behavioral barriers. *Information Resource Management Journal, 2*(1), Winter, 27-39.

Duchessi, P. & O'Keefe, R.M. (1995). Understanding expert systems success and failure. *Expert Systems with Applications, 9*(2), 123-133.

Eierman, M., Niederman, F., & Adams, C. (1995). DSS theory: A model of constructs and relationships. *Decision Support Systems,* 14, 1-26.

Eom, B.S. (2000, March). The contributions of system science to the development of decision support systems subspecialties: an empirical investigation. *Systems Research and Behavioral Science, 17*(2), 117.

Eom, S.B. & Lee, S.M. (1990). A survey decision support systems applications (1971-1988). *Interfaces, 20*(3), May-June, 65-79.

Eom, S.B., Lee, S.M., Kim, E.B., & Somarajan, C. (1998). A survey of decision support system applications (1988-1994). *Journal of the Operational Research Society, 49*(2), 109-120.

Ewusi-Mensah, K. (1997). Critical issues in abandoned information systems development projects. *Communication of the ACM, 40*(9), September, 74-80.

Falk, F. & Miller, N. (1992). *A primer for soft modeling.* Ohio: The University of Akron Press.

Feigenbaum, E., McCorduck, P., & Nii, H.P. (1988). *The rise of the expert company.* New York: Time Books .

Fichman, R. & Keremer, C. (1999). The illusory diffusion of innovation: An examination of assimilation gap. *Information Systems Research, 10*(3), September, 255-275.

Finlay, P.N. & Forghani, M. (1998). A classification of success factors for decision support systems. *Journal of Strategic Information Systems,* 7, 53-70.

Forgionne, G.A. (1991). Decision technology systems: A vehicle to consolidate decision making support. *Information Processing and Management, 27*(6), 679-797.

Forgionne, G. & Kholi, R. (1995). Integrated MSS effects: An empirical health care investigation. *Information Processing and Management, 31*(6), 879-896.

Forgionne, G.A., Mora, M., Cervantes, F., & Kohli, R. (2000). Development of integrated decision making support systems: A practical approach. CD of Proceedings of the AMCIS 2000 Conference (August 10-13), Long Beach, CA, USA.

Fornell, C. (1982). A second generation of multivariate analysis: An overview. In C. Fornell (Ed). *A second generation of multivariate analysis*, (Vol. 1: Methods, pp. 1-21) New York: Praeger.

Forrester, J. (1961). *Industrial dynamics.* Boston: MIT Press.

Forrester, J. (1991). *Systems dynamics and the lesson of 35 years.* On line report no. D-4224-4 found at http://sysdyn.mit.edu/sd-group/home.html

Forrester, J. (1994). Systems dynamics, systems thinking and soft operations research. On line report D-4405-1 found at http://sysdyn.mit.edu/sd-group/home.html

Fowler, P. & Levine, L. (1993). *A conceptual framework for software technology transition.* Technical report CMU/SEI-93-TR-1. Found at www.sei.cmu.edu

Fuentes-Zenón, A. (1990). Systems thinking: Characteristics and main streams. Outlets of Planning and Systems. Mexico: Fac. de Ingeniería, UNAM Press (In Spanish Language).

Fuggetta, A. (2000). Software process: A roadmap. In *Proceedings of the International Conference on Software Engineering.* ACM digital library at www.acm.org

Gelman, O. & García, J.I. (1989). Formulation and axiomatization of the concept of general systems. Outlet of the Mexican Society of Operational Research.

Gill, G.T. (1995). Early expert systems: Where are they now? *MIS Quarterly,* March, 51-81.

Ginzberg, M. (1981). Early diagnosis of MIS implementation failure: Promising results and unanswered questions. *Management Science, 27*(4), April, 459-478.

Goldenson, D. & Hersbsleb, J. (1995). After the appraisal: A systematic survey of process improvement, its benefits and factors that influence success. Technical report CMU/SEI-95-TR-009. Found at www.sei.cmu.edu

Hardaway, D. & Will, R. (1990). A review of barriers to expert system diffusion. ACM digital library, www.acm.org, paper no. 089791-416-3 /90/0010/0619, 619-639.

Huber, George P. (1990). A theory of the effects of advanced information technology on organizational design, intelligence and decision-making. *Academy of Management Review, 15*(1), 47-71.

Huber, G. P. & McDaniel, F. (1986). The decision-making paradigm of organizational design. *Management Science, 32*(5), May, 572-589.

Keen, P. & Scott-Morton, M. (1978). *Decision support systems: An organizational perspective.* MA: Addison-Wesley.

Kellner, M., Curtis, B., deMarco, T., Kishida, K., Schulemberg, M., & Tully, C. (1991). Non-technological issues in software engineering. In Proceedings of the 13th International Conference on Software Engineering. ACM digital library at www.acm.org.

Keyes, J. (1989, November). Why expert systems fail. *AI Expert,* 50-53.

Kivijarvi, H. & Zmud, R.W. (1993). DSS implementation activities, problem domain characteristics and DSS success. *European Journal of Information Systems, 2*(3), 159-168.

Klein, M. & Methlie, L.B. (1990). *Expert systems: A decision support approach.* MA: Addison-Wesley.

Kwon, T.H. & Zmud, R.W. (1987). Unifying the fragmented models of information systems implementation. In R.J. Boland & R.A. Hirschheim (Eds.), *Critical Issues in Information Systems Research* (pp. 227-251) Boston: Wiley.

Lee, B., Barua, A., & Whinston, A. (1997). Discovery and representation of causal relationships in MIS research: A methodological framework. *MIS Quarterly,* March, 109-133.

Leidner, D. (1996). *Modern management in the developing world: The success of EIS in Mexican organizations.* Draft of paper submitted to the ICIS Conference.

Lewin, K. (1951). *Field theory in social science.* New York: Harper and Row.

Lewin, K. (1952). Group decision and social change. In T.M. Newcomb & E.L. Harley (Eds.), *Readings in Social Psychology* (pp. 459-473) New York: Holt.

Liebowitz, J. (1990). *Expert systems for business and management.* New York: Yourdon Press.

Little, D. (1991). *Varieties of social explanation: An introduction to th philosophy of social science.* San Francisco: Westview Press..

Lucas, H. (1975). *Why information systems fail.* New York: Columbia University Press.

Luger, G. & Stubblefield, W. (1993). *Artificial intelligence: Structure and strategies for complex problem solving.* Redwood: Benjamin/Cummings.

Marakas, G. (1998). *Decision support systems in the twenty-first century*. Saddle River, NJ: Prentice-Hall.

McFeely, B. (1996). IDEAL: A users' guide for software process improvement (Tech. Rep. CMU/SEI-96-HB-001). On line at www.sei.cmu.edu

Mintzberg, H. (1990, March/April). The manager's job: Folklore and fact. *Harvard Business Review*, 163-176.

Mohan, L. & Bean, A.S. (1979). Introducing OR/MS into organizations: Normative implications of selected Indian experience. *Decision Sciences*, 10.

Mora, M. & Cervantes-Perez, F. (2000). The role of simulation in business decision making through decision technology systems. In S. Raczyinski (Ed.), *Proceedings of the Fifth International Conference on Simulation and Artificial Intelligence* (February 16-18, pp. 51-58) Mexico: McLeod Institute and Panamerican University.

Mora, M., Cervantes-Perez, F., & Forgionne, G. (2000). Understanding the process of successful implementations of management support systems: A review of critical factors and theories about adoption of new information technology. In CD of Proceedings of the 3rd BITWorld Conference, Mexico, D.F. June 1-3.

Mora, M., Forgionne, G.A & Cervantes-Perez, F. (2000). Decision making support systems: Core theoretical concepts and practice implications. In CD of Proceedings of the 3rd. SSGRR 2000 Conference, SSGRR Institute, Rome, Italy, July 31th – August 6.

Mora, M., Gelman, O., Cervantes-Perez F., Mejia, M., & Weitzenfeld, A. (2002). A systemic approach for the formalization of the information system concept: Why information systems are systems. To be published in J. Cano (Ed.), *Critical reflections of information systems: a systemic approach* (forthcoming, Fall 2002) Hersehy, PA: Idea Group.

Nambisan, S., Agarwal, R., & Tanniru, M. (1999, September). Organizational mechanisms for enhancing user innovation in information technology. *MIS Quarterly, 23*(3), 365-395.

Nandhakumar, J. (1996). Design for success? Critical success factors in executive information systems development. *European Journal of Information Systems*, 5, 62-72.

Newman, M. & Robey, D. (1992). A social process model of user-analyst relationships. *MIS Quarterly, 16*(2), 249-266.

Nishiyama, T., Ikeda, K., & Niwa, T. (2000). Technology transfer macro-process: A practical guide for the effective introduction of technology. In Proceedings of the International Conference on Software Engineering. ACM digital library at www.acm.org

Nolan, R. (1991, July/August). The strategic potential of information technology. *Financial Executive,* 25-27.

Palvia, S.C. & Chervany, N.L. (1995). An experimental investigation of factors influencing predicted success in DSS implementation. *Information and Management, 29*, 43-53.

Poulymenakou, A. & Holmes, A. (1996). A contingency framework for the investigation of information systems failure. *European Journal of Information Systems*, 5, 34-46.

Prescott, M. & Conger, S. (1995). Information technology innovations: A classification by IT locus of impact and research approach. *Data Base Advances, 26*(2 & 3), 20-41.

Rai, A. & Bajwa, D.S. (1997). An empirical investigation into factors relating to the adoption of executive information systems: an analysis of EIS collaboration and decision support. *Decision Sciences, 28*(4), Fall, 939-974.

Rainer, R.K. Jr. & Watson, H.J. (1995). What does it take for successful executive information systems? *Decision Support Systems, 14*(2), 147-156.

Rockart, J.F. (1979). Chief executives define their own data needs. *Harvard Business Review, 57*(2), 81-93.

Rockart, J.F. & DeLong, D.W. (1988). *Executive support systems*. Homewood, IL: Dow Jones-Irwin.

Rockart, J.F. & Tracy, M. (1982, January/February). The CEO goes on-line. *Harvard Business Review*, 82-88.

Rogers, E.M. (1983). *The diffussion of innovations* (3rd Ed.). New York: Free Press.

Rogers, E.M. (1995). *The difussion of innovations* (4th Ed.). New York: Free Press.

Rowe, J., Davis, S. & Vij, S. (1996). *Intelligent information systems: Meeting the challenge of the knowledge era*. Westport: Quorum Books.

Simon, H.A. (1973, May/June). Applying information technology to organization design. *Public Administration Review 33*(3), 268-278.

Simon, H.A. (1997). Administrative behavior: A study of decision-making process in administrative organizations. New York: Free Press.

Software Engineering Institute. (2001). Process maturity profile of the software community 2001 mid-year update. On line at www.sei.cmu.edu

Sowa, J.F. (1984). *Conceptual structures: Information processing in mind and machine*. MA: Addison-Wesley.

Sprague, R.H. (1989). A framework for development of decision support systems. In R. Sprague & H. Watson (Eds.), *Decision support systems: Putting theory into practice*, Englewood Cliffs, NJ: Prentice-Hall.

Sprague, R. H. & Carlson, E.D. (1982). *Building effective decision support systems*, Englewood Cliffs, N.J: Prentice-Hall.

Standish Group. (1999). CHAOS: A recipe for success. Online report at www.standishgroup.com/chaos.html

Turban, E. (1990, May/July). Why expert systems succeed and why they fail. *Decision Line*, pp. not availables.

Turban, E. (1995). Decision support systems and expert systems. *Management Support Systems,* (4th Ed.). Englewood Cliffs, NJ: Prentice-Hall.

Turban, E. & Aronson (1998). Decision Support Systems and Expert Systems (Management Support Systems) Englewood Cliffs, NJ: Prentice-Hal, 5th. Ed.

Turban, E. & Watson, H. (1989). Integrating expert systems, executive information systems and decision support systems. DSS-Transaction, pp. n.a.

Turban, E. & Watkins, P. (1986, June). Integrating expert systems and decision support systems. *MIS Quarterly,* pp. not available.

Tyran, C.K. & George, J.F.. (1993). The implementation of expert systems: A survey of successful implementations. *Data Base, 24*(4), Winter, 5-15.

Udo, G.J. & Guimaraes, T. (1994). Empirically assessing factors related to DSS benefits. *European Journal of Information Systems, 3*(3), 218-227.

Walsham, G. (1995). Interpretative case studies in IS research: Nature and method. *European Journal of Information Systems, 4*(2), 74-81.

Watson, H., Rainer, K., & Houdeshel, G. (1992). Executive information systems: Emergence—development—impact. Boston: Wiley.

Watson, H. J., Rainer, K., & Koh, K. (1991). Executive information systems: A framework for guiding EIS development and a survey of currrent practices. *MIS Quarterly*, March, 13-30.

Welsch, G. (1986). The information transfer specialist in successful implementation of decision support systems. *Data Base,* Fall, 32-40.

William, J.J. & Ramaprasad, A. (1996). A taxonomy of critical success factors. *European Journal of Information Systems, 5*, 250-260.

Xu, L. (2000, March). The contributions of system science to information systems Research. *Systems Research and Behavioral Science, 13*(12), 105.

Yin, R. (1994). *Case study research: Design and methods.* Thousand Oak: Sage.

Young, D. & Watson, H.J. (1995, September). Determinates of EIS acceptance. *Information and Management, 29*(3), 153-164.

Zmud, R. & Apple, L. (1989, February). Measuring information technology infusion, unpublished manuscript. Referenced in R.B. Cooper & R.W. Zmud. Information technology implementation research: a technological difussion approach. *Management Science, 36*(2), 123-139.

SECTION V

CHALLENGES
AND
THE FUTURE OF
DMSS

Chapter XXI

Evacuation Planning and Spatial Decision Making: Designing Effective Spatial Decision Support Systems Through Integration of Technologies

F. N. de Silva
University of Aberdeen, Scotland

R. W. Eglese and M. Pidd
Lancaster University, England

ABSTRACT

Issues concerning the development of Spatial Decision Systems for evacuation planning include realistic modelling of evacuee behavior, decision-making processes that take place during an evacuation, logistics, generating realistic scenarios, validation, technology development and trends for the future. These issues are discussed with reference to the development of a prototype system called CEMPS, which integrates simulation and GIS technology for emergency planning.

INTRODUCTION

The process of emergency planning and management in the present day very much depends on computer-aided emergency management systems which gather and analyse information and data on hazardous emissions, geological activity, meteorology, demography, geography, etc., in order to provide decision support for emergency prevention/mitigation, response and recovery (e.g., Belardo & Wallace, 1981; Fedra, 1998; Herrnberger, 1996). These systems are developed by the unification of various technologies that provide useful functions to aid this decision making process. Technology has a fast evolutionary trajectory that often makes its use attractive but complex. The complexity is intensified when attempting to link two streams of technology to achieve a realistic, usable design/system. The emergency planning process offers an interesting opportunity as a test bed to attempt such a union.

This chapter identifies and analyses the challenging issues faced in using two technologies, namely, simulation modelling and geographical information systems (GIS). A GIS is able to store spatially referenced data and information and provide sophisticated mapping and display facilities. Many contemporary GIS come with built-in analysis tools in addition to their data storage, manipulation and representation tools. The problem and decision making scenario that is generated from an emergency evacuation provides a plethora of interacting elements that have a spatial dimension, i.e., can be related to geographical coordinates of the earth's surface. For instance, locational elements such as shelters, population generation points (houses, workplace, schools, hospitals, etc.), hazard location, etc., and directional elements such as travelling vehicles, wind and other meteorological features, etc., all can be related to a spatial dimension. Thus, in designing a decision support tool for the evacuation planing process, this spatial element plays a dominant role as decisions made also have a spatial dimension. Using GIS technology provides a useful mechanism to tackle problems that have this strong spatial dimension. However, as emphasised by Church, Murray, Figuerosa, and Barber (2000), a GIS by itself cannot provide the complex decision models that are required to tackle real-world problems. Other technology such as simulation modelling is essential to develop a proper usable tool. The issues discussed in this chapter arise from the experiences gained in designing CEMPS (Configurable Evacuation Management and Planning Simulator), which attempts to tackle the spatial decision making aspects of the evacuation planning process. The issues investigated will primarily focus on the behavioural and decision making processes of the various players in the evacuation system, logistics, generating realistic scenarios for testing out contingency plans and the validation of such computer-based decision support tools. Future trends in technology and the evolution of emergency planning and management processes will also be discussed.

INTEGRATING TECHNOLOGIES FOR SPATIAL DECISION SUPPORT

The decision making process relating to any problem situation goes through stages of problem definition, identification of alternatives, analysis and evaluation of alternatives followed by the prescription of the best alternative. Often these problems involve descriptive information with a spatial dimension. The role spatial technologies, such as GIS, play in this planning process is discussed by Batty and Densham (1996). Plunkett (1993) describes an example of how a GIS is used in the nuclear emergency preparedness and response process in southern New Jersey (USA). Here the GIS is used to plot the radioactive plume dispersion and users can interact with the GIS to get further analysis of the crisis. Spatial technologies are thus widely used in all stages of the emergency management process today.

The concept of a spatial decision support system (SDSS) embodies the linkage of GIS and analytical/decision models to produce systems that can especially cope with problems that are of a spatial nature. It is designed to aid in the exploration, structuring and solution of complex spatial problems such as the evacuation process. The aim is to support decision making by the employment of quantitative approaches with the use of geographic information that is stored in a manipulable form within the GIS. The primary advantage is being able to display the critical information related to an incident on maps, satellite images or digital terrains in relation to time in emergency response software using spatial technologies (Mondschein, 1994).

A typical SDSS has four components: **analytical tools** enabling data investigation; **decision models** enabling "what-if" or scenario investigations; **geographic/spatial database**; **and user interface** providing easy access to decision models, database, analytical tools and an attractive and comprehensive display of the output (Densham, 1991). When problems are well structured and are of a static nature (e.g., resource allocation) mathematical programming methods can be built into the SDSS. For dynamic situations, such as the evacuation process, simulation is a popularly used modelling tool (see Fedra & Reitsma, 1990).

The greater part of the evacuation process involves vehicles or evacuees travelling along existing roads and would probably be controlled by the local emergency management personnel and/or the police or armed forces. Simulation offers an efficient way of modelling evacuations because it allows the modeller to build-in what is likely to be realistic behaviour as opposed to making concessionary assumptions for the sake of easy computation when using many analytical models. It is crucial to ensure that evacuation plans are based on realistic assumptions.

Evacuation is a process that combines elements that are geographically referenced on the earth's surface. For instance, evacuees would commence their evacuation journey from an origin location (e.g., home, workplace) where they would be when the warning to evacuate is given. This is a unique spatial coordinate on the earth's surface. As the evacuees travel on their evacuation journey they can be tracked through continuously by using their current spatial location coordinate. This is a powerful asset in tracking the behaviour of elements, such as route choice behaviour of individual evacuees, in the evacuation system. This asset of spatial referencing is made easily accessible via a GIS. Pilot experiments have been carried out in several countries (e.g., Japan, USA) in using GPS (global positioning systems) tracking systems in vehicles whereby the vehicles are assisted in their route choice decisions. GPS and GIS together provide the facility of this type of tracking system in real time. In mass-scale evacuations tracking each individual entity in the system using this technology may prove to be a difficult task to accomplish due to the sheer scale of entities being processed.

Batty (1994) discusses the possible contribution GIS can make to visualise simulation. He identifies two extremes: one where the various components of the GIS can be drawn into the modelling process and the other where modelling can take place within the GIS. A combination of the two is often the case in the design of SDSS, where by using the analytical tools within the GIS some sort of analytical modelling of the data takes place while tailor-made decision models within the SDSS are likely to draw on the display and data analysis facilities of the GIS.

A PROTOTYPE FOR EVACUATION PLANNING

The powerful attributes of both simulation modelling and GIS have been harnessed in the design of the prototype SDSS CEMPS (**Configurable Evacuation Management and Planning Simulator**). The aim was to produce an interactive planning tool that is used to examine simple scenarios where the emergency planners are able to watch a simulation proceed and provide limited interaction to obtain information on the progress of the evacuation. The development of the prototype was also expected to give insight to challenges relating to the integration of a traffic simulator with a GIS in terms of the flexibility and adaptability of related technologies in amalgamation. CEMPS integrates a tailor-made, dynamic, interactive evacuation simulation model with a GIS to provide a system that would be detailed but general enough to be configured as appropriate. Decision modelling tools have also been included through the impressive built-in capabilities of the GIS—ARC/INFO. The role of the GIS here is to define the terrain, road network and related installations, such as the hazard source and shelters, as well as the population to be evacuated, hence making CEMPS configurable from existing GIS data files. Simulation and link routines have been added to enable dynamic interactive modelling. Figure 1 shows a typical output from CEMPS.

CEMPS is an integrated system of four main core components designed for achieving specific design objectives. The **traffic simulation model** uses data from the geographic database and simulates the behaviour of individual evacuating entities. Analytical queries on the current status, such as congestion on roads and available shelter capacity, can also be performed using its functions. The **GIS component** provides dynamic mapping output of the simulation. It includes the database, functions that provide a convenient and consistent form for easy downloading, and GIS-based query and analytical/modelling functions, such as generating the shortest routes to shelters, evacuation zones, population and evacuee queries. The **integrated link** integrates the traffic model with the GIS by controlling and synchronising parallel tasks and performing communication functions between the GIS and simulation model. The **user interface** has been developed with the aid of interface development facilities provided by the GIS and the OpenWindows

Figure 1: An example of the CEMPS display

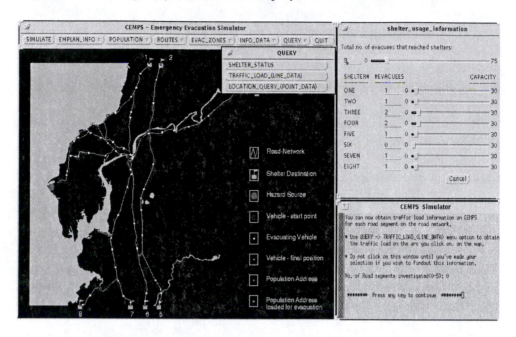

programming environment. This provides menu, interactive and display facilities which cater to a novice user. The details of the design and development of CEMPS can be found in de Silva & Eglese (2000) and Pidd, de Silva, and Eglese (1996).

DECISION MAKING AND EVACUEE BEHAVIOUR

Large-scale evacuations involve the movement of people, voluntarily or involuntarily, to safe places. Understanding the behaviour and decision making process of these people, which is affected by fear, uncertainty and the speed at which things happen, is crucial to the success of the evacuation. Johnson (1985) discusses a theoretical model designed for evacuation decision making in a nuclear reactor emergency basing its design on the intended behaviour of the affected population from a disaster. It stresses the influence of "**distance**" and "**direction**" in the evacuee behaviour. The distance from the hazard source and the direction in which the evacuees travel towards safe areas determine the behaviour of the evacuees in their response pattern and journeys. For instance, the closer a potential evacuee is to a hazard the more quickly the evacuee is likely to respond to a warning. Furthermore, the evacuee is likely to travel away from the hazard source and its looming radioactive plume. A disaster can trigger varying and extreme forms of human behaviour. Studies relating to evacuee behaviour during the Three Mile Island mishap conclude that only a few people used the official shelters and that the majority preferred to find shelter in homes of friends and relatives (Cutter & Barnes, 1982; Sorensen, Vogt, & Mileti, 1987). This means that the routes taken by evacuees were determined by their personal destination goals rather than being predefined to an official shelter. Thus an evacuation can often end up being a fraught and messy situation which the emergency planners must be prepared to cope with, to some degree of efficiency, in order to avoid costly confusion and damage.

Two parallel streams of decision making take place during an evacuation, viz., that of the authorities, i.e., people managing the evacuation operation, such as emergency planners, and that of the individual, i.e., evacuees. The behavioural issues encompass the complications that arise due to the disparity between these two processes. Factors that contribute to the disparity include inadequate information, unclear goals and poorly defined procedures. Klein (1998) discusses the recognition-primed decision (RPD) model that can be used to understand individual decision making behaviour under time pressure, as is the case in evacuation. The model attempts to understand two processes; firstly, how do decision makers size up a situation to recognise which course of action makes sense? Secondly, how do they evaluate that course of action by imagining it?

The disparity issues between the authorities and the evacuees can be analysed by applying this model to the decision making process of these two major groups of players in the evacuation process. An interesting "disaster life-cycle" model that can be used to view human reactions to any type of disaster is discussed by Park (1989) in the context of the lessons drawn by the Three Mile Island incident and the Chernobyl disaster. It is a simple model which summarises human reactions to a disaster by allowing activities and priorities at various stages in coping with a disaster to be examined in context and providing the monitoring of human adjustment at different timescales. Srinivasan, Sundaram, and Davis (2000) discuss the importance of programmability and structuredness in decision making when designing a decision support system. Decision making in the evacuation process and most real-world problem processes lean more towards the unstructured and/or nonprogrammable end. The challenge then is to model the problem and the decision making process with minimal abstraction from the real-world situation.

LOGISTICS

Logistical problems in evacuation can arise during the warning process, when transporting and providing accommodation for large numbers of evacuees or while administering protective measures, etc. (see Efrat, 1991; Lindell et al., 1985). Brandsjö (1988) mentions the enormous procedural difficulties faced during the evacuations associated with the Chernobyl accident. The examples include having to remove large quantities of shoes and clothing from evacuees before they left the area as these contained a high level of radiation and having to find replacement clothing for evacuees, coupled together with the lack of trust in the authorities by the evacuees.

A comprehensive discussion of evacuation planning concepts and decision criteria is reported by Lindell et al. (1985) for the National Environmental Studies

Project of the Atomic Industrial Forum of USA. Covering issues relating to both sheltering and evacuation, it identifies factors, such as the radius of the area within which the public is going to be evacuated, delay time between warning and the start of evacuation, speed of evacuation, and changing meteorological conditions during evacuation, that need to be addressed in planning evacuation activities. Alternative modes of transport, identifying facilities requiring special consideration, such as schools and hospitals, protective health measures for the vulnerable population, etc., also need to be investigated.

In planning evacuations, often the consequences of deciding to end the evacuation are overlooked. The same behaviour and logistic issues largely apply at this stage of the evacuation process. Conflicts can arise between evacuees and public officials about the timing and return of evacuees back to the affected region and there may be procedural difficulties in the return of a large evacuee population to the affected region (Gillespie & Murty, 1991). An overall evacuation plan therefore must include plans for this final aspect of the evacuation process.

SCENARIO GENERATION

In order to increase the range of scenarios that can be generated by the simulator, information is needed on a variety of factors. For example, effects of weather patterns, road accidents, extreme behaviour of individuals, route choice behaviour, timing of any warnings, and the effect of wind speed on the dynamics of the radioactive plume may be used when modelling an incident. One way of including this type of information, which can be of a subjective nature especially where evacuee behaviour assumptions are concerned, is the inclusion of a knowledge base that provides the traffic model with expert information input to the simulation as the need arises. A more complex rule base would need to be developed in order to utilise this information for a more intricate scenario generation process. For example, consider the likely situation in an evacuation where the traffic is directed by the police to various shelters according to the information on traffic congestion, closure of roads and current capacity of shelters. This would restrict the behaviour of the evacuee in making his/her own judgements on route finding on the road network. The information needs to be fed into the simulation via an information base, which releases the necessary information in the appropriate format. Provision of functions to perform multistage/multiphased evacuations further enhances the scenario generation process.

As in the case of the CEMPS traffic simulation model, behaviour functions are designed under various simplifying assumptions. For instance, it is often assumed when behaviour functions are designed that evacuees will respond to a warning to evacuate promptly. Realistically assumptions should reflect the fact that there would be certain delays associated with the time the evacuees actually embark on their evacuation journey. These can be modelled according to a suitable warning-response behaviour pattern. Some statistical methods have been employed for this purpose in evacuation models developed in the past (see Hobeika & Jamie, 1985; Southworth, 1991; Stern & Sinuany-Stern, 1989). This initial behaviour of the evacuees at the start of the evacuation process will determine how the evacuation progresses in the following stages.

The accuracy of predicting evacuee behaviour and the detail required for modelling this behaviour depend on whether the simulator uses a micro, meso or a macro modelling approach. The micro approach concentrates on simulating the behaviour of each individual evacuating entity while the macro approach concentrates on using flow equations that grossly average evacuee behaviour. The meso approach attempts to strike a balance between the two by averaging behaviour among groups/batches of evacuees. The choice between the three very much depends on the trade-offs that need to be made in order to maintain realistic computing power when processing large amounts of data. The flexibility provided for scenario generation increases with the more micro approach adopted for behaviour modelling.

VALIDATING ASSUMPTIONS

A simulator is intended to mimic a real-world system using the actual data associated with the real-world system. It uses assumptions that generally simplify the complex behaviour of this real-world system (Banks, Carson, & Nelson, 1996). These assumptions fall into two categories: **structural assumptions** which involve simplification and abstraction of reality on issues involving the operation and the processes of the system, and **data assumptions** which are based on the collection of reliable data and its proper analysis.

CEMPS is intended for use at different levels of detail the user feels is appropriate. This means that the experimental frame cannot be straightforwardly specified, which in turn makes validation of structural assumptions very difficult. Thus trade-offs are inevitable in providing a balance between flexibility to the user and realistic validation of these assumptions.

The validation of structural assumptions can proceed in several ways. The extent to which evacuee movement is modelled accurately depends on the framework defined for the simulation experiment. Assumptions are typically made on speed of movement of evacuating traffic and behaviour of evacuating vehicles on the road network. The simulated times taken to move evacuating vehicles between two known points on a road network under defined traffic conditions could be compared with those found to be the case in real life. It may be necessary to observe a very large number of vehicle movements on a road network before relying on the data for such a comparison. Similarly, the effect of stochastic occurrences, such as vehicle breakdowns and accidents, as well as control interventions, such as the closure of roads or lanes, could be compared with the effects that these would have in the real-world system. This would be a complex, time-consuming operation but would nevertheless help build confidence in the model. Balci and Sargent (1984) and Miser and Quade (1988) discuss the problems associated with such validation in relation to large-scale military simulations.

The data assumptions, in general, are based on the collection of reliable data and the proper analysis of this data. The data used in this research are those relating to the Heysham nuclear power station and its environs in the northwest of England and have been obtained from reliable geographical data sources. They are static data relating to the spatial location of each data point. The data is geo-referenced according to standard formats and conventions and thus, in this sense, validated in relation to its geographical situation. However, the data that need proper validation and analysis are those data sets that relate to the dynamic behaviour of the elements in the system, such as those relating to the behaviour of the evacuating vehicles on the road network in relation to time and the growing emergency and evacuee behaviour toward warning which would affect the time they start their evacuation journey, etc. This is much affected by the difficulty of obtaining historical data on previous similar incidents.

VALIDATING THE SDSS

Validating a spatial decision support system is by no means a straightforward process and there is no clear-cut formula that is generally applicable. When the SDSS deals with decision making for situations that occur frequently, there is the possibility of comparing the consequences of instances of decisions taken without the aid of the SDSS with those that have been taken with the aid of the SDSS. Such a comparison can be carried out using a suitable method of investigation such as a Turing test (see Norlen, 1972). The purpose of the Turing test is to find out to what extent it is possible to discriminate between the model and the modelled. The testing process in this instance is made simpler due to the fact that the data and information required for the analysis and experimentation are likely to be readily available. Clearly any validation procedure used on an SDSS should include at the least a validation of the output and of any underlying models.

In an SDSS dealing with complex problem situations that are unique or occur rarely, which is the case with emergency situations, validation of its output and underlying models becomes extremely difficult. Historical data are not easy to come by and are often nonexistent or incomplete. In politically or socially sensitive problems like nuclear disasters, access to historical data on the resulting disaster management activities is heavily restricted, preventing public access to information. This is especially so for recent events. One method that can be used in these situations is to make a comparative study of existing decision support tools that are applicable and evaluate the performance of the SDSS in relation to them. This, however, is not a satisfactory method of validation, as the other tools that are compared with the SDSS may not have the same output functions or decision support goals as the SDSS.

According to Norlen (1972) validating a simulation model involves estimating how well the model matches its specifications. This is a difficult task and many suggestions have been made on various approaches to model validation. For example there are standard validating methods such as the three-step approach described by Law and Kelto (1991). Banks et al. (1996) encompasses the idea of maintaining contact with the potential decision makers throughout the design stage, aiming to develop a model that seems reasonable to the user, using historical data for experimentation, and finally the evaluation of the output. In the case of the CEMPS simulation model these methods cannot be applied in full largely due to the lack of historical data and validated experimental data on regional evacuations. Ideally in order to investigate the input-output transformation of an evacuation simulator there should exist several sets of different case study data so that one is able to obtain a reasonable range of outputs for investigating the efficiency of the system. This process can be severely hampered by lack of access to historical data. It is also not appropriate to quote output statistics such as runtime as they depend on factors such as the scenario being investigated, the degree of detail required, the computer hardware and operating system that are used, etc. According to Zeigler (1976) the only way models can be validated is by comparing them against specified experimental frames, placing the model in the context of its intended use. He also observes that a simulation model that has general validity does not exist. Furthermore, Paul and Hlupic (1994) argue that since the real world is dynamic, so are its problems and systems. Thus, they conclude that models cannot be validated against the real-world system they represent, are especially as the real-world system is not static. These viewpoints emphasise the difficulty of validating any simulation model.

IMPLICATIONS OF PROGRESS IN TECHNOLOGY

A flurry of research activity is currently taking place in the development of complex emergency planning and management systems that can handle a disaster that would, for instance, affect the whole of Europe. Of particular interest is the RODOS project (Real-time Online DecisiOn Support) involving major research institutions of several nations of Europe (Kelly & Ehrhardt, 1996; Papamichail & French, 1999). This project has sprung as a result of the lessons learned from Chernobyl and involves developing a decision support system for off-site emergency management that would be broadly applicable across Europe. It also aims to provide greater transparency in the decision process by facilitating improved communication between countries for monitoring data, prediction of consequences, etc. in the event of a future accident that may affect Europe. Another joint European project which also includes the design of tools for evacuation management is the MEMbrain project (Quasar Consultants (A/S), 1993 & 1997). This project involves the development of an integrated software platform for emergency management that includes several components, including a GIS and a decision support system, that will aid public protection and emergency management. The increasingly prominent role GIS play in providing decision support tools for the emergency planning and management process is emphasised by Fedra (1998). He discusses the various risk management and emergency planning systems that have been recently developed or are presently being developed, such as XENVIS, which have firmly based their design on the integration of spatial technology to provide for spatial decision making.

Interesting developments have also taken place recently in devising globally accessible, networked decision support tools for emergency planners using the Internet. One such development is PREMIS, the Pacific Regional Emergency Management Information System, designed to aid civil defence emergency management activities within the state of Hawaii, USA (Hawaii State Civil Defence, 1997). The interesting feature of this system is that it is driven by a GIS called the Integrated Emergency Management Information System (IEMIS)/ Integrated Baseline System (IBS). IEMIS supports the mapping functions while IBS supports computer-based modelling, including the response of transportation networks in evacuations, radiation dose rates, etc.

TRENDS FOR THE 21ST CENTURY

The advancements taking place in computer technology will have a profound effect on the future of SDSS. These include intelligent transport systems (ITS), expert systems technology/knowledge-based decision support architecture, global positioning systems (GPS), etc. The various ways in which ITS technology, such as highway advisory radio, variable message signs, video technology and fog warning systems, can be integrated to enhance decision support in evacuation situations is discussed by Kilim, McFadden, Pal, Karri, and Graettinger (2001). They also discuss how GPS can be used to produce accurate digital data on the transportation network and the location of shelters. Mobile positioning systems can also be developed using GPS technology with mobile communication systems to track moving entities such as evacuating vehicles. The designing of intelligent SDSS by coupling a GIS with an expert system is discussed by Zhu and Healey (1992). Spatial decision making is based on two streams: that of the quantitative, which includes data analysis and modelling, and that of the qualitative, which includes experience, intuition, judgement and specialist expertise. Current GIS concentrate on providing facilities for the quantitative aspects of this process and largely ignore the qualitative aspects of the process, such as the influence of knowledge and personal preferences of the evacuees on their route choice behaviour. The inclusion of expert systems, which perform decision making tasks using rules defined by experts in the area, would greatly enhance the aids for qualitative spatial decision making within GIS, and so also in SDSS. Not only do such advancements affect the future of GIS, they also have a profound effect on traffic simulation models. Ritchie (1990) discusses an artificial intelligence based solution approach to providing decision support to traffic management systems. Such systems focus on multiuser access and processing applications.

The rapid development of Internet technology has a significant effect on how new decision support tools are designed for geographically dispersed problems such as complex emergencies spanning several countries. A typical example would be a regional war where evacuation, resettlement, disease control, logistics of aid distribution, etc. are issues that may require decision making input from several countries. Systems such as HITERM (see Fedra, 1998), which use Internet technology to access monitoring systems to obtain meteorological, traffic and sensor data, also use high-performance computing networks to obtain better real-time solutions to such complex simulation models. Technology, such as GPS, which enables the identification of locations on the surface of the earth to a great degree of accuracy via satellite technology makes it possible for GIS to perform real-time operations to a great degree of spatial accuracy. These advanced technologies, which have already been introduced to real-time emergency management processes, will have a profound effect on the way SDSS are designed in the future.

Significant attempts are being made to harness emergency planning activities and resources available around the world through modern technologies so that disaster preparedness can not only draw in the efforts of local emergency planners but can also draw in expertise, information and resources from all over the globe. One such major effort is the GEMINI project (Global Emergency Management Information Network Initiative), which has directed its efforts not only to develop a global networked system to rapidly access resources and exchange information around the world but also to define standards for information and establish global protocols (Anderson, 1995). Following in the footsteps of the GEMINI project, the GDIN (Global Disaster Information Network; www.gdin.org) initiative aims to improve the effectiveness and interoperability of global systems for sharing natural disaster information, especially maps and data generated by remote and land-based sensors. This project has been set in motion with the collaboration of all players in the emergency planning and management arena, such as national governments, international organisations, NGOs, academia, corporate partners, etc.. The driving force for this effort has been the developments in Internet technology. It is evident that the future of emergency planning decision support is set to strongly focus on a global approach with enormous reliance on GIS, Internet and related technologies.

CONCLUSION

This chapter has attempted to highlight and discuss challenging issues that are encountered in using and merging technologies to design SDSS for evacuation planning. The highlights include realistic modelling of evacuee behaviour, decision making processes that take place during an evacuation, logistics, generating realistic scenarios, validation and technology development and trends for the future. These issues are discussed via lessons learned in developing the prototype SDSS CEMPS, while generic issues are discussed in light of using simulation and GIS technology for designing such systems for emergency planning.

As technology evolves, so will the design challenges and opportunities, stressing a need to tackle successfully the fundamental issues discussed here so that new and evolving technologies are able to aid the decision making process in disaster management, while improving the integrity and reliability of the decisions made.

ACKNOWLEDGMENTS

This research was funded by the UK Economic and Social Research Council (grant reference R000233382). Thanks is due to Prof. Tony Gatrell and Dr. Robin Flowerdew of the Department of Geography, Lancaster University, and the staff of the North West Regional Research Laboratory for their support in the CEMPS project.

REFERENCES

Anderson. (1995). Global Emergency Management Information Network Initiative (GEMINI) - progress report - Halifax summit - June 1995. (http://hoshi.cic.sfu.ca/~g7/progressG7.html)

Balci, O. & Sargent, R.G. (1984). A bibliography on the credibility, assessment and validation of simulation and mathematical models. *Simuletter, 15*(3), 15-27.

Banks, J., Carson, J. S., & Nelson, B. L. (1996). Discrete-event system simulation (2nd ed.). NJ: Prentice Hall.

Batty, M. (1994). Using GIS for visual simulation modelling. *GIS World, 7*(10), 46-48.

Batty, M. & Densham, P. (1996). Decision support, GIS and urban planning. *Sistema Terra, 5*(1), 72-76.

Belardo, S., & Wallace, W. A. (1981). The design and test of a microcomputer based decision support system for disaster management. *DSS-81 Transactions*, D. Young & P.G.W. Keen (Eds.), *Proceedings of the International Conference on Decision Support Systems*, 152-164.

Brandsjö, K. (1988). Nuclear accidents—Chernobyl, a warning. *Disaster Management, 1*(2), 36-41.

Church, R. L., Murray, A. T., Figueroa, M. A., & Barber, K. H. (2000). Support system development for forest ecosystem management. *European Journal of Operational Research*, 121, 247-258.

Cutter, S. & Barnes, K. (1982). Evacuation behaviour and Three Mile Island. *Disasters, 6*(2), 116-124.

Densham, P. (1991). Spatial decision support systems. In D.J. Maguire, M.F. Goodchild, & D.W. Rhind (Eds.), *Geographical Information Systems: Principles and applications*, (Vol. 1, pp. 403-412) Harlow, UK: Longman.

Efrat, E. (1992). The geography of a population mass-escape from the Tel Aviv area during the Gulf War. *The Geographical Journal*, *158*(2), 199-206.

Fedra, K. (1998). Integrated risk assessment and management: Overview and state-of-the-art. *Journal of Hazardous Materials*, 61, 5-22.

Fedra, K. & Reitsma, R. F. (1990). Decision support and geographical information systems. Geographical information systems for urban and regional planning, Research report: RR-90-009, ACA, International Institute for Applied Systems Analysis (IIASA), Laxenburg, Austria.

Gillespie, D. F. & Murty, S.A. (1991). Setting boundaries for research on organizational capacity to evacuate. *International Journal of Mass Emergencies and Disasters*, 9(2), 201-218.

Hawaii State Civil Defence. (1997). Section 3: Pacific Regional Emergency Management Information System (PREMIS) baseline. (http://scd.hawaii.gov/pdc/premis.htm)

Herrnberger, V. (1996). Radiological emergency management. (www.psi.ch/~beer/rem_home.html)

Hobeika, A. G. & Jamie, B. (1985). MASSVAC: A model for calculating evacuation times under natural disaster. In J.M. Carroll (Ed.), *Emergency Planning, Simulation Series*, 15, 23-28.

Johnson, J. H. Jr. (1985). A model of evacuation-decision making in a nuclear reactor emergency. *The Geographical Review*, 75, 405-418.

Kelly, G.N. & Ehrhardt, J. (1996). RODOS—A comprehensive decision support system for off-site emergency management. (*www.scs.leeds.ac.uk/rodos/rodos_rp1.html*)

Kilim, R. R., McFadden, J., Pal, A., Karri, V. R., & Graettinger, A. (2001). *Evaluation of evacuation procedures during extreme weather events for the gulf coast of Alabama.* Paper presented at the *2001 Traffic Records Forum—27th International Forum on Traffic Records and Highway Information Systems.* Retrieved at www.traffic-records.org/forum2001/S_04/McFadden_paper.pdf

Klein, G. (1998). Sources of power: How people make decisions. MA: MIT Press.

Law, A. M. & Kelto, W. D. (1991). Simulation modelling & analysis (2nd ed.). McGraw-Hill, Inc..

Lindell, M. K., Bolton, P. A., Perry, R. W., Stoetzel, G. A., Martin, J. B., & Flynn, C. B. (1985). Planning concepts and decision criteria for sheltering and evacuation in a nuclear power plant emergency. National Environmental Studies Project, Atomic Industrial Forum, Inc., AIF/NESP-031, USA, 202p.

Miser, H. J. & Quade, E. S. (1988). Validation. In H.J. Miser & E.S. Quade (Eds.), *Handbook of systems analysis: Craft issues and procedural choices*, (pp. 527-565) Chichester, UK: John Wiley & Sons.

Mondschein, L. G. (1994). The role of spatial information systems in environmental emergency management. *Journal of the American Society for Information Science*, 45(9), 678-685.

Norlen, U. (1972). Simulation model building: A statistical approach to modelling in the social sciences with the simulation method. Uppsala, Sweden: Almqvist & Wiksell Informationsindustri AB.

Papamichail, K. N. & French, S. (1999). Generating feasible strategies in nuclear emergencies—A constraint satisfaction problem. *Journal of the Operational Research Society*, 50, 617-626.

Park, C. C. (1989). The disaster life cycle and human adjustments: Lessons from Three Mile Island and Chernobyl. In J.I. Clarke, P. Curson, S.L. Kayastha, & P. Nag (Eds.), *Population and Disaster* (Chap. 13, pp. 193-205) Oxford: Institute of British Geographers & Blackwell, 292p.

Paul, R. J. & Hlupic, V. (1994). The CASM environment revisited. In J.D. Tew, S. Manivannan, D.A. Sadowski, & A.F. Seila (Eds.), *Proceedings of the 1994 Winter Simulation Conference*, (pp. 641-648) San Diego, CA: Society for Computer Simulation.

Pidd, M., de Silva, F. N., & Eglese, R. W. (1996). A simulation model for emergency evacuation. *European Journal of Operational Research*, *90*(3), 413-419.

Plunkett, B. (1993, May). In *Proceedings of the Thirteenth annual ESRI User Conference* (pp. 151-155) Redlands, CA: Environmental Systems Research Institute, Inc..

Quasar Consultants. (A/S) (1993). Accident development and evacuation management—Quasar's work-packages. In *MEMbrain, A/S Quasar Consultants-report,* Oslo, Norway, 9p.

Quasar Consultants. (A/S) (1997). MEMbrain. (www.quasar.no/MEMBRAIN/ Membrain.htm)

Ritchie, S. G. (1990). A knowledge-based decision support architecture for advanced traffic management. *Transportation Research A*, *24A*(1), 27-37.

Silva, F. N., de, & Eglese, R. W. (2000). Integrating simulation modelling and GIS: Spatial decision support systems for evacuation planning. *Journal of the Operational Research Society—Special Issue on Progress in Simulation Research*, *51*(4), 423-430.

Sorensen, J. H., Vogt, B. M., & Mileti, D. S. (1987). Evacuation: An assessment of planning and research. Oak Ridge National Laboratory for Federal Emergency Management Agency, ORNL-6376 (FEMA publication RR-9), ORNL, Oak Ridge, TN, 234p.

Southworth, F. (1991). Regional evacuation modelling: A state-of-the-art review. Oak Ridge National Laboratory, Energy Division, ORNL/TM-11740, Oak Ridge, TN.

Srinivasan, A., Sundaram, D., & Davis, J. (2000). Implementing decision support systems: Methods, techniques and tools. *Information Systems Series*, Maindenhead: McGraw-Hill, 161p.

Stern, E. & Sinuany-Stern, Z. (1989). A behavioural-based simulation model for urban evacuation. In *Papers of the Regional Science Association*, 66, 87-103.

Zeigler, B. P. (1976). Theory of modelling and simulation. New York: John Wiley & Sons, 435p.

Zhu, X. & Healey, R. (1992). Towards intelligent spatial decision support. Integrating geographical information systems and expert systems. In *Proceedings of the GIS/LIS '92 Annual Conference*, 877-886.

Chapter XXII

Knowledge Management and Sharing

Bee K. Yew
Illinois Business Training Center, USA

WeiXiong Ho
Callisma Incorporated, USA

Marvin D. Troutt
Kent State University, USA

ABSTRACT

The knowledge economy is driven by growth and development of intellectual capital in organizations. Knowledge is defined to be reusable abstractions that can produce new knowledge and modify existing knowledge. Decision making, which includes task solving, is a common feature of the working organization, and it requires good knowledge as input. This chapter provides a review of the knowledge management (KM) concepts and perspectives, with an introduction to the knowledge management Systems (KMS) and its related technologies. The importance of a knowledge base for KM and knowledge sharing (KS) activities is illustrated for Callisma, a consulting firm. Models for knowledge cycle and conversions are covered to provide further theory for KM research. KS, in particular, is an important concern for a knowledge organization as it is believed that effective knowledge sharing or better knowledge utilization can result in increased organizational capabilities as defined by competitiveness, efficiency, competency, and creativity. The inquiring models based on Kant, Hegel, Locke and Liebnitz mental models are presented to provide an analytical framework for knowledge creating and sharing activities.

INTRODUCTION

The Webster dictionary defines knowledge to be a fact or condition of knowing with a considerable degree of familiarity gained through experience. An individual's knowledge is personal and serendipitous and changes in content, form and applications. Organization knowledge, however, requires an understanding that the collective knowledge of its members ranging from business strategists to customer service representatives is an asset to be deployed for organization success. This collective knowledge is known as the organization intellectual capital. Though not accountable in today's accounting and financial systems, organizations must be active in investing or recruiting knowledge-possessing individuals to continue to exist (Sveiby, 2001a). Managing the knowledge assets of individuals in an organization is quite different from managing its fixed assets. This is because knowledge in an organization is both a driver and an outcome of the continuous learning process, which defines its being.

The management of knowledge or better known as knowledge management (KM), is the recent focus of management and organization theorists, business strategists, and top executives. An objective of KM is to gather, categorize, store, and disseminate a firm's collective knowledge. This can be realized through a system of technologies. KM motivations can be summarized as greater knowledge utilization leading to increased organizational capabilities as defined by competitiveness, efficiency, competency, and creativity.

To capitalize on the knowledge in a work group or in an organization unit, processes and tools must exist for effective knowledge sharing and transfers. A system that rewards individual performance would place an organization on the low end of a hypothetical knowledge sharing scale. Therefore the firm's human resource function needs to enhance its recognition and reward system to include identifying and rewarding members who contributed and shared their knowledge with others in the organization.

For knowledge-driven organizations such as consulting, technology, and pharmaceutical firms, knowledge exploitation means profitability, and long-term survivability. Knowledge repositories of consulting firms such as Ernst & Young's Knowledge Center and Accenture's Knowledge Xchange organize their companies' knowledge. Successful implementations of knowledge repositories allow for knowledge sharing, which benefits the organization at all levels. At the very least an improved business operating synergy can be realized from sharing of knowledge about customer and supplier relationships.

KM repositories not only serve the individual who needs to look up information about a methodology, but work teams that are engaged in customer relationship management (CRM), enterprise resource management (ERP) and business reengineering initiatives in organizations. Such repositories consist of knowledge clusters of routine operating procedures, policies, processes, best practices, objectives, patents, and business intelligence. Well-built links that connect knowledge clusters or nodes (as defined by path efficiency and accessibility) can bring about business success. Companies such as AskMe, Knowledge Research Institute, and

AccessSystem specialize in providing KM for clients through consulting, training, and solution implementations. Other KM initiatives, like the Intellectual Asset Management (IAM) at Dow Chemical, have been proven to be effective by achieving a higher return on its intellectual patents.

Communities of practice or of interest are groups formed within the organization to discuss situations faced and how to solve or tackle specific problems. The coming together of employees' minds from diverse geographical locations, where roles are assumed based on abilities and skills and not on titles or hierarchy, is a structural improvement that fosters knowledge sharing.

The Internet plays a critical role in accelerating the rate of exchange of information and knowledge, and it is an excellent reference model and platform for knowledge sharing. A large part of this chapter's knowledge creating and sharing activities is based on information and knowledge acquired from Internet sources. The focus of this chapter will be to examine the different perspectives on KM and their contributions to designing knowledge-based decision support systems, which is also being referred as knowledge management systems (KMS). In our discussions, we will highlight challenging KM issues faced by corporations of today and the strong connection between KM research and decision support systems (DSS). The chapter concludes with an attempt to organize KM research contributions using the "systems thinking" framework and a KM conceptual framework.

KNOWLEDGE MANAGEMENT SYSTEMS (KMS)

Without question, good knowledge should be beneficial if not necessary for decision making. A KMS is an information system that allows members of an organization to access a knowledge repository of "best practices" documents, course materials, and external knowledge sources (Villegas, n.d.). Such a system will also provide collaborative tools for members to seek or to share expertise in various knowledge domains.

In designing systems for decision making members in an organization, mathematical models and knowledge models based on inductive/deductive rule reasoning models are used. Knowledge systems (which include expert systems) based on predicate calculus are good for narrowing the possibilities type of search in case-reasoning applications, which are relatively well-defined problems. Knowledge management systems, however, require an intelligent content manager, support a nonrestrictive user inquiry language, and offer flexibility to users in creating knowledge documents. A content management feature that can be very useful in evaluating KM contributions from members of the organization is reference-tracing in a document creating process. The integration of KM principles in decision support systems requires an understanding of knowledge creation, types of knowledge and their transferability, and knowledge applicability. Knowledge transfer is a process that refers to the delivery and communication of refined knowledge content in training seminars or courses. We think that contributions from cognitive psychology and economics will provide theoretical frameworks for designing effective knowledge management systems. Decision making within group setting is particularly relevant as present business decisions or solutions are more complex and are solved by teams of individuals with expertise in specific knowledge areas. The economics of knowledge exchanges among key participants assuming the roles of seller, broker and buyer can provide further insight on perceptions of value of information and other factors affecting such transactions. Kanevsky and Housel's learning-knowledge-value-spiral examined the value generated by the knowledge conversion process, and provided a valuation model for corporate knowledge. Such knowledge valuation model allows for the evaluation of the effectiveness of KMS and the management of KM processes in the organization.

The design of a traditional DSS is based on the rational decision model. The only distinction between the problem-solving model and the decision making model is that the problem-solving model is a process of phases of activities with these generic labels: problem definition, generation of alternatives, choice, implementation and evaluation; while the decision making model is a proactive process which requires systematic scanning of the environment for detection of opportunities or threats that would trigger activities in the problem definition phase. As knowledge is an important input in this whole process, the presence of a knowledge base is essential to the development and maintenance of organizational competency. The firm's knowledge would include its members' experiences, business intelligence, and specifics about operations. A knowledge-based DSS or KMS allows a user to gain a better understanding of the firm's past experiences in facing business challenges and to update its knowledge base to reflect changes in its operating environment.

Figure 1: A knowledge management system (KMS)

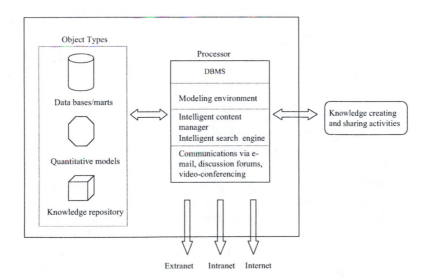

The capabilities of today's decision support systems (DSS) include analytical modeling, database/data warehouse querying, graphing, and reporting, work team collaboration, and desktop management. In comparison, a KMS has a knowledge repository and content management capabilities to support knowledge sharing and creating activities. The integration of knowledge system components into the DSS can be regarded as a system upgrade to meet the knowledge management objectives of an organization. Figure 1 shows a diagram of the components of a KMS.

The user system interface for traditional decision support systems focuses on query-based interactions, which is essentially a sequential, question-answer based interface, with the exception of spreadsheet templates. Such query-based interface components range from standard questions (which require quantifiable inputs as in a mathematical model based DSS) to what is considered to be text-rich query language interface found in a database management system and an expert system. The current technology employed in KMS interface is the "point-click" document link method in enterprise information portals.

In a KMS, the search for knowledge or information is critical. In trying to seek for an answer to a straightforward question on what key factors will have some impact on a client's acquisition decision, a sales engineer may look up "best practices," click on "sales," then click on "successful presentation" in the company's Web portal. Here, the individual will learn about return on investment (ROI) and may next proceed to understand the different types of ROI computations for services and system products. Information about FAQs on the various ROIs would be a link in the intranet web site.

The new generation of search engines is based on the use of context information in user queries. In his paper, Lawrence (2000) discussed the context-based search techniques. Inquirus2, Google and Watson are examples of search engines that employ different strategies in associating explicit and implicit context information. Inquirus2, for example, requests context information through user-selected categories of information such as "Research Paper" and "Personal Homepages" with an added automated learning (intelligent) feature by transforming the user's query with added keywords such as "Abstracts" and "References." Watson is a personalized client-based search service that models the context search information by identifying words that are indicative of the content of document that is being edited by the user. Lawrence also noted that developments are being made in domain-specific search techniques that are able to locate web communities, in which each member in a web community has more links within a community than outside. Member profiling as defined by DelphiGroup (n.d.) refers to the collecting of information related to user interest levels, areas of expertise indicated by work submitted and reviewed, and query habits. We think that profiling of members based on their current project workflow documents is what intelligent search agents should be able to do to deliver relevant knowledge to members' desktops. This is referred to as "push" technology, which is useful for promoting knowledge sharing and transfer. In content management software, indexing is applied to categorize knowledge documents in an organized and intuitive way.

As with any repository technology, the maintenance of knowledge integrity is a concern for a KMS. Changes in rules of competition in the business environment translate to changes in process, product, and relationship knowledge. This calls for a modification of the corporate knowledge base. The task of updating documents in KMS can be aided by an intelligent content management application. Firestone (n.d.) defined content management system functions to be that of processing, filtering, and refining "unstructured" internal and external information in knowledge documents of different formats. It also archives, structures, and stores knowledge documents in KMS. IBM, Microsoft, Sybase, Plumtree, and Hyperion are examples of several KM software technology providers.

Besides contributing to the development of knowledge for accounting/financial reporting, a knowledge creation model is good for understanding factors affecting the explication of hidden or unconscious knowledge in individuals. Nonaka and Takeuchi (1995) described tacit knowledge as deeply rooted in individual's actions and experience, ideals, values or emotions. Their knowledge model consists of four different modes of knowledge creation: socialization, externalization, combination and internalization. Table 1 shows the conversion from one knowledge form to the other for these modes.

Table 1: Conversion from one knowledge form to the other

Modes	Conversion
Socialization	Tacit ⇨ Tacit
Externalization	Tacit ⇨ Explicit
Combination	Explicit ⇨ Explicit
Internalization	Explicit ⇨ Tacit

All these knowledge-creating modes occur in core and supporting business activities of an organization. The data warehousing function, for example, is using online analytical processing (OLAP) and data mining with decision support tools to convert explicit knowledge to tacit knowledge (Burlton, 1998). It is the externalization knowledge-creating mode that draws a greater attention from researchers and practitioners in the KM field. The idea that hidden knowledge of individuals is the "know-how," expertise, and the ability to make sense of a complicated situation characterized by uncertainty, conflicting, and confusing states refers to an untapped knowledge resource that is of value to the organization. The externalization process in individuals is imaginably not easy to mandate. Barriers such as perceived value of transactional exchange, structural and process shortcomings, technology limitations, and personal dispositions need to be addressed. In knowledge-intensive organizations such as consulting firms, members are encouraged to share their knowledge through a performance system that rewards knowledge sharing and activities that lead to it. Technology plays an important role in facilitating such activities. Document management applications, which can provide routing of workflow documents such as reports, white papers, and "best practices," can be thought of as structuralization of the knowledge sharing initiative. The use of document templates for workflow processes allows members to create knowledge in an analytical and complete form.

Communication and collaboration technology includes videoconferencing, e-mail, and Lotus Notes, which support the functioning of virtual work teams whose members are geographically dispersed. A study by Kimble, Li, and Barlow (n.d.) found that a major barrier to virtual team effectiveness is the lack of "a team culture with common communication procedures." The study also concluded that the use of communities of practice (CoP) improves the effectiveness of virtual teams by fostering familiarity among team members.

Table 2: Churchman's inquiring modes and their strategies for gathering information and decision making

Personal Style (Philosopher)	Inquiring Strategy
Synthesist (Hegel)	Seeks conflict and synthesis of contrasting views, gets at underlying assumptions by asking why and why not, and regards data as useless without interpretations.
Idealist (Kant)	Seeks multiple perspectives and ideal solutions and believes in values.
Pragmatist (Singer)	Works from a basis of an eclectic view, emphasizes being innovative and adaptive, and uses a tactical, incremental approach.
Analyst (Leibniz)	Seeks the optimal outcome and operates with quantitative models.
Realist (Locke)	Places importance on "facts" and expert opinions, seeks solutions that meet current needs, serious about getting concrete results, and acts with efficiency and clear-cut correction.

Mental models suggested by Churchman (1971) for designing information systems are based on philosophical-based inquiring modes. A summary of Churchman's inquiring modes and their strategies for gathering information and decision making is provided in Table 2.

From a technologist point of view, inquiring styles can be incorporated in a KMS. As an example, the development of multiple contrasting and complementary views in the documentation of "best practices" is useful because it reveals more contextual information about the case, and underlying assumptions are explicated in the process. Templates that pose questions will assist knowledge contributors in creating these documents that are shared with others within the organization. As discussed earlier, indexing and intelligent searching technologies are applied to retrieve (and to deliver) these archived, up-to-date knowledge contents. We hypothesized that over time the usage of KMS with an inquiring feature will benefit the organization members by enhancing their knowledge competencies.

KM BACKGROUND

Numerous contributions from KM consultants and IT professionals who are knowledge workers provide valuable insights to the challenges of leveraging on the collective knowledge of an organization. These challenges include how to increase the level of knowledge sharing, protect corporate knowledge, and improve the search for relevant pieces of information (Svetvilas, 2001). Not to be neglected in the collection of KM contributions is the theoretical aspect of the field, which consists of abstract ideas, logical arguments or persuasions, principles, models, and frameworks that lay the foundation for applied research.

KM is about recognizing and capturing members' expertise on products and services, technology, processes and relationships and fostering sharing of expertise among members in an organization. In comparison, TQM (total quality management) is meeting customer needs through quality circles and breakdown of interdepartmental barriers to facilitate communications and cooperative performance reviews. There are certain similarities between knowledge and quality. Both concepts have been defined and explained in many different ways, and technology plays an important role in effecting structural changes within the organization to achieve KM and TQM (total quality management) goals. Success in implementing effective KM and TQM initiatives still depends on the human qualities, such as leadership, attitude and trust. Teamwork is highly valued, and members are encouraged to freely exchange knowledge, thoughts, and ideas to improve existing conditions or to come up with innovative business and technological solutions. In Arveson's (1999) model of the relationship between KM and Kaplan and Norton's balanced scorecard, KM is the first step in the chain of causes and effects for strategic success that leads to business process improvement. A TQM concept, business process improvement is a TQM principle based on employee feedback on process improvements.

KM is what was commonly referred to as knowledge transfer within a firm (Villegas, n.d.). Knowledge transfer is very different today from the master-apprentice relationship of the industrial revolution era. Increasingly, organizations are finding that technology and knowledge transfer need to be closely interwoven to take on the dynamics of a fast-changing business environment.

One marketing theme for KM can be as follows: When knowledge is available, whether it is tacit or explicit, the process of relearning such knowledge (due to failure in exploiting it) translates to costly learning experiences for the organization. The importance of having archives in a corporate knowledge base is therefore to reduce cases of "reinventions" and to increase cases of "newly rediscovered" knowledge transfers (Villegas, n.d.). The costs to the organization in reinventing the learning wheel and ineffective knowledge utilization will be conceivably higher if the operating business environment is "wicked" as described by Malhotra (2000a).

The learning organization is defined in DelphiGroup (n.d.) Language of Knowledge as "an organization with the necessary practices, culture, and systems to promote the continuous sharing of experience and lessons known." Being a learning organization may increase the organization's capability in leveraging its knowledge base and prevents it from being phased out in marketplace competition.

An important KM issue is the valuation of a firm's knowledge stock. This is clearly evident from the recent downfall of dot.com companies largely funded by venture capitalists. The overinflated stock price valuations were based in part on the unsystematic approach used in valuation of companie's knowledge stock by investors. Corporate knowledge stock includes marketing prowess, technology innovations, and management ingenuity. Sveiby (2001c) referred to the "invisible" intangible part of the company's balance sheet in annual report as being made up of three components: internal structure, external structure and individual competence. The internal structure includes "patents, concepts, models, and computer and administrative systems," while the external structure is the "relationships with customers and suppliers, brand names, trademarks and reputation." Individual competence, on the other hand, refers to the skills, abilities, experience, and "know-how" of employees.

KM is not a new way of thinking or a management philosophy, as knowledge has long been accepted to be a critical asset that sustains the organization. KM initiatives can be referred to as a formalization of organizational activities in knowledge transfers and exploitations. However, it has been reported that only 2% of intellectual capital of organizations is leveraged, which is equivalent to 2% knowledge capacity utilization. In comparison, 70 to 95% of capacity utilization is achieved in manufacturing industries (Svetvilas, 2001).

ORGANIZATION KNOWLEDGE BASE

Highly intensive knowledge organizations such as consulting firms have knowledge bases for their business and technical knowledge. Figure 2 is an illustration of

Figure 2: Illustration of an extended knowledge base (KB) for Callisma

Knowledge Base of an Organization

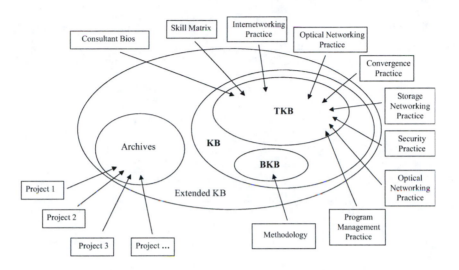

an extended knowledge base (KB) for Callisma, a consulting firm headquartered in Silicon Valley, CA, and in the business of providing technology solutions. The firm's KB consists of the technical knowledge base (TKB) and business knowledge base (BKB). The extended KB includes archives of documents related to project management, such as weekly progress reports, deliverables, project books, billing statements, travel arrangements, and user groups. TKB contains staff biographies and skill matrix, "best practices," product-related experiences, news and updates, white papers, library, and technical notes. The elements of BKB include business lessons learned, methodology, client relations, post-engagement reviews, and pricing. The methodology in BKB represents the firm's general business practice and organization culture and values. From the business perspective, it is the business methodology that differentiates a firm from its competitors. The methodology in BKB provides guidance for each step of the complete business cycle and ensures the success of the project by significantly lowering project cost through prevention of reinventing the wheel, shortening project duration, increasing productivity, and creating values for both the firm and its client.

KM DEFINITIONS

Table 3 provides a table listing of conceptual definitions for KM from online sources.

Is knowledge inclusive of information? Information is static and context-independent. Knowledge, on the other hand, can be regarded as interpretations and

Table 3: Listing of conceptual definitions for KM from online sources

Source	KM conceptual definitions
DelphiGroup (n.d.) www.delphigroup.com	Leveraging of collective wisdom to increase responsiveness and innovation
Acquire Data www.acquire-data.com	Focuses on ways of sharing and storing knowledge to improve speed, efficiency, and competency of members, thereby increasing profitability
Miskie, Ron (n.d.) www.ktic.com	A strategic thinking that produces an increase in one's capacity to take action
Villegas, Robert Jr. (n.d.) www.insmkt.com/kmorder.htm	A system of technologies focused upon the delivery of strategically useful knowledge and expertise, the availability of which facilitates effective collaboration and timely decision making
Hoyt Consulting (2001) www.hoytconsulting.com	Connecting people to people and people to information to create competitive advantage

is intangible. It requires learning and exposure for effective transfer (Villegas, n.d.). Knowledge is referred to as reusable abstractions such as equations, principles, rules, insights, recipes, models, templates, and diagrams which lend to understanding and are valuable in decision making (Lang, n.d.). Knowledge can be defined in terms of its visibility to other members and categories such as product/services, human, process, innovation, and relationship. Knowledge reflects the "know-how" in searching and assimilating relevant information to generate good, feasible solutions to situations. Seiner (2000) defines knowledge as an understanding that is acquired through personal experience or the study of factual information. In an ill- to moderate-structured decision domain and context, knowledge possession includes the ability to filter information by eliminating irrelevant and inaccurate information, and to evaluate multiple, complementary as well as noncomplementary (conflicting) perspectives on the subject. According to Hoyt Consulting (2001), knowledge is based on context and exists in both tacit and explicit forms. The tacit form of knowledge is experiential based and includes insights and intuitions, while the explicit form of knowledge can be described by information in databases, warehouses/marts, manuals, software codes, and guidelines.

KNOWLEDGE CYCLE

The process of knowledge creation in the organization can be described as the knowledge creation cycle, which is comprised of the personal and collective cycles (Hoyt Consulting, 2001). In the personal knowledge cycle, knowledge is created from experiential exposure to information from various sources including e-mails and meetings, moderated by the serendipity factor. Absorption of new filtered information from a variety of sources can further modify, enhance, and improve existing personal knowledge. The collective cycle refers to the categorization, augmentation, and modification of knowledge though contextual understanding. Essentially, this is a process from which information is acquired and shared in the organization.

Knowledge can be further described as synthesized information from multiple sources. The acquisition of knowledge is visualized to be in iterative stages and these stages are labeled as exposure, evaluation, and knowing. In the exposure stage, new information (conflicting and complementary) is encountered through some search and retrieval mechanism. In the evaluation stage, these knowledge artifacts are then examined, filtered, and evaluated for their values in knowledge enhancement. The knowing stage refers to the integration of filtered knowledge artifacts into a current knowledge base.

The LFM-SDM knowledge cycle (n.d.) theorized that the tighter coupling of four steps: knowledge generation, knowledge development, knowledge transfer and knowledge need and use, will result in a greater rate of knowledge production that would then lead to increased organizational competency. The activities in these steps are outlined in Figure 3.

We believe that the design of a KMS system is an undertaking that requires an understanding of the process of knowledge creation and knowledge renewal (or

Figure 3: Activities in the four steps of the LFM-SDM knowledge cycle

Knowledge Steps	Activities
1. Generation	build knowledge base through research, adaptation, discovery & experience
	⇩
2. Development	transform raw knowledge into codified principles and practices
	⇩
3. Transfer	produce documentation and skills to facilitate knowledge delivery
	⇩
4. Need & Use	implement and adjust knowledge to meet customer needs

updating). The creation of web portals, enterprise portals included, is an example of applying knowledge categorizations and associations to facilitate information search. In KMS, the enterprise portal allows users to freely navigate and search for information (both internal and external) through links to knowledge documents stored in a global network of servers.

One should also recognize that a strong adherence to certain beliefs or values could be a hindrance to creative thoughts or approaches to a business situation. Our recommendation for sound decision making is to include contextual information in evaluating a business situation. Loyalty to a system of beliefs and the practice of minimizing risks in decision making, as in the unquestioning mode of applying "best practices," may result in bad business decisions. The issue here is that the "non-inquiry" mode of operation can pose an internal threat to the organization. But how can the non-inquiring way of deciding be discouraged, when there is a penalty for ineffective decisions in a performance-driven company? We think that the payoff in trusting employees to do their best for the company will eventually outweigh the costs of non-rewarded actions. As in the inspiring Maslow's human self-actualization level (1968), the assumption that employees are acting on rationale and have the knowledge to act is one approach to encouraging creativity and calculated risk-taking decisions. This view is supported with an example from Nordstrom's two-sentence policy manual, "Use your good judgement in all situations. There is no additional rule" (Taylor, 1994). Creative decisions, novel approaches to solutions, and non-status-quo actions can only subsist through appropriate recognition and the adoption of a culture that values rational unconventionality. Further support can be found in the learning organization for which there is continuity of new ideas from members resulting in knowledge advancements, new knowledge and addenda to existing knowledge.

KM CONTRIBUTIONS AND SUGGESTIONS

Based on our research, we think that further developments in knowledge sharing, knowledge creation and knowledge metrics will lead to development of effective KMS and improve organizational structures for management of knowledge. Our goal in this final section of our chapter is to try to make sense of a key subset of these contributions by summarizing, organizing and synthesizing them in a meaningful way. Sveiby (2001b) analyzed the contributions in the KM field and concluded that there are two tracks of research: IT track and people track, at two different levels: organization perspective and individual perspective. Rossett and Donello (n.d.) provided a review of KM for training professionals and highlighted two perspectives on KM. The first perspective views KM to be an object that can be captured and transferred. This had led to the technology development to collect and disseminate knowledge. The second views KM to be a process that is unique to each individual. This is responsible for the creation of "communities of practice" (CoP).

KM CONCEPTUAL FRAMEWORK

KM perspectives can be organized into three groups of KM thinking based on the concept of knowledge. The first group embraces the view that knowledge is less visible and intangible; knowledge is hidden and not widely shared among members due to the fact that there is little or no derived value in knowledge sharing activities. The focus here is on shortcomings in management process. Existing management process solutions include formation of CoPs and coupling of KM initiatives with human resources (HR) function.

Another group of contributors looks at KM as information and that it exists everywhere in the organization: memos, e-mail exchanges, intranet discussion forums, project management documents, data warehouse, and manuals. Extracting information and storing it in a meaningful way constitute managing knowledge in an organization. The direction provided is to treat KM as an implementation issue with references to technology solutions such as that of data mining, data warehouses, search engines, content management, and document management.

Finally, the group that looks at knowledge as a creative process requires an understanding of how knowledge is created, stored, accessed or disseminated and used. The LFM-SDM knowledge cycle (n.d.) and Nonaka and Takeuchi's (1995) knowledge conversion modes are examples. Contributions from this perspective include better understanding of factors leading to knowledge creating, sharing and transfer. This has implications in discovery of innovative ways to increase levels of knowledge activities. Drucker (as cited in Arveson, 1999) pointed out that it is the innovations of creative members in an organization that provide the only guarantee for long-term success and competitiveness. This underscores knowledge use as an important but so far little-studied dimension of KM. Creativity can be regarded as highly effective knowledge use. It can surface the kinds of questions that lead to potentially relevant knowledge. Closely related is the way experts solve situational problems that are studied in the field called naturalistic decision making (NDM). Several connections between KM and NDM are discussed in Meso, Troutt, and Rudnicka (2002).

"SYSTEMS THINKING" FRAMEWORK

"Systems thinking" can be applied to an integrated view of KM perspectives. The input-oriented KM research calls for an assessment of current knowledge base, and transformation of the existing knowledge stock to support overall business strategy. A combination of indexing, searching, and push technologies is applied to organize, search, and deliver knowledge artifacts (in repositories) to users. Maglitta (1995) shares this utilitarian approach to knowledge assets in organizations by making references to categorization, intelligent searching, and accessing of data from disparate databases, e-mails and data files. "Best practices" is a common term used to describe case examples of successful implementations of a firm's solutions for its clients. Intranets, groupware, data warehouses, networks, bulletin boards (or discussion forums) and videoconferencing are the "wherever and whenever" solutions to sharing and creating knowledge of processes, procedures, "best practices," fixes, and more (Maglitta 1996, as cited in Malhotra, 2000b). These views hold technology as the KM enabler, and that information and knowledge can be shared and transferred through computer networks.

The output-oriented research emphasizes the goal(s) for applying KM. A good example is a definition provided by Seiner (2000), "knowledge management envisions getting the right information, in the right context, to the right person, at the right time, for the right business purpose stated." Solutions for goal-oriented views are mainly technology driven and are based on recognizing and rewarding employees for their knowledge sharing contributions. "Push" and "pull" technologies, on which intelligent agents and content management are based, are examples of technology solutions.

The process-oriented research focuses on management processes and is paradigmatic with perspectives on the workings of a knowledge organization. An example of a KM paradigm is the information-processing model. In the information-processing paradigm, the focus is on creating repositories for organizational knowledge assets to allow accessibility by members. However, Drucker (1994) pointed out that this would result in insufficient attention given to knowledge transfers and knowledge sharing, and the organization's learning and adaptive capabilities. Another concern for the information-processing model is the lack of consideration for the dynamic environment that motivates adaptations and transformations by organizations through time. Furthermore, the prescribed, static information-processing KM model runs the risk of implementing information technologies that will support the convergence and consensus-oriented mode of decision making. This may limit understanding and interpretations of new situations, thus leading to the generation of routine optimization-based solutions. The decreasing marginal returns from the deployment of technologies to automate, rationalize procedures and reengineer business processes seem to further indicate that the information-processing model is inadequate in shifting the organization from an "economies-of-scale" operation to a knowledge-driven (innovative) enterprise in a more unpredictable, competitive environment. The emphasis on benchmarking and transfer of "best practices" as prescribed by the information-processing model assumes a static and "syntactic" view of knowledge. Such view focuses on capturing, storing, and making knowledge accessible to members based on text-retrieval techniques. The problem is core competencies based on "best practices" today may very well be the "worst practices" in a relatively short time frame (Malhotra, 2000a).

Another process-oriented research focus is the organization perspective, which prescribes the need for sponsorship (and direction) from top management on KM initiatives. Such sponsorship comes in the form of an individual with a formal title of CKO (chief knowledge officer). Brainstorming sessions with CKOs from both private and public sectors conducted by Nielson (n.d.) revealed that there is agreement on major issues from these groups. From these sessions, a CKO's multidimensional focus includes attracting and maintaining high-quality human capital and using KM to achieve competitive advantage and business innovations. The planning role of a CKO involves making sure that the firm's knowledge repositories are in alignment with business strategies. This involves an assessment of current repositories and developing plans for promoting knowledge sharing, refining the organization's knowledge base, and filling existing knowledge gaps in business processes. Other process-oriented research work is the knowledge conversion modes by Nonaka and Takeuchi (1995) and virtual teams (Kimble et al., n.d.). Contributions in communications processes, group managing techniques, and decision making frameworks will have implications for effective knowledge sharing and transfer in group work settings.

In a system, the feedback mechanism is the controlling feature that ensures that the input, process and output components are working together. Models for KM metrics are research work that constitutes the feedback in our KM research framework. The work by Sveiby (2001c) and Kanevsky and Housel's (n.d.) learning-knowledge-value-spiral are examples. The work performance issue must include evaluation of the member on knowledge sharing and transfer activities. Though knowledge by itself is difficult to quantify, activities that lead to knowledge generation/creation, such as white paper contributions and participation in online discussions, are measurable. Further development in the knowledge valuation model for an organization will allow management to gauge its effectiveness in KM.

REFERENCES

Arveson, P. (1999). *The balanced scorecard and knowledge management.* Retrieved September 9, 2001, from http://www.balancedscorecard.org/bscand/bsckm.html

Burlton, R. (1998). *Data warehousing in the knowledge management cycle.* Retrieved July 25, 2001, from http://datawarehouse.dci.com/articles/1998/08/25km2.htm

Churchman, C. W. (1971). *The design of inquiring systems.* New York: Basic Books.

DelphiGroup. (n.d.) *The language of knowledge.* Retrieved June 19, 2001, from http://www.delphigroup.com

Drucker, P. F. (1994). The theory of business. *Harvard Business Review*, September/October, 95-104.

Firestone, J. (n.d.) *Enterprise information portals and enterprise knowledge portals.* Retrieved July 19, 2001, from http://www.dkms.com/EKPandEIP.html

Hoyt Consulting. (2001). *Knowledge management news.* Retrieved July 30, 2001 from http://www.kmnews.com/Editorial/perspectives.htm

Kanevsky, V. & Housel, T. (n.d.) *The learning-knowledge-value-cycle: Tracking the velocity of change in knowledge to value.* Retrieved September 1,

2001, from http://www-bcf.usc.edu/~house1/paper1/valuecycle.html

Kimble, C., Li, F., & Barlow, A. (n.d.) *Effective virtual teams through communities of practice, management science: Theory, method and practice.* Retrieved May 4, 2001, from http://www.mansci.strath.ac.uk/papers.html

Lang, I. (n.d.) *Strategic knowledge management.* Retrieved September 13, 2001, from http://www.assistaum.com/background/skm.html

LFM-SDM. *The knowledge cycle.* Retrieved September 21, 2001, from http://lfmsdm.mit.edu/rkt/knowledge/cycle.html

Maglitta, J. (1995, June 5). Smarten up! *ComputerWorld, 29*(23), 84-86.

Maglitta, J. (1996, January 15). Know-how, inc. *ComputerWorld, 30*(1), 15.

Malhotra, Y. (2000a). Knowledge management and new organization forms: A framework for business model innovation. *Information Resources Management Journal*, 13, 1.

Malhotra, Y. (2000b). From information management to knowledge management: Beyond the "hi-tech hidebound" systems. In K. Srikantaiah, M.E.D. Koenig, & T. Srikantaiah (Eds.), *Knowledge Management for the Information Professional.* ASIS Monograph Series.

Maslow, A. H. (1968). *Toward a psychology of being.* D. Van Nostrand.

Meso, P., Troutt, M. D., & Rudnicka, J. (2002, March). A review of naturalistic decision making research with some implications for knowledge management, to appear. *Journal of Knowledge Management, 6*(1).

Miskie, R. (n.d.). *Documentation and training—Foundation of knowledge management.* Retrieved June 12, 2001, from http://www.ktic.com/topic6/12_KMDOC.htm

Nielson, R. (n.d.). *Knowledge management and the role of chief knowledge officer.* Retrieved August 28, 2001, from http://www.ndu.edu/ndu/irmc/km-cio_role/km-cio-role.htm

Nonaka, I. & Takeuchi, H. (1995). *The knowledge-creating company.* New York: Oxford University Press.

Rossett, A. & Donello, J. F. (n.d.). *Knowledge management for training professionals.* Retrieved September 16, 2001, from http://defcon.sdsu.edu/1/objects/km/defining/index.htm

Seiner, R. S. (2000, November). Knowledge management: It's not all about the portal. *The Data Administration Newsletter.*

Sveiby, K. E. (2001a). *Intellectual capital and knowledge management.* Retrieved August 30, 2001, from http://www.sveiby.com.au/IntellectualCapital.html

Sveiby, K. E. (2001b). *What is knowledge management?* Retrieved July 15, 2001, from http://www.sveiby.com.au/KnowledgeManagement.html

Sveiby, K. E. (2001c). *The invisible balance sheet.* Retrieved July 25, 2001, from http://www.sveiby.com.au/InvisibleBalance.html

Svetvilas, C. (2001). *The human factor.* Retrieved September 30, 2001, from IntelligentKM Feature http://www.intelligentkm.com

Taylor, W. C. (1994, November/December). Control in an age of chaos. *Harvard Business Review,   72*(6), 72.

Villegas, R. Jr. (n.d.) Knowledge management white paper. Retrieved September 12, 2001, from http://www.insmkt.com/kmorder.htm

Chapter XXIII

Decision Making Support Systems: Achievements, Challenges and Opportunities

Guisseppi A. Forgionne
University of Maryland, Baltimore County, USA

Jatinder N. D. Gupta
University of Alabama in Huntsville, USA

Manuel Mora
Autonomous University of Aguascalientes, Mexico

ABSTRACT

Previous chapters have described the state of the art in decision making support systems (DMSS). This chapter synthesizes the views of leading scientists concerning the achievements of DMSS and the future challenges and opportunities. According to the experts, DMSS will be technologically more integrated, offer broader and deeper support for decision making, and provide a much wider array of applications. In the process, new information and computer technologies will be necessitated, the decision makers' jobs will change, and new organizational structures will emerge to meet the changes. The changes will not occur without displacements of old technologies and old work paradigms. In particular, there will be an evolution toward team-based decision making paradigms. Although the evolution can require significant investments, the organizational benefits from successful DMSS deployments can be significant and substantial. Researchers and practitioners are encouraged to collaborate in their effort to further enhance the theoretical and pragmatic developments of DMSS.

INTRODUCTION

In previous parts of the book, we learned about the foundations of decision making support systems (DMSS), the advanced technologies that are delivered by such systems, the organizational and management issues created by DMSS, and the range of DMSS applications. Decision making support systems involve various creative, behavioral, and analytic foundations that draw on a variety of disciplines. These foundations give rise to various architectures that deliver the fundamental support concepts to individual and group users. A variety of public and private sector applications have been presented. These applications include scheduling of railway services, urban transportation policy formulation, health care management, decision making in the pharmaceutical industry, banking management, and entertainment industry management. The reported and other applications draw on advanced information technologies (IT) to physically deliver support to the decision maker. The advanced IT presented includes intelligent agents, knowledge-based procedures, ripple down rules, narratives, and synthetic characters.

Once created, DMSS must be evaluated and managed. A variety of approaches have been suggested to measure DMSS effectiveness. There are economic-theory-based methodologies, quantitative and qualitative process and outcome measures, and the dashboard approach. These approaches suggest various organizational structures and practices for managing the design, development, and implementation effort. Most of these approaches suggest much more user involvement than had heretofore been practiced, and they also suggest a larger role for specialists outside of traditional information systems practitioners to carry out the technical design, development, and implementation tasks. Despite the technical progress, a key challenge persists—how to reduce DMSS implementation failures in organizations.

The suggested changes and developments discussed in various chapters of this book present unique challenges and opportunities for DMSS professionals. The issues discussed in this book revolve around integration of technologies and knowledge sharing and management. To gain further insights about DMSS achievements, challenges, and opportunities, we asked recognized leaders in the field for their views. This chapter presents those views and examines the implications for DMSS research and practice.

KEY QUESTIONS

The knowledge presented in this book suggested several key unresolved DMSS issues. These unresolved issues resulted in five key questions to be addressed. The suggested questions are listed in Figure 1. To provide perspective on the key issues, we asked 12 leading DMSS professionals to answer Figure 1's questions.

The professionals were selected on the basis of their demonstrated accomplishments and reputation within the DMSS community. Figure 2 provides the profiles of these 12 experts, where anonymity is preserved for privacy and other reasons.

Figure 1: Questions for DMSS experts

1) **What are the key achievements obtained through the research and the practice of DMSS in the last 20 years (1981-2001)?**

2) **What are the research issues and practical problems that have yet to be resolved in the field?**

3) **What are the 3-5 characteristics for the next generation of DMSS for all management levels?**

4) **What are the core concepts on DMSS that are essential for future DMSS architectures?**

5) **What are the main trends and challenges in the development of DMSS from a practical perspective?**

Figure 2: Profile of DMSS experts consulted

Expert	Profile
Expert 1. (*)	Longtime professor, widely published and cited author of DMSS articles, and highly respected consultant in the field. Key research is focused on organizational impacts of EIS.
Expert 2. (*)	Longtime professor, widely published and cited author of DMSS articles and books, and longtime consultant in the field. Key research is focused on effectiveness of integrated DMSS.
Expert 3. (**)	Longtime professor, widely published and cited author of DMSS articles and books, and highly respected consultant in the field. Key research area is focused on DSS.
Expert 4. (**)	Longtime professor, widely published author, developer of early DMSS concepts, and highly respected information systems consultant. Key research area is focused on theoretical and practical foundations of managerial decision making.
Expert 5. (*)	Longtime professor, widely published and cited author of DMSS articles and books, and highly respected consultant in the field. Key research area is focused on spatial DSS.
Expert 6. (*)	Longtime professor, widely published and cited author of DMSS articles, editor of a major DMSS journal, and highly respected consultant in the field. Key research area is focused on theoretical and practical foundations of DMSS.
Expert 7. (*)	Longtime professor, widely published and cited author of DMSS articles, editor of a premier Web site on DMSS, and respected consultant in the field. Key research area is focused on typologies of DMSS.
Expert 8. (**)	Longtime professor, widely published and cited author of DMSS articles and books, editor of major DMSS journals, pioneer in the field of DSS, and highly respected consultant in the field. Key research focused on decision analysis and systems engineering.
Expert 9. (*)	Longtime professor, widely published and cited author of DMSS articles, and highly respected consultant in the field. Key research area is focused on intelligent DMSS.
Expert 10. (**)	Longtime professor, widely published and cited author of DMSS articles and books, pioneer in the field of DSS, and highly respected consultant in the field. Key research area is focused on foundations of DSS.
Expert 11. (**)	Longtime professor, widely published and cited author of DMSS articles and books, and highly respected consultant in the field. Key research areas focused on DSS, EIS, and ES/KBS.
Expert 12 (*)	Longtime professor, widely published and cited author of DMSS articles and books, pioneer in DMSS field, member of editorial board of major DMSS journals, and highly respected consultant in the field. Key research area is focused on EIS and business intelligence.

Note: (*) indicates a completed e-interview, while (**) indicates no response.

EXPERT OPINIONS

An e-mail letter of invitation, along with Figure 1's questions, was emailed to the group of 12 experts. Responses were received from 7 of the 12. Many attempts were made to achieve a response from the remaining 5, but were not successful.

The e-interview answers offer a rich set of ideas provided by a unique worldwide collection of experts in the DMSS field. Diverse research streams as well as balanced theoretical and practical perspectives result in disparate views. The experts' verbatim responses to Figure 1's questions are reported, in the order received, in Tables 1-5.

Key DMSS Achievements

Table 1 presents the expert opinions regarding the key achievements achieved in decision-making support systems (Question 1). According to Table 1, the experts feel that the key achievements in the field are: (a) the evolution of DMSS software and hardware, (b) the implementation of DMSS in a variety of organizations and (c) the creation of DMSS-tailored design and development strategies. However, different experts have different opinions about these characteristics. All agree that (a) is key, three agree that that (b) is essential, and only one thinks that that (c) is vital. These responses implicitly suggest that DMSS have been recognized as a unique type of information system.

Table 1: Expert opinions on the key achievements of DMSS

Expert 12: By 1980, the conceptual foundation for DSS was well established. At that time, however, there was still a heavy emphasis on model-based DSS. This was due in large part to the number of academicians with management science backgrounds who became interested in DSS. Over time, it has become clear that data-based DSS is where most of the practical applications are. As a result there is now much more attention given to the management of data, as seen by the popularity of data warehouses. A key achievement is the evolution of DMSS software. It is now possible to deliver systems that are easier to use, have far superior display capabilities, much greater functionality, and with the ability to accommodate the needs of a much more diverse user base. Through research, we now have a thorough understanding of what is required to successfully develop and implement DMSS.
Expert 7: In some ways the key achievements have come more from applied research and practice than from academic research. Researchers at a number of universities made substantial contributions to the development of group DSS and their research stimulated many studies related to the use of group technologies in organizations. Vendors have worked to implement DSS products using graphical user interfaces and this has increased the accessibility of query and reporting tools, decision models and expert system technologies. Improved products have not however led to many new empirical studies related to how DSS impact decision behavior or decision quality.
Expert 2: One key achievement has been the development conceptually of important stand-alone DMSS, such as DSS, EIS, ES, and idea processing, that conceptually support the decision making process. Another key achievement has been the implementation of such systems in a variety of public and private organizations, with resulting major financial and management benefits. The final achievement has been the creation of DMSS-tailored design and development strategies, such as the adaptive design strategy, and organization structures, such as DSS planning teams, for implementing DMSS.

Table 1: Expert opinions on the key achievements of DMSS (continued)

Expert 6 and Expert 1: The key feature of the evolution of the DMSS field can be traced to the evolution of hardware and software used for the development and use of DMSS systems; in particular, spread of PCs and distribution of information and processing power to large numbers of users. The creation of development tools that encourage the rapid development of personal DMSS such as spreadsheets or DSS toolkits has also been a key feature of the evolution of DMSS, such that most systems are now developed by end users. There has also been a move towards open systems and an evolution towards more and more integrated systems including DBMS and data warehouses. Each DBMS is now more or less a basic DMSS on which the decision maker can rely to base their reasoning. The development and spread of EIS-type systems which improve the ability of managers to analyze situations in real time and identify subtle changes in the environments quicker have also been a key achievement of this period.
Expert 9: The developments and achievements in the past 20 years will guide us in understanding the coming evolution of decision support technology. The key developments and achievement are: 1) development of the decision making support systems concept, 2) powerful decision making support tools, including data warehouse, online analytical processing (OLAP), data mining and Web-based decision making support systems, 3) collaborative support systems, along with group decision making support systems, virtual teams, and executive information systems, 4) optimization-based decision making support models, 5) user interfaces, and 6) intelligent agents.
Expert 5: DMSS has successfully synthesized information technology and decision science techniques to provide systems of real value to decision makers. This hasn't happened in all fields, but it has set the scene for further developments.

Research Issues and Practical Problems

Table 2 presents the expert opinions regarding the research issues and practical problems remaining for decision-making support systems (Question 2). According to Table 2, the experts feel that the research issues and practical problems in the field are: (a) providing quality data for decision support, (b) managing and creating large decision support databases, (c) model management and model reuse, (d) building knowledge-driven DMSS, (e) improving communication technologies, (f) developing a uniform and comprehensive scheme, (g) developing an effective toolkit, (h) developing and evaluating a synergistic integrated DMSS, (i) collecting insights about the neurobiology of decision support for managers' less structured work, (j) the application of agent and object-oriented methodologies and (k) developing DMSS though well-established methodologies. However, different experts have different opinions about these characteristics. Two agree that (e), (f), and (h) are key, and one of each of the experts thinks that (a), (b), (c), (d), (g), (i), or (j) is vital.

In summary, the opinions seem to focus on the deployment of new and advanced information technology (IT) to improve the quality of the overall DMSS design. This collective opinion suggests that DMSS implementation problems are not perceived as critical. On the other hand, the literature suggests that implementation of information systems, in general, is a complex and critical problem in practice (Standish Group, 1999, pp 1). Implicitly, then, the expert opinion suggests that advanced IT progress can be used to reduce implementation failures.

Next Generation DMSS

Table 3 presents the expert opinions regarding the nature of the next generation decision-making support systems (Question 3). According to Table 3, the experts

Table 2: Expert opinions on research issues and practical problems

Expert 12: A continuing practical problem will be providing quality data for decision support. Data warehousing is working on this but the large amounts of dirty legacy data and the organizational issues that are required to have clean data are huge.

Expert 7: The research issues related to DSS should still read like a long shopping list. A few questions stand out for me including: How can changes in the user interface impact the utility, perceived usefulness and effectiveness of a specific category of decision support system? How does the metadata available to a user impact the usefulness of a data-driven DSS? How does interactive video and voice change the dynamics and results of a synchronous meeting where some participants are geographically dispersed? As far as practical problems, they are perhaps fewer in number than 20 years ago, but more important because of the increased number of DSS users and their evolved expectations. Managing and creating large decision support databases remain difficult tasks. Model management and model reuse remain difficult tasks related to building model-driven DSS. Representing knowledge and capturing knowledge from experts in useful domains for decision support is certainly not a trivial task. Despite extensive commentaries, anecdotes and studies, building Knowledge-Driven DSS seems more like a mysterious art than a routinized, well-understood development methodology. Finally, communications technologies have improved tremendously, but much needs to be done to insure that systems are available when needed and perform satisfactorily and that needed capabilities for interactive video are provided and integrated with other decision support and collaboration tools.

Expert 2: A major research issue is to develop a uniform and comprehensive scheme to measure and evaluate DMSS effectiveness. Most schemes evaluate some process or outcome measure in a nonintegrated and incomplete manner, leading to divergent and conflicting results from DMSS experiments. Another major research issue deals with the development of an effective toolkit for users to independently create working DMSS. DSS generators are incomplete, and programming languages are too technical for such purposes. A final issue is to develop and evaluate a synergistic integrated DMSS that would support all phases of the decision making process in an integrated and comprehensive manner. Most integration schemes still support only selected phases or steps of the DMP and in a nonintegrated manner.

Expert 1 and Expert 6: There is a still a strong need for a better integration of decision theory, especially as regards future uncertainty and our understanding of its implication for the design of decision support systems. We have only just begun to collect some insights about the neurobiology of decision and this will probably change our perspectives on decision support. At a conceptual level, not enough is understood yet about the ways managers utilize information and make decisions, and the linkages between these two activities. Nearly 30 years after the publication of Mintzberg's seminal work on the nature of managerial work, we still cannot state with certainty how managers' less structured tasks should be supported. In addition, practitioners and researchers must move towards the solution of problems that span the boundaries of organizations such as the management of supply chains and the optimization of distribution networks. Researchers and practitioners must also work towards the application of agent and object methodologies for building DMSS more easily and developing more effective systems.

Expert 9: There are several areas in which DMSS researchers should resolve: 1) identify areas where tools are needed to transform uncertain and incomplete data into useful knowledge, 2) be more prescriptive in effective decision making through use of intelligent systems, 3) exploit advancing software tools to improve the productivity of decision making time, and 4) assist DMSS practitioners in improving their core knowledge of effective decision making support.

Expert 5: There is a continuing need to research the appropriate decision representations for DMSS to better exploit the potential available in the use of information technology. Further work is needed to ensure that practical implementations are directed at the decision representations of interest to the decision maker rather than those that closely model the computer representation of problems.

feel that the nature of the next generation DMSS will involve: (a) the use of portals, (b) the incorporation of previously unused forms of artificial intelligence through agents, (c) better integration of data warehousing and data mining tools within DMSS architectures, (d) creation of knowledge and model warehouses, (e) the integration of creativity within DMSS architectures, (f) the use of integrated DMSS as a virtual team of experts, (g) exploitation of the World Wide Web, (h) the exploitation of mobile IT and (i) the incorporation of advanced IT to improve the user interface through video, audio, complex graphics, and other approaches. As before, however, different experts have different opinions about these characteristics. All agree that (b) is key, three agree that (c) is essential, two agree that (a) is critical, and only one thinks that (d), (e), (f), (g) or (h) is vital. Among the latter, each stresses a different factor. In summary, the experts implicitly recognize the relevance of improving the DMSS user interface through the deployment of advanced IT.

Core DMSS Architectural Concepts

Table 4 presents the expert opinions regarding the core elements needed in future decision making support system architectures (Question 4). According to

Table 3: Expert opinions on next generation DMSS

Expert 12: A major advance will be the use of portals to deliver customized information and functionality for all users. These portals will both provide the information that people need and also help people avoid having more information available than they can possibly sort through. These portals will also be used to seamlessly deliver both structured and unstructured data. Another advance will be the use of event alerts to inform people of mission-critical developments. These alerts will be delivered through a variety of mediums and devices – e-mail, voice mail, pagers, PDAs, etc. Voice will also be increasingly important, probably on the output rather than the input side, at least initially.
Expert 7: There won't be a single next generation for decision support. Some characteristics that will appear in some decision support systems include greater customization, more integration with other systems, interactive voice and video over IP, voice-driven user interfaces, and more powerful representations including 3-D graphics and more realistic, graphical business and process simulations. I'm looking forward to "Roller Coaster Tycoon" or "Roller Coaster Designer" like decision support simulation.
Expert 2: The main characteristics will be: (1) the incorporation of previously unused forms of artifical intelligence, such as machine learning, robotics, agents, and speech recognition, into DMSS architectures to provide direct technical support for DMSS processing tasks, (2) better integration of data warehousing and data mining tools within DMSS architectures to facilitate data filtering and focusing for the purpose of populating the DMSS database, (3) creation of knowledge and model warehouses to facilitate the population of DMSS model bases, (4) the integration of creativity within DMSS architectures to stimulate and facilitate user-initiated model building and alternative evaluation, and (5) the use of integrated DMSS as a virtual team of experts to facilitate user problem-solving.
Expert 6 and Expert 1: • Flexibility of use/Intuitive interface • Intelligent information filtering features • Assisted search for relevant information • Exploitation of the World Wide Web as a source of information and a key channel for connectivity • Support for group/organizational/interorganizational decision making
Expert 9: DMSS technology of the future for all management levels will be enhanced by mobile tools, mobile e-services, and wireless protocols, such as wireless applications protocol (WAP), wireless markup language (WML), and NTT DoCoMo i-Mode. Thereby this leads to ubiquitous access to information and decision making support tools.
Expert 5: Systems will evolve to accommodate higher order decisions, providing support at this level by allowing complex database and modeling operations to be conducted transparently to the user. These systems must flexibly adapt to the varying requirements of uses and the characteristics of the technologies used to deliver them. Systems will incorporate some form of artificial intelligence to facilitate this.

Table 4, the experts feel that core DMSS architectural concepts are: (a) Web technology, (b) accessibility, (c) security, (d) effective data, idea, and knowledge management, possibly through the use of smart agents, (e) effective model management, (f) effective dialog management, (g) EIS-like features, (h) incorporation of basic and common DMSS functionalities, (i) mobile computing and (j) user-centric design. Again, however, different experts have different opinions about these characteristics. All agree that (d) is key, but only one thinks that (b), (c), (e), (f), (g), (h), (i) or (j) is vital. Among the latter, each expert identifies a different factor. Implicitly, however, distributed DMSS, through Web-based, mobile computing and accessibility concepts, is suggested as a critical factor.

DMSS Trends and Challenges

Table 5 presents the expert opinions regarding the trends involved in and the challenges presented for decision making support systems (Question 5). According

Table 4: Expert opinions on the core DMSS architectural concepts

Expert 12: Web technologies will be at the core of future DMSS architectures – for all of the obvious reasons. At the client end, the data access tool must be cheap, easy to maintain, readily available, intuitive, and easy to learn. Also key will be data warehouses and operational data stores. A lack of quality data is at the core of many DMSS failures. Also look for decision support architectures to be increasingly integrated with operational systems. And finally, information will be delivered to users in a plethora of ways.

Expert 7: The core concept is accessibility, but security issues need to be addressed more systematically than they have been in recent years. The issue of database backup is a problem in terabyte-sized warehouses that will only get worse.

Expert 2: The same as they have been in concept since the beginning of DMSS evolution: (1) effective data, idea, and knowledge management to facilitate the user's organization of data, information, and knowledge and the structuring of conceptual models, (2) effective model management to facilitate the user's operationalization of decision models, evaluation of alternatives, and generation of decision recommendations and explanations for the recommendations, and (3) effective dialog management to facilitate the user's ability to utilize the DMSS computer technology to perform the needed processing tasks and feedback loops and to assist the user in presenting and interpreting processing results. The challenge remains to accomplish these functions in an effective manner.

Expert 1 and Expert 6: EIS-like features such as exception reporting and drill down have proven that they can truly help executives in the search for problems and their diagnosis of the current situation. Smart agents that can accelerate the search and retrieval of data in large warehouses using OLAP, for example have also delivered significant benefits. We also think that the three basic architectures of DMSS (see our chapter) will remain in force: centralized, hierarchical, and network.

Expert 9: Over the past two decades, decision making support systems research has evolved to include some additional concepts, such as group support systems. This, in turn, evolved to provide idea generation and communications facilities to support team problem-solving. In the next generation, mobile tools, mobile e-services, and wireless Internet protocols will mark the next major set of developments in DMSS for all management levels. The Internet/Web and telecommunication technology (including wireless mobile technology) can be expected to result in organizational environments that will connect more globally. Organizations will interact with more diverse political, social, economic, and cultural environments.

Expert 5: There needs to be a continued focus on the user-centric nature of systems, accommodating the users' needs wherever and whenever required. The next generation of DMSS will include many systems that incorporate distributed operation in various forms. Web-driven systems will evolve into systems that can interact with mobile devices; further development is required to achieve this.

to Table 5, the experts feel that DMSS trends and challenges are: (a) availability of DMSS packages for specific organizational functions, such as customer relationship management, (b) system functional and technical integration, (c) reducing software tool costs, (d) consolidation and innovation, (e) the creation of a technology role for the decision maker through the DMSS application, (f) the integration of the decision maker into the design and development process for DMSS, (g) developing effective design and development tools for user-controlled development, (h) accommodating the structural changes in the organization and job duties created by DMSS use, (i) developing measures of DMSS effectiveness, (j) recognizing the group dimension of organizational decision making, (k) incorporating the cognitive dimension of human

Table 5: Expert opinions on DMSS trends and challenges

Expert 12: A major trend is toward customer relationship management. CRM is already well established in some industries like financial services, retail, and telecommunications but look for it to spread even more. As part of CRM, the use of data mining to better understand customers will grow.

Also look for more packaged decision support applications. They will be task- and industry-specific, such as fraud detection in financial services. A continuing challenge will be a priori establishing the business value of proposed DMSS applications. Look for Microsoft to continue to lower the cost of software for doing the basic MDSS work. SQL Server 7 with OLAP Services is just the beginning. Also look for companies wanting to manage huge amounts of data. Petrabyte data warehouses are just around the corner.

Expert 7: The main trends seem to be consolidation and innovation. The "older" business intelligence and modeling and analysis vendors seem to be ready for a wave of mergers and other joint activities. Innovation is still possible in this product space and the examples of Web portals suggest that more innovation is both possible and likely. There is certainly a need for new products in most of the decision support categories.

Expert 2: The main trends are system functional and technical integration, the creation of a technology role for the decision maker through the DMSS application, and the integration of the decision maker into the design and development process for DMSS. The main challenges are to develop effective design and development tools for user-controlled development, to accommodate the structural changes in the organization and job duties created by DMSS use, and to develop measures of DMSS effectiveness that are understood and accepted by decision makers.

Expert 6 and Expert 1: In years to come, DMSS as a field of research will have to work hard towards proving its practical relevance to managerial decision making and towards proving that better quality decision making, sticking to human cognitive traits, can be delivered through the support of decision makers by computer-based systems. This will require that the group dimension of organizational decision making is taken into account in the design of future systems. The cognitive dimension of human decision making will also have to be taken into account.

The development of smart agents and features that support the acquisition, assessment and filtering of information on the Web and in large databases must be pursued and further improved. Finally, the distribution of DMSS expertise in the firm and the communication between IS-oriented staff and managers in other business areas must be improved so that required systems are developed in a timely fashion.

Expert 9: The main trends can be observed in the development of DMSS. 1) The increasing sophistication of model-based DSS software. Most major decision making support systems software developers have Websites and offer downloading software for further exploration, e.g., Application Service Provider (ASP) model. 2) How the Web is supporting more collaboration and interactivity in DMSS. With the application of intranets and enterprise resource planning (ERP) systems, entire organizations interact via technology with little or no face-to-face interaction. 3) The rise of the Web as a common platform from which to extend the capabilities of DMSS to a large number of users. 4) How the business intelligence is supporting decision making support systems.

Expert 5: Future DMSS will facilitate interaction with other systems using ubiquitous networking and support is needed for open standards such as XML for data interchange. Richer forms of data, such as spatial data, need to be accommodated in all types of DMSS. These enhanced facilities for complex data interchange must be made in a way that does not introduce additional user complexity; the users must continue to be focused on the decisions.

decision making, (l) utilization of smart agents and features, (m) distribution of DMSS expertise through collaborative technologies, (n) incorporating rich data, information and knowledge representation modes into DMSS and (o) focusing user attention on decisions rather than technical issues.

However, different experts have different opinions about these characteristics. Two agree that that (b) is key and only one thinks that (a), (c), (d), (e), (f), (g), (h), (i), (j), (k), (l), (m), (n) or (o) is vital. Among the latter, each expert cites a different factor. Common themes suggested by the disparate expert opinion are: (a) the DMSS should focus decision makers on the decision process rather than technical issues and (b) DMSS development may require specialized and new IT professionals.

CONCLUSIONS

In some ways, the DMSS field has not progressed very much from its early days. There is still significant disagreement about definitions, methodologies, and focus. Experts vary on the breadth and depth of the definitions. Some favor analytical methodologies, while others promote qualitative approaches. Some experts focus on the technology, while others concentrate on managerial and organizational issues. There does not seem to be a unified theory of decision making, decision support for the process, or DMSS evaluation.

In spite of the diversity, opinions are consistent regarding some key DMSS elements. Most experts recognize the need for problem-pertinent data, the role of the Internet in providing some of the necessary data, the need for system integration within DMSS architectures and between DMSS and other information systems, and the importance of artificial intelligence within DMSS processing. The DMSS concept also continues to be successfully applied across a variety of public and private organizations and entities. These applications continue to involve the user more directly in the design, development, and implementation process.

The trends will create DMSS that are technologically more integrated, offer broader and deeper support for decision making, and provide a much wider array of applications. In the process, new information and computer technologies will be necessitated. New roles for artificial intelligence will emerge within DMSS architectures, new forms of decision technology and methodology will emerge, and new roles will be found for existing technologies and methodologies.

As the evolution continues, many tasks that had been assigned to human experts can be delegated to virtual expertise within the DMSS. With such consultation readily available through the system, the decision maker can devote more effort to the creative aspects of management. Support for these tasks can also be found within DMSS. In the process, the decision maker can become an artist, scientist, and technologist of decision making. The DMSS-delivered virtual expertise can reduce the need for large support staffs and corresponding organizational structures. The organization can become flatter and more project-oriented. In this setting, the decision maker can participate more directly in DMSS design, development, implementation, and management. Such changes will not occur without displacements of old technologies and job activities, radical changes in physical organizations, and considerable costs. As the reported applications indicate, however, the resulting benefits are likely to far outweigh the costs.

While the experts do not foresee DMSS implementation issues emerging in the future, Mora, Cervantes-Perez, and Forgionne (2000) and Mora et al. (in chapter 20 of this book) show that the DMSS implementation process is still an open challenge to practitioners and researchers. Complementary or emergent research approaches such as the systems approach will be required to understand the complexity of the full DMSS process as a whole. Only then will DMSS implementation and practice realize the full potentials of this powerful technology.

A key global trend is a growing organizational interest in the disparate forms of DMSS. A primary challenge is getting successful development and implementation of DMSS across organizations in the face of disparate views among the decision makers, experts, and support personnel.

Thus, even though much has been accomplished in the field of DMSS, considerable work still lies ahead to successfully design, develop, implement, and use decision making support systems. Researchers and practitioners are encouraged to participate in this intellectual endeavor.

ACKNOWLEDGMENT

The authors acknowledge the contributions of those unnamed experts who provided responses to the key questions asked. Without their help and participation, this chapter would not have been possible. In addition, Ran Wang, a doctoral student at the University of Maryland, Baltimore County, prepared summaries of the contents in Tables 1-5, identified factors from the summaries, and prepared some of the final document. Her valuable assistance is gratefully acknowledged.

REFERENCES

Mora, M., Cervantes-Perez, F., & Forgionne, G. (2000). Understanding the process of successful implementations of management support systems: A review of critical factors and theories about adoption of new information technology. In CD of *Proceedings of the 3rd BITWorld Conference*, Mexico, D.F. June 1-3.

Standish Group. (1999). CHAOS: A recipe for success. Retrieved at www.standishgroup.com/chaos.html

About the Authors

Manuel Mora is an associate professor in the Autonomous University of Aguascalientes (UAA) from 1995 and an Eng.Dr(c). from the Engineering Graduate School of the National Autonomous University of Mexico (UNAM). Previously he was an instructor professor at Monterrey Tech System (ITESM) at Monterrey and San Luis Potosí cities and a lecturer for graduate programs at the Autonomous University of Nuevo Leon (UNAL) and the Institute of Technology of Aguascalientes (ITA). He received his B.S. in Computer Systems Engineering in 1984 and his M.Sc. in Computer Sciences with Artificial Intelligence as major area in 1989, both from the Monterrey Tech (ITESM). In the last 5 years, he has published, presented and served as reviewer of several papers in refereed international conferences in USA, Europe and Mexico. He has been also guest co-editor for special issues on DMSS for the *Information Resource Management Journal* (IRMJ) and the *Journal of Decision Systems* (JDS). His current research interests are: the organizational design and implementation of Integrated Decision Making Support Systems and Theoretical Foundations of Information Systems, using in both research streams the Systems Approach as the theoretical frame. Associate Professor Mora is also currently a member of the Association of Information Systems (AIS) and the Association for Computing Machinery (ACM).

Guisseppi A. Forgionne is professor of information systems at the University of Maryland, Baltimore County (UMBC). Prof. Forgionne holds a B.S. in commerce and finance, an M.A. in econometrics, an M.B.A., and a Ph.D. in management science and econometrics. He has published 25 books and approximately 150 research articles and consulted for a variety of public and private organizations on decision making support systems theory and applications. Dr. Forgionne's work has appeared in *Interfaces, The European Journal of Operations Research, Information & Management, Decision Support Systems, Information Systems Engineering, The Journal of Information Systems Management, International Transactions on Operational Research, OMEGA, Science, Information Processing and Management, Computers and Operations Research, The International Journal of Geographical Information Systems*, and other refereed journals. His research has been funded through competitively earned grants, and his work has been recognized with many national and international awards. Dr.

Forgionne also has served as a department chair at UMBC, Mount Vernon College, and Cal Poly Pomona.

Jatinder N. D. Gupta is currently an eminent scholar of management, professor of management information systems, and chairperson of the Department of Accounting and Information Systems in the College of Administrative Science at the University of Alabama in Huntsville, Huntsville, AL. Most recently, he was a professor of management, information and communication sciences, and industry and technology at Ball State University, Muncie, IN. He holds a B.E. in mechanical engineering from Delhi University, M. Tech. in industrial engineering and operations research from the Indian Institute of Technology in Kharagpur, India, and a Ph.D. in industrial engineering (with specialization in production management and information systems) from Texas Tech University. Coauthor of a textbook in operations research, Dr. Gupta serves on the editorial boards of several national and international journals. Recipient of the Outstanding Faculty and Outstanding Researcher awards from Ball State University, he has published numerous papers in such journals as *Journal of Management Information Systems, International Journal of Information Management, INFORMS Journal of Computing, Annals of Operations Research*, and *Mathematics of Operations Research*. More recently, he served as a coeditor of a special issue of *Computers and Operations Research* on neural networks in business and a book entitled *Neural Networks in Business: Techniques and Applications*. His current research interests include information and decision technologies, scheduling, planning and control, organizational learning and effectiveness, systems education, and knowledge management. Dr. Gupta is a member of several academic and professional societies including the Production and Operations Management Society (POMS), the Decision Sciences Institute (DSI), and the Information Resources Management Association (IRMA).

* * *

Frédéric Adam is a lecturer in the Business Information Systems Group at University College Cork in Ireland and a senior researcher with the Executive Systems Research Centre (ESRC). He holds a Ph.D. from the National University of Ireland and Université Paris VI, France. His research has been published in the *Journal of Strategic Information Systems, Decision Support Systems*, the *Journal of Information Technology, Systèmes d'Information et Management* and the *Journal of Decision Systems,* for which he is an associate editor. He is the coauthor of *A Manager's Guide to Current Issues in Information Systems* and *A Practical Guide to Postgraduate Research in the Business Area* (Blackhall Publishing, Dublin, Ireland).

B. Adenso-Díaz is a professor of operations management in the Industrial Engineering School at Universidad de Oviedo, Spain. He worked for seven years in the Spanish National Steel Company and has been a visiting professor at the

University of Colorado. He has authored three books and published articles in scientific journals such as *European Journal of Operational Research, International Journal of Production Research, Omega, Interfaces, Production and Operations Management, International Journal of Operations & Production Management, Journal of the Operational Research Society*, etc. He is an associate editor of *Journal of Heuristics* and a member of INFORMS and POMS.

Donald Bain works at the European Commission Joint Research Centre, Institute for the Protection and Security of the Citizen in Italy, where he is head of the Decision Support and Integrated Assessment Sector. Although originally a political scientist he has spent the last 25 years as a science policy advisor, specialising in technology assessment and futures studies. In recent years he has been the JRC's project manager for several multi-partner European projects in the transport sector, including UTOPIA.

Francisco Cervantes-Pérez received his B.S. in mechanical electrical engineering in 1978 from the National Autonomous University of Mexico (UNAM), an M.Sc. in electrical engineering in 1982 from the same university, and his Ph.D. in computer and information sciences from the University of Massachusetts at Amherst in 1985. He is currently a full professor at the Department of Computer Engineering and the director of the master's in information technology and administration at the Mexico Autonomous Institute of Technology (ITAM). His research interests are: the analysis of the dynamic and computational properties shown by neuronal systems underlying sensorimotor coordination behaviors in living animals; and the synthesis of neural and schema-theoretic models to build automata that solve practical problems in robotics, nonlinear control, and pattern recognition.

Charu Chandra has been an assistant professor in industrial and manufacturing systems engineering at the University of Michigan-Dearborn, USA, since September 1998. Prior to this, Charu was a postdoctoral fellow at Los Alamos National Laboratory, Los Alamos, NM, and at the University of Minnesota, Minneapolis, MN, USA. He is involved in research in supply chain management. He teaches courses in information technology, operations research and supply chain management. His master's and Ph.D. degrees are in industrial engineering and operations research from the University of Minnesota and Arizona State University, USA, respectively.

R. W. Eglese is currently head of the Department of Management Science in the Management School at Lancaster University, England. After taking his first degree in mathematics at Cambridge, he obtained an M.A. in operational research from Lancaster. He worked in the Operational Research Department of British Rail before joining the staff of Lancaster University in 1979. His research interests include solution methods for various types of vehicle routing problems and he is currently working on a number of such projects sponsored by industry. He is also a member of the Council of the Operational Research Society. His university web page is: http://www.lums.lancs.ac.uk/mansci/Staff/eglese.htm.

Nicholas V. Findler is a professor emeritus at the Department of Computer Science and Engineering and the Department of Mathematics as well as a director emeritus of the Artificial Intelligence Laboratory, Arizona State University, Tempe, AZ, US. His current research interests include artificial intelligence, heuristic programming, applications of distributed artificial intelligence and intelligent agent systems, decision support systems, simulation of cognitive behavior, human-machine systems, decision making, theory of strategies, computational linguistics, information and knowledge retrieval, and expert systems. He has worked in various areas of artificial intelligence since 1957, authored and coauthored over 210 refereed articles and wrote/edited/contributed to 43 books. His awards include: ACM Recognition of Service Award; Recognition of Service Award by the Council for International Exchange of Scientists; Senior Fulbright Scholar on three occasions (sabbaticals); NATO Research Scientist on three occasions; Centennial Award of Merit by the president of Arizona State University; fellow of the British Computer Society; senior member of the IEEE; Medal of Merit by the rector of the University of Helsinki, Finland; and awards from universities in North and South America, Europe, Asia and Oceania.

Lee A. Freeman is an assistant professor of MIS at the University of Michigan—Dearborn. He has a B.A. from the University of Chicago, and he received both his M.B.A and Ph.D. in information systems from Indiana University. His teaching interests include systems analysis and design, end-user computing, and electronic commerce; and his primary research interests include the conceptualization and use of information systems knowledge, systems analysis and design, and electronic commerce. He has published in *MIS Quarterly*, *Information Systems Frontiers*, the *Journal of IS Education*, *Failures and Lessons Learned in Information Technology Management*, and the *Handbook of IS Management*, among others.

Ovsei Gelman-Muravchik received his B.S., M.Sc. and Ph.D. in physics and mathematics from the University of Tbilisi, Georgia. Since 1976 he has lived in Mexico and he is a full researcher in the Center of Instruments of the National Autonomous University of Mexico (UNAM). He also is a faculty member of the Engineering Institute, of the Graduate Engineering School and the Graduate Accounting and Management School at UNAM. In the last 30 years, he has published a vast quantity of papers for national and international congresses, journals and books, developed several consulting activities and contributed strongly to the diffusion of the systems science in Mexico. His current research interests are: organizational cybernetic, systems science, risk management, interdisciplinary research on disasters and decision-making support systems.

Rick Gibson has over 20 years of software engineering experience and is authorized by the Software Engineering Institute to lead assessments of software organizations. In this role, he has extensive domestic and international experience in the conduct of evaluations and the subsequent development of process maturity improvement action plans for software organizations. He is currently the department chair and an associate professor at American University, Washington, DC, for the Department of Computer Science and Information Systems. His responsibilities, as a faculty member, include teaching graduate courses in software engineering, decision analysis, and knowledge management. He has published a variety of books, book chapters, and journal articles on software development and quality assurance.

M. Goitia-Fuertes is a computer engineer from Universidad de Oviedo, Spain. She has been working in different engineering companies as a system analyst, database designer and Web technologies expert. She has collaborated as well in research projects related to decision systems in such various subjects as railways modeling and waste management nets.

Richard T. Herschel is an associate professor of management and information systems at St. Joseph's University in Philadelphia. He received his Ph.D. in MIS from Indiana University, an M.A.S. in Business Management from John Hopkins University, and a B.A. in journalism from Ohio Wesleyan University. Dr. Herschel's research interests include knowledge management, organizational communication, decision making, and group support systems. His articles have appeared in *Information Strategy: The Executive's Journal, Computers in Human Behavior,* and *Small Group Research*. He has also published a book entitled *Organizational Communication in a Technological Society*.

WeiXiong Ho received the Ph.D. degree in electrical engineering from the Southern Illinois University at Carbondale. His research has spanned across a wide spectrum of topics, from residue number systems, to signal processing, to neurocomputing, to fuzzy processing systems, to data mining, to decision support systems, to knowledge management, to his most recent focus on communication network modeling and simulation. Dr. Ho is currently a senior network consultant at Callisma. His works focus on the field of network communications, including modeling and simulation, capacity planning, and operations management.

Beverley G. Hope is a faculty member in the School of Information Management at Victoria University of Wellington, New Zealand. Beverley's research focuses on information needs for quality initiatives, performance measurement, quality of online service delivery, electronic commerce, and IS education. In her work she takes a holistic or system view of organizations and the issues that face them. She has presented and published at many regional and international conferences in information systems, decision sciences, and evaluation and acts as referee for several international conferences and journals. Beverley completed B.S. and M.B.A. degrees at the University of Kansas and a Ph.D. at the University of Hawaii at Manoa.

Peter B. Keenan has been a member of the Department of Management Information Systems at University College Dublin, Ireland, since 1990. Before joining UCD, he developed logistics software for a number of large Irish organizations. Currently his research interests include geographic information systems (GIS) in business, spatial decision support systems and the use of the Internet for decision support. He holds degrees from the National University of Ireland: bachelor of commerce (1984), master of management science (1985) and Ph.D. (2001).

Antonio Leal is a professor of business administration for the Department of Business Administration and Marketing at the University of Seville, Spain. He is the author of five books on management. He has published several articles and he has authored numerous international conference proceedings. He has been a visiting professor at different European and Latin American universities. His research interests include management support systems, knowledge management, total quality management, benchmarking, organisational culture, and change management.

Marcelo Mejía-Olvera received his B.S. in biomedical engineering in 1982 from the Metropolitan Autonomous University (UAM). He also has M.Sc. studies in computer sciences from the UAM and the National Autonomous University of Mexico (UNAM) and an M.Sc. in informatics networkings from the Superior School of Electricity at France. In 1989, he received his degree of doctor in informatics, from the University of Rennes I at France. Currently he is a full professor and the head of the Computer Department in the Mexico Autonomous Institute of Technology (ITAM) and a member of the Doctoral Advising Committee at the National Autonomous University of Mexico (UNAM). His current research interests are: computer networking design and software engineering.

Hamid Nemati is an assistant professor in the Information Systems and Operations Management Department at the University of North Carolina at Greensboro. He received his doctorate degree from the University of Georgia. He has extensive professional experience as an analyst and has consulted with a number of major corporations. His current research and publications are in the areas of decision support systems, data warehousing, data mining and knowledge management.

Pirkko Nykänen received her Ph.D. in computer and information sciences from Tampere University, Finland. She has been working with health information systems and especially with decision support and knowledge-based systems since the 1980s. Her major research interests deal with health information systems, decision support, conceptualisation and interoperability of systems, and evaluation of information technology products and applications in health care. Dr. Nykänen has been working as a visiting researcher at Lille University, Center for Medical Informatics, France, at the National Research and Development Centre for Welfare and Health, Centre of Excellence for Information and Communication, Finland, and at Pennsylvania State University, School of Information Sciences and Technology, USA.

M. Pidd is professor of management science in the Management School at Lancaster University, England. He is known for his work in computer simulation and in approaches to modelling. Amongst his publications are two books, both published by John Wiley: *Computer Simulation in Management Science*, now in its 4th edition, and *Tools for Thinking—Modelling in Management Science*; he is working on the 2nd edition of the latter. He is the immediate past-president of the Operational Research Society and is the holder of two current EPSRC research grants related to decision support. His personal web page is: http://www.lancs.ac.uk/staff/smamp/default.html.

Giuliano Pistolesi, cofounder and vice president of ThinkinGolem, Italy, has worked in computational simulation of cognitive systems by AI and ALife techniques for about 8 years. He holds an M.Sc. in cognitive psychology and a Ph.D. in medical informatics from the University of Rome "La Sapienza." He is also a research fellow at the National Research Council (CNR), Institute for Cognitive Science and Technology, where he is involved in a project for the simulation of social behavior by intelligent agents and complex systems theory. At ThinkinGolem he is primarily involved in several R&D projects regarding intelligent user interfaces, natural language processing systems, and synthetic characters for HCI.

Jean-Charles Pomerol is a professor of computer science at the Université Pierre et Marie Curie (UPMC) in Paris (France), where he is vice-chancellor for research in charge of technological transfer. For 6 years he headed UPMC's Artificial Intelligence Laboratory. He was also with the French National Center for Scientific Research (CNRS) as a project manager for information science and technology from 1995 to 2000. The first part of J. -Ch. Pomerol's career was devoted to game theory and convex analysis and later turned to AI, computer aided decision and 'intelligent' decision support systems. He has published a number of books on expert systems, decision support systems and multi-criterion decision making (with Barba-Romeo) and numerous papers in international journals such as *European Journal of Operational Research*.

D. J. Power is a professor of information systems at the College of Business Administration, University of Northern Iowa, Cedar Falls. He has a PhD in Business Administration from the University of Wisconsin-Madison, has developed decision support software and systems, and has examined impacts of DDS on managers. Prof. Power's book, *Decision Support Systems: Concepts and Resources for Managers*, was published in 2002 by Quorum Books. Also, he has authored many book chapters, proceedings papers and more than 20 articles for the major journals of his field. Prof. Power is a pioneer developer of computerized decision support systems. He is the chair of the association for information systems special interest group on decision support and analytical information systems (SIG DSS). Prof. Powers is editor of DSSResources.com, the knowledge repository about computerized systems that support decision making, and the bi-weekly DSS News e-newsletter.

Debbie Richards is currently a senior lecturer at Macquarie University in Sydney, Australia. She completed a Ph.D. at the University of NSW, Sydney, in 1999 under the supervision of Paul Compton. Her thesis describes an approach for retrospectively generating conceptual models from propositional knowledge-based systems using formal concept analysis. These models can be compared and the approach is being applied to the identification and reconciliation of system requirements from different stakeholders. She began working in the computer industry in 1980 and has performed various roles including data control officer, operator, programmer, analyst and MIS manager. Her industry experience with management was the catalyst of her interest in decision making support systems.

Francesco Mazzeo Rinaldi works at the European Commission Joint Research Centre (JRC), Institute for the Protection and Security of the Citizen (IPSC), Italy. He has an M.Sc. in environmental management and a Ph.D. in environmental economics. He has specialized in building multi-criteria decision support tools for environmental and socioeconomic problems, particularly in the public sector. In the last few years he has been involved in the management of several international projects. These have involved developing and applying integrated decision support systems with special emphasis on sustainable water and waste management, industrial impact assessment and alternative urban transport options and collaborating with the main actors involved in order to integrate all possible viewpoints and stimulate compromise solutions.

José L. Roldán is an assistant professor of business administration for the Department of Business Administration and Marketing at the University of Seville, Spain. In 2000 he obtained a Ph.D. from the University of Seville on a dissertation titled "Executive Information Systems: Emergence, Implementation and Organisational Impact." He has published three books and several articles on management aspects. He has authored diverse proceedings and conference papers. He has been a visiting professor at the Technical University of Brno (Czech Republic) and at the Central American University of San Salvador (El Salvador). His current research interests focus upon executive information systems, knowledge management and structural equation modeling.

F. N. de Silva is a lecturer in management science at the University of Aberdeen, Scotland. Her research interests lie in the design of decision support tools for emergency planning, for which she has obtained support funding from major UK funding councils. She is currently involved in developing a collaborative network of

European disaster experts and practitioners, for which funds are being sought from the European Union. On a wider scale her research work on disaster management involves her in the Global Disaster Information Network (GDIN), pioneered by United Nations agencies such as UNHCR, US Department of State, Emergency Management Australia, various NGOs, industry, academia and other national and international bodies which seek to tackle global issues of information and resource sharing during emergencies.

Alexander V. Smirnov is deputy director for research and head of the Computer Aided Integrated Systems laboratory at St. Petersburg Institute for Informatics and Automation of the Russian Academy of Sciences, Russia. He received his degrees—Dipl.-Ing. (1979), Ph.D. (1984), and D.Sc. (1994)—at St. Petersburg, Russia. He is a full professor at St. Petersburg State Technical University and St. Petersburg State Electrical Engineering University. His current research is in areas of corporate knowledge management, multiagent systems, group decision support systems, virtual enterprises, and supply chain management. He published more than 150 research papers in reviewed journals and proceedings of international conferences, books, and manuals.

David Steiger is an associate professor of management information systems at the University of Maine, Orono, ME. He received his B.S. in electrical engineering and M.B.A. from the University of Texas at Austin and a Ph.D. in information systems/management science from Oklahoma State University. Between his M.B.A. and Ph.D. degrees he spent 15 years in various analysis and managerial positions in industry, applying the concepts of information systems and decision support. Prof. Steiger's research interests include knowledge management, decision support systems, model analysis and inductive artificial intelligence technologies. His research has been published in *Information Systems Research, Management Science, Journal of Management Information Systems, Interfaces, INFORMS Journal On Computing, Decision Support Systems, European Journal of Operational Research, Journal of Knowledge Management, Journal of Data Warehousing* and *Annals of Operation Research*.

Natalie Steiger is an assistant professor of management at the University of Maine, Orono, ME. She received her doctorate degree from North Carolina State University. She has an extensive professional and managerial experience. Dr. Steiger has published numerous professional and scholarly papers and has presented nationally and internationally. Prof. Steiger's research interests include simulation, knowledge management, decision support systems, and large-scale optimization technologies.

M. J. Suárez-Cabal is an associated professor in the Computing Department (Universidad de Oviedo), where she is teaching computer systems. She is pursuing a Ph.D. degree, working on the automation of testing generation in software engineering using metaheuristic techniques. She has collaborated in research projects related to optimization and task and resources programming, where heuristic methods have been used, and she has participated in conferences and published papers on the subject.

Marvin D. Troutt is director of the Center for Information Systems, Management and Information Systems Department, and a professor in the Graduate School of Management at Kent State University. He received a Ph.D. in mathematical statistics from the University of Illinois at Chicago. He is an associate editor of *Decision Sciences* and a fellow of the Decision Sciences Institute. His publications have appeared in *Decision Support Systems, Journal of Knowledge Management, Decision Sciences, Management Science, Journal of Operational Research Society* and others. His current research interests include knowledge management, data mining and decision support.

J. Tuya is a professor of software engineering at the Universidad de Oviedo, Spain. He has obtained a Ph.D. in computer sciences with his main area of research being the field of software quality assurance, software process improvement and formal software verification. He has published in different international conferences and journals and is member of professional associations such as IEEE, IEEE/CS and ACM.

Linda Volonino is a professor of MIS and director of the master's in telecommunications management at Canisius College, in Buffalo, NY, where she is currently developing postgraduate certificate programs in customer interaction management (CIM) and computer security. She teaches courses and professional workshops on fact-based, data-driven CRM. She is an associate editor of the *Journal of Data Warehousing* and a contributing author and has been a research associate with The Data Warehousing Institute. Dr. Volonino coauthored *Accounting and Information Technology* (2001), a textbook for the Arab Society of Certified Accountants (ASCA).

Hugh J. Watson is a professor of MIS and a holder of a C. Herman and Mary Virginia Terry Chair of Business Administration in the Terry College of Business at the University of Georgia. He is the author of 22 books and over 100 scholarly journal articles. He is the senior editor of the *Journal of Data Warehousing* and a fellow of The Data Warehousing Institute. Hugh is the senior director of the Teradata University Network and the consulting series editor for John Wiley & Sons series in Computing and Information Processing.

Harold W. Webb is an assistant professor at the University of South Florida. He received his M.B.A and Ph.D. in management information systems from Texas Tech University. His work experience includes the development of advanced information systems requirements for the United States Army. His research interests are behaviorally oriented and include the effects of information technology on learning at the individual and organizational level. His research interests also extend to the behavioral aspects of software testing as well as decision support systems, and electronic commerce.

Alfredo Weitzenfeld-Reitel is a professor in the Computer Engineering Department at the Mexico Autonomous Institute of Technology (ITAM). He received his B.S. in electrical engineering from Israel's Institute of Technology (TECHNION). He has an M.Sc. in computer engineering and a Ph.D. in computer science, both from the University of Southern California, where he was a research assistant professor. He is the cofounder and director of the CANNES Laboratory for Brain Simulation at ITAM. He is a member of the Mexican National Research System (SNI) as well as a member of the Doctoral Advising Committee at the National Autonomous University of Mexico (UNAM).

Rosemary H. Wild is an associate professor at the California Polytechnic State University in San Luis Obispo and has also taught at the University of Hawaii, the University of Arizona, and San Diego State University. Dr. Wild teaches courses in management information systems, production and operations management, and quantitative analysis. Her research interests include knowledge management, knowledge-based systems, and models of e-commerce. She is currently working on a complex knowledge management system for US Navy manpower management. Dr. Wild has an M.S. degree in systems and industrial engineering and a Ph.D. in management information systems, both from the University of Arizona.

Surya B. Yadav is the James and Elizabeth Sowell Professor of Telecom Technology and the head of the ISQS department, Texas Tech University, Lubbock, TX. He has over 16 years of teaching, research, and systems development experience in the area of information systems. He received his Ph.D. degree in business information systems from Georgia State University. His research interests include research methodology, adaptive systems, and electronic commerce. He has published in several journals including *Communications of the ACM, IEEE Transactions on Software Engineering, IEEE Transactions on Systems, Man, and Cybernetics, and Decision Support Systems*.

Bee K. Yew is director of IT research at Illinois Business Training Center and an independent consultant in the software industry. She received a doctor of business administration from the Southern Illinois University at Carbondale. She has taught in Western Michigan University and Arkansas Tech University. Her publications are found in the *Journal of Operational Research Society, Journal of Higher Education Management* and others. Her research interests include knowledge management, decision support, data mining, fuzzy logic and neurocomputing applications.

Index

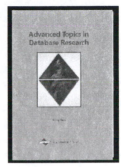